MAYA PALACES AND ELITE RESIDENCES

**The Linda Schele Series
in Maya and Pre-Columbian Studies**

This series was made possible through the generosity of

WILLIAM C. NOWLIN, JR., AND BETTYE H. NOWLIN

The National Endowment for the Humanities
and the following donors:

Elliot M. Abrams and
    AnnCorinne Freter
Anthony Alofsin
Joseph W. Ball and
    Jennifer T. Taschek
William A. Bartlett
Elizabeth P. Benson
Boeing Gift Matching Program
William W. Bottorff
Victoria Bricker
Robert S. Carlsen
Frank N. Carroll
Roger J. Cooper
Susan Glenn
John F. Harris
Peter D. Harrison
Joan A. Holladay
Marianne J. Huber
Jānis Indrikis
The Institute for Mesoamerican
    Studies
Anna Lee Kahn
Rex and Daniela Koontz

Christopher and Sally Lutz
Judith M. Maxwell
Joseph Orr
The Patterson Foundation
John M. D. Pohl
Mary Anna Prentice
Philip Ray
Louise L. Saxon
David M. and Linda R. Schele
Richard Shiff
Ralph E. Smith
Barbara L. Stark
Penny J. Steinbach
Carolyn Tate
Barbara and Dennis Tedlock
Nancy Troike
Donald W. Tuff
Javier Urcid
Barbara Voorhies
E. Michael Whittington
Sally F. Wiseley, M.D.
Judson Wood, Jr.

Maya Palaces and Elite Residences

AN INTERDISCIPLINARY APPROACH

Edited by Jessica Joyce Christie

UNIVERSITY OF TEXAS PRESS
AUSTIN

Library of Congress Cataloging-in-Publication Data
Maya palaces and elite residences : an interdisciplinary approach / edited by Jessica Joyce Christie.
    p.   cm. — (The Linda Schele series in Maya and pre-Columbian studies)
Includes bibliographical references and index.
ISBN 978-0-292-72598-0
1. Maya architecture. 2. Mayas—Dwellings. 3. Mayas—Kings and rulers.
4. Palaces—Latin America. 5. Latin America—Antiquties. I. Christie, Jessica Joyce, 1956– II. Series.
FI435.3.A6 M37   2003
972.81′016—dc21   2002015037

This volume is dedicated to **LINDA SCHELE**

Contents

Acknowledgments

Linda Schele inspired all of us in many ways, but she was particularly instrumental in my own career: she accepted me as her doctoral student in the Department of Latin American Studies at the University of Texas in Austin and thus paved my way to becoming a Mayanist, which has been one of the most fortunate developments in my life.

After completing my dissertation on Classic Maya Period Ending ceremonies and their cosmological symbolism, I turned my attention to the architectural spaces in which such rituals may have taken place and my primary interests shifted to palaces. Tending to be a loner by nature, I followed Linda's admonitions to teamwork and organized a symposium entitled "Maya Palaces and Elite Residences" at the annual conference of the Society for American Archaeology in 1998. This volume is the outcome of the symposium.

I have found myself in the middle of a growing and very dynamic debate about Maya residential architecture, its form, function, and meaning, and the degree to which houses may reflect aspects of Maya political structure and social organization. Later in the same year, 1998, two conferences related to the topic of my symposium were held. One was entitled "Ancient Palaces of the New World: Form, Function, and Meaning" and was organized by Susan Toby Evans and Joanne Pillsbury at Dumbarton Oaks; the other, "Royal Courts of the Ancient Maya," was put together and recently published as two volumes by Takeshi Inomata and Stephen D. Houston. I feel that this form of "palace activism" is very much in the spirit of Linda Schele and at least strives to continue her legacy. I would like to conclude with her words from her convocation address at the College of Art Association Conference in 1995, which hangs above my desk:

For me collaboration is a central requirement for my work, because in my field no one discipline or one person can any longer command all the knowledge and methodologies that are required for successful research. The only effective way I have found to break out of the box created by my own limited experience and imagination is to combine myself with others who have different kinds of experience and imagination. That is the heart of multidisciplinary approach. It is what I teach by example and instruction. And in it, there is no winning or losing—only the work.

Furthermore, I would like to thank all the participants for their contributions, and in particular Arthur Demarest and E. Wyllys Andrews for advising me in the publishing process, and Thomas Guderjan for showing me Blue Creek, not just on paper but the real site, and having me with my son in his camp. I would also like to extend my gratitude to Michael Dixon, technical consultant at East Carolina University, and graduate student Margie Labadie, who with their superior computer knowledge have been of great help in putting together the final manuscript.

MAYA PALACES AND ELITE RESIDENCES

Introduction

This volume brings together scholars in archaeology, anthropology, art history, and epigraphy. They will investigate residential architecture at a number of different Maya sites, but they all will analyze architectural form and associated artifacts, as well as iconographic and epigraphic information, with the goal of reconstructing use and function of specific rooms and houses and what such reconstructions might reveal about ancient Maya social organization. The authors will look at two categories of residential architecture: palaces and residences. Both of these categories are similar in form and layout—they consist of gallery-like structures, on low platforms, that surround courtyards. They differ in that palaces are usually larger in size, are built of stone masonry and with corbeled vaults, have more sculptural decoration, and are located closer to the ceremonial core of a city. Most scholars assume that ruling families both lived in palaces and conducted government business from them but that elite residences were used exclusively as dwellings. Individual authors will define these architectural categories further and bring them to life as they discuss how palaces and elite residences were built and used in different Maya cities.

This introduction will begin with a brief outline of Maya history followed by a chronological overview of approaches taken and directions of research in Maya studies. The history of research will demonstrate the need for the interdisciplinary perspective pursued in this volume. Finally, the authors of the individual chapters and their topics will be introduced.

Interest in Maya palaces was raised when early European explorers discovered their ruins in the nineteenth century.

Continuing on this terrace, we stopped at the foot of a second, when our Indians cried out "el Palacio," "the palace," and through openings in the trees we saw the front of a large building richly ornamented with stuccoed figures on the pilasters, curious and elegant; trees growing close against it, and their branches entering the doors; in style and effect unique, extraordinary, and mournfully beautiful.

We had reached the end of our long and toilsome journey, and the first glance indemnified us for our toil. For the first time we were in a building erected by the original inhabitants, standing before the Europeans knew of the existence of this continent, and we prepared to take up our abode under its roof. (Stephens [1841] 1988: 278)

Maya palaces were first mentioned in the literature by Spanish writers, who described certain Maya structures as *palacios,* as well as by early explorers whose vision of Maya ruins was colored by eighteenth-century Romanticism, as the above excerpt from John L. Stephens' account of Palenque illustrates. Based on their physical appearance as large building complexes with a high density of rooms, the so-called *palacios* reminded early visitors of European Renaissance and Baroque palaces. It filled them with awe and surprise to stumble across examples of monumental architecture constructed of fine stone masonry in a tropical jungle far removed from any trace of Western civilization.

Rain forest covered much of the Maya area, which extended from the present Mexican state of Chiapas in the west to the Copan Valley located in Honduras in the east, and from the coast of Yucatan in the north to the Guatemalan highlands in the south. In the Late Preclassic from approximately 200 B.C. to A.D. 250, the earliest public monumental structures were erected by the Maya. These were primarily temple buildings with ornate facades decorated with stucco sculpture in Maya cities in northern Belize and in the Peten such as Cerros, Lamanai, El Mirador, Tikal, and Uaxactun. During the Classic period from about A.D. 250 to 900, Maya culture reached full maturity. Maya cities were governed by individual rulers who battled each other to expand territories and influence or attempted to forge political and marriage alliances to increase their power. These rulers were the generous patrons who commissioned the construction of temple buildings and palaces, as well as the carving of their portraits on stone stelae and the written documentation of their accomplishments in life. During the Late Classic, the artistic output dramatically increased and there is mounting evidence that social stratification became more complex. In particular, the elite class gained in size and influence.

Beginning in the ninth century, most Maya cities were being abandoned, with only a small local resident population remaining. Contacts with other areas of Mesoamerica, specifically central Mexico, were increasing. Maya culture rose once again in the Yucatan peninsula in the Postclassic, approximately from the tenth century to the Spanish conquest, in centers such as Chichen Itza and Mayapan. However, Postclassic cities were no longer ruled by one individual but by a council or multiple government in which several independent lineages were represented. As a consequence, Maya art, which since Preclassic times had attempted to make kingship sacred, changed.

This was the Maya culture the Spanish encountered when they arrived in the Yucatan in the sixteenth century. Bishop Diego de Landa was one of the first to write about Maya houses. His description of thatched dwellings still fits most rural Yucatecan houses of today. He also addressed the layout of towns and hierarchy of space when he observed that temples and the houses of the lords, priests, and most important people stood in the central areas while the houses of the lower class were found at the outskirts of towns (Tozzer 1941: 62).

It was not until the twentieth century that the term "palace" and how it was applied to Maya architecture came under academic scrutiny. Early researchers classified architectural entities that they assumed to be residential as palaces. There was no agreed-upon definition as to what exactly constituted a palace with regard to form or function. The palace category was primarily a convenient tool to distinguish temple buildings from other types of architecture; temples usually have single rooms and sit on high pyramidal substructures, while palaces are multichambered and rest on low platforms—a description which applies to most Maya buildings that are not temples.[1]

In his report on Tikal, Alfred Tozzer discussed buildings of what he called the "residential type" (1911). He outlined several characteristics of "residential" structures: they contain large numbers of rooms and may be two stories high, the plans often exhibit two rows of parallel longitudinal rooms and one or two transverse rooms at either end, residential buildings are frequently arranged around courts (Tozzer 1911: 96–98). Based on such formal elements alone, Tozzer concluded that these structures had the function of residence.

At the same time, Tozzer noted a close physical connection between residential and religious structures. He suggested that many residences "were probably the homes of the priests" and that, together with temples, they may have formed a court (Tozzer 1911: 98).

Herbert Spinden's understanding of palaces was quite similar to that of Tozzer. He defined as palaces large buildings with multiple rooms that sat on low terraces and were usually arranged around courts. Like Tozzer, he deduced a residential function from the above formal and material aspects (Spinden 1913: 98).

His vision was also forward-reaching when he considered the numerous small mounds seen near temples and palaces at the large sites of Yucatan to be dwellings of the "common people" (Spinden 1913: 99). This observation foreshadows the current debate over the hierarchy of residences and their owners. Spinden also realized that palaces could have experienced changes in plan and grown over time and that function could have changed in this course. All of these are issues for which archaeology at some sites has now provided material evidence.

Ledyard Smith reiterated Spinden's position (1913) in his report on Uaxactun (1950). He used formal categories for what constituted a palace that were similar to Tozzer's and Spinden's and made a clear point that the material form of an archaeological palace determined the function of a residence. However, he cautioned that some buildings may have been used for residential as well as ritual purposes or may have changed from a temple into a dwelling. Like Spinden, he differentiated "palaces" and "dwellings of the common people" (Smith 1950: 71–72).

By 1962, in his report on Mayapan, Smith was more aware of the ambiguities associated with the term "palace." He avoided the term altogether and instead established categories of building types under which he discussed excavated structures. These types of buildings are "dwellings of the poor or unimportant," "dwellings of the wealthy or important," kitchens, oratories, group altars, and group shrines, as well as miscellaneous structures. The main criterion he used to distinguish the dwellings of the poor from those of the wealthy was size. He further noted that the dwellings of the wealthy are almost always arranged in a group and located in the vicinity of the ceremonial center (Smith 1962: 217–218). He listed the number of large and really elaborate residences as "probably not more than 50" (Smith 1962: 218) but did not explore what this number might reflect about social structure and political organization at Mayapan. Altogether, Smith's work was important because he advocated more complex building functions that were not limited to religious/ritual or residential uses.

Linton Satterthwaite was the first scholar to propose a new and more objective archaeological approach to reconstructing the function of Maya palaces. In the 1930s, he excavated the palaces on the Acropolis of Piedras Negras. Based on formal elements, he distinguished two plan-types among palace buildings. He defined the term "palace" by these plan-types but was very careful not to assign any functional significance (Satterthwaite 1935).

He observed that form alone was insufficient to deduce domestic use of a building and that this kind of conclusion would have to be backed up by material remains of such domestic activities as eating and sleeping. Satterthwaite himself found insufficient evidence for eating and sleeping in the Acropolis palaces. He also described the discomforts associated with living in these palaces: their narrow interior spaces, darkness, and humidity, as well as the difficulty of moving daily supplies, particularly water, up the steep hill of the Acropolis. In Satterthwaite's opinion, the Acropolis palaces were nonresidential and rooms containing benches with backscreens might have been used for formal audiences and receptions (Satterthwaite 1933).

John Eric Thompson expressed his belief that Maya cities were ceremonial centers which were filled with life only on special occasions and that Maya royalty and priests must have lived in thatch-roofed houses at the periphery of the ancient cities (Thompson 1963: 48–49). Like Satterthwaite, he stated that stone buildings were unsuited for permanent habitation: "They had no chimneys and no windows, although some rooms had small vents in the walls. Moreover, they were damp and ill lit" (Thompson 1959: 57–58). He suggested that stone buildings could only have been used for secret rites and for storage of paraphernalia.[2]

In summary, Satterthwaite as well as Thompson present the view that the primary function of palaces was public in nature and not residential. In their opinion, palaces may have provided spaces for formal audiences, political receptions, religious ceremonies, and storage of precious items.

By the 1960s, most researchers began to realize that the function of Maya palaces was neither strictly residential nor strictly public. Expanding archaeological data provided evidence that palaces had multiple functions: they were used as living spaces but also housed religious as well as political events. All the authors represented in this volume share this concept.

The reason that the ambiguity of function has been fully recognized is the explosion of newly available data. In the past decades, there has been a burst of settlement pattern surveys in the lowland Maya area that have documented new palace-type structures not only in city centers but also in further outlying areas. One of the earliest and most comprehensive projects was the work at Tikal sponsored by the University Museum of the University of Pennsylvania and directed by William R. Coe and William A. Haviland. Fieldwork was carried out for over ten years from 1956 to 1969, and the results were published in a series of Tikal reports. Tikal Report 13 was written by Dennis E. Puleston and documents the settlement survey of Tikal, while Reports 19 through 22 focus on residential areas. Excavations in the residential areas were supervised by Haviland and Marshall J. Becker, who identified numerous new palace-type structures (Coe and Haviland 1982).

Another large-scale survey was the Copan Valley Settlement Pattern Project of Harvard University, which was carried out from 1975 to 1977 under the direction of Gordon Willey. The principle goal of the project was to establish the extent of occupation and to begin an analysis of site size and layout. An initial typology of sites based upon size, arrangement, height, and construction materials was created (Hendon 1987: 51–55). The most informal grouping of structures identified are small, low, isolated platforms which occur in the more remote parts of the valley. Types I through IV conform to the plaza or *plazuela* (small square) arrangement, in which a rectangular courtyard area is surrounded on all four sides by structures oriented inward (see also Ashmore 1981). There is an increase in the number of plazas, buildings, height, and quality of construction from I to IV. The top of the hierarchy of sites constitutes a major center, in this case the Main Group at Copan, which is seen as the focal point of a regional system. This site typology, which is applicable to most Maya cities, demonstrates that Maya residential architecture is very complex. If one agrees that architecture reflects social structure, then one has to conclude that Maya social organization must have portrayed a similar degree of complexity.

After the Harvard Project ended, work at Copan continued as the Proyecto Arqueológico Copán Primera Fase (PAC I) from 1977 to 1980, directed by Claude F. Baudez, and as PAC II from 1981 to 1984 under the direction of William T. Sanders. PAC II was designed to focus specifically on the Late Classic period in the Copan Valley. In addition, extensive, long-term excavations were carried out in Las Sepulturas (Hendon 1987: 55–57). The work in Las Sepulturas, in particular, has provided a wealth of new information about elite residences in the Late Classic. Julia Ann Hendon thoroughly documented the structural remains and the associated artifacts and used these data as the basis of her functional analysis (Hendon 1987). It is important to note that Hendon's work constitutes one of the recent, more holistic approaches which is not limited to architectural form—as the research of early scholars was—but places equal emphasis on artifacts as well as sculptural decoration.

But what do the data from Las Sepulturas tell us about the position its inhabitants held in Maya social hierarchy, their relationships with other residents in the Copan Valley, and about Maya social organization in general? Diane and Arlen Chase (1992) address these questions with great clarity and careful consideration of data from throughout Mesoamerica. They criticize the traditional cut-and-dried two-division model of Mesoamerican societies that have been viewed as having two tiers consisting of nobles or elites and commoners or non-elites (Chase and Chase 1992: 7–9). The archaeological evidence from Las Sepulturas, as well as from many other Maya cities, shows a large number of high-status residences that were occupied by an elite class which was probably large in numbers and not homogeneous. Excavations have uncovered variations in the quality of construction and decoration which are probably indicative of gradations in the social status, as well as occupation, within the elite class itself. In describing the problem of identifying elites, Chase and Chase observe that, "based upon both archaeology and ethnohistory, it would seem that Classic and Postclassic Mesoamerican social organization was less clear-cut than a simple two-class system, for there appear to have been varying intermediate categories of individuals" (1992: 11). They argue that a series of variables has to be analyzed, some of which fall outside the purview of archaeology. Thus, it is becoming increasingly clear that an interdisciplinary approach is required in order to understand the function and the role palaces and elite residences played in Maya society.

Two such variables to be considered are iconography and epigraphy. In 1960, Tatiana Proskouriakoff was the first to recognize that Maya inscriptions record historical information (Proskouriakoff 1960). Accepting her profound insights, the new generation of epigraphers deciphered texts from a historical perspective and began to reconstruct entire dynastic histories of Maya cities (Schele 1976–1997). Textual and iconographic analyses combined made it possible to understand the interactions and relationships between Maya sites (Schele and Freidel 1990). In the 1990s, epigraphic and iconographic studies enriched and complemented archaeological investigations in many ways. A nice example is Structure 5D-46 in the Central Acropolis at Tikal. Harrison had suspected for some time that this was the clan house of the ruler Great-Jaguar-Paw when archaeologists located a cache vessel deposited under the west stairs of 5D-46. The inscription on the pot records that it was made for the dedication of the "holy structure of Great-Jaguar-Paw"—thus clearly identifying him as the owner (Schele and Freidel 1990: 464–465).

Traditionally, archaeology as well as art history and epigraphy have focused on the material remains of a bygone culture, such as standing walls, artifacts, carved monuments, and painted walls. Anthropology, on the other hand, looks at cultural behavior and therefore how architectural space was used and how it constitutes another variable to be integrated into an interdisciplinary approach. In the mid-1980s, Bill Hillier and Julienne Hanson lamented "the absence of any general models relating spatial structure to social formations" (1984: 26). They advocated that society be "described in terms of its intrinsic spatiality" and space be described "in terms of its intrinsic sociality" and proposed "a broad theory of the social logic of space and the spatial logic of society" (1984: 26). According to Hillier and Hanson (1984), the primary purpose of architecture is the ordering of space, and they outline a syntax model of space in the form of a morphic language whose primary elements are closed and open architectural spaces. Their principal argument, derived from syntax theory, is that spatial organization is a function of social solidarity as defined by Durkheim (Hillier and Hanson, 1984: 142). Mechanical solidarity, which is a form of social integration forged through similarities of group belief and structure, requires a segregated and dispersed space that separates the constituent social groups and helps them maintain their individual identity. Organic solidarity, in contrast, is a form of social integration forged through an interdependence based on differences, for example, the division of labor. This type of solidarity requires an integrated and dense space to facilitate the numerous social encounters needed for the exchange of information and material that ties together the mutually interdependent social entities (Ferguson 1996: 21). Hillier and Hanson further distinguished between what they called correspondence and noncorrespondence sociospatial systems (1984: 256–261). In a correspondence system, spaces and social groups correspond to each other. Encounters result from physical proximity through membership in a spatial group and the system is strong locally. In a noncorrespondence system, a split occurs between spatial groups and transpatial groups, which are other types of social associations not defined by residence. Transpatial groups must interact across space to relate individuals in different spatial groups to each other, and therefore the system tends to be globally strong (Ferguson 1996: 22).

Other scholars share Hillier and Hanson's view of the close relation that exists between architecture, space, and society. Susan Kent has shown that segmentation in various parts of culture, behavior, and cultural material, such as architecture, increases with the development of sociopolitical complexity (1990: 5).

While the pure space syntax model clearly has shortcomings—for example, it cannot address changes in access due to remodeling efforts without independent evidence from archaeological data[3]—it can and should be applied to Maya architecture because it will enrich our understanding of palaces, elite residences, and their inhabitants, as well as their relationship to the rest of Maya society. Especially Maya elites from different cities might be compared and contrasted following the model of a noncorrespondence system. One application of Hillier and Hanson's syntax model of architectural space to Maya archaeology is demonstrated by Liendo Stuardo (this volume).

The main purpose of this volume is to present an interdisciplinary approach and bring together scholars in archaeology, anthropology, art history, and epigraphy, as well as information from a number of different Maya sites, to see what kind of formal and functional patterns in palaces and elite residences can be isolated and in which ways they reflect the structure of Maya society. The majority of the chapters focus on one specific Maya city. Both Loa Traxler and E. Wyllys Andrews and colleagues, for instance, take the reader to Copan. Traxler outlines the development of residential architecture underneath the Acropolis during the Early Classic. The earliest constructions were made of adobe, and one patio group has been identified as the residence of the founder of the Copan royal lineage, Yax K'uk' Mo'. Traxler shows how the adobe structures were replaced by masonry buildings over time. Andrews and coauthors introduce the Late Classic residences in Group 10L-2 south of the Acropolis. They identify the private houses of Yax Pasaj, the final ruler in the dynasty started by Yax K'uk' Mo', and assign functions to most of the other buildings. The evidence for their interpretation is primarily architectural layout and furniture, sculptural decoration, and hieroglyphic inscriptions. Together, the two chapters clearly describe the similarities and changes in palace architecture at Copan from the Early to the Late Classic.

Takeshi Inomata and Daniela Triadan present a special situation at Aguateca. This Maya city was attacked in the early ninth century, most of the elite residences were burned, and the site was abandoned. Because of this rapid departure of the inhabitants, Inomata and Triadan encountered in these structures unprecedented assemblages of in situ domestic artifacts that form the basis of their functional analysis. One of the buildings was identified as the house of a high-status scribe. Arthur Demarest, Kim Morgan, Claudia Wolley, and Héctor Escobedo explore the role natural geography played in the design of the Murciélagos palace complex at Dos Pilas. Demarest and colleagues demonstrate that a subterranean system of caves and springs impacted the plan of this palace and was strategically used to sanctify and legitimize the power of the Dos Pilas ruler. Peter Harrison's work concentrates on the Central Acropolis at Tikal. His reconstruction of function takes into consideration information derived from epigraphy and iconography, and in this respect Harrison's chapter greatly enhances the interdisciplinary approach of this volume. Thomas Guderjan, Robert Lichtenstein, and C. Colleen Hanratty report transformations and changes in elite residences at the site of Blue Creek from the Early Classic to the Late Classic. They use their data to draw conclusions about changes in social structure. James Ambrosino's chapter is a very thorough analysis of the artifactual material associated with a palace structure at Yaxuna. He points out the need to examine the formation processes of material deposits before interpretations of Maya palace function is advanced.

The remaining four chapters discuss formal elements and possible uses of palaces and elite residences at multiple sites. Edward Kurjack presents a general hierarchy of houses in the Yucatan and explores function from an anthropological perspective, addressing numerous forms of cultural behavior, such as defense, economic production, and migration between villages. Jeff Kowalski analyzes form and reconstructs domestic and political functions of several specific Maya palace buildings in the Yucatan Peninsula. He identifies possible Council Houses or Popol Nahs at Dzibilchaltun and Uxmal which beg for a revised definition of the Late Classic Maya institution of kingship.[4] Rodrigo Liendo Stuardo investigates access patterns in royal compounds by means of graphical analysis employing space syntax models. His results demonstrate differences in access and layout between Classic palaces in the southern lowlands and Early Postclassic structures in the northern Yucatan. Liendo Stuardo also discusses what the changes in elite architecture might reveal about the political organization of Postclassic centers. My chapter looks at a very common tripartite floor plan in Maya residences. The approach is structural and the interpretation is based on principles of Maya cosmology and worldview as these are represented in iconography and in the inscriptions.

NOTES

1. This is exactly the issue this volume is aiming to clarify. The palace category established by early scholars is so broad and general that it has become nearly devoid of meaning. The goal is first of all to demonstrate archaeologically that a particular building was the highest-status residence at a site and then to narrow down the distinctions between palaces and elite residences.

2. Peter Harrison rejects Thompson's argument because he feels it is "based upon ethnocentrism, which must be inadequate for a functional analysis" (Harrison 1971: 220). I would counter that smoke, darkness, and humidity are universal, uncomfortable experiences to individuals no matter what their time period or culture. That the Yucatec Maya in the 1930s shared such feelings is reported by Robert Wauchope. He observed that when a family had achieved a certain amount of wealth and prestige, they sometimes desired to build a masonry house of the Spanish type. Wauchope visited five of these masonry structures in the village of Chan Kom and "in each case found the house almost devoid of furniture, the entire family living in a bush house (generally called a kitchen) in the back yard. The front house was a dis-

play; its owners found themselves more comfortable in the old-style hut to which they were more accustomed" (Wauchope 1938: 141).

While the more recent archaeological data have demonstrated that Maya cities were not empty ceremonial centers as Thompson had claimed, I nevertheless think it is quite possible that royal and noble families maintained secondary dwellings in the form of thatched-roof houses at the outskirts of their cities, to which they re-treated between official events and in which some members of the extended family, especially small children, may have permanently lived.

3. Ferguson presents a critical evaluation of Hillier and Hanson's space syntax theory (1996: 23–24).

4. While the existence of Popol Nahs has been established at southern lowland cities such as Copan and Palenque, Classic Maya government has been viewed as a kingship institution based on one monarch in most of the literature since the 1960s. This understanding was derived from the discoveries in epigraphy that Maya texts recorded the accomplishments of historical rulers. However, it is becoming increasingly clear that the epigraphic data mismatch data from archaeology. I think we have to strongly emphasize that the history written on stone monuments was politically manipulated to spread the belief that the power of kingship was absolute. On the other hand, the evidence from archaeology, especially the large number of high-status residences, points to the fact that Maya social hierarchy was rather stratified, with numerous intermediate positions of political and/or religious power in between the king and commoners. I am aware that some of these intermediate elite members have been identified by title and name (see Harrison, this volume), but the focus of Maya inscriptions, as well as iconography, is typically on the authority of the king.

REFERENCES

Ashmore, W. A.
1981 Some Issues of Method and Theory in Lowland Maya Settlement Archae-ology. In *Lowland Maya Settlement Archaeology*, edited by W. Ashmore, 37–69. Albuquerque: University of New Mexico Press.
Chase, D. Z., and A. F. Chase (eds.)
1992 *Mesoamerican Elites: An Archaeological Assessment.* Norman: University of Oklahoma Press.
Coe, W. R., and W. A. Haviland
1982 *Introduction to the Archaeology of Tikal, Guatemala.* Tikal Report 12, University Museum Monograph 46. Philadelphia: University of Pennsylvania.
Ferguson, T. J.
1996 *Historic Zuni Architecture and Society.* Tucson: University of Arizona Press.
Harrison, P.
1971 The Central Acropolis, Tikal, Guatemala: A Preliminary Study of the Functions of Its Structural Components during the Late Classic Period. Ph.D. dissertation, University of Pennsylvania.
Hendon, J. A.
1987 The Uses of Maya Structures: A Study of Architecture and Artifact Distribution at Sepulturas, Copan, Honduras. Ph.D. dissertation, Department of Anthropology, Harvard University.
Hillier, B., and J. Hanson
1984 *The Social Logic of Space.* Cambridge: Cambridge University Press.
Inomata, T., and S. Houston (eds.)
2001 *Royal Courts of the Ancient Maya.* 2 vols. Boulder: Westview Press.

Kent, S. (ed.)
1990   *Domestic Architecture and the Use of Space.* Cambridge: Cambridge University Press.
Ortiz, A.
1969   *The Tewa World: Space, Time, Being, and Becoming in a Pueblo Society.* Chicago: University of Chicago Press.
Proskouriakoff, T.
1960   Historical Implications of a Pattern of Dates at Piedras Negras, Guatemala. *American Antiquity* 25: 454–475.
Satterthwaite, L.
1933   *Description of the Site, with Short Notes on the Excavations of 1931-32.* Piedras Negras Preliminary Papers 1. Philadelphia: University Museum, University of Pennsylvania.
1935   *Palace Structures J-2 and J-6.* Piedras Negras Preliminary Papers 3. Philadelphia: University Museum, University of Pennsylvania.
Schele, L.
1976–1997   *Notebooks for the Maya Hieroglyphic Workshops.* Austin: University of Texas.
Schele, L., and D. Freidel
1990   *A Forest of Kings.* New York: William Morrow.
Smith, A. L.
1950   *Uaxactun, Guatemala: Excavations of 1931-1937.* Carnegie Institution of Washington Publication 588. Washington, D.C.
1962   *Residential and Associated Structures of Mayapan.* Carnegie Institution of Washington Publication 619. Washington, D.C.
Spinden, H. J.
1913   *A Study of Maya Art: Its Subject Matter and Historical Development.* Memoirs of the Peabody Museum of American Archaeology and Ethnology, vol. 6. Cambridge, Mass.: Harvard University.
Stephens, J. L.
[1841] 1988   *Incidents of Travel in Central America, Chiapas & Yucatan.* London: Century.
Thompson, J. E. S.
1959   *The Rise and Fall of Maya Civilization.* Norman: University of Oklahoma Press.
1963   *Maya Archaeologist.* Norman: University of Oklahoma Press.
Tozzer, A. M.
1911   *A Preliminary Study of the Prehistoric Ruins of Tikal, Guatemala.* Memoirs of the Peabody Museum of American Archaeology and Ethnology, vol. 5, no. 2. Cambridge, Mass.: Harvard University.
1941   *Landa's Relación de las Cosas de Yucatán: A Translation.* Papers of the Peabody Museum of American Archaeology and Ethnology, vol. 18. Cambridge, Mass.: Harvard University.
Wauchope, R.
1938   *Modern Maya Houses: A Study of Their Archaeological Significance.* Washington, D.C.: Carnegie Institution of Washington.

CHAPTER ONE

Elite Residences at Blue Creek, Belize

*Thomas H. Guderjan, Robert J. Lichtenstein,
and C. Colleen Hanratty*

Introduction

The purpose of this chapter is to examine elite residences at the site of Blue
Creek in the upper Río Hondo drainage of northwestern Belize. This is the
first overview of the topic resulting from current research at Blue Creek.
It is also very much a work in progress. While we have been successful in
answering many questions about the elite residences and Blue Creek in
general, we still have many important unresolved issues, meaning that this
is also an agenda for future research. In this chapter, we will attempt to
apply what we understand of elite residences at Blue Creek to the goal of
understanding the structure and dynamics of the community as a whole.

There are three specific goals here. First, we will present what is currently known of the elite residences at Blue Creek from both survey and
excavation data. This presentation is structured by use of a morphological typology of such residences. Second, the chronology of these residences
illuminates aspects of both the Early and Late Classic periods and the transition between them. Then, the geographic contexts of these residences
will be examined to begin the process of understanding the sociopolitical
structure of Blue Creek.

The greater Blue Creek area has been divided into several zones of study.
Atop the Río Bravo escarpment, in the central public precinct or Core Area,
we find two plazas composed of several public ritual, residential, and multi-
functional structures. Adjacent to the Core Area is a series of elite residential complexes known as the Western Group. Surrounding the Core Area
and Western Group is the settlement zone, which in turn has been divided
into a number of broad environmental categories. These categories include
the open flatlands of the Belize coastal zone below and to the east of the
escarpment, the high ground along the top of the escarpment, and finally

the hill and bajo (low-lying area) terrain found above and to the west of the escarpment. Excavations at Blue Creek in northwestern Belize (Figure 1.1) have been underway since 1992 (Guderjan et al. 1994; Guderjan and Driver 1995; Guderjan, Driver, and Haines 1996; Driver, Clagett, and Haines 1997). Over the years, we have been able to develop a picture of the architectural history of Blue Creek that shows it to have a unique chronology. The initial planning and construction of Blue Creek's monumental core district was anything but unusual, with early construction phases of buildings in the Main Plaza and much of the other public architecture being undertaken during the Late Preclassic. At Structure 4, on the Main Plaza, a massive dedicatory cache of obsidian blades, cores, jade, chert bifaces, and other objects marked the beginning of Blue Creek's life as an independent kingdom (Guderjan 1998). Sometime later during the mid–Early Classic, the front of Structure 9 was decorated with plaster *ajaw* (glyph of abstracted face meaning lord) masks, denoting it as an ascension house for rulers (Haines 1995, Grube, Guderjan, and Haines 1995).[1] At about the same time, Structure 1, the largest building on the Main Plaza, was a tall, graceful temple with a columned superstructure (Driver 1995). This unique building is the earliest columned building in the southern lowlands and perhaps the earliest in the Maya world. The only known similar building is Structure 1 at Ake' in Yucatan (Roys and Shook 1966). While we expect that Structure 1's status as the "earliest" columned building will someday be usurped, its presence clearly indicates that Blue Creek was participating in architectural innovation at the time. This was no backwater community.

Another marker of affluence and influence at Blue Creek is the presence of large quantities of jade during the Late Preclassic and Early Classic periods (Guderjan and Pastrana 2001). Much of this jade is found in ritual settings, such as the Structure 4 shaft caches as well as burial settings such as Tomb 5 (Lichtenstein 2001) and Tomb 7 (Guderjan and Hanratty, 2001). Furthermore, jade artifacts have been found disbursed throughout all social and economic contexts at Blue Creek. In total, more than 1,500 jade artifacts have been recovered from Late Preclassic and Early Classic contexts.

Such innovation and wealth seems surprising, as Blue Creek is best characterized as a medium-sized center rather than a large one. However, its strategic location probably has a great deal to do with its success in the Early Classic period. Situated on top of the Bravo escarpment, Blue Creek is very near the navigable terminus of the Río Hondo, so mercantile and other canoe traffic would have stopped at Blue Creek. Ethnohistoric and archaeological data both suggest that the Bravo escarpment marks a cultural as well as physiographic transition. The eastern Peten (above the escarpment) and

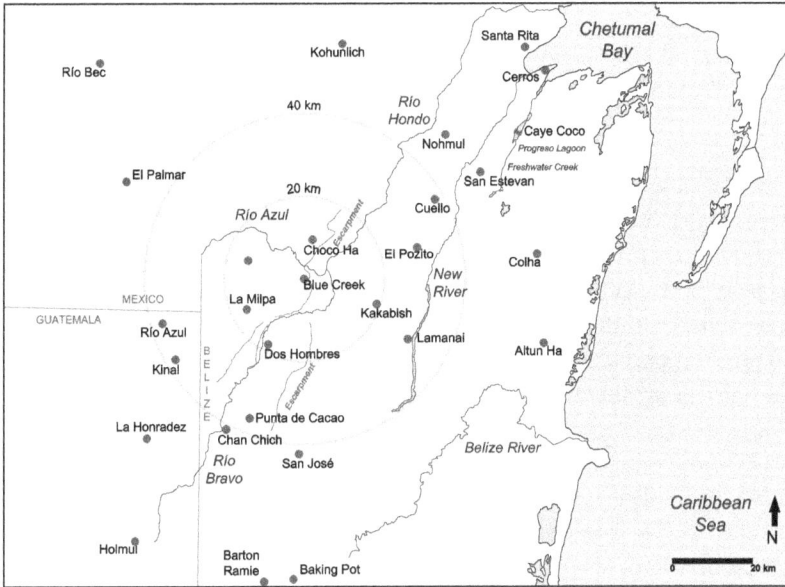

FIGURE I.I. Location of Blue Creek.

the coastal Belize zone (below the escarpment) are distinct cultural zones (A. Chase and D. Chase 1985, Guderjan 1997, Houk 1996, Roys 1957). So, Blue Creek was at a transition point on an economic lifeline that connected distinct cultural zones. Blue Creek also controlled important agricultural resources, as it overlooks vast arable land, much of which was ditched by the Maya for intensive agriculture (J. Baker 1997). Under the circumstances, the city would be expected to have thrived. And thrive it did; during the Early Classic, Blue Creek saw major construction after major construction.

However, this came to an abrupt end at approximately A.D. 500. At some time before then, the Blue Creek Maya gutted the center of Structure 4 and constructed a stone-lined shaft into the building as they refilled their excavation. In this shaft, during a single ceremony at approximately A.D. 500, they deposited more than nine hundred jade adornments, including four "bib-heads" and other anthropomorphic and zoomorphic artifacts, *incensarios*, and other objects (Guderjan 1998, Pastrana 1999). Aside from the ostentatious display of wealth and the conspicuous consumption of symbols of power represented by the massive deposit, the bib-heads are of particular importance. They have been found in Late Preclassic contexts at Cerros and Nohmul and an Early Classic context at Chan Chich (Houk 1998). These have been interpreted as K'inich Ajaw, the Sun God (Hammond 1986). Further, Schele and Freidel (1990) link them to the personage of the ruling king.

We have several possible explanations for this act, such as the death of a king ending a royal lineage (Guderjan 1996) or the beginning of a war (Kent Reilly, personal communication, 1996). In Guderjan's current view, Blue Creek was a small but wealthy independent polity until the A.D. 500 event. At that time, it was taken over by one of several possible neighboring polities, probably one of those to the east such as Kakabish or Lamanai or possibly La Milpa to the west. The decapitation of the polity is seen by the virtual cessation of construction of public buildings. In addition, we see an almost complete absence of jade at Blue Creek after this event, which may also be attributable to the loss of political independence (Guderjan and Pastrana 2001). Regardless of which interpretation bears out, it is clear that we cannot contemplate this Maya center without recognizing that it had a dynamic political history during its millennium and a half of existence. It is equally clear that the interpolity political and economic relationships of the Classic period were anything but static, even within a regional area such as northwestern Belize.

Perhaps shortly afterward, but at about the same time, the columned superstructure of Structure 1 was razed to accommodate the addition of a minor construction and a small royal tomb (Tomb 4). The individual interred in Tomb 4 may have been the last of Blue Creek's independent rulers or another member of the ruling elite (Driver 1995). While a few other small additions exist, construction of public architecture came to a nearly complete halt after A.D. 500. However, Blue Creek did continue on as a small city throughout the Late Classic, only to be ultimately abandoned in the mid-to-late ninth century A.D.

Despite the radical changes that marked the transition to the Late Classic at Blue Creek, the city continued to thrive economically. Elite residences were almost uniformly expanded and the population seems to have continued to grow in the residential area known as Chan Cahal, as well as the settlement zone in general (Lichtenstein 2000). It also appears, though it is a bit uncertain yet, that the ditched-field systems continued to be used and perhaps were expanded. So agricultural productivity remained stable or grew.

We also now have an increasingly clear picture of the structure of the small city of Blue Creek (Figures 1.2, 1.3). The monumental architecture and public precinct of the city are situated on top of the Bravo escarpment (Figure 1.4), affording views of at least 10 mi. to the east. Within and adjacent to the public precinct are the twelve elite residences that will be consid-

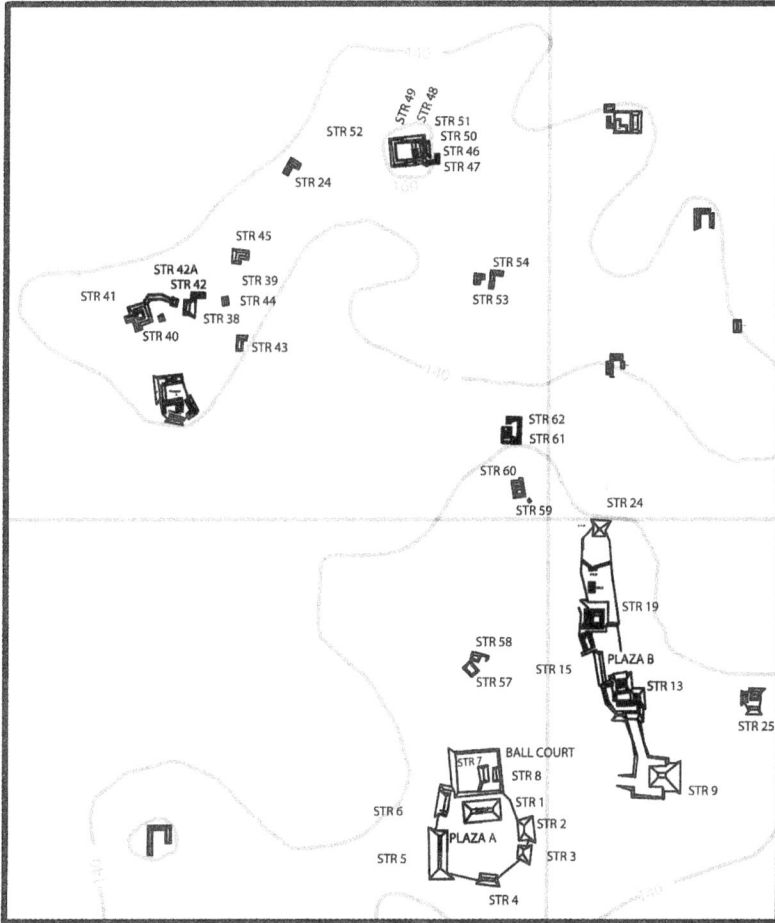

FIGURE I.2. Blue Creek: Core Area and Western Group.

ered in this chapter. However, these do not constitute all of the elite residences known at Blue Creek. On prominent knolls along the escarpment,
both north and south of the public precinct, are dozens of additional courtyards, plazuelas, and patio groups. To the west of the escarpment is a zone
of rolling hills and small bajos. On top of virtually all of these hills are other
prominent residences, often associated with groups of smaller residences.

Below the escarpment to the east, the situation seems to be somewhat
more complex. The eastern landscape is less rugged than the west, the
major relief being provided by low terraces of the Río Bravo. Much of the
land is very low lying and was seasonally inundated prior to recent flood

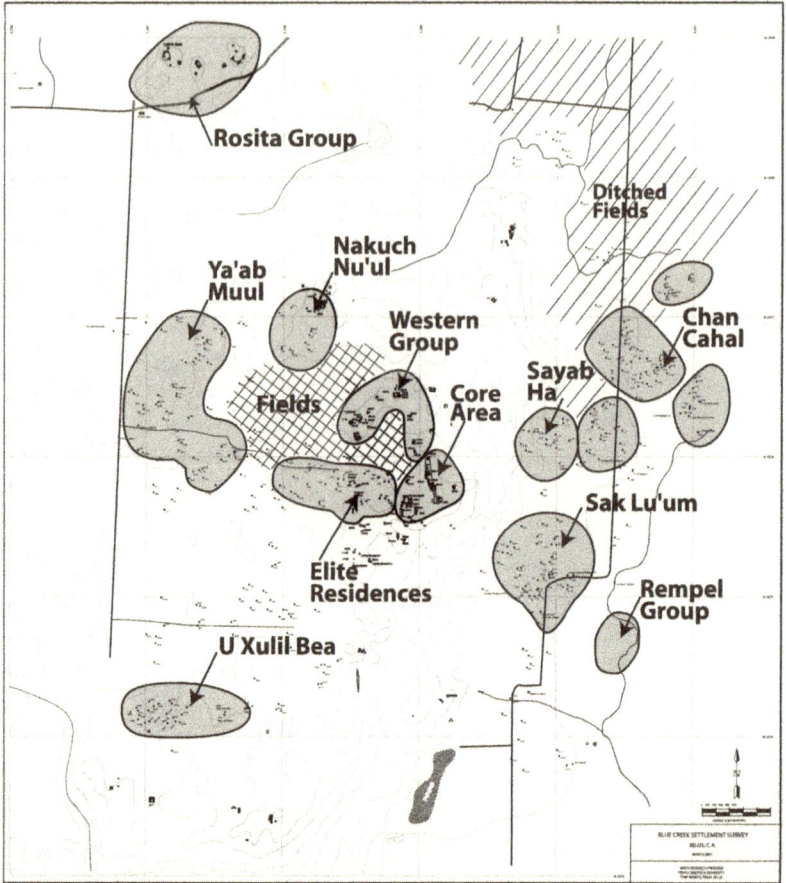

FIGURE I.3. Schematic map of Blue Creek site components.

control efforts. We have identified an extensive network of ditched agricultural fields in such low-lying areas (J. Baker 1997). Ditched fields surround
the terraces, upon which we have found complexes of settlement, in effect,
residential barrios. For example, one of these, known as Chan Cahal, consists of twenty-six housemounds, a large open platform, and a small shrine.
Excavations have shown that these Late Classic housemounds often over-
lie Late Preclassic and Early Classic middens and residences (Clagett 1997,
Lichtenstein 1999, 2000, Popson and Clagett 1999).

While the Chan Cahal residences appear to be some of the most humble
found at Blue Creek, the people of Chan Cahal had a surprisingly high access to a variety of exotic goods. Jade artifacts, for example, have been re-

covered from caches, burials, and midden deposits. The Chan Cahal jade collection now numbers more than two hundred pieces.

Several barrios similar to Chan Cahal exist below the escarpment, each having its own character. One commonality among them is the presence of a single or limited number of high-status residences within each barrio. Additionally, some barrios contain examples of monumental public ritual architecture of some kind. We have also found monumental buildings at the Rempel complex, southeast of the core zone of the site. This group includes a few monumental buildings and elite residences. Another, the Rosita Group, was long ago identified to the northwest of the public precinct (Guderjan 1991). It is possible that these groups defined the limits of the city of Blue Creek.

Elite Residences

There are three general criteria that are used here to identify elites and their associated residences: spatial, architectural, and material assemblage. Spatial indicators of elite status include relative degrees of access restriction to bounded exterior spaces, location in relation to the central precinct (Pendergast 1992: 63), location in relation to critical resources, and viewshed, which analyzes what can be seen from a certain vantage point. Architec-

FIGURE 1.4. Photo of site from air, showing location on escarpment.

tural scale (Harrison 1970), complexity, and form (Pendergast 1992: 63) are often used as identifiers of elite presence. The final criterion involves the material assemblage or certain elements of it. The possession of a wide assortment of artifacts such as luxury goods (Coggins 1975: 5), trade wares, exotic materials, and material representations of elite ideology (Iannone and Conlon 1993) have all been used to identify elite presence. While the presence of any of the above aspects in isolation sheds little light on the identification of an elite presence, an examination of these criteria taken together can and often does make a persuasive case.

While numerous elite residences exist within the greater Blue Creek area, this chapter focuses upon the thirteen residences within and adjacent to the public precinct. Largely following Ashmore (1981), we have defined four types of elite residences: patio groups, plazuelas, courtyards, and range buildings. The defining differences among the first categories are relative degrees of access and bounded exterior spaces. The patio group is the most open and accessible, with external space bounded by structures on two or three sides. Plazuelas have exterior space bounded on all sides by structures, but access is relatively free and unrestricted between structures. Courtyards have the most restricted access. External space is bounded on all sides by either multiple abutting structures or by the wings of a single structure (Loten and Pendergast 1984: 7). The fourth category, range buildings, is qualitatively different. These are long, narrow buildings with one or two rows of rooms usually of vaulted stone construction. Generally, these structures exist in isolation, but occasionally they have small additions and associated structures. The term is often used to describe buildings with a range of potential functions in the Maya area. However, at Blue Creek and nearby sites such as Kakabish or El Pozito all of them appear to be residential. Importantly, three of the categories really represent somewhat arbitrary divisions of a range of variation. In fact, patio groups can be remodeled into courtyards and plazuelas.

The area of Blue Creek under consideration in this chapter includes at least thirteen such residences (Figure 1.2). Starting in the central core and moving out, we find the Structure 19 and Structure 13 courtyards flanking Plaza B. Considerable work has been undertaken at these residences (Gilgan 1996, 1997; Lichtenstein 1996, 1997). Located on a hill slightly to the east of Plaza B and Structure 9, the next group to be encountered is the Structure 25 patio group. While excavations in this group were completed some time ago (Guderjan et al. 1994), recently Helen Haines returned to the area to excavate the Middle and Late Preclassic components found within this group's platform (Haines and Wilhemy 1999). Moving south

Table 1.1. *Elite Residences at Blue Creek (within or near the public precinct)*

Major Structure	Type of Residence	Location	Excavation Reports
Structure 28	Range building	South of Plaza A	
Structure 13	Courtyard	Public precinct (Plaza B)	Gilgan 1996, 1997
Structure 19	Courtyard	Public precinct (Plaza B)	Lichtenstein 1997
Structure 25	Patio group	East of public precinct	
Structure 37	Plazuela	Western Group	Hanratty & Driver 1997; Hanratty 1998
Structure 41	Courtyard	Western Group	Lichtenstein 2002
Structure 43	Patio group	Western Group	
Structure 45	Patio group	Western Group	
Structure 46	Courtyard	Western Group	Ek 2002
Structure 54	Patio group	Western Group	
Structure 58	Patio group	Western Group	
Structure 60	Patio group	Western Group	Currid 2002
Structure 61	Courtyard	Western Group	

from Plaza A, the first structures to be encountered are those of the Structure 28 Group. With a range building, open patio space, and at least one *chultun* (underground chamber), this group could very well be an elite residence. However, it must be noted that David Driver (personal communication, 2000) disagrees and sees Structure 28 as a public/administrative building. The last area to be considered here is that known as the Western Group, a group of ten residential complexes that stretch in an arch to the west of Structure 24, the northern major building at the site. This virtually unbroken string of residences is situated on top of prominent hills and consists of the Structures 33, 37, 41, 43, 45, 46, 54, 58, 60, and 61 complexes. Excavations have been conducted at four of these; the Structure 37 plazuela, the Structure 41 and Structure 46 courtyards, and the Structure 60 patio group (Hanratty and Driver 1997; Hanratty 1998; Ek 2002; Currid 2002; Lichtenstein 2002).

Residences of the Core Area
The elite residences of the Core Area have been designated the Structure 19 and Structure 13 courtyards, and define the north and south ends of Plaza B respectively. These are the most central and presumably housed the politically most important families of Blue Creek.

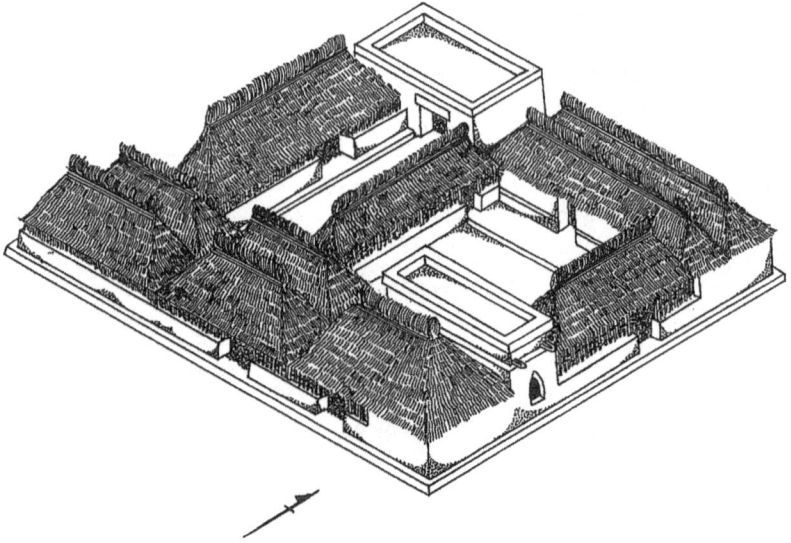

FIGURE 1.5. Structure 19 reconstruction drawing.

The Structure 19 Courtyard Defining the northern extent of Plaza B, the Structure 19 courtyard complex was clearly the residence of one of Blue Creek's most powerful elite families. The complex consists of a low platform upon which are at least fourteen interconnected rooms and passageways surrounding two very private courtyards (Figure 1.5), covering about 650 m² with 160 m² of courtyard space. With construction beginning in the latter part of the Early Classic and continuing to its final form in the Late Classic, the Structure 19 courtyard is a truly agglutinative complex.

The architecture of Structure 19 is an amalgam of construction styles. While some rooms have low masonry walls that supported pole and thatch superstructures, other rooms were vaulted or have beam and mortar roofing. At various points throughout the occupation of this complex, new walls were added either to create new rooms or to restrict or alter routes of access. The formation of rooms can be seen in several places on the south side of the complex, with the dividing walls that created both Rooms G and E as well as the restricted area in the east end of Room C. An example of restriction and alteration of access routes can be found by examining Courtyard A. Early in this area's history, access was easily obtained from Plaza B by a direct and open route. Later, after a series of structural additions and alterations, access became quite tortuous and convoluted, requiring a person to navigate a number of passageways and rooms before entering Courtyard A.

The artifact assemblage recovered includes a wide variety of ceramics, as well as flaked and ground stone tools. From simple to complex and from local to exotic, the ceramics from Structure 19 include plain ware storage jars, ollas, plates, and bowls, as well as polychromes, cylinder vases, censers, and central peninsular slate wares. The stone artifact assemblage contains obsidian blades and basalt metates from Highland Guatemala, granite metates and slate from the Maya Mountains, and an assortment of biface tools manufactured from local materials. The residents of Structure 19 clearly had access to material resources from local, regional, and long distance exchange networks.

At least four primary burials were encountered in the excavations of this complex. One other burial had been badly damaged by looters. It had been placed in a bench in the north end of a room on the west side of the complex. Associated with the material inside this bench were the shattered remains of an incised Chilar Fluted cylinder vase. In a room on the southeast corner of the complex three individuals were found; one had been interred in an intrusive subfloor pit and two others were found in the construction fill of two superimposed benches. The fourth individual was found in an intrusive subfloor pit in a connecting room just south of the previous room.

While none of the undisturbed burials had any associated grave goods, one did show evidence of a postburial ritual event. The grave of an adult male interred in one of the benches had been opened prehistorically and its long bones and cranium removed. This practice of opening and removing bones has been interpreted by some as an event connected to the raising of status for a deceased ancestor (McAnany 1998).

Several points are important regarding the Structure 19 courtyard. First, its location adjacent to one of the two major plazas at Blue Creek argues for the central importance of its inhabitants. This is strongly supported by its early construction date. At this stage in our investigations, the Structure 19 courtyard is the earliest known elite residence in the central core. Further, in some respects this is the most elaborate of the site's elite residences. In particular, flanking the courtyard to the west are support structures possibly inhabited by servants of the courtyard's residents. The continuity of occupation by a single lineage is likely, given the repeated use of Room F for mortuary purposes. There were at least three burial events. We have obtained a corrected radiocarbon date from the earliest of these burials (Burial 10) of A.D. 555–675 (BC 53; DRI18329; AMS; 1335 BP ±60 years). While we would prefer a somewhat earlier date, this assay tends to support the idea that these interments began in the Early Classic and range into the Late Classic period, spanning the dramatic events of A.D. 500. Nevertheless, it does appear likely that this is a "palace" of the rulers of Blue Creek in the

Early Classic. The fact that occupation was continuous through the Late Classic does lead us to believe that we are dealing with a single lineage occupying the structure throughout its history.

As we will see in the following discussions of the Structure 13 and 46 courtyards, as well as the Structure 37 plazuela, several of the residences of Blue Creek's Terminal Classic period elite were ritually terminated by the deposition of massive amounts of artifacts smashed across the faces of certain structures. While there is no evidence of these termination rituals having occurred at the Structure 19 courtyard, middens encountered in the southernmost (Room B) and the westernmost (Room H) rooms have been interpreted as evidence of a reduced population living here at the end of the Terminal Classic period.

The Structure 13 Courtyard The Structure 13 courtyard represents both continuity and a departure from the pattern seen at the Structure 19 courtyard. Like its counterpart on the other side of Plaza B, the Structure 13 courtyard flanks this expansive plaza, placing the two residences at a level of equal stature. Dramatically unlike the Structure 19 courtyard, the Structure 13 courtyard was not originally constructed as a residence. Instead, its original Early Classic function was as an open, public triadic group. The group was originally composed of two temples: Structure 13 on the north side and Structure 12 on the east side. Later, the plaza platform was expanded laterally to the west and Structure 10 was added to the complex. While we have not conducted penetrating excavations into Structure 10 or 13, a centerline trench into Structure 12 revealed an important set of Early Classic dedicatory caches, which clarify the building's construction date (Gilgan 1997).

At a later point in time, the plaza was transformed from sacred space to secular, residential space. The facades of Structure 12 and presumably Structure 13 were reworked, and two new buildings were added. Structure 11 was appended to Structure 12 and Structure 14 was added to Structure 13, forming a bounded, restricted-access exterior space. Structure 14 was a single-room, stone-roof building. Similarly, Structure 11 was a three-room structure, with its easternmost room stone-roofed and its two rooms to the west thatch-roofed. This structure was probably built in a series of expansions that progressively restricted the external space of what was to become the Structure 13 courtyard.

The reworked facades of Structures 12 and 13 were interesting in architectural form. Unlike most Maya buildings that have staircases built along their central medial axis, both of these had vertical walls as basal sections

Structure 13 Courtyard

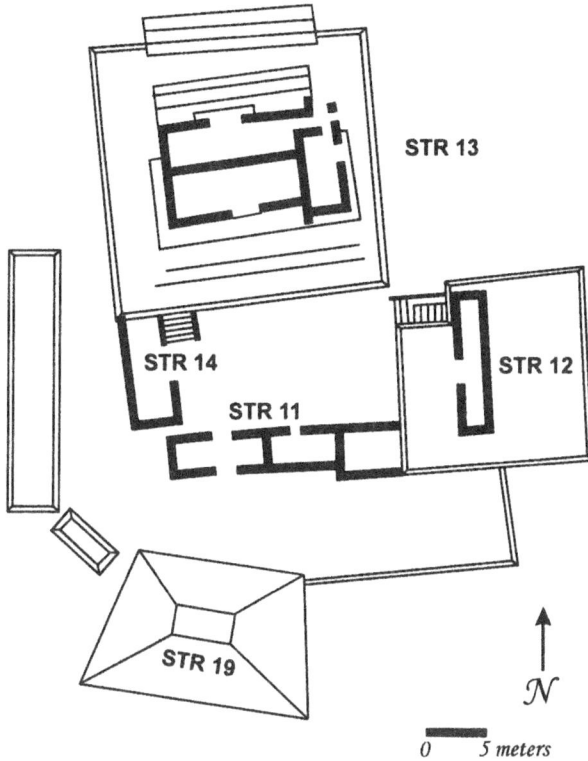

FIGURE 1.6. Structure 13 courtyard.

of the facades and small staircases on their left corners. These staircases led into a set of rooms along the front of the buildings. In the case of Structure 12, a doorway on the medial axis then led to the second and highest tier of rooms, and another doorway led out the back of the building. In the case of Structure 13, a person would have needed to walk through the front set of rooms to the far right side of the building to gain access to the double row of vaulted rooms which topped the building.

While these renovations created private space, they were also planned so that public access to Structure 10 remained possible and so that people could pass by the courtyard as they went into and out of Plaza B.

The implications of this transformation are important. Perhaps this is only a reflection of the ruling lineage of Blue Creek needing more residential space. Certainly, we can argue that expansion of the elite class did occur in the Late Classic (A. Chase 1992; A. Chase and D. Chase 1992), and it follows that elite residences must have expanded and increased in number. Further, that is just what we are considering as an explanation for the growth of the Western Group, a sort of elite suburbia. However, it is agreed that other mechanisms may be at play here. Without going too far out on this particular limb, it is enough to say that the events of A.D. 500 altered the trajectory of Blue Creek as a city and independent polity in a dramatic way. If the deposit at Structure 4 represents preparations for warfare (Guderjan 1998), further monumental construction ceased to occur, and we no longer see evidence of Blue Creek as an independent polity, then the transformation of Structure 13 could mean something quite different. Perhaps Blue Creek lost the war and was ruled by another city. It is possible that this transformation represents the installation of a vassal ruler.

The Structure 25 Patio Group The Structure 25 patio group (Figure 1.7) is located atop a hill in the central core. While it appears on the surface not to be a residence of note, there are a number of factors that argue against such a conclusion. First to be considered is the group's location and viewshed. To the east there is a commanding view of the Belizean coastal zone and the residences below the escarpment. To the west this group overlooks Plaza B and, possibly more importantly, directly overlooks Structure 9, one of the most significant ritual structures found at this site. This kind of spatial relationship is not one to be taken lightly. The psychological impact of viewed associations is a powerful tool that was not likely to have been overlooked by the ancient Maya. The next piece of spatial information to be taken into account is how the exterior space of this group is organized and defined. The group is composed of three structures that are arranged in a U-shaped configuration, with the open end facing to the east. On level terrain patio groups generally do not appear to have very much in the way of access restriction to their external spaces. That, however, is not the case for this particular group. The steep gradient of the hill that the Structure 25 group is constructed upon effectively serves to create a natural restriction of access across the eastern boundary of this group's exterior space. The next major aspect of this group to be examined is its architectural form. Constructed on a raised platform during the Late Classic (Guderjan et al., 1994), the structures that make up this group have low masonry walls with basal moldings, and probably supported pole and thatch superstructures. A large plastered bench, a feature often thought to be diagnostic of residential architecture, was encountered in one of this group's structures. Structure 25 is a platform for a perishable building with a low frontal tier. Under-

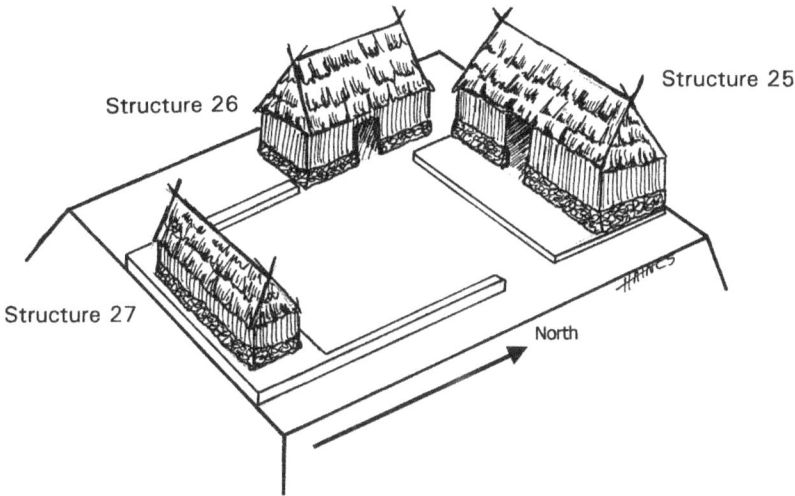

FIGURE I.7. Structure 25 patio group.

lying this group are significant Preclassic deposits that include at least one burial, as well as an impressive cache of obsidian blades and spent cores (Haines and Wilhelmy 1999).

While the Structure 25 patio group is geographically close to the public architecture, the energetics and complexity of construction lead us to believe that it was not inhabited by the highest political stratum of Blue Creek. Nevertheless, its location indicates that it was of sufficient importance to be considered in this discussion.

The Structure 28 Group The only range building that has a possible residential function near the public precinct, Structure 28, is located 150 m south of Plaza A. The building is unexcavated, though an excavation in front of the building indicates a Late Preclassic or Early Classic construction date. Further, evidence from a looters' trench shows it to have been built in at least two construction phases. Ceramics recovered from the trench date to the Classic period. Structure 28 is oriented north-south and is 35 m long, 15 m wide, and 3–4 m tall. It appears to consist of a double row of vaulted rooms on a relatively low platform. The area east of the building has been leveled to be an open patio, and there is one small ancillary building on the south side of the patio. Again, Driver (personal communication, 2000) believes Structure 28 had a public/administrative function rather than residential. This is the only range building of this type near the precinct, but two others are known. One is near the residential barrio of

Sayap Ha', and the other is about a kilometer south of the public precinct in a setting much like that of Structure 28. While we include Structure 28 in this discussion, the function of such buildings remains ambiguous. Until we devote more field research to them, we will be uncertain of their role within the Blue Creek settlement hierarchy.

The Western Group

The Western Group is a large arching, but otherwise linear, complex of elite residences. Within this area are found the following residences: Structures 37, 41, 43, 45, 46, 54, 58, 60, and 61 complexes. While these are grouped according to their proximity to each other and general location within the site, there is considerable variability within them as a group.

Plazuelas

Within the Western Group residences, there is only one plazuela, the Structure 37 plazuela. However, others have been located within the greater Blue Creek area.

It is evident that the events that took place throughout the site reflect a period of drastic social and political change during the Early Classic–Late Classic transition. With the wane of Blue Creek's central power, the elite population's influence over the Late Classic site plan is evident in residential construction and modification, such as those identified within the Structure 37 plazuela. After A.D. 500, this reorganization is evidenced by a pronounced shift in the focus of Core Area construction programs, changes in ritual activities, and a transformation of Classic material symbols of elite power.

The Structure 37 plazuela forms the anchor for the Western and is located atop a 14 m tall hill that lies 600 m northwest of Plaza A. An elite residential group, its final construction form is composed of seven buildings, Structures 31–37, arranged around two distinct exterior areas designated A and B. The northern exterior space (A) is defined by Structure 35 to the south, Structure 36 to the west, and Structure 37 to the north. The patio is not bounded by a structure on its east side, leaving an open view of the site core. The southern exterior space (B) is bounded by Structure 35 to the north and west, Structure 31 to the south, and Structures 33 and 32 to the east. Structure 34 lies within the center of this exterior space.

Intensive excavations and preliminary ceramic analysis have revealed that only two of these structures, Structure 34 and Structure 37, were in place prior to the Late Classic period. During the Early Classic period, Structure 37, a 1.0 m tall platform, defined the northern portion of the

Structure 37 Plazuela

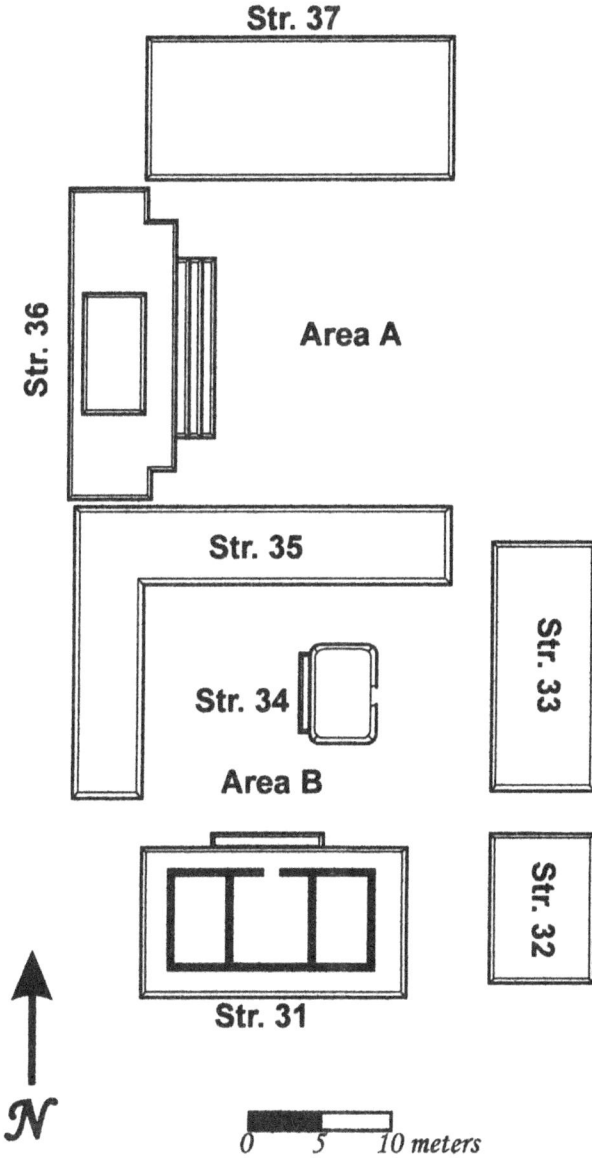

FIGURE 1.8. Structure 37 plazuela: planview.

group. This phase was constructed directly upon a natural outcrop of bedrock. A plaster floor was then laid directly upon the bedrock, extending eastward and southward from the construction. Later during the Classic, Structure 37 was extended eastward. During the construction of this platform, Burial 37 was placed on the floor. The body was covered with the large boulders that were utilized as construction fill for the extension. Unfortunately, the osteological evidence that remained was in very poor condition. However, the badly disturbed remains were identified as belonging to an adult female. There were no grave goods recovered in association with this burial.

Excavations have revealed that Structure 34, a small platform, capped an Early Classic tomb. Tomb 7 was recovered from beneath the Early Classic plaza floor and was dug directly into bedrock. Recovered within the construction fill directly above the tomb and lying on the Early Classic floor was a concentration of shells. This shell density increased as excavations penetrated the Early Classic plaza floor and moved closer to the tomb's capstones. Tomb 7 consisted of a formally constructed chamber that measured 3.25 m × 2.11 m and possessed cut limestone walls and capstones. The complete skeleton of an adult male was recovered oriented perfectly north-south (zero degrees) in a partially flexed position; it was lying on its right side. Placed directly above its skull was a red-slipped plate with a kill-hole; a small polychrome bowl was recovered below this plate. A jade pendant in the form of an acrobat and a triangular jade bead were recovered from within the left portion of the jaw. (It should be noted that these jade pieces were most likely placed around the man's neck and were recovered from within the jawbone due to the decomposition of the body.) The phytolith evidence recovered revealed the presence of a woven burial mat beneath the body (Bozarth, personal communication, 2001). Ceramic analysis of the burial goods indicates that this interment dates to the Late Preclassic/Early Classic transitional period.

Recovered at the foot of Tomb 7 and directly above its capstones was Cache 49. This cache consisted of two red ware bowls placed lip to lip. Recovered from within one bowl were the remnants of a smashed jade bead, jade flakes, numerous marine shells, pieces of coral, fish bones, a stingray spine, charcoal, and red ocher. In addition, phytolith analysis revealed that there were numerous sponge spicules present. Ceramic analysis of Cache 49 indicates that this event also dates to the Late Preclassic/ Early Classic transitional period.

A crypt was recovered 2.3 m to the west of Tomb 7 and was also capped by the construction of Structure 34. This crypt was recovered in a *chul-*

tun that measured 1.6 m × 1.6 m. The crypt itself was placed within the westernmost portion of the *chultun*. The crypt measured 1.30 m × 0.60 m and possessed precariously balanced capstones and walls that were constructed out of limestone. The badly preserved skeleton was identified as an adult male. The body was recovered oriented north-south (zero degrees) in a tightly flexed position and was lying on its left side. The only burial object recovered in association with his crypt was a red-slipped ceramic pendant. The entire *chultun* appeared to have been burned due to the high density of charcoal recovered from the fill. Based upon the ceramic analysis of the sherds recovered within the fill of the *chultun* and in conjunction with the crypt, this interment has been dated to the Late Preclassic/Early Classic transitional period.

In addition to the identification of the ritual activities beneath Structure 34, a cache was recovered within the center of Area B, directly under the plaza floor. Cache 36 consisted of two shallow bowls placed lip to lip. Recovered from within these vessels were three cylindrical jade beads, one cylindrical coral bead, and two pieces of raw coral. An Early Classic expanded-stem, long-blade, chert biface was found in association with the cache. The ceramic analysis of Cache 36, in conjunction with the lithic data recovered, indicates that this ritual caching event dates to the Early Classic period.

The remaining buildings identified within the plazuela were all constructed during the Late Classic period. As such, the open public ritual space of this area was transformed into a high-status residential space. Each structure is comprised of a masonry substructure (1–2 m in height), and two of these buildings, Structures 31 and 37, possess masonry superstructures as well. This shift from public ritual to private residential space underscores the fundamental Late Classic shift in architecture, as well as the change in the nature of ritual activities. This evidence correlates to similar activities identified within the site core (Guderjan 1996).

In addition to the architectural forms identified as being Late Classic, Cache 37 was recovered from beneath Area B's plaza floor, approximately 2 m south of Cache 36. This cache consisted of twenty-two expanded stem, long-blade, chert bifaces, a 30 cm long laurel leaf biface, twenty-one prismatic obsidian blades, and an elaborate, perforated chert eccentric. While straight or expanded-stem projectile points are relatively rare in the Maya lowlands, at Barton Ramie and Altar de Sacrificios they do occur within the Late/Terminal Classic. The obsidian analysis from Cache 37 indicates the obsidian source as El Chayal. The ceramic analysis of Cache 37, in conjunction with the lithic data recovered, indicates that this event dates to the Late/Terminal Classic period. Similar caches of this form and date can be found at other sites, such as El Baúl (Thompson 1948).

The caching activities noted at the Structure 37 plazuela indicate a transition of ritual activities from the Early Classic to the Late Classic period. During the Early Classic, exterior Area B functioned solely as a sacred space. However, with the placement of Cache 37 and the construction of the remaining structures that formed the plazuela, a divergence from traditional ritual activities occurred. Chert bifacial tools replaced jade objects in ritual caching events. However, though the form of the caches recovered transformed over time, the continued use of exterior Area B as a ritual space remained constant.

The Terminal Classic would prove to be a turbulent period for the elite inhabitants of the site. Massive amounts of portable goods were ritually deposited against the baselines of Structure 36, Structure 34, and Structure 31. The artifact assemblage recovered from the deposits within the plazuela included over 14,190 Late Terminal Classic sherds. In addition to the ceramics identified, 428 pieces of lithic debitage and 203 special finds were recovered from these deposits. Of the Special Find database, 36 percent consisted of chert biface fragments, 35 percent were identified as obsidian blades, 8 percent as chert cores, and 7 percent as metate fragments. The remaining 14 percent consisted of a variety of items such as ceramic appliqués, figurines, beads, stamps, whistles, mano fragments, armatures, spindle whorls, hammerstones, projectile point knives, scrapers, and counterweights.

These problematic features have been dubbed special deposits. Similar deposits have been identified within the Structure 13 courtyard, within the site core, and at Courtyard C-7 at Dos Hombres (Houk 1998). Archaeological experience has shown that the Maya were not in the habit of depositing trash within living spaces. As such, it is theorized that these events may represent the pattern of ritual residential termination noted at Yaxuna (Suhler 1996), Blackman Eddy (Garber et al. 1998), and Floral Park (Glassman, Conlon, and Garber 1995). These ritual middens show promise of providing an especially valuable form of secondary deposit. These features can allow for the documentation and comparison of contemporaneous activities in sites throughout the region. The results of such can provide a valuable database for establishing an artifactual chronology of the area.

After A.D. 500, construction of monumental architecture in the site core nearly ceased. Nonetheless, Blue Creek remained an active and vibrant community as construction and modification of medium and large residences for the elite members of the community increased at an unparalleled rate, especially within the residential area we have dubbed the Western Group. The dramatic shift of sacred, ritual space to residential space, noted both within the site core and within the Structure 37 plazuela, underscores the transition of power to the elite inhabitants of the site during this time period. In addition, the change in ritual activity and representations of material wealth and power can be inferred from the caching activities identified throughout this plazuela during these periods.

Courtyards From the architecturally complex but relatively open access of the plazuela group, this study now moves to the complex residences of the Western Group, which have a higher degree of restriction of access to their exterior bounded spaces. While a number of courtyard complexes have been identified across the greater Blue Creek area, only three are located within the Western Group, i.e., Structure 41, 46, and 61 courtyards (Figure 1.9).

The Structure 41 courtyard (Figure 1.9A) has a highly restricted access exterior bounded space, the formation of which appears to be the result of a continued program of construction and expansion begun during the Early Classic period. A continuous series of additions and alterations were executed throughout the Early Classic and most of the Late Classic period. This and the Structure 19 courtyard are the only completely enclosed courtyards known at Blue Creek, although others exist at nearby sites such as La Milpa, Dos Hombres, and Punta de Cacao (Guderjan 1991, Houk 1996).

Material recovered from the construction fill below the north and east sides of the complex date to later in the Early Classic period. A dedicatory cache consisting of a single inverted Late Classic period plate was found below a badly eroded staircase on the western side of the courtyard. The most substantial constructions appear to date to the Late Classic period.

From the highly restricted and compact Structure 41 courtyard we now move to the larger and slightly more open Structure 46 courtyard complex. This complex is composed of Structures 46, 47, 48, 49, 50, 51, and 52 (Figure 1.9B). To date, test excavations have been carried out on a number of these structures. The general chronological trend observed in the Western Group holds true here. The earliest constructions in this complex date to the Early Classic period. Later and more massive expansions clearly date to the Late Classic period. Spatially, there are three external bounded spaces, one large and somewhat open and two smaller and somewhat more restricted.

Structure 50, built in two phases, occupies the east side of Area A. Furthermore, it serves to define the boundary between Areas A and B. Like Structure 34 in Area B of the Structure 37 plazuela group, Structure 50 is

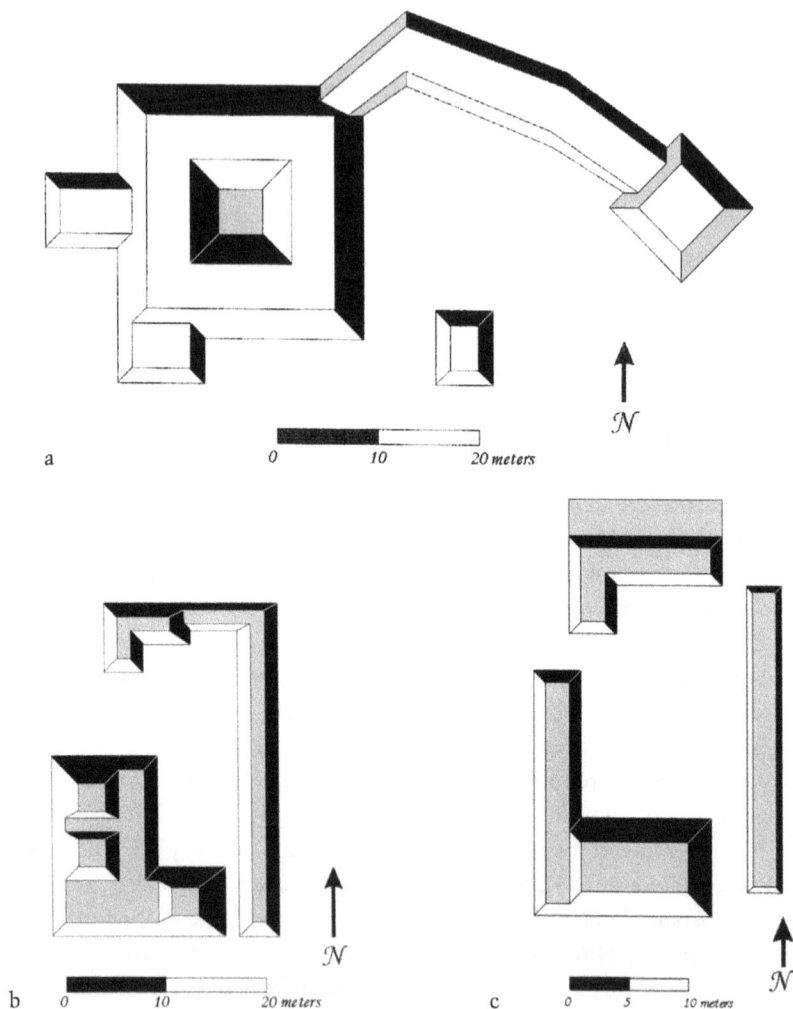

FIGURE 1.9. Example planviews of courtyard groups. (a) Structure 41. (b) Structure 46. (c) Structure 61.

a central focus feature dedicated to elite private ritual and ancestor veneration. A looter's trench penetrating the eastern flank of this structure revealed the presence of a small but well-constructed burial crypt within the center of the mound. While to date little securely datable material has been recovered from this structure, initial observations point to an Early Classic period construction for at least the first phase, Structure 50-I.

As with investigations at the Structure 13 courtyard and Structure 37 plazuela, excavations at Structure 50 have revealed the presence of a large deposit of material remains, smashed across one face of the structure. However, unlike the above-mentioned deposits, a close examination of the stratigraphy at Structure 50 reveals that this deposit was not laid down until after the structure had begun to collapse.

After the large and complex forms of plazuelas and courtyards, the next category to be considered is the patio group. This is a simpler spatial form that was often, through time and continued occupation, transformed into the previously discussed spatial categories.

Patio Groups At the smallest end of the range of variability are the patio groups: the Structure 43, 45, 54, 58, and 60 patio groups, which largely consist of L-shaped buildings generally facing the east and have no apparent eastern side enclosures (Figure 1.10). To be clear, each of these sits atop a substantial hill that was "sculpted" into a flat, very well defined external space. Thus it was probably not necessary to use walls or buildings to define space. To date, the Structure 60 patio group is the only tested member of this category that lies within the scope of this chapter.

Architecturally, Structure 60 consists of a central structure with low platforms to the north and south. The north side platform is bounded on the east side by a low extension of the central structure, thus defining the patio space of this group. Temporally, Structure 60 appears to be an anomaly as far as the Western Group is concerned. The general trend of construction observed so far is that relatively minor construction episodes occurred in the Early Classic, with subsequent massive Late Classic expansions. While Structure 60 certainly has two clear construction phases, ceramic analysis of construction fill has dated both of these to the Early Classic period. To be certain, however, surface deposits and sheet middens at Structure 60 also clearly show use and occupation throughout the Late Classic period.

Spatial and Temporal Variability of Elite Residences

We have defined three primary types of elite residences at Blue Creek: plazuelas, courtyards, and patio groups. An additional type, range buildings, is also known at Blue Creek. However, our understanding of these is again uncertain.

Of the three primary types considered here, plazuelas are the most complex and energy-intensive, as well as the least common. Only the Structure 37 plazuela is among the elite residences considered here. However, two other significant plazuela complexes have been discovered in the settle-

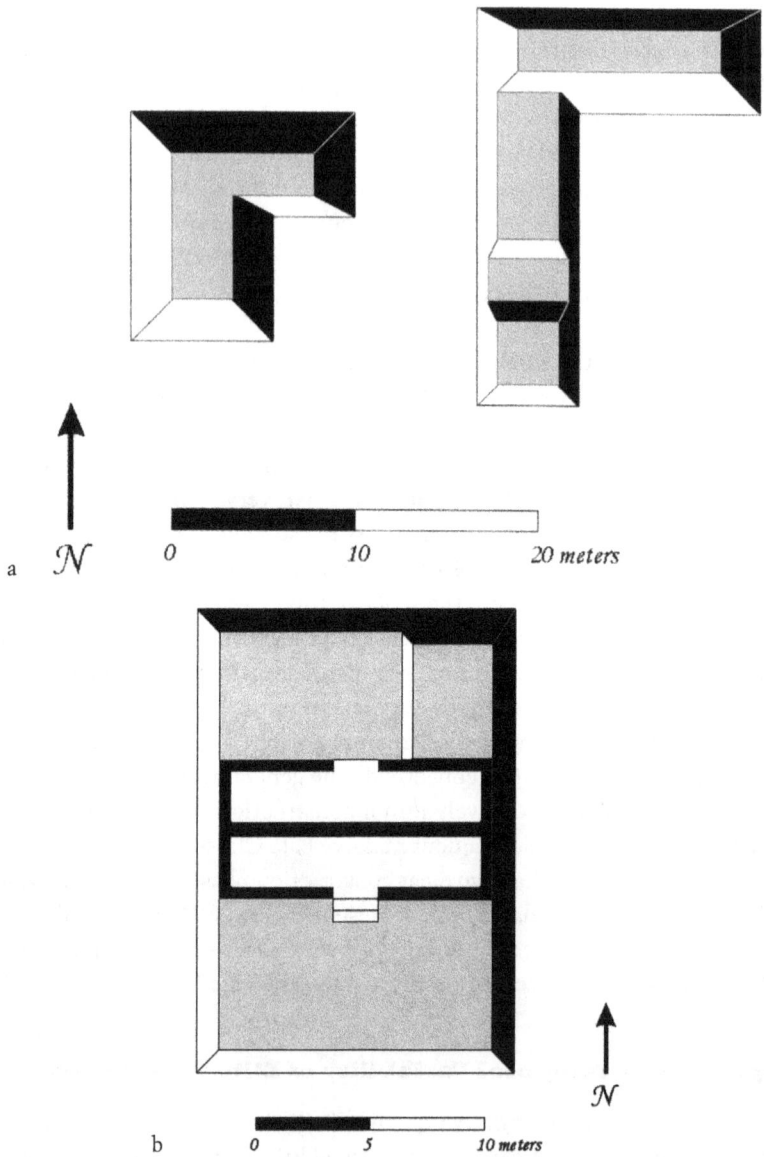

FIGURE 1.10. Example planviews of patio groups. (a) Structure 54. (b) Structure 58.

ment zone of the Blue Creek ruin. The first is the Structure 2C-6 plazuela, at the center of the settlement zone community of Nukuch Muul, located 1.6 km northwest of the site core. The second is the Welker plazuela, located approximately 1.4 km to the northeast of the site core along the top of the escarpment. While no temporal data have been recovered from these complexes, some spatial aspects of these groups have been noted. All three of these complexes are located atop prominent hills with commanding views of the surrounding region. The Welker plazuela boasts a view off the escarpment as far as the horizon. The 2C-6 Group forms the central focus of its barrio.

Courtyards, a more common feature in the greater Blue Creek area, constitute five of the thirteen residences treated in this chapter. We also know of several other courtyards that are well within the settlement zone. Most of these are found on hilltops along the crest of the Bravo escarpment to the north and south of the Core Area.

The exceptions to the courtyard pattern are the Structure 19 courtyard and the Structure 13 courtyard. The Structure 19 courtyard is an extremely complex compound that saw numerous modifications over its several century life. The Structure 13 courtyard was originally a small public group and was transformed into secular, residential space probably in the latter part of the Early Classic or early part of the Late Classic. Importantly, there are no other palaces or temple-palaces in the site core. So, these courtyards apparently functioned as the homes of the most important families. While the Structure 19 courtyard was built in the Early Classic, the transformation of the Structure 13 courtyard was later. This may be related to the events of A.D. 500—the massive caching of jade and other objects at Structure 4 and the general cessation of construction of public monumental architecture after that time. This could have been the result of the installation of a vassal lord by a conquering ruler who left the Blue Creek ruling lineage in place. It has also been seen as Blue Creek developing a bilateral ruling lineage, conforming to a historic Yucatecan model. A third possibility is that Structure 13 simply reflects a Late Classic expansion of the elites, as seen at other sites. Nevertheless, these two courtyards are the most centrally located and most complex elite residences at Blue Creek. This fits well with the postulated general growth of elites throughout the region. Chase and Chase (A. Chase and D. Chase 1992; A. Chase 1992) have argued that such a process occurred at Caracol, and Awe has made the same argument for Cahal Pech (Iannone 1994). Further, numerous other sites exhibit considerable construction of elite residences in the Late Classic. In some of these cases, the process of secularization also occurred, so it is equally possible that the changes in the Structure 13 courtyard were simply part of that larger social and political process.

Patio groups are quite common, forming fully half of the sample under consideration. All but one of these are located in the Western Group. However, many others are found elsewhere at Blue Creek, particularly on hilltops along the Bravo escarpment. Though we do not have accurate data at this time, we can reasonably say that there are probably twice as many patio groups as courtyards. In addition, other patio groups are found on hilltops west of the site core, which overlook small bajos. It is very possible that patio groups were occupied by a "middle," or managerial, class who served the ruling lineage and "upper" class.

The locations of elite residences are important (Table 1.2). Of the thirteen considered in this chapter, four are located in or very near the core, and the other nine make up the Western Group, closely associated with the core. The central location, size, complexity, and restricted-access exterior spaces found in the Structure 19 and Structure 13 courtyards argue strongly for the residents of these complexes to be members of Blue Creek's most powerful ruling lineages. The Structure 25 and 28 Groups, as well as the residences of the Western Group, were occupied by those elites who were apparently one step removed from the rulers. It is possible that these individuals were seeking to establish themselves as an ideological elite, as opposed to an economic elite. A line of evidence in this direction has been recovered from the Structure 37 plazuela, in the form of a significant cache of assorted lithics that included an elaborate eccentric (Hanratty 1998). Lithic caches that contain eccentrics may have been used by the Maya elite to define and solidify sociopolitical relationships. Finally, various elite and high-status residences are found throughout the rest of the settlement zone. While some of these residences occur in relative isolation, most appear associated with the various barrios that have been identified both above and below the escarpment. Whether associated with commanding views of the surrounding landscape or with critical resources such as water management or prime agricultural lands, the residents of these groups may have formed an economic elite that was socially distinct from the elite residents found in and near the central precinct. Alternately, several of these complexes may have been secondary residences of the elite households of the Core Area and Western Group.

The elite and other high-status residences of the settlement zone generally occur in one of three overlapping contexts: the high ground along the top of the escarpment, the hilltops to the west of the escarpment, and the various barrios. The Welker plazuela and the SHB courtyard are examples

Table 1.2. *Locations of Elite Residences at Blue Creek*

Location	Examples
In Core Area	Structure 28, Structures 13 & 19 courtyards, Structure 25 patio group
Western Group	See Table 1.1
Along crest of escarpment	SHB, Welker plazuela
Hilltops west of public precinct	Numerous
Residential barrios	Range building at Sayap Ha'
Residential barrios	Range building at Sayap Ha'
Outlying mound groups	Rosita, Nukuch Muul

of the isolated residences located along the top of the escarpment. Complex elite residences are found atop most of the hills found to the west of the escarpment. While some barrios have only a single patio group, others exhibit a wider variety. The barrio of Sayap Ha', for example, 1.2 km northeast of the core, contains a large range building, a courtyard, and several patio groups, as well as a twin temple mound ritual complex.

What we know of the temporal aspects of elite residences is still limited by lack of excavation. Large-scale work has only been undertaken at four residences, the Structure 25 patio group, the Structure 13 courtyard, the Structure 19 courtyard, and the Structure 37 plazuela. The Structure 25 patio group was not constructed until the Late Classic, though there probably were perishable structures at that location in the Early Classic. The Structure 19 courtyard was initially constructed in the Early Classic and saw continual minor remodelings from then until A.D. 850. The Structure 13 courtyard was transformed from sacred public space to secular residential space near the end of the Early Classic. Finally, the Structure 37 plazuela was initially constructed in the Early Classic and massively remodeled during the Late Classic.

Consequently, we see a possible shift in construction emphasis between the Early Classic and the Late Classic. In the Early Classic, public monumental construction was rapid and large-scale at Blue Creek. Possibly related to the events of A.D. 500, this virtually ceased in the Late Classic.

Instead of public monumental construction, a significant amount of Late Classic construction and remodeling of elite residences seems to have occurred. While Blue Creek was not building public structures in the Late Classic, it certainly was a thriving small center. It also appears to have been at its population peak in the Late Classic. The possible reasons for this may be the conquest of Blue Creek by another kingdom (Guderjan 1998). Alternatively, we may only be seeing a shift in emphasis from public display to privatizing and competition for status among the elite.

Abandonment Rituals in the Blue Creek Courtyards

One last point about the elite residences at Blue Creek has to do with the final act of abandonment of the site. At the end of Tepeu 2 times, approximately A.D. 850, Blue Creek was abandoned, and throughout the site ritual destruction of portable objects marked the event. These events are often termed "termination rituals," but "abandonment rituals" is probably a better term. In earlier excavations, such deposits were believed to be postoccupational debris (Thompson 1939; see also Mock 1998 for a current consideration of such deposits).

Importantly, after considerable excavation of public buildings, we have only seen a single case of a large-scale abandonment ritual: hundreds of pottery vessels were smashed onto the front of Structure 3 on the Main Plaza.

On the other hand, large-scale abandonment rituals occurred in three of the elite complexes so far investigated, the Structure 13 courtyard, the Structure 46 courtyard, and the Structure 37 plazuela. Interestingly, no such ritual took place at the Structure 19 courtyard or the Structure 25 patio group. A similar pattern of elite residential abandonment seems to be the case at the site of Dos Hombres (Houk 1996) to the south, but abandonment rituals at Belize Valley sites such as Floral Park were focused on the public architecture (Mary Brown, personal communication, 1997; James Garber, personal communication, 1997). In closing, two final points of interest should be noted. The poststructural collapse deposition of the deposit on the Structure 46 courtyard and the evidence for a reduced population living at the Structure 19 courtyard provide evidence that the termination and abandonment of the Blue Creek elite residences resulted from a process and not a single event. Whatever did occur at Blue Creek seems to have focused either animosity or veneration on the elites of the city. How this will play into our understanding of the demise of Late Classic civilization is yet to be seen.

ACKNOWLEDGMENTS

We offer our thanks to the members of the staff of the Blue Creek project who have aided this chapter by both their physical and intellectual efforts. In particular, we express our appreciation to David Driver, Helen Haines, Laura Kosakowsky, and Lorraine Williams-Beck, each of whom has contributed ideas to this treatment. They do not, by the way, necessarily agree with our interpretations and speculations. In addition, Colleen Popson, Jason Renaud, and the late Bill Welker contributed several summers of fine effort toward the goals of the project. Tom Dolezal continues to assist us by maintaining our computer mapping database, and he provided a number of figures used in this chapter. Finally, thanks to all of the students and volunteers of the Blue Creek project, without whom the project would not be possible.

NOTE

1. However, Karl Taube (personal communication, 1996) disagrees, arguing that the maize god is represented.

REFERENCES

Ashmore, Wendy
1981   *Maya Settlement Patterns.* Albuquerque: University of New Mexico Press.
Baker, Jeff
1997   Investigations in the Ditched Agricultural Fields. In *The Blue Creek Project: Working Papers from the 1996 Field Season,* edited by W. David Driver, Heather L. Clagett, and Helen R. Haines, 71–78. San Antonio, Tex.: Maya Research Program, St. Mary's University.
Bey, George, III, Craig A. Hansen, and William Ringle
1997   Classic to Postclassic at Ek Balam, Yucatan: Architectural and Ceramic Evidence for Defining the Transition. *Latin American Antiquity* 8 (3): 237–255.
Chase, Arlen
1992   Elite and the Changing Organization of Classic Maya Society. In *Mesoamerican Elites: An Archaeological Assessment,* edited by Diane Z. Chase and Arlen F. Chase, 30–49. Norman: University of Oklahoma Press.
Chase, Arlen, and Diane Chase
1985   Postclassic Temporal and Spatial Frames for the Lowland Maya: A Background. In *The Lowland Maya Postclassic,* edited by Arlen F. Chase and Prudence M. Rice, 9–22. Austin: University of Texas Press.
1992   Mesoamerican Elites: Assumptions, Definitions, and Models. In *Mesoamerican Elites: An Archaeological Assessment,* edited by Diane Z. Chase and Arlen F. Chase, 3–17. Norman: University of Oklahoma Press.
Clagett, Heather
1997   Household Archaeology at Blue Creek, Belize: A Step beyond Functionalism. Paper presented at the annual meeting of the Society for American Archaeology, Nashville, Tenn.
Coggins, Clemency
1975   Painting and Drawing Styles at Tikal: An Historic and Iconographic Reconstruction. Ph.D. dissertation, Department of Anthropology, Harvard University.
Currid, Demori
2002   Excavations in the Structure 60 Courtyard. In *Working Papers of the Blue Creek Project: The 1998 and 1999 Field Seasons,* edited by Thomas H. Guderjan and Robert L. Lichtenstein. Fort Worth: Maya Research Program, Texas Christian University.
Driver, W. David
1995   Architecture and Ritual at Structure 1. In *Archaeological Research at Blue Creek, Belize: Progress Report of the Third (1994) Field Season,* edited by Thomas H. Guderjan and W. David Driver, 27–33. San Antonio, Tex.: Maya Research Program, St. Mary's University.

Driver, W. David, Heather L. Clagett, and Helen R. Haines (eds.)
1997   *The Blue Creek Project: Working Papers from the 1996 Field Season.* San Antonio, Tex.: Maya Research Program, St. Mary's University.

Ek, Jerry
2002   Excavations in the Structure 46 Courtyard. In *Working Papers of the Blue Creek Project: The 1998 and 1999 Field Seasons,* edited by Thomas H. Guderjan and Robert L. Lichtenstein. Fort Worth: Maya Research Program, Texas Christian University.

Freidel, David, Linda Schele, and Joy Parker
1993   *The Maya Cosmos: Three Thousand Years on the Shaman's Path.* New York: William Morrow.

Fried, M.
1967   *The Evolution of Political Society.* New York: Random House.

Garber, James F., W. David Driver, Lauren A. Sullivan, and David M. Glassman
1998   Bloody Bowls and Broken Pots: The Life, Death, and Rebirth of a Maya House. In *The Sowing and the Dawning: Termination, Dedication, and Transformation in the Archaeological and Ethnographic Record of Mesoamerica,* edited by Shirley Boteler Mock, 124–133. Albuquerque: University of New Mexico Press.

Gilgan, Elizabeth
1996   Excavations in the Structure 13 Courtyard and Complex. In *Archaeology at Blue Creek, Belize; Papers of the Fourth (1995) Field Season.* Edited by Thomas H. Guderjan, W. David Driver, and Helen R. Haines. San Antonio, Tex.: Maya Research Program, St. Mary's University.
1997   Excavations in the Structure 13 Courtyard Group. In *The Blue Creek Project: Working Papers from the 1996 Field Season,* edited by W. David Driver and Heather Clagett, 33–39. San Antonio, Tex.: Maya Research Program, St. Mary's University.

Glassman, David M., James M. Conlon, and James F. Garber
1995   Survey and Initial Excavations at Floral Park. In "The Belize Valley Archaeology Project: Results of the 1994 Field Season." Department of Archaeology, Belmopan, Belize. Photocopy.

Grube, Nikolai, Thomas H. Guderjan, and Helen R. Haines
1995   Late Classic Architecture and Iconography at the Blue Creek Ruin, Belize. *Mexicon* 17 (3): 51–56.

Guderjan, Thomas H.
1991   *Maya Settlement in Northwestern Belize.* Culver City, Calif.: Labyrinthos.
1996   Investigations at the Blue Creek Ruin, Northwestern Belize. In *Los investigadores de la cultura maya,* 330–354. Campeche, Mex.: Universidad Autónoma de Campeche.
1997   Archaeological and Ethnohistorical Data: A Re-Appraisal of the Chetumal Province. Paper presented at the annual meeting of the Society for American Archaeology, Nashville, Tenn.
1998   The Blue Creek Jade Cache: Early Classic Ritual in Northwest Belize. In *The Sowing and Dawning: Termination, Dedication, and Transformation in the Archaeological and Ethnographic Record of Mesoamerica,* edited by Shirley Mock. Albuquerque: University of New Mexico Press.

Guderjan, Thomas H., and W. David Driver (eds.)
1995   *Archaeological Research at Blue Creek, Belize: Progress Report of the Third (1994) Field Season.* San Antonio, Tex.: Maya Research Program, St. Mary's University.

Guderjan, Thomas H., W. David Driver, and Helen R. Haines (eds.)
1996   *Archaeological Research at Blue Creek, Belize: The 1995 Season.* San Antonio,
       Tex.: Maya Research Program, St. Mary's University.
Guderjan, Thomas H., Helen Haines, Michael Lindeman, Dale Pastrana, Ellen
       Ruble, and Pam Weiss
1994   *Excavations at Blue Creek: The 1992 and 1993 Field Seasons.* San Antonio,
       Tex.: Maya Research Program, St. Mary's University.
Guderjan, Thomas H., and C. Colleen Hanratty
2001   A Non-Royal Elite Lineage at Blue Creek: Evidence from Burials, Caches, and
       Architecture. Paper presented at the Sixth European Maya Conference, Ham-
       burg, Germany.
Guderjan, Thomas H., and Dale Pastrana
2001   Patterns of Maya Jade Disposal at Blue Creek, Belize. Paper presented at the
       annual meeting of the Society for American Archaeology, New Orleans.
Haines, Helen R.
1995   Summary of Excavations at the Temple of the Masks. In *Archaeological Re-
       search at Blue Creek, Belize: Progress Report of the Third (1994) Field Season,*
       edited by Thomas H. Guderjan and W. David Driver, 73–99. San Antonio, Tex.:
       Maya Research Program, St. Mary's University.
Haines, Helen R., and David Wilhelmy
1999   Excavations in the Structure 25. In *Working Papers of the Blue Creek Project
       from the 1997 Field Season,* edited by W. David Driver, Helen R. Haines, and
       Thomas H. Guderjan. San Antonio, Tex.: Maya Research Program, St. Mary's
       University.
Hammond, Norman
1986   The Emergence of Maya Civilization. *Scientific American* 255 (2): 106–115.
Hanratty, C. Colleen
1998   Excavations at the Structure 37 Courtyard, Blue Creek, Belize. Paper pre-
       sented at the annual meeting of the Society for American Archaeology, Seattle.
Hanratty, C. Colleen, and W. David Driver
1997   Excavations in the Structure 37 Courtyard. In *The Blue Creek Project: Work-
       ing Papers from the 1996 Field Season,* edited by W. David Driver and Heather
       Clagett. San Antonio, Tex.: Maya Research Program, St. Mary's University.
Harrison, Peter D.
1970   The Central Acropolis at Tikal, Guatemala: A Preliminary Study of the Func-
       tion of Its Structural Components during the Late Classic Period. Ph.D. dis-
       sertation, Department of Anthropology, University of Pennsylvania.
Houk, Brett A.
1996   The Archaeology of Site Planning: An Example from the Maya Site of Dos
       Hombres, Belize. Ph.D. dissertation, Department of Anthropology, University
       of Texas at Austin.
1998   *The 1997 Season of the Chan Chich Archaeological Project.* San Antonio,
       Tex.: Center for Maya Studies.
Iannone, Gyles
1994   Ancient Maya Social Organization and the Concept of Middle Class: An As-
       sessment. In *Belize Valley Archaeological Reconnaissance Project: Progress
       Report of the Sixth (1993) Field Season,* edited by Jaime J. Awe. London: Insti-
       tute of Archaeology, University College.
Iannone, Gyles, and James M. Conlon
1993   Elites, Eccentrics, and Empowerment in the Maya Area: Implications for the
       Interpretation of a Peripheral Settlement Cluster near Cahal Pech, Cayo Dis-

trict, Belize. *Papers from the Institute of Archaeology* 4: 77–89. London: University College.

Lichtenstein, Robert

1996 Preliminary Report of the Excavation of the Structure 19 Courtyard. In *Archaeology at Blue Creek, Belize: Papers of the Fourth (1995) Field Season*, edited by Thomas H. Guderjan, W. David Driver, and Helen R. Haines. San Antonio, Tex.: Maya Research Program, St. Mary's University.

1997 The Structure 19 Courtyard. In *The Blue Creek Project: Working Papers from the 1996 Field Season*, edited by W. David Driver, Heather Clagett, and Helen Haines, 39–53. San Antonio, Tex.: Maya Research Program, St. Mary's University.

1999 The Blue Creek Settlement Testing Program. In *Working Papers of the Blue Creek Project from the 1997 Field Season*, edited by W. David Driver, Helen R. Haines, and Thomas H. Guderjan. San Antonio, Tex.: Maya Research Program, St. Mary's University.

2000 *Settlement Zone Communities of Blue Creek*. Occasional Paper 2. Fort Worth: Maya Research Program, Texas Christian University.

2001 Tomb 7: A Late Preclassic Burial at Blue Creek. Paper presented at the annual meeting of the Society for American Archaeology, New Orleans.

2002 Excavations in the Structure 61 Courtyard. In *Working Papers of the Blue Creek Project: The 1998 and 1999 Field Seasons*, edited by Thomas H. Guderjan and Robert L. Lichtenstein. Fort Worth: Maya Research Program, Texas Christian University.

Loten, Stanley, and David Pendergast

1984 *A Lexicon for Maya Architecture*. Toronto: Royal Ontario Museum.

McAnany, Patricia A.

1998 Ancestors and the Classic Maya Built Environment. In *Function and Meaning in Classic Maya Architecture*, edited by Stephen D. Houston, 271–298. Washington, D.C.: Dumbarton Oaks Research Library and Collection.

Mock, Shirley Boteler (ed.)

1998 *The Sowing and the Dawning: Termination, Dedication, and Transformation in the Archaeological and Ethnographic Record of Mesoamerica*. Albuquerque: University of New Mexico Press.

Pastrana, Dale

1999 Analysis of Jades from Structure 4. In *Working Papers of the Blue Creek Project from the 1997 Field Season*, edited by W. David Driver, Helen R. Haines, and Thomas H. Guderjan. San Antonio, Tex.: Maya Research Program, St. Mary's University.

Pendergast, David M.

1992 Noblesse Oblige: The Elites of Altun Ha and Lamanai. In *Mesoamerican Elites*, edited by Diane Chase and Arlen Chase, 61–77. Norman: University of Oklahoma Press.

Popson, Colleen, and Heather Clagett

1998 Excavations at Chan Cahal. In *Working Papers of the Blue Creek Project from the 1997 Field Season*, edited by W. David Driver, Helen R. Haines, and Thomas H. Guderjan. San Antonio, Tex.: Maya Research Program, St. Mary's University.

1999 Excavations at Chan Cahal. In *The Blue Creek Project: Working Papers from the 1997 Season*, edited by W. David Driver, Helen R. Haines, and Thomas H. Guderjan, 71–84. San Antonio, Tex.: Maya Research Program, St. Mary's University.

Roys, Ralph

1957   *Political Geography of the Yucatan Maya.* Washington, D.C.: Carnegie Institution of Washington.

Roys, Ralph, and Edwin Shook

1966   *Preliminary Report on the Ruins of Ake, Yucatan.* Memoir 20, Society for American Archaeology.

Schele, Linda, and David Freidel

1990   *A Forest of Kings.* New York: Morrow.

Suhler, Charles

1996   Excavations in the North Acropolis, Yaxuna, Yucatan, Mexico. Ph.D. dissertation, Department of Anthropology, Southern Methodist University.

Thompson, J. Eric S.

1948   *An Archaeological Reconnaissance in the Cotzumalhuapa Region, Escuintla, Guatemala.* Carnegie Institution of Washington Publication 574; Contributions to American Anthropology and History, no. 44. Washington, D.C.

Tourtellot, Gair, III

1988   *Excavations at Seibal, Department of Peten, Guatemala: Peripheral Survey and Excavations, Settlement and Community Patterns.* Memoirs of the Peabody Museum of Archaeology and Ethnology, vol. 17. Cambridge, Mass.: Harvard University.

CHAPTER TWO

At Court in Copan

PALACE GROUPS OF THE EARLY CLASSIC

Loa P. Traxler

The Acropolis of Copan preserves generations of royal architecture and represents one of the best archaeological case studies for the evolution of a Classic Maya center. Each major construction phase consistently emphasized specific locations within this royal precinct (Sharer, Fash, et al. 1999; Fash 1998). Two locations, Structure 10L-16 and Structure 10L-26, figure most prominently in this evolution (Figure 2.1), and imagery along with texts relate these loci to the founder of the Classic era dynasty, K'inich Yax K'uk' Mo'. Recent and ongoing investigations associate the earliest large-scale architecture of the Acropolis stratigraphy in these loci to the time of the founding in A.D. 426.

The South Group of the early Acropolis, located beneath the area of Structure 10L-16, was dominated by puddled adobe architecture yet also included the first cut masonry residences of the Acropolis sequence (Figure 2.2). One building, Structure Hunal, was likely the residence of the founder. This royal group was quickly developed with sequential masonry construction in monumental proportions, becoming the massive core of the Acropolis (Sharer, Traxler, et al. 1999).

To the northeast of this royal group stood additional patio groups of adobe architecture. These groups were maintained as adobe facilities, alongside the expanding masonry Acropolis, until they were rebuilt as masonry courtyard groups on terrace platforms extending from the Acropolis, probably around A.D. 470. At the point when the adobe patio groups were rebuilt as masonry courtyard groups, we have clear evidence of what scholars traditionally call palace structures in Classic Lowland Maya architectural style. These structures exhibit the characteristics of residential buildings of highest elite construction, and their location in relation to the early Acropolis summit suggest they formed a palace compound for the ruler's extended household and court.

This chapter considers, based on the stratigraphic history of these groups and continuities of specific locations and forms, whether the term "palace compound" accurately describes not only the masonry architectural groups but also the earlier facilities with mixed architectural traditions within the center of Copan. This chapter suggests that the South Group built by the founder represents the first palace compound of the Copan Acropolis, even though its architectural character differs from both the masonry compounds seen at Copan later in the Early Classic and those seen further afield during the Late Classic.

This chapter also evaluates the early stratigraphy and chronology of the Great Plaza. The evidence of adobe architecture in the Acropolis sequence prompted a review of the published excavation reports by Cheek (1983; Cheek and Kennedy Embree 1983) and more recent excavation data from the plaza area (Fash et al. 1992; Williamson 1996; Fash 1998). These data, as well as comparison with the current understanding of the Acropolis stratigraphy, suggest the entire Great Plaza was established as part of a redesigned polity center during the reign of the founder, K'inich Yax K'uk' Mo' (Traxler n.d.).

Early Acropolis Architecture

Beneath the Acropolis, the South Group and the Northeast Group were dominated by puddled adobe architecture. The adobe matrix consists of clay and soil with few inclusions of stone or cultural debris, generally speaking. This adobe architecture was not constructed from loads of river clay piled one atop another, but rather from masses of carefully mixed and prepared adobe formed in place into platforms, walls, and stairways.

Adobe substructures supported thin-walled adobe superstructures, roofed with perishable materials. Substructures varied in height and number of terraces, but most had a single vertical face which rose less than 1.5 m high. Cobble footings in several structures gave additional, internal support to the terrace bases. Adobe stairways provided access to the structures and were constructed without cobble or flat stone interior support. The surfaces of the adobe structures received a thin coating of clay mixed with red pigment. This surface on some structures was noted to be more sandy in texture, perhaps resulting from a loss of surface clay through longer exposure to weather during the structure's use-life. Postholes and post footings were located in association with several platforms, indicating they were protected with perishable roofs supported by large posts. The height of the thin-walled superstructures is not known because all were

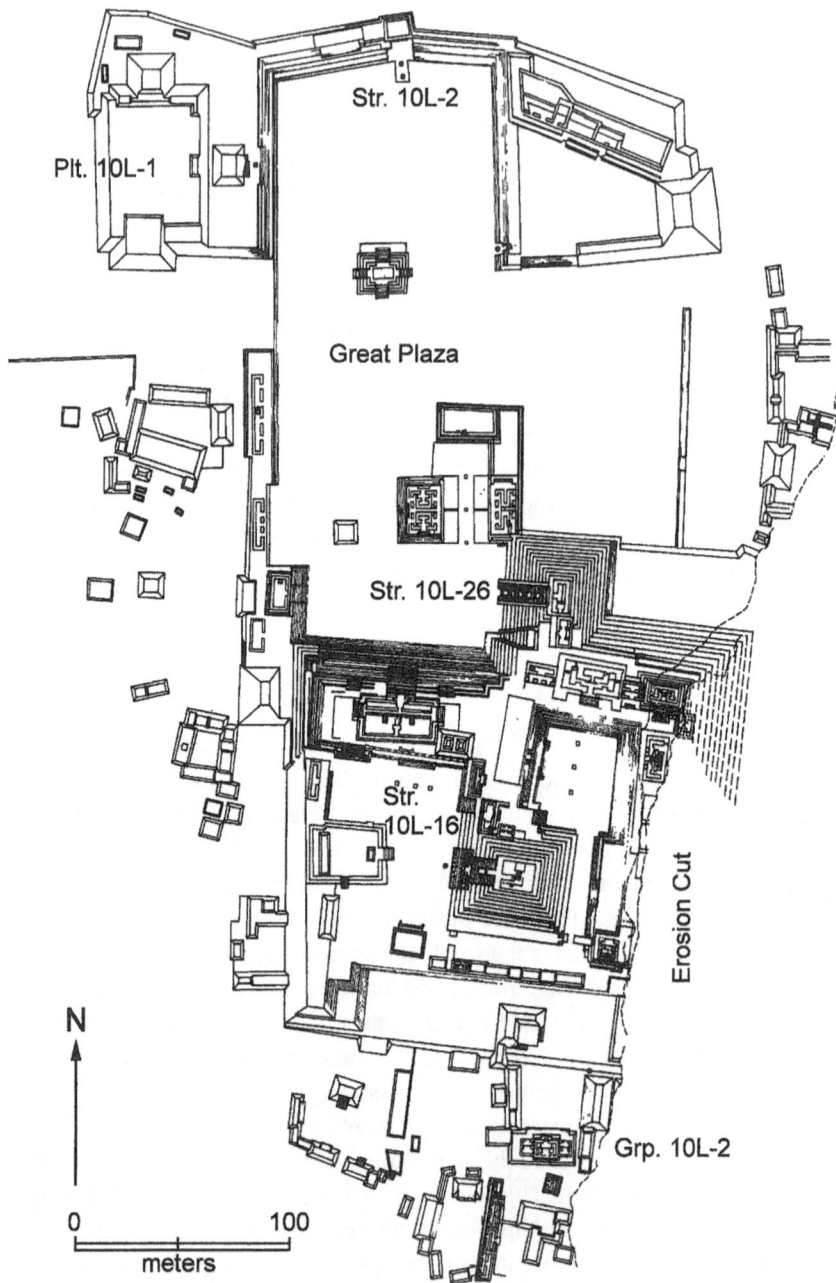

FIGURE 2.1. Principal group of Copan. The Acropolis represents four centuries of stratified royal architecture, culminating with Structure 10L-26 at its northern limit and Structure 10L-16 at its highest point near the center. (Redrawn from Fash 1991)

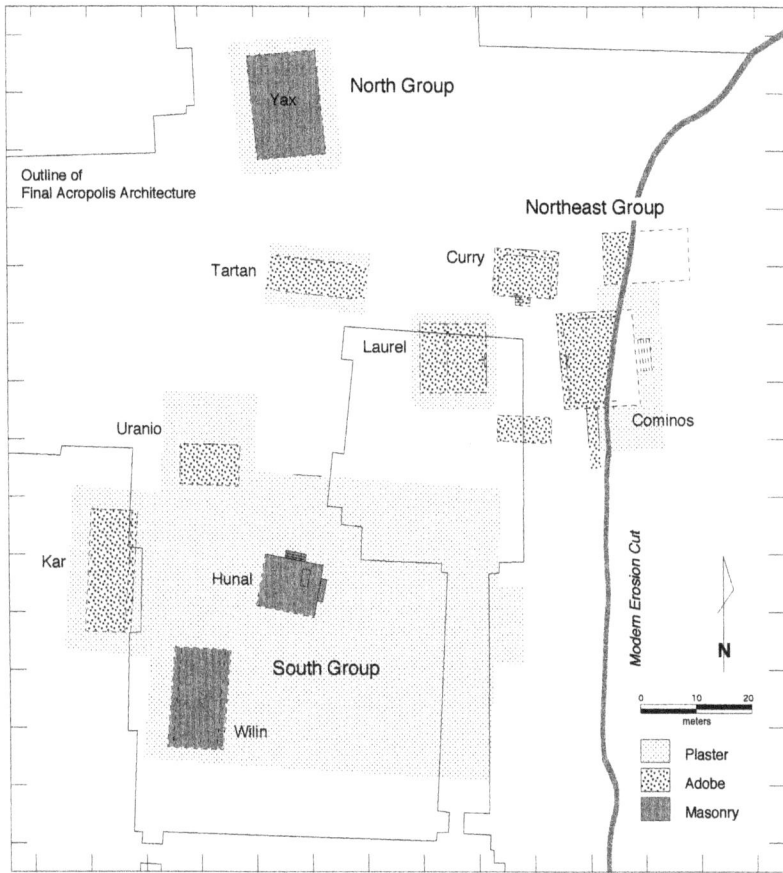

FIGURE 2.2. Plan of early architectural groups beneath the Acropolis ca. A.D. 430. The North Group underlies Structure 10L-26; the South Group underlies Structure 10L-16. (Plan by author)

mostly destroyed, leaving only the low stubs of exterior walls. There is evidence, however, for wattle-and-daub construction for at least one building. Two buildings preserve evidence of their interior floors finished with a thin whitewash surface.

The structures defined rectangular patio areas. Renovations over time added new structures to patio groups or expanded the area of existing structures. The patio areas were surfaced with various materials. Some structures were initially surrounded by a skirting floor of coarse plaster extending less than 2 m beyond the terrace bases. Other patios had cobble surfaces with gravel ballast; some were paved with flat stones. Throughout the Acropolis stratigraphy, all these early patio surface types ultimately were replaced with formal plaster floors, laid with crushed stone ballast and thick lime plaster surfaces.

South Group and Adjacent Patios

The South Group lies at the base of the Acropolis sequence beneath the area of the Late Classic Structure 10L-16 (Figure 2.2). This group was constructed in the early fifth century A.D., according to several lines of evidence including radiocarbon assays, ceramic associations, and stratigraphic ties to inscriptions with absolute dates. The South Group stood on a slight rise from which the terrain sloped downward to the river farther east. At the center of the group, four structures were arranged around a plastered patio. The eastern and southern structures of this group were masonry structures for much of their use-life; however, excavations in Structure Hunal on the east side show it replaced an initial adobe structure with evidence of pole supports for roofing (Sharer et al. 1998). Recent excavations penetrated Structure Wilin to the south and revealed evidence for several apparently adobe predecessors. The western structure of the group, Structure Kar, was maintained as an adobe structure with modifications during the occupation of the group. Sharer (1996) and Sedat (1997) interpret these three buildings as residential facilities based on their locations and low substructures, their lack of exterior decoration, and the general absence of ceremonial deposits.

The substructure of Hunal had a *talud-tablero* profile and stairway access on its north side. There were two stages of summit buildings. The second stage was largely destroyed, but wall stubs provide evidence for interior rooms with a cordholder preserved in one jamb of an offset doorway. The cut stone debris in the overlying construction fill preserved fragments of elaborate painted murals which probably decorated the building's interior rooms. About the time when Hunal's second stage superstructure was destroyed, a tomb chamber was built within the substructure. This chamber held the remains of an adult male who, based on skeletal analysis, burial furnishings, and associated inscriptions, was probably the founder of the Classic era dynasty of Copan, K'inich Yax K'uk' Mo' (Sharer 1997). Based on the various lines of evidence, this patio group was likely his residential group, and although later construction covering Hunal transformed this building into a memorial structure to K'inich Yax K'uk' Mo', the group probably remained the residence of his son and successor, Ruler 2, for several years.

Access to the buildings of the South Group was restricted by low adobe perimeter walls at the limits of the plaster patio surface on at least the north and west sides. On the sloping land to the east, an expansive fill deposit leveled the ground and supported a 2 m high cobble perimeter wall running north-south. This cobble wall probably served to define the eastern limit of the South Group, as well as the eastern limit of an area of adobe patio groups to its northeast (Figure 2.2).

In the adjacent Northeast Group, the adobe structures defined at least four patios. Additional patios may have existed in ancient times to the east and southeast, but modern river erosion has destroyed a significant portion of the eastern Acropolis which covered these areas. The patios in the Northeast Group had evidence of flat-stone cobble or gravel paving around their structures initially, and plaster paving was used later in many areas. A cobble perimeter wall oriented north-south separated two patios, and in time a two-terraced adobe structure, Structure Cominos, incorporated this wall and straddled its northern end.

Structure Laurel defined the east side of another patio area further to the west, which was bounded by other structures to the north and south. Laurel faced west and had two floor levels with at least two rooms on the upper floor level. The interior floors of these rooms were surfaced with multiple thin layers of white plaster wash and clay. In some areas these laminate, or sliplike, surfaces preserved a red color, and at least four layers of the surfaces were preserved. Cominos and Laurel also defined a patio between them with additional structures on the patio's northern and southern limits. In its initial phase, the northern structure of this patio area, Structure Curry, had the highest summit in the area, with evidence of a central doorway accessed by stairs leading up from the patio.

These adobe patio groups were distinct from the South Group and never incorporated masonry structures. While the South Group was aggressively developed with masonry architecture during the reign of the founder's son, the adobe patio groups outside it were maintained, and structures were added over time. These groups were probably the residential areas for the extended household of the ruler and his close court officials (Traxler 2001; Sharer, Traxler, et al. 1999; Traxler n.d.).

Special Adobe Structures

Many structures which comprise these patio groups are interpreted to be predominantly residential, although various activities, including administrative tasks and ceremonial events, are assumed to have unfolded there. While the majority of structures had no evidence of ceremonial activities associated with them, there were specialized ceremonial facilities within these patio groups. Within the South Group a sequence of adobe platforms on the north side of the patio (Sharer, Fash, et al. 1999) began with a 1 m high construction, Structure Uranio (Figure 2.2), which covered a burial in seated position with jade-inlaid teeth. This structure was encased by the construction of a higher, two-terraced platform, Structure Cobalto, which was surrounded with ritual deposits of carbon, shattered jade, and carved jade objects, indicating it was a more specialized, ceremonial facility.

A monumental three-terraced adobe platform, Structure Maravilla, later covered Cobalto (see Sharer, Traxler, et al. 1999: fig. 1). Preserved evidence indicated an adobe superstructure stood atop Maravilla, probably once sheltered by roofing supported by massive wood corner posts found in situ at the platform base. On the west side, adobe steps on the terraces gave access to the summit of the platform. These stairs in time were augmented with an outset masonry staircase rising from the formal plaster surface of the patio group. This three-terraced adobe structure remained in use for a great length of time, even though the masonry terraces of the expanding early Acropolis surrounded and encroached upon it (Sharer et al. 1994; Sedat 1997).

A second example of a specialized ceremonial facility lay outside the South Group, in the Laurel patio group (Figure 2.2). The northern structure of the patio, Structure Tartan, evolved through time to become a more specialized facility. It began as a simple adobe building with a whitewashed interior floor, slightly raised above the patio surface and surrounded by a skirting floor of coarse plaster. This structure was later renovated, with a low interior adobe bench added and the patio area covered by a formal plaster surface. On this plaster patio floor in front of Tartan on the south side, a series of human profile faces were painted with iconographic details (Figure 2.3). These faces were uncovered in two areas not far apart and very close to the foundation line of Tartan. Later renovation of the area covered the paintings, and another, more elaborate adobe structure stood in this location.

The structure built covering Tartan, called Structure Negra, had a different surface finish than other adobe structures. A small patch of the original exterior surface preserved evidence of a whitewash undercoat covered with a finish of bright red paint. When this structure was terminated, ritual deposits of ash, broken pottery, and clay left on the patio surface bracketed the underlying painted figures. The demolished remains of Structure Negra covered these layered deposits and spread over an extensive area. The demolition was capped with the remains of burned posts and roofing, as well as other remains suggestive of burned textiles. The painted faces, the ash deposits marking their location, the elaborate surface finish of Negra,

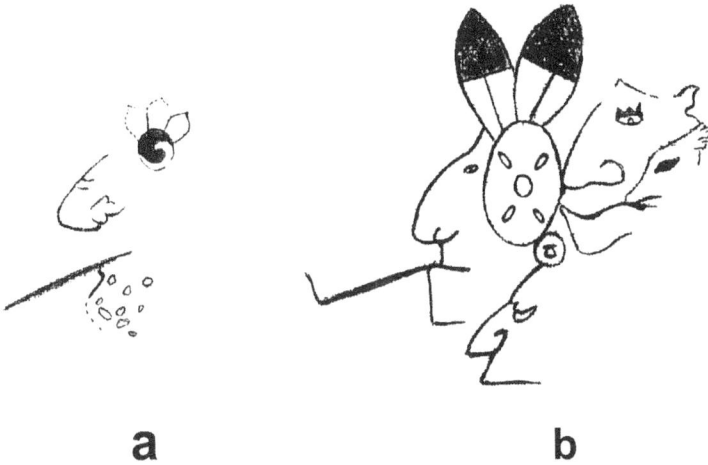

a   b

FIGURE 2.3. Anthropomorphic faces painted on plaster patio surface in front of Structure Tartan. (a) Single face measures 8 cm in height. (b) Group of three faces measures 12 cm in height. (Feature excavation and field drawing by Charles Golden)

and its dramatic termination all seem to indicate this location was the site of ritual activities in the Northeast Group.

The Royal Palace Compound

The South Group, with its mixed architectural styles and construction media, does not fit the traditional Classic Maya architectural pattern of a palace compound. However, based on the evidence that indicates it included the likely residence of the dynastic founder, the varied facilities within its perimeter walls, and its subsequent transformation into the initial stages of a monumental Acropolis during the reign of the founder's son, Ruler 2, it is proposed that the South Group be considered a royal palace compound. The northeast adobe patio groups combine with the South Group to form a more extensive palace compound providing residential facilities and ritual spaces for activities integral to court life.

Diverse Architectural Traditions

The Acropolis excavations suggest the majority of elite architecture from the first centuries of the Early Classic in the Copan Valley relates strongly to the earthen architecture of the Maya Highlands and other Southeast Region sites. This tradition derives from the Late Preclassic elite and monumental architecture documented at highland sites, including Kaminaljuyu (Kidder, Jennings, and Shook 1946; Cheek 1977) and El Portón (Sharer and Sedat 1987), as well as Chalchuapa (Sharer 1978) and Yarumela (Dixon et al. 1994) in the Southeast Region. Numerous adobe structures at these sites resemble those at Copan in their general construction and form. The techniques used to finish structure surfaces, however, differ significantly. Earthen structures at these other sites typically were finished using a thick layer of clay and crushed talpetate (consolidated volcanic ash) as the final protective surface.

While adobe structures underlie most Acropolis construction loci, there is one important exception to this pattern. That exception is north of the patio groups discussed up to this point and lies beneath the area of Late Classic Structure 10L-26 (Figure 2.2). The stratigraphic sequence in this area, here referred to as the North Group, began with leveling fill and subsequent construction of a masonry structure known as Yax (Williamson 1996; Fash 1998; Sharer, Fash, et al. 1999). Little of Structure Yax remains, but this masonry structure stood surrounded by a skirting floor of coarse plaster. It is not known exactly when Yax was built or how long it was used, but it was replaced by Structure Motmot (see Sharer, Traxler, et al. 1999: fig. 1), built directly over its location probably in A.D. 435. Motmot was built in lowland Maya architectural style with elaborately modeled stucco decoration and outset panels. Patolli boards were found both on the summit and to the east of the structure, suggesting that ritual activities took place there.

The construction date of Motmot is derived from an inscribed stone marker set in the plaza floor in front of the structure. Current interpretation of the marker text (Fash 1998; Schele, Fahsen, and Grube 1994) suggests Motmot was the ceremonial facility built for the events related to the completion of the 9th Bak'tun of the Long Count cycle on 9.0.0.0.0 (A.D. 435) mentioned in the text and celebrated during the reign of K'inich Yax K'uk' Mo'. The plaza floor establishes the contemporaneity of Motmot and Ballcourt I (Williamson 1996; Strömsvik 1952) and provides a crucial temporal anchor to the Acropolis stratigraphy.

In contrast to Yax and Motmot, the first preserved masonry structure of the South Group, Hunal, was built in central Mexican style with a low substructure with a *talud-tablero* profile. The *talud-tablero* design with its sloped terrace base below a framed panel was in vogue at both highland and lowland sites during the Early Classic. At Kaminaljuyu earthen architecture built in *talud-tablero* style frequently incorporated stone to stabilize these complex facades. As already mentioned, Hunal was probably the residence of the founder who, according to the inscriptions, came from somewhere other than the Copan Valley. The fact that at Copan the construction methods used for Hunal relied on cut-stone masonry with a lime plaster finish rather than earth and stone with a clay-talpetate finish may indicate K'inich Yax K'uk' Mo' had closer ties with the Maya lowlands than with the highlands. There seems to be a dramatic surge in masonry construction at Copan after ca. A.D. 440, and the puddled adobe tradition for elite construction at the center begins to wane during the Early Classic with the influx of these foreign masonry architectural styles.

Adobe Architecture and the Great Plaza

With the documentation of puddled adobe architecture in Acropolis excavations (see Sharer, Traxler, et al. 1999), other evidence of this construction tradition was sought in the data from previous research programs. The excavations carried out by Charles Cheek as part of the PAC (Baudez 1983; Cheek 1983) revealed the early stages of masonry construction in the evolution of the Great Plaza (Cheek 1983, 1986; Cheek and Spink 1986). A close review of the report and section drawings from this important work reveals evidence in several areas for puddled adobe structures beneath the masonry Plaza architecture.

Over the course of two field seasons, Cheek opened some four hundred excavation units over the entire expanse of the Great Plaza. This energetic program sought to establish the architectural development of the Plaza and to link its stratigraphy with the sequences of Acropolis Structures 10L-11 and 10L-26, known at that time from the tunnels previously excavated by the Carnegie Institution of Washington. In addition to the plaza excavations, Cheek supervised the investigation of Structure 10L-4 in the central area of the Plaza (Cheek and Milla Villeda 1983) and Structure 10L-2 at its northern limit (Cheek and Kennedy Embree 1983).

In the Great Plaza, Cheek characterized the initial level of the northern sector as fill of an extensive leveling construction contemporary with the initial masonry structures of the Plaza's southern sector. In his summary of the early sequence of Plaza construction, Cheek noted that 10L-4-4th was the initial structure of the northern sector of the Plaza (Cheek 1983: 202).

Beneath Structure 10L-2 (Figure 2.4), Cheek and Kennedy identified the vestiges of a structure based on the limits of a flat stone pavement and a series of post holes within a volume of fill (Cheek and Kennedy Embree 1983: fig. F-6). They interpreted this volume of fill (Layer 10e) as the core of a masonry structure, Structure 10L-2-3rd, which had been largely destroyed. They reasoned that the post features (Features 35, 36 and 37) resulted from fill-retaining techniques used during the original construction (Cheek and Kennedy Embree 1983: 105). It now seems more likely that

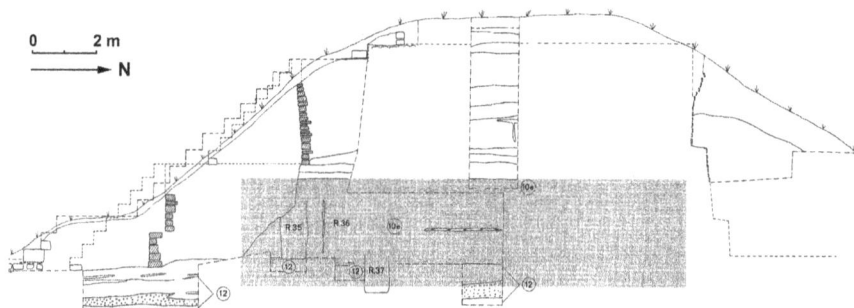

FIGURE 2.4. Section drawing of Structure 10L-2. Gray area indicates possible extent of initial adobe structure in this location, Structure 10L-2-3rd, based on fill layer 10e. (Redrawn from Cheek and Kennedy Embree 1983: Figure F-6)

the fill and the post features are the remains of an earthen substructure with posts that supported a perishable roofing of some design. This roofing would be similar in concept to that proposed for Structure Maravilla beneath the Acropolis, which had preserved remains of sizable wood corner posts (Sharer et al. 1994; Sedat 1997). The stone pavement was probably not contemporary with the construction of this adobe structure and perhaps was added later, following a pattern documented for other adobe structures beneath the Acropolis.

The fill of the earthen Structure 10L-2-3rd was the same as that used to level the Plaza in this area. It contained sherds of Bijac and early Acbi ceramic phases (dated to ca. A.D. 200–400 and ca. A.D. 400–600, respectively), as well as the Preclassic Uir phase. (In excavations beneath Structure 10L-26, this same type of leveling fill is documented underlying Structure Yax, which began the sequence of architecture preserved in the North Group.) There is no preserved facade of Structure 10L-2-3rd, but the fill indicates it measured at least 2.1 m high. It seems likely that Features 35, 36, and 37 are the remains of postholes within the mass of this structure (Cheek and Kennedy Embree 1983: fig. F-6). They were recorded as burned clay features, from which an archaeomagnetic date was reported of A.D. 575 ± 17 (Cheek and Kennedy Embree 1983: 108). This date, however, probably relates to the burning and demolition of the earthen structure at the time it was replaced with a masonry version, Structure 10L-2-2nd.

Elsewhere in the Plaza, Structure 10L-sub-1 was located beneath the central sector (see Cheek 1983: fig. C-6) and was constructed facing north, oriented, it would now seem likely, facing Structure 10L-2-3rd. The remnants of its northern facade are detected as the vertical profile of fill Layer 4 in the section drawing (Cheek 1983: fig. C-14d). Cheek referred to this fill as the probable remains of a destroyed structure, but it is likely to be the actual structure facade. It seems possible, based on the fill descriptions and ceramic associations, that Structure 10L-sub-1 was contemporary with or even predated Structure 10L-sub-2, located to the southwest (Cheek 1983: fig. C-6), which Cheek considered to be the earliest structure of the Great Plaza, and that both predate the construction of Ballcourt I in the North Group.

Associated with Structure 10L-sub-1 were two caches of Bijac phase ceramics, including mammiform tetrapods and a cache vessel with an appliqué face similar to vessels from Kaminaljuyu of this time (Kidder, Jennings, and Shook 1946). Also associated with the structure on its eastern side was a cache of obsidian blade fragments found between two posthole features, one of which would have been near the corner of the structure. Other posthole features are suggested by the southern edge of the frontal platform and its plastered surface, both of which were added later to the north side of the structure.

The fills of these plaza structures are similar to those of the adobe structures beneath the Acropolis. The rather homogenous clay fills contained few artifact inclusions, showing little or no use of construction stone, and preserved evidence of wooden posts and corner posts used to support roofing. The plaza and patio surfaces surrounding them varied. These structures tend to underlie later phase structures, meaning there was in the Plaza, as elsewhere, continuity in locations for buildings over long spans of time.

It is clear that the Great Plaza was an extensive area with formal limits marked by adobe architecture from the beginning of its sequence. The northern, southern, and southwestern limits of the Plaza hold evidence of structures contemporary with the leveling of these plaza sectors. The stratigraphy of the southern sector ties directly into the stratigraphy of Structure 10L-26 and its associated hieroglyphic dates. These connections suggest the entire polity center was reconfigured in the early fifth century A.D.

Recent test excavations directed by Fash (personal communication, 1998) on the summit of Platform 10L-1 at the northwest corner of the Great Plaza revealed Bijac fills beneath the Late Classic masonry architecture of the platform surface. Fash has suggested, based on the ceramic lots and the general layout of the platform, that this complex predates the dynastic era. Based on the observations presented in this chapter, it seems possible that the Platform 10L-1 complex was built initially as an adobe facility rather than a masonry one.

Future excavations may confirm the predynastic dating of the Platform 10L-1, and it is possible that Structure 10L-sub-1 and its Bijac cache deposits date to the predynastic time as well. If further synthesis of the recent excavation data supports the theory that K'inich Yax K'uk' Mo' redesigned the polity center around A.D. 427, then discussion can continue to explore the motivation to relocate his royal center to the south of this complex (Sharer 1996; Traxler 2001). It is clear that the South Group was constructed away from the Platform 10L-1 complex and that this change left the complex standing at the northern limit of the polity center.

Early Acropolis Courtyard Groups and the Expanding Palace Compound

The adobe patio groups beneath the Acropolis grew through time but ultimately were replaced by masonry architecture. The transition from adobe architecture to masonry began early in the South Group. There the construction of Hunal began a long sequence of masonry buildings, and the entire group was transformed into the masonry Acropolis within the span of about twenty years (Sedat 1996; Sharer, Traxler, et al. 1999). The patio structures of the Northeast Group remained in use alongside the Acropolis for some time, with renovations and new structures added. Based on architectural links to the North Group sequence late in the reign of Ruler 2 (ca. A.D. 470) and completed by the reign of the fourth ruler, Cu-Ix (ca. A.D. 480), these adobe patios were rebuilt as masonry courtyard groups on masonry platforms which extend the terraces of the Acropolis (Figure 2.5). These new courtyard groups fit a traditional conception of lowland Maya palace compounds (Traxler 1996, n.d.).

In the Northeast Group the two highest adobe buildings, Structures Cominos and Curry, were kept open for some period of time after their substructures and all of Structure Laurel to the west were buried by a high masonry platform extending out from a preexisting terrace of the Acropolis. In a tunnel operation exposing the south side of Cominos, the ballast of the plaster floor of the engulfing platform is seen abutting the adobe building exterior (Figure 2.6). How long these earthen buildings were used after their substructures were buried is difficult to quantify, but they were ultimately demolished and replaced by masonry substructures and buildings positioned directly over them (Figure 2.5, center). The fact that the earthen buildings were maintained for a period of time on the masonry platform, then replaced with masonry buildings directly over them, suggests a continuation of similar activities in this group as it changed from an earthen to a masonry facility.

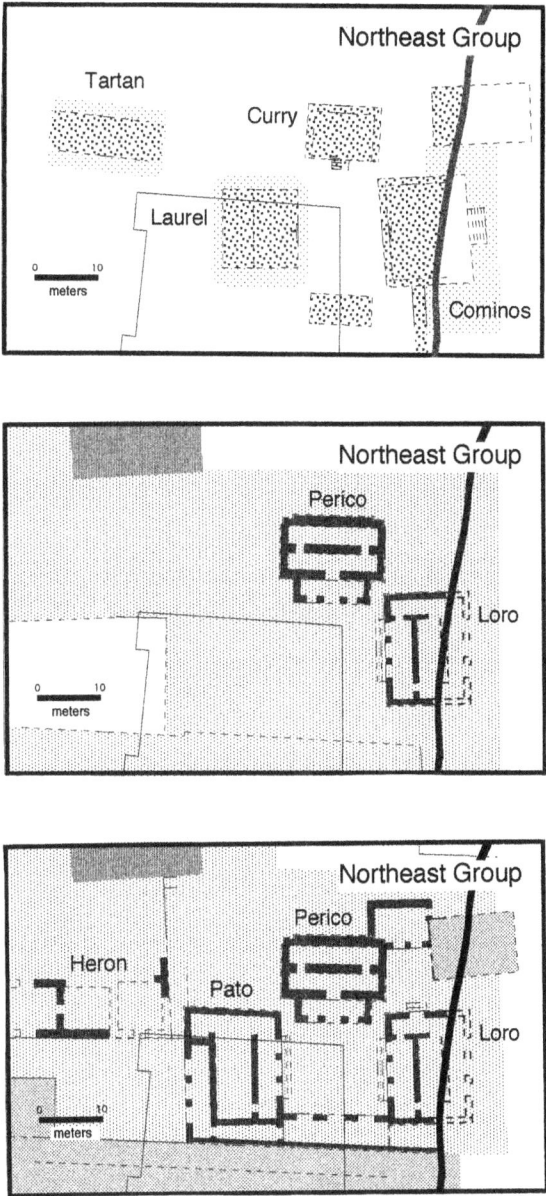

FIGURE 2.5. Evolution of architecture in Northeast Group from (top) initial adobe structures around patios with varied surfaces to (center) initial masonry structures atop masonry terrace and (bottom) additional masonry structures enclosing plastered courtyards. (Plans by author)

FIGURE 2.6. South facade of Structure Cominos exposed in tunnel excavation. Sub-flooring of masonry terrace is shown abutting the adobe structure. (Photo by author)

The large multiroom buildings, Structures Loro and Perico, were the initial constructions of the masonry group. The initial masonry platform was later expanded, and several buildings were added (Figure 2.5, bottom). The masonry buildings defined a series of courtyards arranged east to west, using the northern upper terrace of the Acropolis as their southern boundary. The buildings stood upon low substructures with broad steps across their long facades. The wide interior spaces of these buildings and their rather narrow walls suggest that they probably were not vaulted but likely had plastered, timber roofs behind masonry facades. The exception to this was the northern structure of the central courtyard, Perico, which had thicker walls and more narrow rooms, indicating it was probably vaulted. This building also was more elaborately decorated with modeled and painted stucco than the other courtyard structures.

Each building had multiple entryways from the courtyard to the outer rooms. The wide exterior doorways let in light and allowed residents to pursue activities both inside and out. The courtyards could easily have been used for domestic activities as an extension of the residence. The open character of the outer rooms with their multiple doorways contrasts with the restricted access for the interior rooms. No direct passage was possible from one side of a building to the other, and many interior doorways had cordholders on either side that allowed curtains or other types of screening to close off parts of a building. These interior rooms were quite large. The central room of Structure Pato measured 5.5 m across and 15 m long, with only one known doorway allowing access to it. These architectural spaces would accommodate large numbers of people at any given time, with the innermost rooms maintaining restricted access.

These courtyard groups had close access to the river, which was important for a variety of reasons—from concerns of domestic life to concerns of transportation and communication. Their prominent location would allow observation of river traffic for political and economic ends. The area of sheltered space in these courtyard groups is significant. Some of this space could have served as storage, allowing the ruler and nobility to directly manage some polity resources. In sum, the architectural plan and features suggest a variety of possible activities and interests served by these structures. Several characteristics of residences are present, and their scale suggests they could accommodate many people either as residents or visitors.

These masonry court buildings were renovated and expanded over time, and eventually the courtyards were almost completely enclosed, restricting access from the outside. These courtyard groups are interpreted as the palace compound of the ruler's extended family and court. This interpretation is based on several lines of information. The groups are residential in character yet include a more specialized masonry building on the northern side of the central courtyard. The large east and west structures seem to combine residential, administrative, and storage facilities. One structure preserved the remains of an interior hieroglyphic mural, and all had elaborate iconographic decoration in modeled and painted stucco on the exterior facades. Most importantly, their spatial context—being located adjacent and connected to the elevated Acropolis and serving as an intermediate connection between it and the North Group—sets them apart from all other residential groups at the time. The pattern of large east and west structures with a higher north structure is an enduring pattern for the royal palace compounds of Early Classic Copan.

The masonry palace compound as a unit is even more spatially distinct than its adobe predecessor. It stood on an elevated zone between the highest summit area of the early Acropolis (Sedat 1996; Sharer, Traxler, et al. 1999) and the North Group with the Ballcourt (Strömsvik 1952; Fash 1991; Williamson 1996; Fash 1998). Terraces and anciently destroyed stairways would have clearly defined its limits and the communication between these areas. While the compound did change through time, its organization in courtyard-focused groups remained constant, with the pattern of large structures on the east and west sides of the main courtyard and a taller structure on the north.

Expanding Royal Compound

The additions and renovations to the courtyard structures eventually exhausted the available space, and at some point, probably during the reign of the fifth or sixth ruler, the initial courtyard groups were demolished and covered over with new platform construction. The courtyard groups were rebuilt at the same level but further to the north, at the base of the platform named Purple (Figure 2.7). The new construction followed the pattern of the previous groups. The building on the west side of the main courtyard, Structure Aguila, was a new version of the large multiroom structure with its long parallel rooms and transverse end rooms (Miller and Morales 1997; Sharer, Miller, and Traxler 1992). This building defined two courts, one to the west which included structures built against the eastern terraces of the North Group, and a court to the east which unfortunately was greatly destroyed by modern river erosion. The northern building of the main court sat on the highest substructure, following the pattern seen in the previous courtyard and patio groups.

Recent investigations indicate that instead of an absolute displacement of the courtyards to the north, as reported previously (Sharer, Miller, and Traxler 1992; Traxler 1996), the compound in fact expanded, integrating a new courtyard defined on the surface of Platform Purple (covering the initial masonry courts) with the courtyard groups at the base of the platform's north side defined previously (Sharer, Traxler, et al. 1999; Miller and Morales 1997; Traxler n.d.).

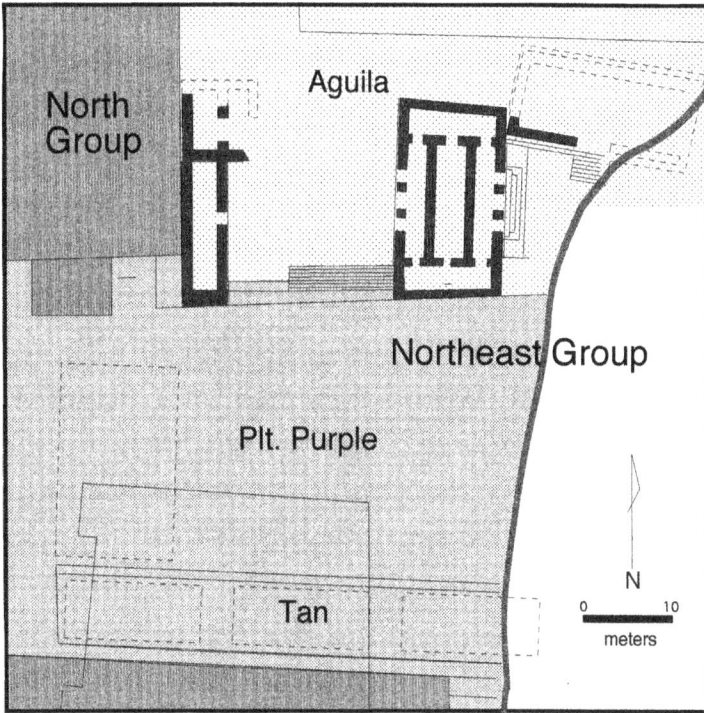

FIGURE 2.7. Later masonry courtyard architecture of Northeast Group. Platform Purple covered courtyard group shown in Figure 2.5c. (Plan by author)

The substructure called Structure Tan preserved evidence of multiple buildings upon it, indicated by short wall stubs, plaster scars, and painted red lines that were used as construction guides. Previous reports discuss Tan as an isolated structure facing north, with little other evidence of structures on the surface of Purple. However, evidence of another substructure and associated building forming the west side of a large courtyard with Tan has recently been documented. Remains of buildings on both of these low substructures are similar to earlier residential facilities, although Tan had at least one cache of charcoal and shattered jade pieces placed within it. Later construction on the northern limit of Platform Purple integrated the large courtyard on its surface with the courtyards below by way of a broad staircase.

By A.D. 500 the palace compound had expanded horizontally, covering more area, as well as vertically, integrating two levels of monumental residential construction and associated structures. One could conclude from the dating of the stratigraphy and the dramatic expansion of these groups from one architectural phase to the next that the growth of the palace facilities supporting the royal court was rapid. Certainly by the reign of the fifth and sixth rulers of the Copan dynasty, the royal palace compound was extensive in area and complex in its range of facilities and their spatial integration.

Summary and Closing Thoughts

The earliest structures in almost all areas of the Copan Acropolis were built using puddled adobe construction. This tradition resembles and likely derives from Preclassic architecture of the Maya Highlands and the Southeast Region. This cultural affiliation, expressed also in ceramics and other material culture, suggests that the people of Proto Classic and Early Classic Copan were more closely connected with highland Maya peoples than the lowland Maya of the Peten. The arrival of K'inich Yax K'uk' Mo' and the founding of the Classic era dynasty of Copan in A.D. 426 represents a shift in cultural affiliation of the highest elite and coincides with the construction of masonry architecture in foreign styles as well as a reconfiguration of the polity center.

The South Group was part of the new configuration. It incorporated adobe and masonry architecture within a restricted group defined by perimeter walls. This group included structures that likely were the residence of K'inich Yax K'uk' Mo' and his royal household. Alongside this royal group stood the other patio groups of adobe architecture that were probably the residential facilities for the extended royal household and court. Together, these groups represent the earliest royal palace compound known at Copan. To the north of this compound stood the ceremonial facility and ballcourt referred to in this discussion as the North Group. At present this is the only known group of the early Acropolis that was initiated with masonry construction. Its focal structure, Yax, may have been built for ceremonies related to the dynastic founding and its successor, Motmot, for ceremonies related to the completion of the 9th Bak'tun in A.D. 435.

Beyond the South and North Groups, the Great Plaza extended farther northward. It was defined by architecture on all sides from its initial phase, including adobe construction underlying Structure 10L-2 and elsewhere (Traxler n.d.). At the northwest corner of the Great Plaza stands Platform 10L-1, which Fash has suggested may preserve an earlier predynastic royal complex. The complex may have been constructed initially of adobe architecture, given the cultural affiliations between Copan and the Maya Highlands during predynastic times.

Recognized first in the sealed strata of the Acropolis, puddled adobe architecture is now recognized elsewhere in the Copan Valley, including the Late Preclassic ballcourt at Los Achiotes excavated recently by Canuto (2002). The long-running discussions (Fash 1983; Webster and Freter 1990; Fash and Sharer 1991) concerning the relatively few Proto Classic and Early Classic settlement areas in the Copan Valley should in the future take into account these recent discoveries. The use of adobe construction for elite architecture during the Proto and Early Classic periods may be difficult to detect at sites where mounds have less protection afforded by overlying masonry architecture than is the case in the polity center.

The South Group was rapidly transformed into the monumental early Acropolis, alongside which the more open patio groups of adobe continued. These groups in time were rebuilt as masonry courtyard groups (ca. A.D. 470–480). They are interpreted as the palace compound of the extended royal household and court of the later Early Classic rulers. This masonry palace compound expanded further in time, with its latest version beneath the Acropolis integrating multiple platform levels.

The South Group and adobe patios formed the earliest identified version of the royal palace compound. The summit of the expanding early Acropolis and the adjacent courtyard groups formed later sequential versions of the same facility. Based on a comparison with the early Acropolis architecture, Group 10L-2, excavated recently by Andrews and his colleagues (Andrews and Fash 1992; Andrews 1996, n.d.) represents the Late Classic version of this royal facility. These compounds were essential for the activities of the ruler and his court, and for this reason they were replicated over time, preserving the essential structural components of their design.

ACKNOWLEDGMENTS

This research is part of a program of investigation begun in 1989 and sponsored by the University of Pennsylvania Museum under the direction of Robert J. Sharer. Our program, the Early Copan Acropolis Program (ECAP), was one facet of the Proyecto Arqueológico de la Acrópolis de Copán (PAAC), directed by William L. Fash, which in cooperation with and support from the Instituto Hondureño de Antropología e Historia brought together archaeologists and other specialists to investigate the development of the Copan Acropolis (Fash and Sharer 1991; Sharer, Miller, and Traxler 1992; Sharer, Traxler, et al. 1999; Fash 1998).

The ECAP has received generous funding from the University of Pennsylvania Museum, the National Geographic Society, National Science Foundation, Foundation for the Advancement of Mesoamerican Studies, the Selz Foundation, the Maya Workshop Foundation, and several private donors.

The efforts of many colleagues involved in the various programs of the PAAC form the basis of this chapter. Special thanks go to Ellen Bell, Charles Golden, and Marcello A. Canuto for their assistance in the field with the excavations in the Northeast patio groups. Responsibility for any errors or misrepresentation of the work by Copan colleagues, however, belongs to the author.

REFERENCES

Andrews, E. Wyllys, V
1996 A Late Classic Royal Domestic Compound at Copán. Paper presented at the sixty-first annual meeting of the Society for American Archaeology, New Orleans.
n.d. The Organization of a Royal Maya Residential Compound at the Center of Copan. In *Copan: The Rise and Fall of a Classic Maya Kingdom*, edited by William Fash and E. Wyllys Andrews V. Santa Fe: School of American Research Press. In preparation.
Andrews, E. Wyllys, V, and Barbara W. Fash
1992 Continuity and Change in a Royal Maya Residential Complex at Copan. *Ancient Mesoamerica* 3: 63–88.
Baudez, Claude (ed.).
1983 *Introducción a la arqueología de Copán, Honduras*. 3 vols. Tegucigalpa: Secretaría de Estado en el Despacho de Cultura y Turismo and Instituto Hondureño de Antropología e Historia.
Canuto, Marcello-Andrea
2002 A Tale of Two Communities: The Role of the Rural Community in the Sociopolitical Integration of the Copan Drainage in the Late Preclassic and Classic Periods. Ph.D. dissertation, University of Pennsylvania.
Cheek, Charles D.
1977 Excavations at the Palangana and the Acropolis, Kaminaljuyu. In *Teotihuacan and Kaminaljuyu*, edited by William T. Sanders and J. W. Michels, 1–204. Pennsylvania State University Monograph Series.
1983 Las excavaciones en la Plaza Principal, resumen y conclusiones. In *Introducción a la arqueología de Copán, Honduras*, vol. 2, edited by Claude Baudez, 319–348. Tegucigalpa: Secretaría de Estado en el Despacho de Cultura y Turismo and Instituto Hondureño de Antropología e Historia.
1988 Construction Activity as a Measurement of Change at Copan, Honduras. In *The Southeast Maya Periphery*, edited by Patricia A. Urban and Edward M. Schortman, 50–71. Austin: University of Texas Press.
Cheek, Charles D., and Veronica Kennedy Embree
1983 La Estructura 10L-2. In *Introducción a la arqueología de Copán, Honduras*, vol. 2, edited by Claude Baudez, 93–141. Tegucigalpa: Secretaría de Estado en el Despacho de Cultura y Turismo and Instituto Hondureño de Antropología e Historia.
Cheek, Charles D., and Daniel E. Milla Villeda
1983 La Estructura 10L-4. In *Introducción a la arqueología de Copán, Honduras*, vol. 2, edited by Claude Baudez, 37–91. Tegucigalpa: Secretaría de Estado en el Despacho de Cultura y Turismo and Instituto Hondureño de Antropología e Historia.
Cheek, Charles D., and Mary Spink
1986 Excavaciones en el Grupo 3, Estructura 223 (Operación VII). In *Excavaciones en el área urbana de Copán*, vol. 1, edited by William T. Sanders, 27–154. Tegucigalpa: Secretaría de Cultura y Turismo and Instituto Hondureño de Antropología e Historia.

Dixon, Boyd, L. R. V. Joesink-Mandeville, Nobukatsu Hasebe, Michael Mucio, William Vincent, David James, and Kenneth Petersen
1994   Formative-Period Architecture at the Site of Yarumela, Central Honduras. *Latin American Antiquity* 5: 70–87.
Fash, William L.
1983   Maya State Formation: A Case Study and Its Implications. Ph.D. dissertation, Harvard University.
1991   *Scribes, Warriors, and Kings: The City of Copan and the Ancient Maya.* London: Thames and Hudson.
1998   Dynastic Architectural Programs: Intention and Design in Classic Maya Buildings at Copan and Other Sites. In *Function and Meaning in Classic Maya Architecture,* edited by Stephen D. Houston, 223–270. Washington, D.C.: Dumbarton Oaks Research Library and Collection.
Fash, William L., and Robert J. Sharer
1991   Sociopolitical Developments and Methodological Issues at Copan, Honduras: A Conjunctive Perspective. *Latin American Antiquity* 2: 166–187.
Fash, William L., Richard V. Williamson, Carlos Rudy Larios, and Joel Palka
1992   The Hieroglyphic Stairway and Its Ancestors: Investigations of Copan Structure 10L-26. *Ancient Mesoamerica* 3: 105–116.
Kidder, Alfred V., Jesse D. Jennings, and Edwin M. Shook
1946   *Excavations at Kaminaljuyu, Guatemala.* Carnegie Institution of Washington Publication 501. Washington, D.C.
Miller, Julia C., and Alfonso Morales
1997   Espacios variables: El desarrollo de la Acrópolis de Copán en el Clásico Temprano. *Yaxkin* 16: 24–30.
Schele, Linda, Federico Fahsen, and Nikolai Grube
1994   *The Floor Marker from Motmot.* Copan Note 117. Copan, Honduras: Copan Acropolis Archaeological Project and Instituto Hondureño de Antropología e Historia.
Sedat, David W.
1996   Early Stages in the Evolution of the Copan Acropolis. Paper presented at the sixty-first annual meeting of the Society for American Archaeology, New Orleans.
1997   The Founding Stage of the Copan Acropolis. ECAP Papers 2. Philadelphia: Early Copan Acropolis Program and Instituto Hondureño de Antropología e Historia.
Sharer, Robert J. (ed.)
1978   *The Prehistory of Chalchuapa, El Salvador,* vols. 1–3. University Museum Monograph 36. Philadelphia: University Pennsylvania Press.
Sharer, Robert J.
1996   Los patrones del desarrollo arquitectónico en la Acrópolis de Copán del Clásico Temprano. *Yaxkin* 14: 28–34.
1997   Initial Research and Preliminary Findings from the Hunal Tomb. ECAP Papers 5. Philadelphia: Early Copan Acropolis Program and Instituto Hondureño de Antropología e Historia.
Sharer, Robert J., and David W. Sedat
1987   *Archaeological Investigations in the Northern Maya Highlands: Interaction and the Development of Maya Civilization.* University Museum Monograph 59. Philadelphia: University Museum, University of Pennsylvania.
Sharer, Robert J., William L. Fash, David W. Sedat, Loa P. Traxler, and Richard Williamson
1999   Continuities and Contrasts in Early Classic Architecture of Central Copan. In

Mesoamerican Architecture as a Cultural Symbol, edited by Jeff Karl Kowalski, 220–249. New York: Oxford University Press.

Sharer, Robert J., Julia C. Miller, and Loa P. Traxler
1992 Evolution of Classic Period Architecture in the Eastern Acropolis, Copán: A Progress Report. *Ancient Mesoamerica* 3: 145–159.

Sharer, Robert J., David W. Sedat, Loa P. Traxler, Ellen E. Bell, Christine Carrelli, Fernando López, and Christian Wells
1998 Investigaciones de la programa de la Acrópolis Temprana de Copan: Temporada de 1998. Manuscript on file with Instituto Hondureño de Antropología e Historia, Copán.

Sharer, Robert J., David W. Sedat, Loa Traxler, Christine Carrelli, and Ellen Bell
1994 Investigaciones de la programa de la Acrópolis Temprana de Copan: Temporada de 1994. Manuscript on file at the Centro de Investigaciones del Instituto Hondureño de Antropología e Historia, Copán.

Sharer, Robert J., Loa P. Traxler, David W. Sedat, Ellen E. Bell, Marcello A. Canuto, and Christopher Powell
1999 Early Classic Architecture beneath the Copan Acropolis: A Research Update. *Ancient Mesoamerica* 10: 3–23.

Strömsvik, Gustav
1952 *The Ball Courts at Copan, with Notes on Courts at La Unión, Quirigua, San Pedro Pinula, and Asunción Mita.* Carnegie Institution of Washington Publication 596. Washington, D.C.

Traxler, Loa P.
1996 Los grupos de patios tempranos de la Acrópolis de Copán. *Yaxkin* 14: 35–54.
2001 The Royal Court of Early Classic Copan. In *Royal Courts of the Ancient Maya,* vol. 2: *Data and Case Studies,* edited by Takeshi Inomata and Stephen D. Houston. Boulder: Westview Press.
n.d. Evolution and Social Meaning of Court Group Architecture of the Early Classic Acropolis, Copan, Honduras. Ph.D. dissertation, University of Pennsylvania.

Webster, David, and Ann-Corinne Freter
1990 Settlement History and the Classic Collapse at Copan: A Redefined Chronological Perspective. *Latin American Antiquity* 1: 66–85.

Williamson, Richard V.
1996 Excavations, Interpretations, and Implications of the Earliest Structures beneath Structure 10L-26 at Copan, Honduras. In *Eighth Palenque Round Table,* edited by Merle Greene Robertson, Martha J. Macri, and Jan McHargue, 169–175. San Francisco: Pre-Columbian Art Research Institute.

CHAPTER THREE

A Multipurpose Structure in the Late Classic Palace at Copan

E. Wyllys Andrews V, Jodi L. Johnson, William F. Doonan, Gloria E. Everson, Kathryn E. Sampeck, and Harold E. Starratt

Behind a facade of shared symbolic culture at lowland Maya sites lies a confounding variety of royal and elite architectural remains. This diversity of building forms and arrangements must reflect different patterns of royal behavior. Architectural and spatial contrasts among Maya sites may, therefore, help us to understand how social, political, and religious organization varied from one Maya site to another. Some differences may derive from age, geographic location, and size, but contemporary sites of roughly similar size in one area often exhibit strikingly dissimilar groups of important buildings and plazas. Recording the forms and interpreting the functions of such royal constructions is the first step in understanding the organization and activities of the group that lived in them.

The focus of this chapter is a linked set of Maya buildings near the house of the last ruler in the Copan dynasty. Although hieroglyphic inscriptions do not tell us what this complex was or who built it, the buildings and spaces that surround Structure 10L-41 help us to infer its context and how it may have served the royal Copan Maya.

Just south of the Acropolis at the Classic Maya site of Copan lies a complex of Late Classic structures arranged around several courtyards (Figure 3.1). Many of the buildings are large and vaulted, with sculpted figures and motifs on their upper facades. Group 10L-2, known locally as El Cementerio, lies in full view from the south edge of the Acropolis. Three adjacent courtyards and a few other large buildings today form this group (Figure 3.2), but the Copan River, which undercut and washed away the east side of the Acropolis, probably also carried away part of Group 10L-2. Symmetry suggests that one or two courtyards on its east side were lost to the river.

From 1990 through 1994, Tulane University excavated all of the structures around Courtyards A and B, including about fifteen major buildings

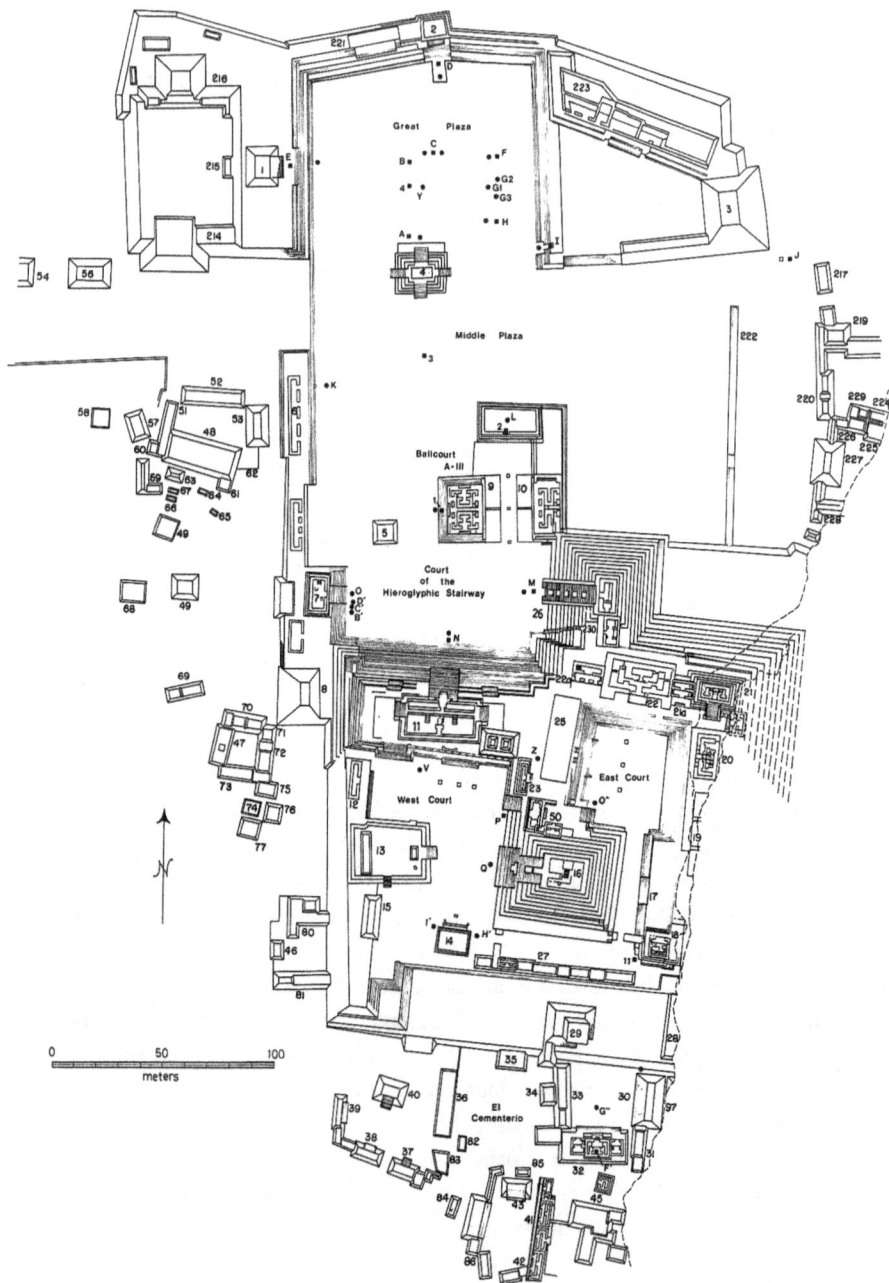

FIGURE 3.1. The Acropolis, Great Plaza, and Group 10L-2 (south) at Copan. This map is taken from the 1983 map of the site as published in Fash 1991, Figure 8, courtesy of William L. Fash. It does not reflect changes resulting from more recent investigations.

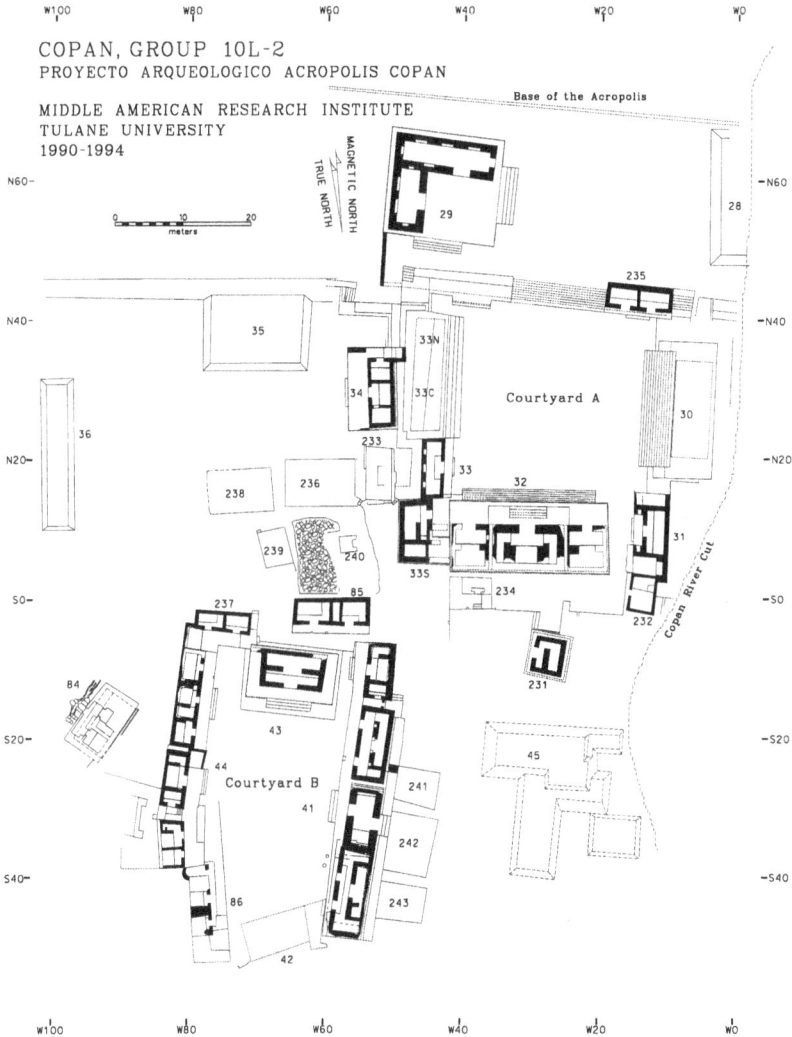

FIGURE 3.2. Group 10L-2, Copan. This map is based on the Tulane University excavations of 1990–1994.

and their supporting platforms, roughly an equal number of smaller buildings (Andrews and Fash 1992; Doonan 1996), and also an area west of Courtyard A that contained several platforms, originally occupied by noble families but later apparently used as a work area (Starratt 2001).[1] Nearly all the large structures contained the remains of earlier buildings and platforms, and after recording the latest construction stage, we exposed as much of the interior constructions as was necessary to determine the form of the earlier buildings inside, or as much as was possible without removing the remains of the final construction phase.

Carved monuments from excavations in Group 10L-2 bear the name Yax Pasaj, the sixteenth and final ruler in the dynasty started by K'inich Yax K'uk' Mo' early in the fifth century A.D. (Fash 1991: 80–81). One of these, Altar F', originally sat on the bench in the central room of Structure 10L-32, the most prominent building in the group, at the south end of Courtyard A. Structure 10L-32 was probably Yax Pasaj's house. Another altar was associated with Structure 10L-30, next to 10L-32. It commemorates A.D. 783, the end of Yax Pasaj's first *k'atun* in office. These two structures were built about the same time, shortly after Yax Pasaj came to power in 763. They are his two largest residential structures, although they are far smaller than the public and ritual buildings he commissioned on the Acropolis. The king's few monuments in Group 10L-2 are also less impressive, designed more for a small audience than were his monuments on the Acropolis.

The residence of Yax Pasaj contains structures of many shapes and sizes, and we believe they served different purposes. Many were lived in, but some were not. Yax Pasaj's house consisted of one large central building with a full-breadth stairway that narrows to steps of massive blocks leading to a wide doorway. A huge bench with side screens and two free-standing inscribed altars dominated this room, where he probably received visitors. This building was flanked by two smaller, slightly lower, and more private ones, where the ruler and members of his family may have slept. Figures of the ruler as a young man adorn the upper facades. Inside 10L-32 are the remains of an earlier vaulted building with an elaborately sculpted facade and a large, looted tomb that probably contained Yax Pasaj's father, who is not mentioned in the known Copan inscriptions. A still earlier platform was encountered inside this one, but little is known about the building that stood on it. It did not contain a big tomb.

Structure 10L-30, Yax Pasaj's second structure in Courtyard A, also had a stair nearly as broad as the two-tiered platform. The central steps of this stairway consisted of huge blocks similar to those used in the upper stair of 10L-32. Its summit was large and open and did not support a building; it was perhaps used for rituals and dances of the lineage or families of Group 10L-2. Inside the latest platform are the remains of a similar precursor, associated with the same plaster floor as the earliest building inside 10L-32.

In the southeast corner of Courtyard A, between 10L-30 and 10L-32, is Structure 10L-31, a probable residence. One vaulted room with a full-length bench is fronted by an antechamber with large side niches. A small unvaulted building to the south (10L-232) was eventually connected to 10L-

31 by an open-fronted vaulted room with a huge niche in the middle of its rear wall.

Structure 10L-33, on the west side of Courtyard A, also contained a full-length bench in a single vaulted room, here with three niches above the bench. Its upper facade bore founder's glyphs (T600) with goggle-eyes, closely associated with Yax K'uk' Mo', the founder of the dynasty. The facade was surmounted by a two-part beveled cornice. An L-shaped addition of two or three rooms to the south of 10L-33 also bore founder's glyphs. Attached to the north end of 10L-33 was then built, in two stages, a long stepped platform with a broad stair and a large upper surface, probably for public rituals and dances.

At the north end of Courtyard A, on a broad, 4 m high terrace projecting south from the base of the Acropolis, is a large L-shaped building that bore extensive sculptural decoration on all sides. The main motif on Structure 10L-29, repeated about ten times on the upper facade, is a rectangular panel with stylized serpent heads protruding from the four corners, similar to what have been called "ancestor cartouches" at Palenque and Yaxchilán, although the panels on 10L-29 do not contain human figures. Below each panel were the head, shoulders, and arms of a man. The figures have supernatural attributes, including a forehead with three deep wrinkles, a prognathic lower face, and large ears. These features suggest the monkey-men gods on the Reviewing Stand of 10L-11 in the West Court and, more generally, the monkey-faced patron of scribes at Copan and other sites. Structure 10L-29 contained no benches but instead eight or nine large wall niches for offerings. We interpret this unusual building as an ancestral shrine, or *way-bil* (Freidel, Schele, and Parker 1993: 189–190), and the deities as patrons of the ancestors of the group that built this temple.

Of the seven major constructions on or just above Courtyard A, then, four appear to have been houses of an important family that claimed a relationship to the founder of the dynasty and that produced the last king in the Copan dynasty. Two were high, flat-topped platforms for rituals, and the last was probably a shrine to the ancestors and their supernatural patrons.

Courtyard B, which we investigated next, was accessible only through a passage at its northeast corner, near the southwest corner of Courtyard A. Its smaller buildings suggested to us that more of Courtyard B might have been devoted to domestic use than of Courtyard A, much of which was constructed for ritual and display that unfolded in front of Yax Pasaj's house.

After excavating them, we judged the structures along the north, west, and south sides of Courtyard B to have been domestic. These showed, however, great variation in size and architectural quality, ranging from a vaulted room with excellently squared and finished masonry at the center of Structure 10L-44, on the west, to tiny subdivided rooms of rougher stonework and perishable materials in 10L-86, at the southwest corner of the courtyard.

The great differences among excavated houses were an important finding of our project, documenting a considerable range of wealth and status among members of this group, differences that were maintained through time and successive building phases.

Midway through the Late Classic period, a small shrine with two rooms but no benches and no sculpture (Structure 10L-43) was built at the center of the north end of Courtyard B, adding a clearly nondomestic structure to the courtyard.

Structure 10L-41, Courtyard B

The focus of the remainder of this chapter is Structure 10L-41, which runs the full length of the east side of Courtyard B (Doonan, Everson, and Sampeck 1993; Hohmann and Vogrin 1982: 57–58, figs. 229–242; Johnson 1993). Its length, well-shaped facing stones, and multiple rooms suggest that it might have been what archaeologists sometimes call "palaces"— large, multiroom buildings on relatively low platforms lived in by royalty but used also for administration and ritual. It is far from clear, however, what the purpose of 10L-41 was. We cannot be sure how most of it was used or that most of it was domestic. Although individuals did live in at least one building that formed part of 10L-41, the other three are different from structures at Copan that are thought to be domestic. These usually contain one bench that covers much of the floor and one door that opens onto the bench. Because most of its exterior and large parts of its interior were partially cleared by the Peabody Museum in 1892 and 1893 (Shorkley 1892–1893), no undisturbed trash deposits remained near it when we returned to it in 1993 to tell us what activities went on inside the rooms or on the terrace outside. In the absence of such middens, we must use the architecture itself and any caches, burials, or accidental deposits inside the structure to infer function.

The platform, just over 1 m high and 34 m long, supports four vaulted buildings that differ from each other in their internal arrangements, if not so much in their external size and shape (Figures 3.3, 3.5, 3.7). All went through two or three episodes of enlargement. The northern building is the smallest and the latest, separated from the next by a passage. The southern three started as separate structures but grew closer together, forming a nearly continuous facade on a single platform. The platform, bearing a two-part beveled cornice similar to the superior molding of 10L-33 in Courtyard A, forms a terrace in front of the four buildings.

The northern building, 10L-41A, was a domestic structure that post-dated the three buildings to its south. It had a central room with a wide bench along the entire back wall, a smaller north room with a raised floor but no bench, and a south room with a low bench covering most of the room and its own doorway on the south side. In the fill of the center room, about a meter under the bench surface, was a Sepultura Unslipped cache pot with appliquéd cacao pods at the front upper corners and a high-relief human face between them, painted yellow with red eyes. Beside the cache pot was a small speleothem (a limestone cave formation), and inside it were two small, ovoid jade plaques, three juvenile *Spondylus* shells, a piece of oyster shell, and a piece of fire-cracked chert (Figure 3.4).

Buildings with similar interior arrangements are common at Copan and are believed to have been sleeping and living quarters. For example, the internal arrangement of 10L-41A is like that of Structure 10L-44B, across Courtyard B, although they are reversed. Structure 10L-44B is the central, and the only vaulted, house on the west side of Courtyard B, where all of the buildings were domestic. Because 10L-41A also shares specific architectural and masonry features with Yax-Pasaj's late buildings on Courtyard A, such as size and quality of facing stones, shape of vault stones, and details of fill and floor construction, we think it was built early in his reign, about the same time as his Structures 10L-30 and 32. Yax Pasaj may have built this house for one of his relatives.

Structures 10L-41B, 41C, and 41D formed a unit, linked at least in their final construction phase by one sculptural program (Figure 3.5). They are also about the same size, but most formal similarities end there.

Structure 10L-41B is one long room with two wide doorways facing the courtyard. The wide front half of the room is one step above the level of the terrace outside, and the back half of the room consists of a broad, high bench running the full length of the rear wall. Two massive piers rise from the front of the bench along the room centerline, supporting long parallel vaults on each side. This construction is unusual, because two parallel vaulted spaces would normally have defined two separate rooms, whereas here the space was designed as one room with a huge bench. The two exterior doorways open onto the two piers, which are blank except for a niche in the bench face below each. The three wide openings onto the bench between the piers were therefore partly hidden from observers standing outside of the doorways.

a

b

FIGURE 3.3. Structure 10L-41, from a photography tower near the center of Courtyard B. (a) 10L-41A. (b) 10L-41B. (c) 10L-41C. (d) 10L-41D. Structure 10L-41A-1st (construction phase V) is shown in May 1994, after consolidation of the existing masonry. The views of 10L-41B, C, and D (all construction phase III) date to March 1993, after the final construction phase of each structure had been cleared.

c

d

a

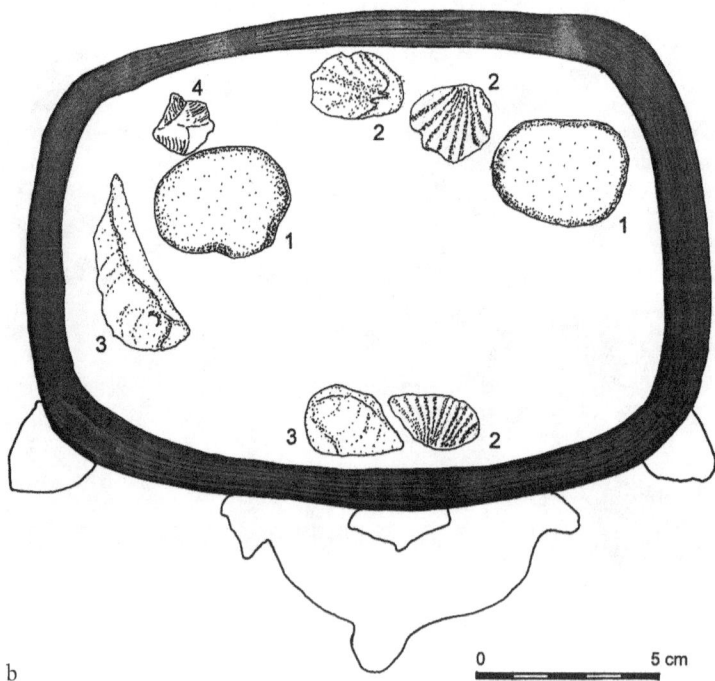

b

0   5 cm

Structure 10L-41C, the central building of the original three, is a large room with an off-center doorway facing the steps leading up from the courtyard. A rear doorway leads to a narrow stair up the back of the platform. The south interior end-wall has a niche, with a low rise in floor level in front of it. This niche and the space in front of it were likely the focus of activities in 10L-41C. A low step is set against the north inside wall. This room could have held many individuals, and the rear door shows that passage was intended through the room and out the back.

Structure 10L-41D, built at the same time as 41C, is unlike its companions. Two doorways facing the courtyard step up to a narrow interior space with a second, lower step up after one enters the room. A huge central bench is flanked by two side chambers with niches. Structure 10L-41D is therefore similar to the larger and slightly later 10L-32 on Courtyard A, but several features distinguish it. The doorways, like those of 10L-41B, open onto high masonry screen walls. In most domestic rooms at Copan the doorway opens directly onto the bench. In Structure 10L-41D (as in 41B), the bench was not visible from outside and the front bench screen walls coming out from the side screens provided additional privacy, as did a short dividing wall on the south side of the bench. Two round pedestals, probably for stone incense burners, had fallen off the platform and lay on the courtyard floor, indicating that rituals took place in front of 10L-41C and 41D. Of the three buildings, however, 41D looks most like elite domestic structures at Copan.

Of the four buildings in a line, Structures 10L-41B and 41C, then, seem the most different from buildings thought to be Late Classic Copan high-status residences. Structure 10L-41B, however, contained three child burials that dated to the final and the penultimate construction phases. These would normally be interpreted as indicating occupation by families. On the surface of the 10L-41B bench lay the only in situ refuse in Structure 10L-41: four small Late Classic ceramic cups, three manos, and a metate fragment. Two of the cups were smashed, and at least one of the manos was driven into the plaster surface of the bench when the wall and vaults collapsed. These items indicate domestic use of 41B just before the building fell, but whether these final inhabitants were the same as those who used this structure throughout the Late Classic period is not known.

FIGURE 3.4. Structure 10L-41A, Cache 1, placed in the fill of 10L-41A-1st, a meter under the surface of the bench along the back wall of the central room (construction phase V). The vessel has appliqué cacao pods and a human face painted yellow with red eyes. Beside it rested a small limestone cave formation. (a) Sepultura Unslipped cache pot. (b) Diagram of the offerings inside the cache pot. (1) Jades. (2) *Spondylus* shells. (3) Oyster shells. (4) Fire-blackened chert.

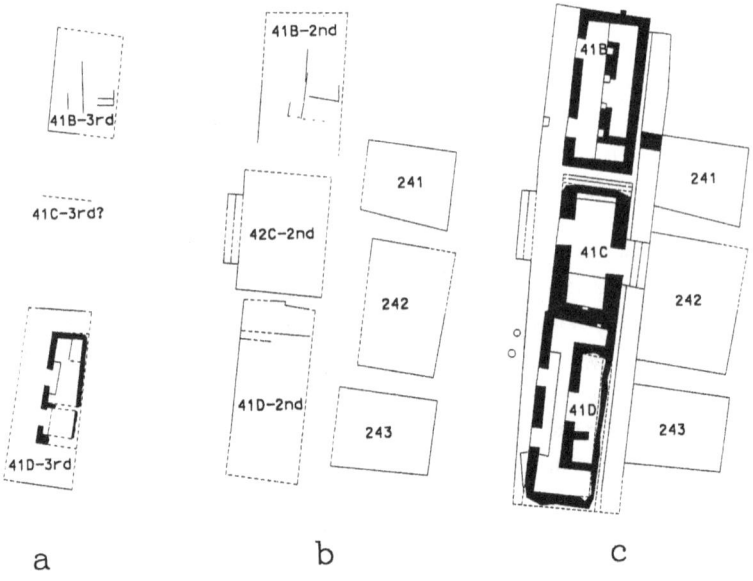

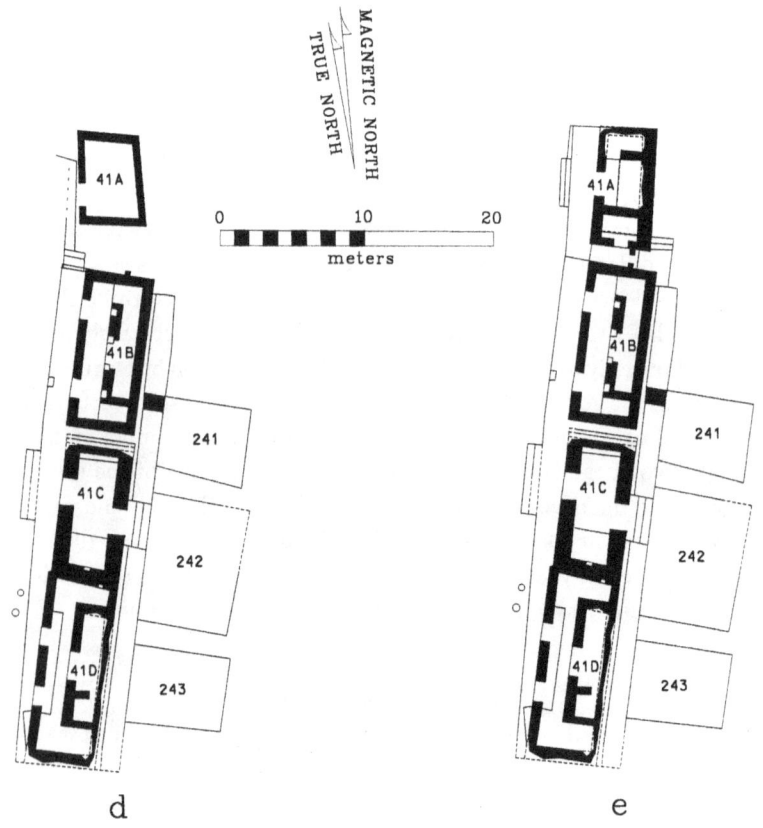

a   b   c

d   e

The remains of earlier constructions are buried under each building of 10L-41. The first platforms and superstructures were probably erected not long after A.D. 650, and the entire complex (except 10L-41A) was rebuilt two times before Yax-Pasaj's reign began in A.D. 763. At each rebuilding, it appears that the original internal arrangements of two or three structures were at least partially recreated (Figure 3.5).

The two earlier constructions that are partially preserved inside 10L-41B-1st show similarities to the final building, although only a few traces of 10L-41B-3rd and -2nd remained intact in the later fill. Atop platforms comparable to the final one were long buildings, and inside both early buildings, running north-south, was the face of a bench that appeared to run much of the length of the building. It divided the room roughly in half, as in the final construction period. In the second phase (10L-41B-2nd) the bench had been rebuilt, and parts of both bench facing walls remained. A further similarity of 10L-41B-3rd and -2nd to the final superstructure is that the raised half of the room, atop the bench, had one or more cross-walls.

Structure 10L-41C-1st, the central structure, contains the remains of one or two earlier platforms inside it. The walls of the platform preceding the final structure (10L-41C-2nd) could be traced, but we found no evidence of a superstructure. Although it seems likely that 41C-2nd did support a building, we cannot know if its internal configuration was similar to that of its successor. Inside the north facing wall of 41C-2nd, and roughly parallel to it, was a crude wall of cobbles. This may be the only remaining facing of 10L-41C-3rd. The line of stones was so rough that we are not certain that it was a wall, but two lines of evidence suggest that it was. The first is a thin layer of tuff subfloor ballast in the fill of 41C-2nd, above the highest course of this possible facing wall. The ballast was probably the remains of a platform surface for 41C-3rd. The platform fill is also different above and below the ballast, indicating a different source and a different date. Second, we know that 10L-41C-2nd was built after 41B-3rd and 41D-3rd. This means that if there had been no 41C-3rd, the earliest construction phase of this three-building complex would have been 41B-3rd and 41D-3rd, with a large gap between them. The integrity of the complex through time as a three-building unit makes a two-building initial period unlikely.

FIGURE 3.5. Structure 10L-41, construction phases I–V. (a) Phase I. (b) Phase II. (c) Phase III. (d) Phase IV. (e) Phase V. Construction phase I probably started Courtyard B early in the Coner phase, in the first part of the reign of Ruler 12 (Smoke Imix), which lasted from A.D. 628 to 695. The final enlargement, including only 10L-41-1st, is thought to date to shortly after Yax Pasah, the final ruler in the Copan dynasty, acceded in A.D. 763.

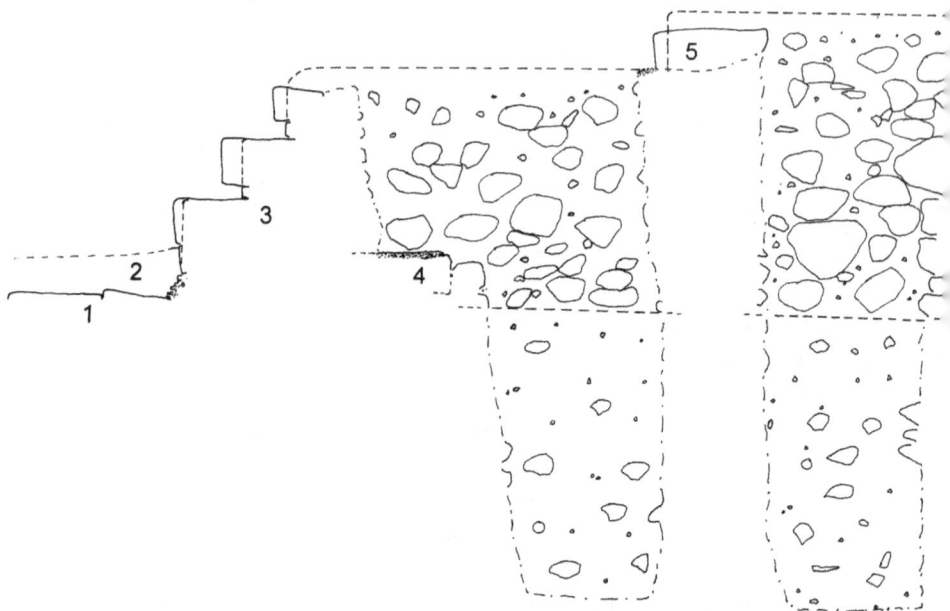

FIGURE 3.6. Transverse sections of Structure 10L-41.
3.6a. Structure 10L-41A, west-east section through the doorway of the central room.
(1) Early flagstone floor of Courtyard B. (2) Level of the final courtyard plaster floor.
(3) Stairway. (4) East edge of the Structure 10L-43 terrace extension. (5) Doorway and
step up to the central room of 10L-41A-1st. (6) Bench in the central room of 10L-41A-
1st. (7) Plaster floor inside 10L-41A-2nd. (8) East (rear) building wall of 10L-41A-1st.
(9) Level of the plaster floor overlying a cobble ballast.

The penultimate building inside 10L-41D-1st was dismantled, and we
learned little about it, but the earliest of the three (10L-41D-3rd) shows
some similarities to the final one, although 41D-3rd was much smaller and
of much rougher masonry. Instead of one large room with a huge, screened
bench and side chambers, 10L-41D-3rd contained two small vaulted rooms,
each of which had about a 10 cm step up just inside the door. The C-shape
of the step in the larger north room is similar to that in 41D-1st. The north

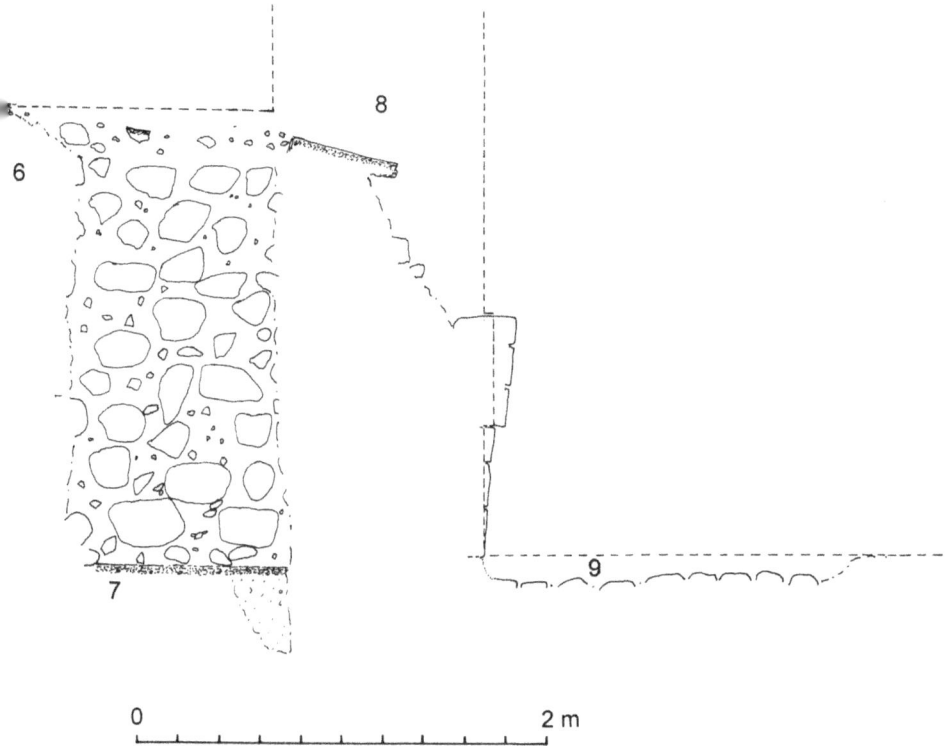

room, which had a small bench at its northeast corner, possibly for ritual objects, bore zones of red paint on the floor. The rooms of 10L-41D-3rd were too small to live in and must have been used for rituals. This interpretation reinforces our belief that the final-phase building, because of the high front- and side-screens on the bench, the hidden bench access, the lateral chambers with niches, and the pedestals that originally rested on the platform outside, was both a residence and a ritual structure.

Structure 10L-41A, built after A.D. 763 by Yax Pasaj at the north end of this long structure, had one earlier platform inside it, but 10L-41A-2nd was also built late in the Courtyard B sequence, after the southern three had reached their final forms. We know nothing about the building that must have stood on the earlier platform, but it may have been a domestic structure, as was its successor, 10L-41A-1st.

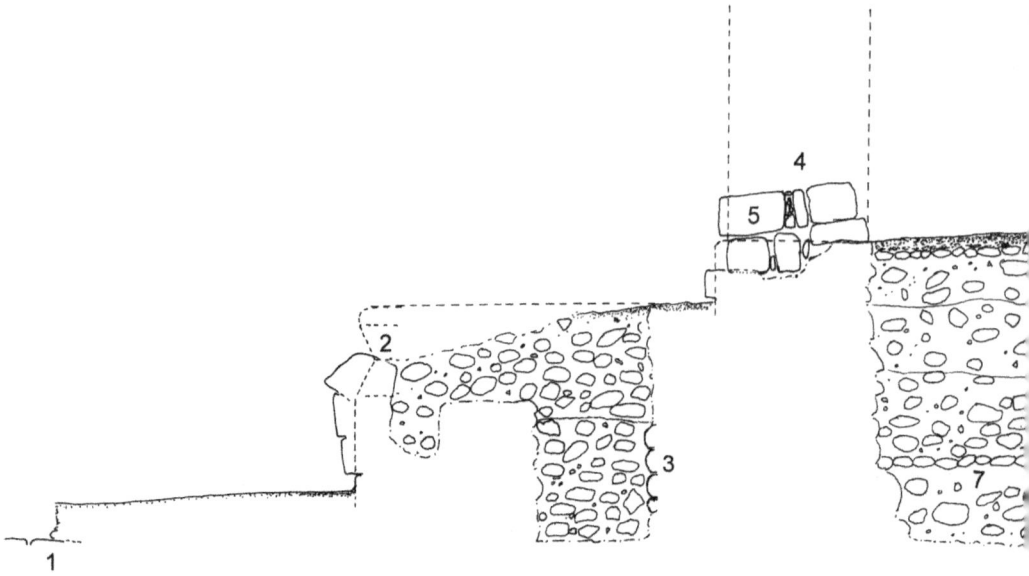

3.6b. Structure 10L-41B, west-east section through the north edge of the north doorway. (1) Early limestone slab floor of Courtyard B. (2) Two-part beveled cornice of platform. (3) West platform wall of 10L-41B-3rd. (4) West, central, and east superstructure walls of 10L-41B-1st. (5) Elevation of the north jamb of the north doorway. (6) Elevation of the north side of the niche in the bench face. (7) Lower (front) plaster and cobble floor of 10L-41B-3rd. (8) Central wall of 10L-41B-3rd. (9) Upper (rear) plaster floor of 10L-41B-3rd. (10) Terrace on the east side of 10L-41B, C, and D.

Although Structure 10L-41 was enlarged and its buildings were rebuilt one or two times, the architects created similar interior arrangements each time. The continuity in form argues for continuity of function from one building phase to the next. Structure 10L-41 is therefore not a chance assortment of superstructures or even a group of slightly different domestic units, but rather a planned set of at least three contiguous buildings that formed a coherent complex of different floor plans, maintained through time.

Three platforms at least a meter high (Structures 10L-241, 242, and 243) were constructed behind 10L-41 and were eventually joined to it by a low terrace that runs along its east side (Starratt 1994). Excavations in 1893 (Shorkley 1892–1893) removed their fill, leaving the remaining exterior wall faces to collapse. We know nothing about their interiors or the buildings

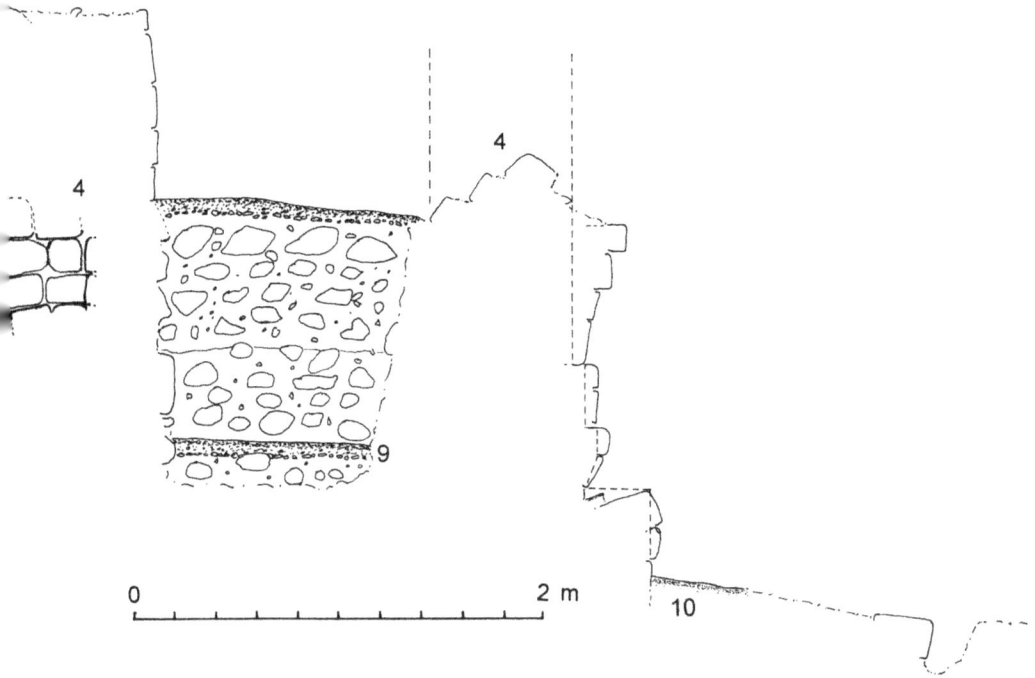

atop them. The facing walls are of well-dressed, squared stones, like those of the final phase of 10L-41 itself, with which they were apparently contemporary. One of the platforms (10L-241), however, contains an earlier wall of squared facing stones inside it, parallel to 10L-41. This wall shows that at least one of the platforms, and perhaps all three, contained more than one construction phase. We have no evidence here of the rough facing stones used in the earliest phases of 10L-41, however, and therefore have no indication that early versions of these platforms go back as far in time as 10L-41 itself.

Structures 10L-241, 242, and 243 must have supported unvaulted buildings used by individuals who had regular access to 10L-41 and Courtyard B. The occupants may have been relatives of the owners or primary users of 10L-41, lesser officials, temporary occupants, or servants.

Much of the recovered sculpture of 10L-41, unearthed and removed from the building a century earlier, was found in piles nearby. The hypothetical reconstruction (Figure 3.7) and analysis of the sculpted facade by Jodi L. Johnson (1993; personal communication, 2000) therefore relies heavily on the positions of the relatively few stones found in 1993 inside the rooms

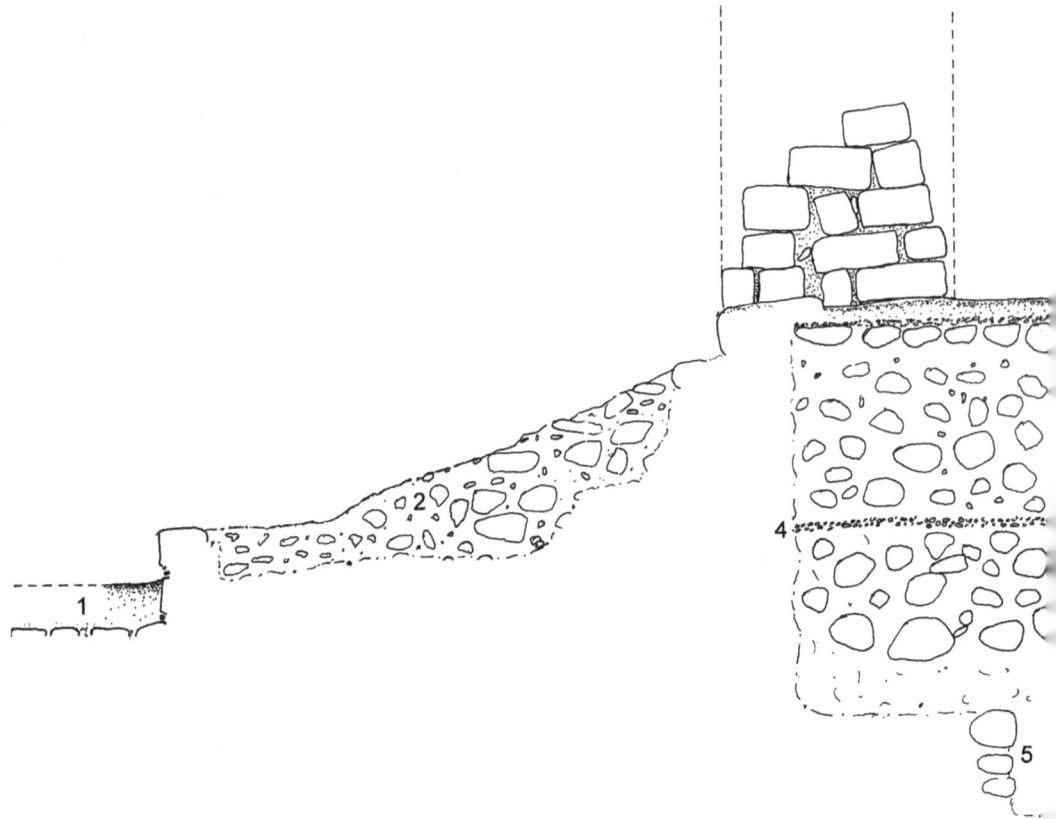

3.6c. Structure 10L-41C, oblique west-east section through west and east doorways, showing the north jamb of each doorway in elevation. (1) Plaster floor of the courtyard with the earlier flagstone floor below it. (2) Western stairway of three risers, with one step remaining in place at its base. (3) Exterior facing of the east side of 10L-41C-1st platform, with the east stairway built against it. (4) Ballast of what was probably the floor of 10L-41C-3rd. (5) Early Classic cobble wall, the lowest and earliest structure encountered beneath Structure 10L-41.

where they originally fell. The 1892–1893 piles of sculpture did provide a clue to the distribution of the sculpture motifs, however, as we will argue below.

Sculpture was probably limited to the facades of the three southern superstructures, as no sculpture was found in the masonry fall of 10L-41A. This house, with its own stairway, was built after the southern three buildings, and its platform lacked the beveled cornice of 41B, 41C, and 41D. Unlike the southern three, it was a residence without other apparent functions.

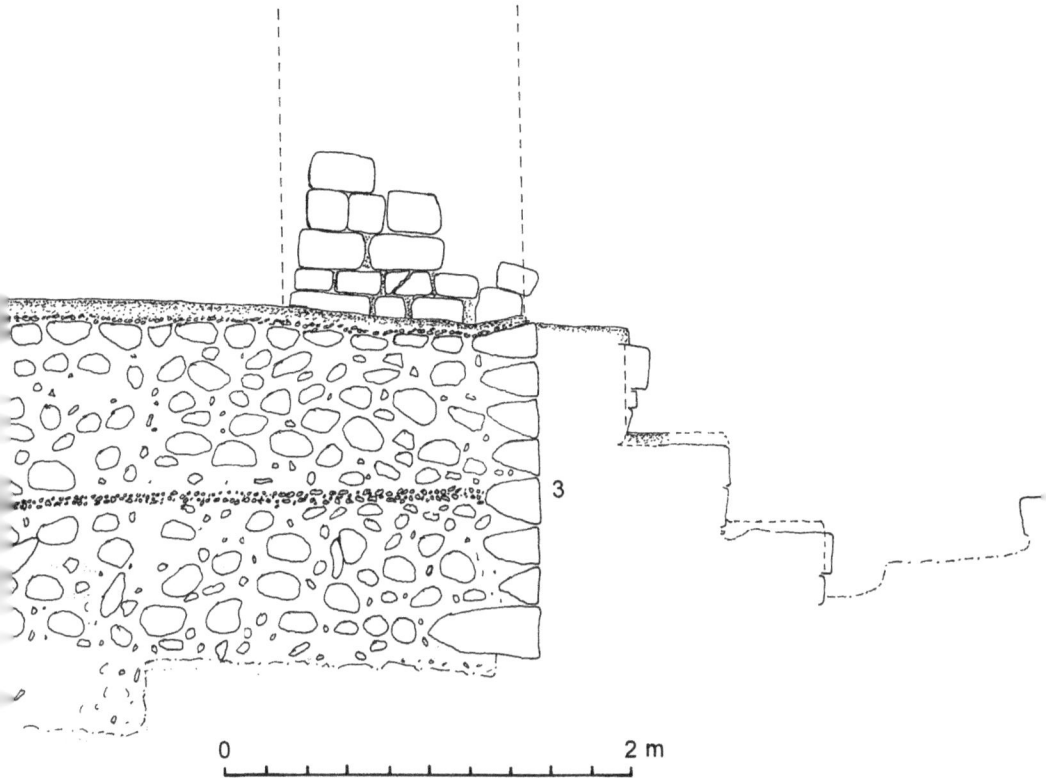

Four motifs—roof ornaments, *cauac* assemblages (stone), Ik niches, and little human heads—were found in the collapsed walls and vaults of 10L-41C and 41D. The roof ornaments, of which seven are known from our excavations and from the early piles, show flowering vegetation, perhaps maize sprouts. The largest and most common motif, consisting of *cauac* assemblages with stepped borders, may have hung from the cornice of 10L-41C and 41D. Thirteen Ik-shaped niches, possibly with the small human heads at their base, may have been placed in the lower facade. No fragment of these motifs was found in the wall fall of 10L-41B.

The three other motifs known from 10L-41 included Venus glyphs, skybands (crossed bands), and Tlalocs, which are goggle-eyes bordered by little scrolls (*ch'ok*, or sprout). Unlike those of Structure 10L-33, these goggle-eyes are not accompanied by the founder's glyph associated with the founder of the Copan dynasty.

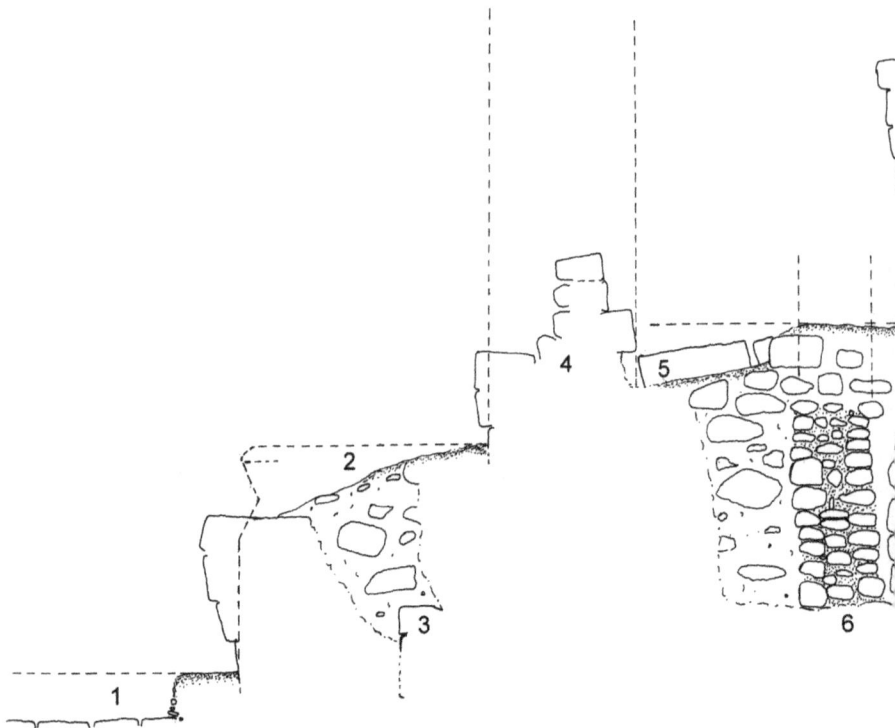

3.6d. Structure 10L-41D, west-east section, showing the north wall of the east (central) room of 10L-41D-1st in elevation. The east and west walls and the bench of the north room of 10L-41D-3rd are shown, as well as the west face of the low platform on which 10L-41D-3rd rested. (1) plaster floor of Courtyard B and the earlier flagstone paving below it; (2) upper surface of the 10L-41D-1st terrace; (3) west platform face of 10L-41D-3rd; (4) west, central, and east superstructure walls of 10L-41D-1st. (5) 10L-41D-1st, step to the upper floor level in the west (front) room, shown in elevation, with both the lower floor and the projected upper floor level indicated. (6) 10L-41D-3rd, north jamb of doorway in the north room. (7) 10L-41D-3rd, elevation of the north wall (south face) between the west wall and the bench in the north room. (8) 10L-41D-3rd, east wall of the north room.

None of these three were found in our excavations, but they were well represented in the nearby sculpture piles. The Peabody Museum cleared more debris from 10L-41A and 41B than from 10L-41C and 41D, so there was far less opportunity to find fallen sculpture in place around 10L-41B. The Venus glyphs, skybands, and Tlalocs were, however, concentrated in the northern sculpture piles, especially those closest to 10L-41B, and they

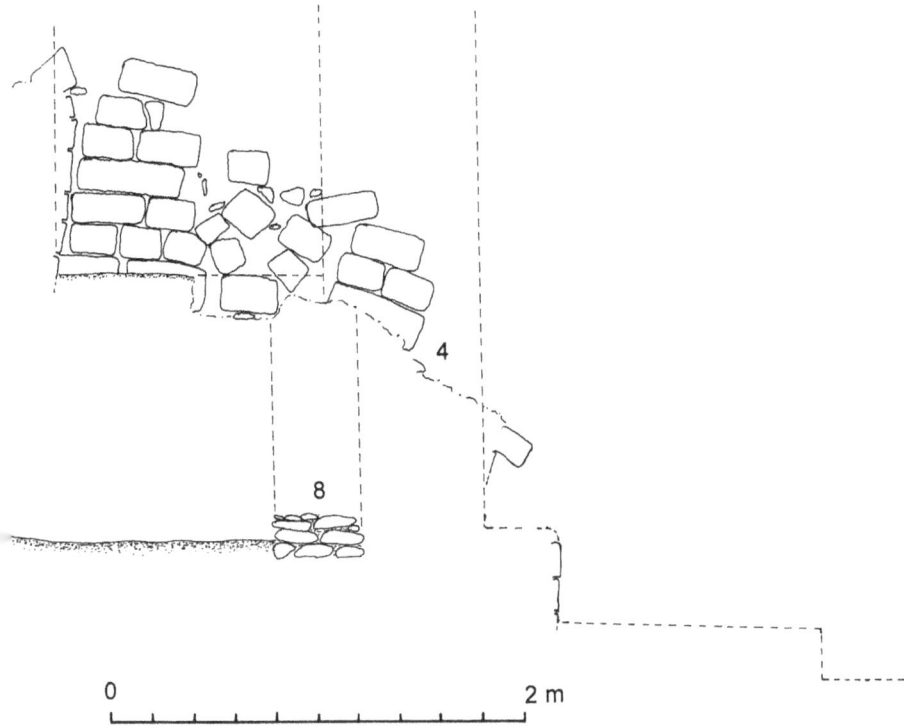

may have been limited to the facade of Structure 10L-41B. Figure 3.7 shows these motifs on all three buildings.

Given the limited evidence of fallen sculpture from our recent excavations in 10L-41B, it is difficult to place these three motifs on the facade. Their placement on the cornice in the reconstruction drawing (Figure 3.7) was suggested by their relatively long tenons. The tenons of these stones probably had to be long, because the cornice would have projected beyond the plane of the facade below it. The position of the Venus glyphs on the cornice (shown in a line near its center) is hypothetical. The alternating placement of the Tlalocs and the skybands is also speculative, but it is based on their consistently similar height.

Linda Schele and Nikolai Grube suggested in 1993 to Johnson that the iconography of 10L-41 refers to Tlaloc-Venus warfare, because of the goggle-eyes and Venus glyphs. They wondered if the buildings housed young noblemen in training for warfare, ritual, or administration. The reconstruction of

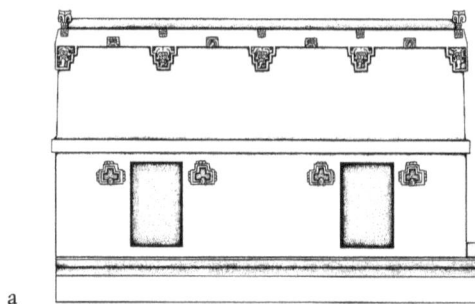

a

FIGURE 3.7. The facade sculpture of Structures 10L-41B, C, and D, a hypothetical reconstruction by Jodi L. Johnson. All of the sculpture had fallen from its original position, and most carved pieces were collected into piles during the Peabody Museum excavations in 1892–1893. The placement of motifs on the facade is therefore based on a relatively few fragments excavated in 1993 that still remained where they had fallen and on the overall frequency of remaining motif elements. The Venus, skyband, and Tlaloc motifs are shown on the cornice of all three structures, but, as suggested in the text, they may have been limited to Structure 10L-41B. (a) Structure 10L-41B. (b) Structures 10L-41C and D.

the facades suggested above, with Venus, Tlaloc, and skyband motifs limited to 10L-41B, might limit Schele and Grube's idea to this building and its two predecessors.

Ethnohistoric evidence of men's or youths' houses is available, and archaeologists have occasionally attempted to identify Maya buildings as boys', men's, or priests' houses. We refer to some of these writings by modern authors here, although we believe the range of functions of Structure 10L-41 ultimately remains unclear.

Men's houses are recorded in ethnohistoric and early colonial records from the Maya area and from central Mexico. Aztec communities had houses for young commoners training to be warriors and also "priestly residences" of primarily religious character for the children of nobles who became warriors, priests, or traders (Carrasco 1971: 356–357). In the Maya lowlands, communal houses for men were noted at the time of Spanish contact or shortly afterward for the Yucatec (Landa in Tozzer 1941: 124), Chol (Thompson 1938: 596), and Chontal (Scholes and Roys 1948: 36, 38, 43). Men's houses were also recorded among the highland Guatemala Pokomam (Miles 1957: 769) and Kekchi (Thompson 1938: 603, 1970: 172). The Chol house seems to have held both religious idols and men during their wives' pregnancies.

If we are to judge from these ethnohistoric data, the Maya had only one type of men's house, rather than separate ones for commoners and

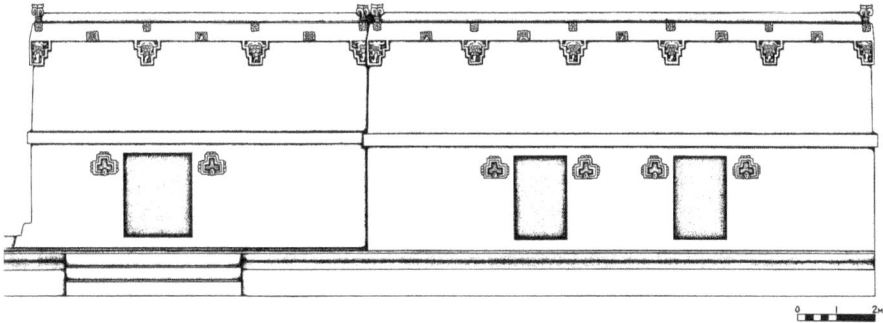

nobles, but the early Maya sources are less informative than those of central Mexico and are perhaps incomplete in this matter. Recent Maya ethnographers have not reported men's houses in today's smaller, simpler, and acculturated communities. The modern Chorti of eastern Guatemala, for example, who may be descendants of the Classic inhabitants of Copan, have no men's house (Wisdom 1940).

Archaeologists have suggested that certain kinds of structures at Maya sites were men's houses. At Mayapan, abandoned little more than a century before Landa's account, Proskouriakoff (1962: 89) wrote that colonnaded halls "probably served as living quarters for unmarried boys being trained in the arts of war and ritual." These were large, one-room structures "lacking the privacy of rear compartments," usually with two rows of columns supporting the roof and therefore providing much open interior space. A bench along the rear and end walls may have been for sleeping, sitting, and other activities. Semi-perishable buildings with domestic refuse behind the hall may have been kitchens. The openness and size of these colonnaded halls, of which Proskouriakoff (1962: 90) counted 21 in the Main Group, remind one of the "large houses . . . open on all sides" described by Landa (Tozzer 1941: 124) in northern Yucatan. Landa did not say how many men's houses were in a town.

Twenty years later, Carmack (1981: 385) suggested the colonnaded halls at Mayapan were "probably lineage houses." He thought their openness, many columns, long benches, and spatial relationship to other buildings made them equivalent to the Quiché "long structures" resting on platforms about a meter high at the highland Quiché capital of Utatlan. Carmack (1981: 287–290) believed the Utatlan long structures, with their length, many entrances, and multiple stairways, were "clearly the 'big houses' of the documentary sources . . . where the ruling lords met to set public policy." He interpreted the twenty-four Utatlan big houses described in ethnohistoric sources as "primarily administrative centers" for the Quiché lineages. Long, open-fronted buildings similar to the Mayapan colonnaded halls have recently been mapped at Late Postclassic Zacpeten (D. Rice, P. Rice, and Pugh 1998: Figures 7, 8). Following Carmack, the Rices suggest they were lineage and administrative structures.

Identification of Classic-period youths' or men's houses, houses for individuals engaged in periodic rituals, or lineage administrative halls has been more difficult. The openness of colonnaded Postclassic constructions was unknown before the end of the Classic period. Pollock (1965: 441) noted that there was little direct evidence for men's houses or similar buildings. He thought that the variety in size and interior arrangement of "palaces" suggested many functions. If Classic-period men's houses did exist, their forms were different enough from what came later that we cannot easily identify them.

Harrison's (1970) functional analysis of Maya royal and noble domestic architecture of the Central Acropolis at Tikal utilized patterned differences in form, size, location, access, and other attributes to establish formal categories of domestic buildings. These included permanent and temporary residences of several kinds, and also nonresidential "special oratories" and "storehouses." The residences included "priestly residences or seminaries," which lacked burials and caches but bore sculpture, "men's ceremonial houses" near temples, and large "boys' premarriage houses." Most of these categories were suggested ultimately by ethnohistoric sources. The building plans in the Central Acropolis at Tikal are different from those in Group 10L-2 and elsewhere at Copan, however, and none is like 10L-41.

Just east of the northeast corner of the Great Plaza at Copan, resting on the massive platform that defines the east side of this plaza, is a large, four-room building that may have been a communal house combining several of the functions mentioned above. Structure 10L-223, excavated by Charles Cheek and Mary Spink (1986), has rooms that are larger than those of Copan buildings considered to be permanently residential, with benches covering half of each room. It lacked masonry internal divisions to create private spaces and carried no architectural sculpture. Each of the four rooms remained different through at least the last two of four major alterations, indicating a pattern of formal continuity through successive renovations, as documented in 10L-41. Cheek and Spink (1986: 91, fig. 33) suggest that one room was a priestly residence, another was a dormitory for students or for men isolated before ceremonies, and the other two, including a sweat bath, were for ritual purification or other activities. The differences between the interior spaces of Structure 10L-223 and those of probable permanent dwellings at Copan, and the maintenance of different room forms through successive renovations, as the excavators argue, point to a series of special uses for this unusual structure.

Summary and Conclusions

Although Group 10L-2 was occupied from the Late Preclassic period until the Late Classic abandonment of Copan sometime before A.D. 900, Courtyards A and B do not appear to have been laid out until the Late Classic period, when they were occupied by a group that claimed relationship to the founder of the Copan dynasty. Courtyard A and the early houses inside Structure 10L-32 were almost certainly the home of the group head from this time through the reign of the last king, Yax Pasaj.

The Late Classic royal palace at Copan included many domestic and special-purpose buildings around three, and possibly as many as five, courtyards south of the Acropolis. The houses, with benches for sleeping, ranged in size and quality from Yax Pasaj's huge, vaulted five-room complex to small, simple one-room units occupied by servants or low-ranking relatives. The variation in structures that were not intended primarily as living quarters is just as great, including in Courtyard A two large flat-topped platforms for dances and other ceremonies and a shrine to the ancestors and patron deities of the lineage. In the adjacent Courtyard B, the nonresidential buildings include a smaller shrine or temple, as well as the focus of this chapter, a line of three, and later four, vaulted buildings on a meter-high platform, each different from the others.

Structure 10L-41 dominated Courtyard B from its inception to its destruction and abandonment. The internal arrangements of its three vaulted buildings are different, and the differences were maintained through two enlargements that spanned a century. Not one of the three was a typical Copan noble residence, although 10L-41B and 41D may have been lived in. 10L-41B, with its large open corridor and its high, partly screened bench and four niches, possibly combined ritual and formal interaction of nobles with lower-ranking individuals. The Tlaloc-Venus warfare imagery that may have been limited to the facade of this one building has raised the possibility that it had something to do with warfare, perhaps housing young men training for battle. Structure 10L-41C, with a raised area leading to a niche at the end of the room, would also have allowed rituals with several participants. Structure 10L-41D was perhaps an audience room, but its privacy and darkness set it apart from, for example, Yax Pasaj's house, 10L-32, in which the throne is in full view of anyone standing outside the door. If anyone lived permanently in 10L-41D, it is likely to have been a priest, and its use must have been partly for rituals.

The possible uses suggested here for 10L-41 are not incompatible with the overall interpretation of the complex as a place to train young nobles in the arts of ritual, war, and administration, suggested by the iconography of at least 10L-41B. The three platforms connected to the back of 10L-41 might have been where men or boys slept. A midden excavated behind 10L-243 suggests a domestic occupation. No direct evidence, however, supports the idea that 10L-41 was a men's house.

Structure 10L-41, with three attached platforms behind it, must reflect a combination of communal, administrative, ritual, and residential use. Three buildings were used for rituals involving numerous participants. The two structures with large benches may have been used for audiences with high-ranking individuals or for rituals conducted by a small number of individuals. It is unlikely that the main purpose of any of the original three structures was domestic, although 10L-41A, a house for a member of the royal family, was added to the complex during Yax Pasaj's reign. Finally, unlike 10L-223, a large special-purpose building located beside the Great Plaza that probably served the nobility of the entire kingdom, Structure 10L-41, was built and used by only one segment of Copan noble society. Its patrons most likely belonged to or were affiliated with one corporate descent group, whose members not only claimed descent from the founder but also produced the final ruler of the dynasty.

The term "palace" has often been applied in the Maya lowlands to well-built, vaulted, individual buildings of varying sizes, as in E. B. Kurjack's chapter in this volume. It is also often employed today to refer to arranged groups of different kinds of structures used for royal residence, audiences and administration, and public and private ritual, and sometimes as a physical embodiment or symbol of the cosmological and mythological underpinnings of religion and the social order, as in the chapter in this volume by Demarest, Morgan, Wolley, and Escobedo. It is equivalent to the "royal Maya court," as illuminated by Inomata and Houston (2001), Webster (2001), and others. At Copan, the Late Classic royal court or "court complex" (Webster 2001: 141) included all of the monuments and architecture on the Acropolis and the great plazas north of it, as well as the royal residential complex in Group 10L-2. I think it is useful at Copan to think of Yax Pasaj's residential complex as his palace, thereby distinguishing it spatially and conceptually as a division of the larger royal court. At many Maya sites the royal residential areas may not be separable from more public constructions, but at some, such as Tikal, the division will be useful.

The royal palace during the reign of Yax Pasaj, then, incorporated all of the buildings around several contiguous courtyards in Group 10L-2, one or more of which may have been washed away by the Copan River. The palace of the ruler included the neighborhood in which he was raised, with its mix of nobles and commoners, elaborate and simple residences, buildings for public ceremony and private ritual, and adjacent storage, work, and food preparation spaces. The functions, sizes, and quality of construction of these buildings; their relationships to each other; and the proximity of this group to the more public royal structures on top of and to the north of the Acropolis reflect the social and political organization of the royal court and the history of the noble line into which the realm's last king was born.

NOTE

1. The Tulane University investigations in Group 10L-2 are part of the Copan Acropolis Archaeological Project (PAAC), which has included investigations by the Honduran Institute of Anthropology and History (IHAH), Northern Illinois University, Harvard University, the University of Pennsylvania, and the Middle American Research Institute at Tulane. The Tulane research was supported by the National Geographic Society and by funds from the U.S. Agency for International Development administered by IHAH. Rudy Larios supervised the consolidation of the buildings around Courtyards A and B in Group 10L-2 for the PAAC.

We are grateful for support, many extra kindnesses, and the pleasant and invigorating company provided by our many colleagues at Copan. Among these are William L. Fash, director of the PAAC; Barbara W. Fash, who has been responsible for most of the analysis of sculpture in Group 10L-2; Robert J. Sharer, director of the University of Pennsylvania research; Ricardo Agurcia F., director of the excavations for IHAH; David Stuart, whose interpretations of the hieroglyphic inscriptions in Group 10L-2 have illuminated the individuals who lived there; Rudy Larios V.; and Fernando López. The Group 10L-2 excavations were carried out by many highly skilled citizens of Copán Ruinas and were supervised by graduate students from Tulane University and elsewhere. Our understanding of this ancient settlement is a result of their work. Cassandra R. Bill has analyzed the ceramics from Group 10L-2 (1997), and all studies of the growth of this complex rely upon her interpretations. The maps of Group 10L-2 and Structure 10L-41 were prepared by Kathe Lawton and Jim Aimers in AutoCAD and MicroStation.

Much of the story of what happened in Group 10L-2 has been informed by the late Linda Schele's readings of the inscriptions. We are grateful for her insights and her hard work, and we miss her enthusiasm.

REFERENCES

Andrews, E. Wyllys, V, and Barbara W. Fash
1992   Continuity and Change in a Royal Maya Residential Complex at Copán. *Ancient Mesoamerica* 3: 63–88.
Bill, Cassandra R.
1997   Patterns of Variation and Change in Dynastic-Period Ceremonies at Copán,

Honduras. Ph.D. dissertation, Department of Anthropology, Tulane University, New Orleans.

Carmack, Robert M.
1981 *The Quiché Mayas of Utatlán: The Evolution of a Highland Guatemala Kingdom.* Norman: University of Oklahoma Press.

Carrasco, Pedro
1971 Social Organization of Ancient Mexico. In *Archaeology of Northern Mesoamerica,* edited by Gordon F. Ekholm and Ignacio Bernal, part 1, pp. 349–375. *Handbook of Middle American Indians,* vol. 10, Robert Wauchope, general editor. Austin: University of Texas Press.

Cheek, Charles D., and Mary L. Spink
1986 Excavaciones en el Grupo 3, Estructura 223 (Operación VII). In *Excavaciones en el área urbana de Copán,* vol. 1, edited by William T. Sanders, 27–154. Proyecto Arqueológico Copán, Segunda Fase. Tegucigalpa: Secretaría de Cultura y Turismo, Instituto Hondureño de Antropología e Historia.

Doonan, William F.
1996 The Artifacts of Group 10L-2, Copán, Honduras: Variation in Material Culture and Behavior in a Royal Residential Compound. Ph.D. dissertation, Department of Anthropology, Tulane University.

Doonan, William F., Gloria E. Everson, and Kathryn E. Sampeck
1993 Excavations in Structure 10L-41, Group 10L-2, Copán, 1993 (Operation 48/10). Field report on file at the Middle American Research Institute, Tulane University, and the Centro de Investigaciones, Instituto Hondureño de Antropología e Historia, Copán.

Fash, William L., Jr.
1991 *Scribes, Warriors and Kings: The City of Copán and the Ancient Maya.* New York: Thames and Hudson.

Freidel, David, Linda Schele, and Joy Parker
1993 *Maya Cosmos: Three Thousand Years on the Shaman's Path.* New York: William Morrow.

Harrison, Peter D'Arcy
1970 The Central Acropolis, Tikal, Guatemala: A Preliminary Study of the Functions of its Structural Components in the Late Classic Period. Ph.D. dissertation, Department of Anthropology, University of Pennsylvania.

Hohmann, Hasso, and Annegrete Vogrin
1982 *Die Architekur von Copán (Honduras): Vermessung-Plandarstellung-Untersuchung der baulichen Elemente und des räumlichen Konzepts.* 2 vols. Graz, Austria: Akademische Druck-u. Verlagsanstalt.

Inomata, Takeshi, and Stephen D. Houston
2001 Opening the Royal Maya Court. In *Royal Courts of the Ancient Maya,* vol. 1: *Theory, Comparison, and Synthesis,* edited by Takeshi Inomata and Stephen D. Houston, 3–23. Boulder: Westview Press.

Johnson, Jodi Lynn
1993 The Sculpture of Structure 10L-41, Group 10L-2, Copán, 1993 (Operation 48/11). Field report on file at the Middle American Research Institute, Tulane University, and the Centro de Investigaciones, Instituto Hondureño de Antropología e Historia, Copán.

Miles, Susanna W.
1957 The Sixteenth-Century Pokom-Maya: A Documentary Analysis of Social Structure and Archaeological Setting. *Transactions of the American Philosophical Society* 47: 731–781. Philadelphia.

Pollock, Harry E. D.
1965 Architecture of the Maya Lowlands. In *Archaeology of Southern Meso-america*, edited by Gordon R. Willey, part 1, pp. 378–440. *Handbook of Middle American Indians*, vol. 2, Robert Wauchope, general editor. Austin: University of Texas Press.
Proskouriakoff, Tatiana
1962 Civic and Religious Structures of Mayapan. In *Mayapan, Yucatan, Mexico*, by H. E. D. Pollock, Ralph L. Roys, T. Proskouriakoff, and A. Ledyard Smith, 87–169. Carnegie Institution of Washington Publication 619. Washington, D.C.
Rice, Don S., Prudence M. Rice, and Timothy Pugh
1998 Settlement Continuity and Change in the Central Petén Lakes Region: The Case of Sacpetén. In *Anatomía de una civilización: Aproximaciones interdisciplinarias a la cultura maya*, edited by Andrés Ciudad Ruiz et al., 207–252. Publicaciones de la S.E.E.M., no. 4. Madrid: Sociedad Española de Estudios Mayas.
Scholes, France V., and Ralph L. Roys
1948 *The Maya Chontal Indians of Acalan-Tixchel: A Contribution to the History and Ethnography of the Yucatan Peninsula.* Carnegie Institution of Washington Publication 560. Washington, D.C.
Shorkley, George
1892–1893 Peabody Museum Honduras Expedition. Copan, 1892–93. Notes taken by Geo. Shorkley. Catalog no. 93-27A. Cambridge, Mass.: Peabody Museum, Harvard University.
Starratt, Harold E.
1994 Excavations in Structures 10L-84, 10L-240, 10L-241, 10L-242, and 10L-243, Group 10L-2, Copán, 1994 (Operations 48/11, 48/16, and 48/17). Field report on file at the Middle American Research Institute, Tulane University, and the Centro de Investigaciones, Instituto Hondureño de Antropología e Historia, Copán.
2001 Excavations in El Cementerio, Group 10L-2, Copán, Honduras. Ph.D. dissertation, Department of Anthropology, Tulane University.
Thompson, J. Eric S.
1938 Sixteenth and Seventeenth Century Reports on the Chol Mayas. *American Anthropologist* 40: 584–604.
1970 Lowland Maya Religion: Worship. In *Maya History and Religion*, 159–196. Norman: University of Oklahoma Press.
Tozzer, Alfred M. (ed. and trans.)
1941 *Landa's Relación de las Cosas de Yucatán.* Papers of the Peabody Museum of American Archaeology and Ethnology, vol. 18. Cambridge, Mass.: Harvard University.
Webster, David L.
2001 Spatial Dimensions of Maya Courtly Life: Problems and Issues. In *Royal Courts of the Ancient Maya*, vol. 1: *Theory, Comparison, and Synthesis*, edited by Takeshi Inomata and Stephen D. Houston, 130–167. Boulder: Westview Press.
Wisdom, Charles
1940 *The Chorti Indians of Guatemala.* Chicago: University of Chicago Press.

CHAPTER FOUR

Palaces of the Royal Court at Tikal

Peter D'Arcy Harrison

Introduction

This chapter will deal with a number of aspects of the analysis of palace architecture in general, with specific examples drawn from the city of Tikal.[1] The first topic is analysis by form in the quest for identification of function. Second is a consideration of the nature of residence and its varied manifestations. Third is an examination of the reality of a royal court for the lowland Maya and specifically at Tikal. This examination is performed by means of a cross-cultural comparison with two other societies that have been recognized as utilizing the institution of the royal court. Supporting evidence for the existence of a royal court is found in the evidence of personal titles present in the lowland inscriptions and also in the iconography of scenes from Maya painted vessels. These considerations lead to a definition of the royal court for the ancient Maya and to conclusions of the functions of such a court at Tikal.

Palaces at Tikal

Surveys and excavations of the architecture of Tikal have demonstrated that structures identified by the term "palace" are distributed in a variety of locations around the city. Detailed excavation of such structures has been achieved in only a few groups within the confines of the greater city. The most extensive investigations of a palace group at Tikal were performed in the Central Acropolis, located adjacent to the ceremonial nucleus of the city, the Great Plaza. A number of other individual palaces were investigated at different loci of the site by a number of archaeologists participating in both the Pennsylvania Project (1955–1969) and the Proyecto Nacional under the direction of Juan Pedro Laporte (1979–1989). During the Pennsylvania Project, Bill Haviland excavated Group 7F-1, which included

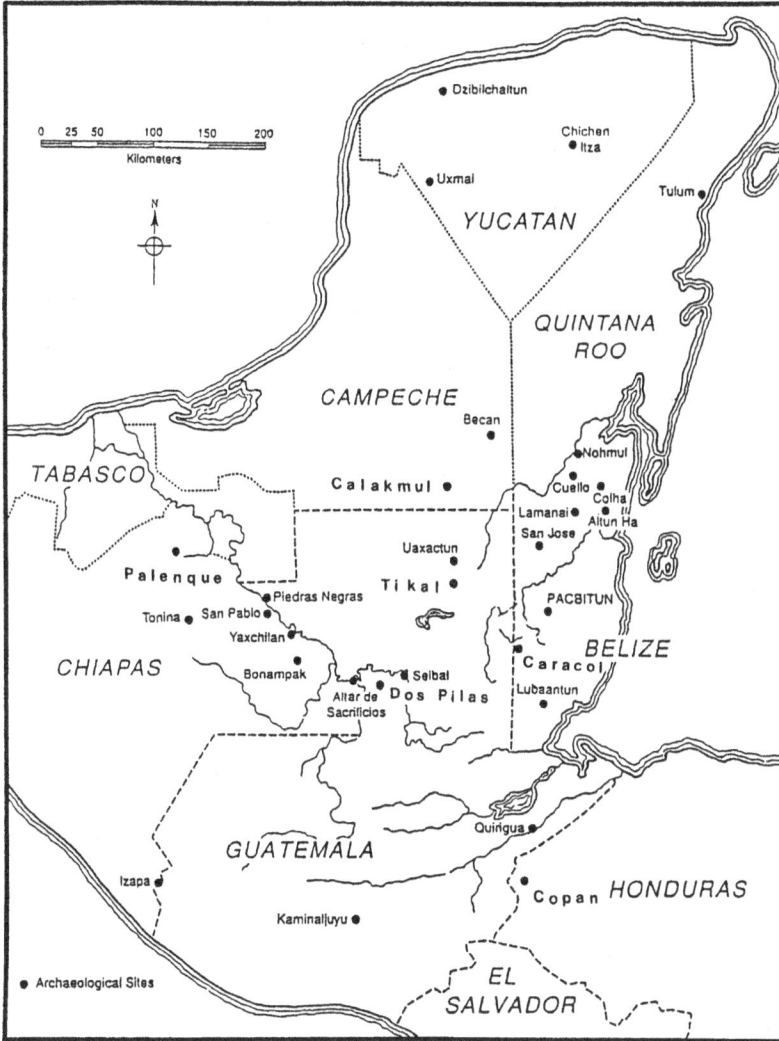

FIGURE 4.1. The Maya lowlands with the location of Tikal among its neighbors.

major palace structures and is interpreted as an elite residential group. In addition to the Central Acropolis, Harrison worked in the West Plaza where the large, raised palace Structure 5D-15 was at least partially cleared and tunneled. Another significant excavation and stabilization project took place in the major complex known as G Group, where the Guatemalan investigators Rudy Larios and Miguel Orrego were in charge (Orrego and Larios 1983). Additionally, some consolidation and clearing was accomplished around the environs of the building known as the "Bat Palace," a group raised on a ceremonial platform that supports Structures 5C-11, 12, and 13. Despite these varied locales around the city of Tikal, few of the investigations actually cleared whole structures or were able to define their most intricate details. Other groups or structures still retain standing architecture that clearly identifies their palace functional associations (more on this below) but have been subjected to no investigation other than the basic mapping. An outstanding example is F Group, prominently located between the twin-pyramid groups of Q and R to the north and with the Mendez Causeway to the south. There are other important and even central palace groups about which we know nothing other than their plan configuration with occasional bits of standing architecture. Among these are a complex well to the south of the Great Plaza that includes Structures 6D-42 through 62, not to mention the palaces which top the South Acropolis (see Figure 4.3). However, the existing information provides a pattern for a structure type referred to in the literature as "palace" and which is found scattered around the city of Tikal displaying a wide variety of size and shape, number of rooms, and varied numbers of elevating platforms.

The excavations which have been achieved allow the opportunity to introduce some order in the perception of their differences and similarities. It has been noted often that the term "palace" is borrowed from the European lexicon and assumes residence as the primary function, with an opposition to "temple" as the other Maya monumental structural form, which has a primarily assumed religious function (Harrison 1996). Evidence to hand indicates that the real situation is more complex than this simple opposition, but the modes of defining and separating the variety of building forms still cause analysts to stumble. One focus of this chapter is to demonstrate order in the analysis of palaces at Tikal, centering on those of the Central Acropolis which are most familiar and more completely excavated. This exercise will require a number of steps. First, defining what is meant by the term "palace" in the Maya lowlands is made difficult by many variables: location, size, shape, interior and exterior complexity, occurrence in clusters, and occurrence alone. Some of these architectural entities are sited low on the surrounding terrain, while others are raised high above it by platforms in the manner associated with temples. Further, modification of many structures over time has occurred both in different methods of change and in different intensities of such change.

As a category, the term "palace" is a deception. The buildings artificially brought together under this rubric do not serve the same—and often not even similar—functions. The evidence suggests that some palaces served a

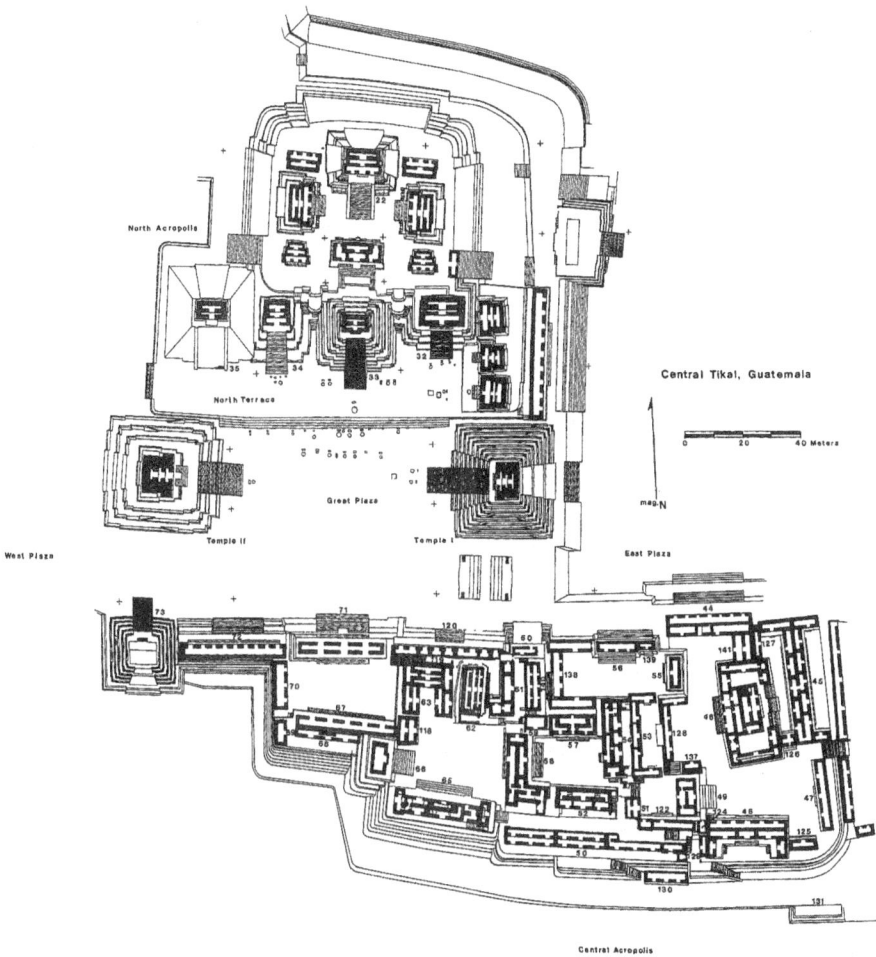

FIGURE 4.2. The ceremonial core of Tikal with the North Acropolis and Central Acropolis in close proximity, showing an opposition of sacred (north) and secular (south).

few and specific functions while others served many (Harrison 1970). The variety of still unsorted evidence forces us to conclude that we are faced with a huge complexity of cultural expression at the city of Tikal alone. Efforts to compare palaces from one city to another increases the complexity level, as individual community expression enters into the equation. This does not suggest that the analysis of Maya architecture is hopeless— only that recognition of a higher level of complexity than has been expressed in the existing literature is still required.

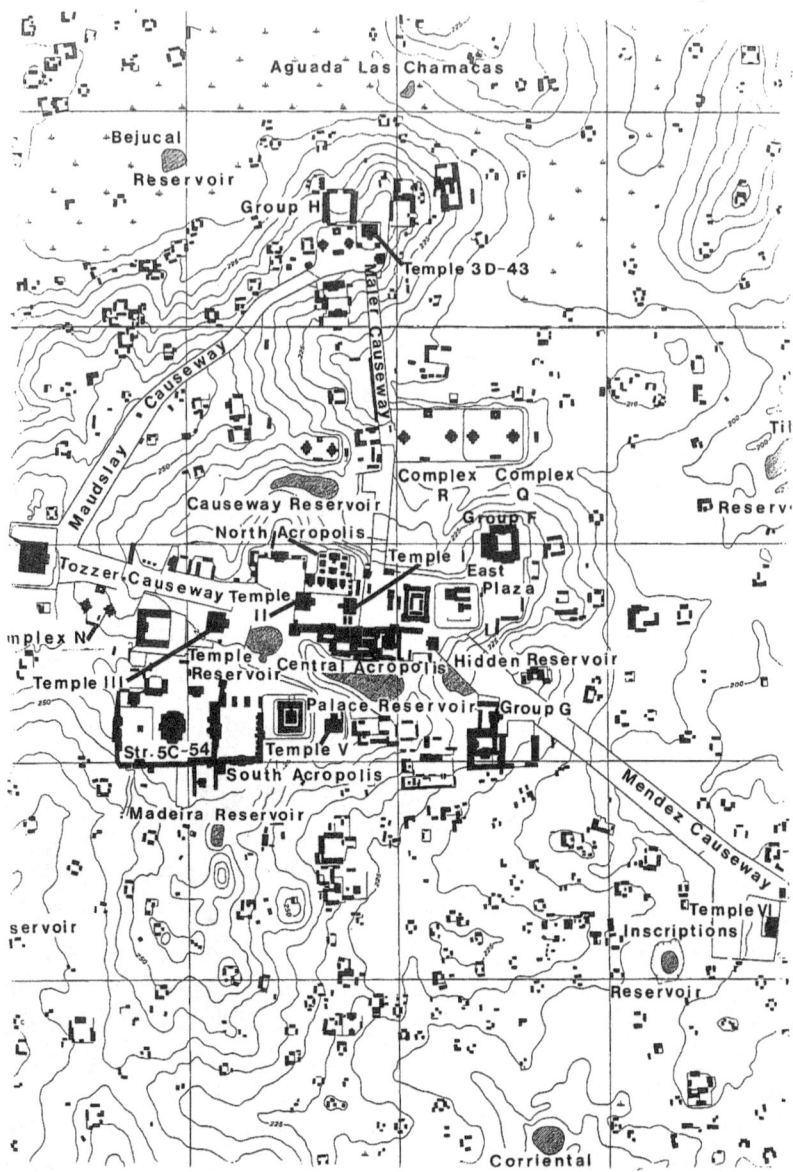

FIGURE 4.3. General map of Tikal, including the locations of Palace Groups F and G, as well as other palace and ceremonial groups of importance.

Analysis by Variety in Form

The original analysis of palace functions made from the data retrieved from the Central Acropolis during excavations performed from 1964 through 1967 appears only in a still unpublished dissertation (Harrison 1970). During the time period of this work, there existed a preconception that palace structures served the primary function of elite residence, and it was of some interest that the preliminary analysis did not support this thesis. For the first time, the features of variability were identified. The hypothesis that "form follows function" applied to a specific and detailed data set forced the conclusion that a multiplicity of functions existed in the Central Acropolis, of which only one was residence.

Rather than force some abstract formula of analysis upon the architectural data, the technique we used in the Central Acropolis allowed the data to sort themselves into variations of form. In order to perform such an analysis, one basic variable, along with its varietal positions, had to be selected. The most obviously objective variable was floor plan. Comparison of the available floor plans within the Central Acropolis showed a distribution of tandem and transverse rooms as the principal feature that distinguished one building from another. These two room arrangements offer four possible variables in a simple to most-complex progression. These are: (1) no-tandem/no-transverse, which by definition is a single-room structure; (2) no-tandem/transverse, which can be either a two- or three-room structure; (3) tandem/no-transverse, which can be multiple-room but without transverse rooms; (4) and finally tandem/transverse, a variety that is most complex and can offer a large number of room arrangements.

In order to further differentiate the structures, all other known archaeological features were added into the equation. These included features that were both primary to the initial construction of the building, as a well as those that were secondarily added to the structure. The latter have the greatest variety, including the introduction of secondary beams, benches, and even additional stories to the original building. Even these variables have a range of simple to complex. The distribution of such features, especially the secondary ones, correlated well with the complexity of room plan, in the sense that the more complex plans were subject to more intense use of secondary features (Harrison 1970).

The resulting analysis produced clusters of traits associated with different floor plans. The most complex plan was also associated with the most types of other features, such as secondary niches, subspring beams that may have supported curtains, and a multiplicity of bench forms including one type interpreted as a bed. This cluster is viewed in the analysis as

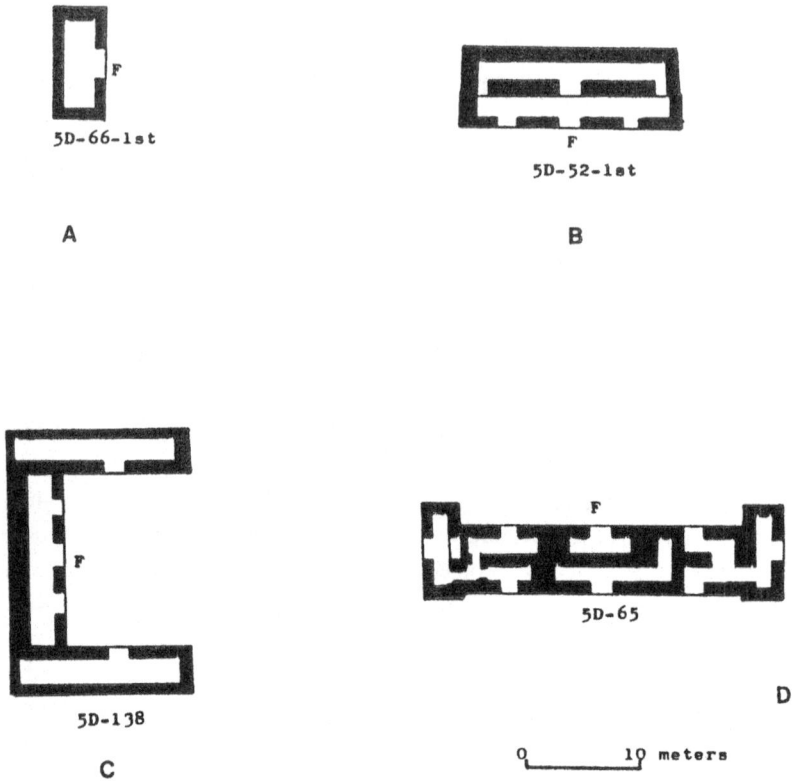

FIGURE 4.4. Examples of the four types of floor plans in the Central Acropolis. (A) No-tandem/no-transverse. (B) Tandem/no-transverse. (C) No-tandem/transverse. (D) Tandem/transverse.

having supported the function of residence, which fits well with a number of buildings in the Central Acropolis. However, only one excavated building, 5D-46, offered all the features that were expected of a permanent residence, including the presence of burials. The interesting conclusion that a number of structures indicated residential function by their attributes and form, yet only one excavated structure produced evidence of permanent residence, led to a new consideration: the nature of residence.

The Nature of Residence

Much has been learned since this initial analysis in 1970. Several fronts of investigation have led to confirmation of some of the original identifications of function, while other concepts have changed. Developments in epigraphy, as well as new fieldwork at other sites, have led to a focus on the function and location of a royal court that is recognized as having many more functions than simple family residence. There is, in fact, a difference between the simple concepts of "residence" and "residents." While the former has a family reference and can be associated with ideas of "clan houses" with great longevity and having important anthropological association with lineage, the latter is more transitory. For example, the Central Acropolis could well have had a population at any given time of a high number of residents (e.g., 500), and still only have contained one or two family residences that were permanently occupied by a nuclear or extended family. A major difference in these two types of residence is that those individuals who resided permanently in one place had no other place where their bodies could have been included in a population count. However, the temporary "residents" did have another place of residence within the confines of the city and should not be included in a population count that depends upon numbers of habitations. The temporary resident was undoubtedly an important component of the fabric of a royal court but not a factor in population counts. This is an important and usually overlooked factor when population counts of major city-sites have been calculated.

FIGURE 4.5. Structure 5D-46, the one excavated structure interpreted as a family residence. The central core is Early Classic, while the side patios are Late Classic additions. Shown after excavation and consolidation. Photograph, 1966.

Because of the centralized location of the Central Acropolis adjacent to the Great Plaza, it is a fair assumption that the permanent residences belonged to the ruling family or their near relatives. While this may be true, knowledge of other events in the city over time indicates that permanent family residence was neither a prominent nor stable factor in the Central Acropolis. While it is easy to conceive of the nature of permanent elite family residents, and more will be said of this below, the other residents were more esoteric, probably ritual, in nature. These were people who lived in the palace complex for a variety of reasons for nonpermanent, and likely short, lengths of stay. Some stays were related to the function of the court, possibly by courtiers with visiting privileges. Others were for more ritualistic reasons. Some groups who may have been residents for such functions include men and/or women on temporary retreat for religious, possibly purification, purposes; scholars—young people temporarily resident for the purpose of learning the arts of aristocracy, such as literacy, painting, architecture, and warfare; visiting ball teams associated with the ritualization of simulated warfare through the medium of the ball game; visiting dignitaries and diplomats from other cities or state regimes; and of course the support staff: servants with a wide range of duties and social status, providing the sumptuary setting that befits a royal court as well as the defense of its occupants. It is likely that the royal precincts were the location of the production of those types of craft that were made by the hands of the elite themselves. The carving of ceremonial objects of stone and wood (Houston and Stuart, with Taube 1998), the painting of ceramic vessels, the production of objects sacred to the family, are all pursuits that were appropriate to the confines of the royal palaces. Structure 5D-65, known also as Maler's Palace, was a structure of temporary residence and multiple functions. The many thrones/benches in this building suggest either the roles of reception by a ruler or the seat of a great teacher.

Establishing the Existence of Royal Courts

The first public presentation which addressed the palace function as an expression of a royal court was made in a symposium at the ninety-fifth annual meeting of the American Anthropological Association; it was titled "The Royal Courts of the Classic Maya: An Anthropological Perspective."[2]

A number of lines of evidence were invoked at this time to establish the veracity of the concept of a royal court for the lowland Maya. These lines of evidence included cross-cultural comparisons with the features of other

FIGURE 4.6. Artist's reconstruction by Terry Rutledge of Structure 5D-65, Maler's Palace, during its prime occupation. Approximate date A.D. 800.

societies, both ancient and modern, that are recognized by anthropologists as having supported a royal court. My own contribution to this symposium included a comparison of the Maya with the court of Louis XIV of France in the seventeenth century and the court of the Inka rulers of Peru in the fifteenth century. Specific features which identified the courts of these societies were compared with the culture of the Classic Maya. These included (a) the role of ancestors as a validation of power; (b) association of the dynastic family with the church/temple (that is, the dominant religious body of the culture), including the physical relationship between the royal place of residence and the church/temple; (c) the use of livery as ritual identification; and (d) the use of thrones as the symbolic seats of power, diplomacy, and jurisprudence.

   In each of the three compared societies, the evidence for all of these features was present in comparable form, and these comparisons are described below.

The Role of Ancestors as Validation of Power

Louis XIV. A common theme of royal courts is the divine right of kings, in which the right to rule is invested from the patrilineal line of descendancy, by which the ultimate sanctifier of the position is a divine being. Louis XIV's right to rule came from his father and from God. Disagreement with his opinion was considered a sin. That he chose the sun as his personal symbol of vitality and was known as the Sun King is perhaps a coincidence that enhances comparison with American cultures wherein the sun *was* the overriding deity and source of ultimate power. When Louis ascended to the throne, he was legally considered to be the master and owner of the bodies and property of 19 million men and was saluted as a "visible divinity." However, the ancestral kings, although revered as the line of divine power, were not openly worshipped, as in other societies (*Encyclopaedia Britannica*, 15th ed.; Mitford 1966).

Inka. In Inka society, not only were the ancestors the source of power for the living king, but the old rulers did not lose either their power or their wealth upon their death. Rather, the Inka cult of the dead was perhaps the most intense in culture history, wherein the royal court of one ruler never ceased to exist but became one of a succession of royal courts with the dead ancestors at its core. These royal courts had a physical architectural entity known as the *kancha*, which was quadrangular in form with an inner courtyard. The deceased ruler was mummified and continued in death to hold his properties, entourage, and decision-making abilities carried out through family descendants. Only the government office was passed on to the eldest son. This extraordinary system results in some interesting comparisons with the Maya at Tikal (see below). A major difference between the Inka and Maya is that storage of the dead Inka king, and eventual burial of his entourage and family, took place within the confines of his *kancha*, while the Maya did not bury royalty within the confines of the residential (palace) complexes. Such burial was separate and associated with the church/temple, comparable to the European practice of burying kings in the church, not in the palace (Brundage 1967; Hyslop 1990).

Lowland Classic Maya. Classic period Maya seem to have established their divinity during their lifetimes, but ancestors, who were the source of power and succession, were revered as gods. The reality of Maya succession is in some doubt, especially at Tikal where the succession of office was strictly recounted by numbered rulers after the named, recognized founder-king, Yax Ehb' Xook. The best-known dynastic line was that of Jaguar Claw, but breaks in the familial line of descent are certain on several occasions. The use of mythological or assumed descent is common at the city of Palenque as well, where reference to ultimate right of descent from a divine being was used on more than one occasion, demonstrating that while accounting for ancestry was extremely important to the Maya, in reality it was not always observed. The political exigencies of power, by conquest or merely palace revolt, often determined the identity of the individual in power. Legitimization after the fact was a matter of producing a public record that satisfied convention (Marcus 1992).

Association of the Dynastic Family with the "Church"

Louis XIV. During this regime the ideological association of family and church was very strong, with the power of the head of the church falling below that of the king, although it was the king's responsibility to protect and uphold the precepts of the church. God and ruler intertwined in a reciprocal service of goals.

However, the physical association was not necessarily a close one. In fact, Louis XIV moved the location of his court to his largest architectural project, Versailles, to escape the noise and health dangers of the Paris of his time, thus leaving behind the close physical association that had previously bonded the king and the church. Of course, chapels were included as part of the structure of the new royal palace, so that in a sense the church came with Louis, when he distanced the court from Paris. Later, he moved the government offices to Versailles as well, so that all sources of power were centralized at the location of his residence.

Inka. The seats of government, wealth, and society were located in the *kancha*, or home compound of the ruler. With the capital city of Cuzco as the example, the holy temple (church in this analogy) was located at the site center associated with a public place or plaza. The successive *kanchas* were arranged around this religious focal point but were not public places themselves. Local matters seem to have been adjudicated from within the *kancha*, while matters of conquest were conducted from the public plaza (more about this under the topic of thrones). As mentioned earlier, burial or storage of the dead took place in the *kancha*, not in the temple (church). Religion was much more focused upon the cult of the dead than upon worship of deities external to the society, such as the various aspects of the Sun God, even though this deity was considered ancestral to the living (or dead) rulers. Observation of the divine right of kings was not translated into a close association of the office with the "church," as was the case with Louis XIV. The strongest element of the religion was ancestor worship. Burial practice contrasts with that of both Louis' time and with the Classic Maya, excepting in the prominence of ancestor worship.

Lowland Classic Maya. The Maya court, or palace groupings as we know them, excludes the burial of kings, which instead is associated with the temples (the church). The North Acropolis of Tikal is known to have served as a sacred necropolis over a long period of time, including the Classic period. However, it was not the exclusive place of burial of kings. The court apparently shifted temporarily to the region of the Lost World Pyramid (5C-54) for a time during the Early Classic (Laporte 1990), and then returned to the environs of the Great Plaza. The Central Acropolis has long been considered the main focal point of what we now recognize as the functions of a royal court. Many of the palaces found here contain features commensurate with functions of judiciary, diplomacy, schooling, and even royal residence. One such structure, 5D-46 (already mentioned; see Figure 4.5), is known, by association with an inscription on the dedicatory vessel buried at the time of construction, to be the house of Jaguar Claw the Great—that is, the clan house, the seat of the court. The Central Acropolis complex grew by expansion over the centuries and suffered some considerable destruction of buildings in the course of its occupation.

Consideration of the *kancha* practice of the Inka leads one to reassess the features of the many palace groups at Tikal as a whole. A number of *kancha*-like complexes do exist, dating to the Late Classic period. These include the palace groups referred to earlier as Group F, Group G, the Bat Palace, and a group around Structure 6D-42 for which the date is not known. For some of these palace groups, it is possible to infer the ruler who built them by association with other buildings. All of these groups have a physical similarity to the quadrangular *kancha* of the Inka, but they do not include royal burials within the limits of known excavation. If these later complexes are truly analogous to the Inka *kancha*, as royal courts, the association with religious structures is ephemeral and much less clear than in the case of the Central Acropolis (see Figure 4.2). There is indication that the construction of these later palace complexes was associated with an expansion of the perceived cosmos of the city, that is, the east and west architectural markers were expanding outward, away from the Great Plaza, by the construction of new religious buildings, notably Temples VI and IV (Harrison 1999).

Summary. Comparison of the Maya shows a partial conformity to the fifteenth-century Inka model and also partial conformity with the seventeenth-century French model. Overlap occurs. The comparison has led to the observation that a *kancha*-like architectural configuration may have emerged at Tikal during the eighth century, suggesting that some change took place in the court pattern.

The Use of Livery as Ritual Identification

The term "livery" is used here to mean any form of symbolic identification worn about the body or carried as a special privilege. It may take the form of designs identifying the family clan, the individual, or the political entity governed. Designs on clothing, headdress, and banners all constitute items of livery and are used to separate the royal court members or its leaders from commoners. The usage in battle of identifying banners is traditional in almost all societies that engage in warfare, not just in high civilizations.

Louis XIV. Louis was entitled to the emblems of the Bourbon dynasty which produced him, to the emblems of the country of France, which he owned, and the emblem that he adopted as his own personal insignia, the sun disk. His personal motto was "None his equal," which exemplified the individuality and arrogance that personal livery can project. Louis' emblems were carried in war, worn at court, and loaned to favorites as an outward display of loyalty on their parts. The long and elaborate wigs that were a fashion of the time found longevity in the court of jurisprudence, not just in France, but also in England. Although this was just a fashion, not an item of livery, its projection as a symbol of one prime function of the court is of particular interest in comparison with other societies.

Inka. In royal processions, not only were the physical emblems in the form of staffs of office and banners carried for the Inka, but his robes were particular to the individual: "Affixed to poles carried by selected servitors in the *kancha* came the sandals, the coca bag and the 'king's robe,' the *capac uncu*, that rich tunic with its singular and unrepeatable pattern woven solely for that ruler. Each ruler could be recognized by this state garb alone. The tunic of Manco Capac, for instance was a rich red around the shoulders, a belt of three bands of [abstract square designs] around the middle, and a skirt of plain blue" (Brundage 1967: 45–46). Similarly, each of the Inka rulers, living or dead, had a singular and individual livery.

Lowland Classic Maya. For the Maya, the sources of information are far less secure, but the topic invokes other bodies of source information: the data contained on painted vessels, both provenienced and unprovenienced; other sources of Maya iconography, such as carved stelae; and sixteenth-century colonial accounts, all of which supply some information on this topic. Headdresses depicted on carved stelae and painted vessels are a lively source of information. These iconographic sources indicate that symbols contained within headdresses were capable of distinguishing, not just the city of origin, but also the family clan of the wearer. Hummingbirds attending water lily flowers, owls, jaguar paws (with claws), and crocodiles are a few of the livery emblems derived from nature that were displayed by Maya rulers. The latter two are distinctive not just of Tikal but of other sites such as El Mirador and Calakmul. The remains of an actual crocodile skeleton were recovered from the tomb of the Early Classic ruler at Tikal named Yax Nuun Aiin I, as well as a crocodile emblem carved in jade from the same tomb.

Tatiana Proskouriakoff (1950) began the study of the ornamentation of dress, and others have continued in this line (Miller, Taube, Houston), but to date there does not exist a comprehensive analysis of this topic of such enormous potential. The sacred palanquins of the rulers of Tikal and Calakmul are featured in written accounts of wars conducted out of Tikal. Of course, only victorious accounts are found in the texts of the lintels on Temples I and IV at Tikal, which purportedly describe victories over Calakmul and Naranjo. The giant figures depicted on these carved palanquins were the livery of either the victorious or the conquered ruler.

Summary. Livery is a common characteristic of each of the royal courts in this sample, one which served as a significant feature of royal identification and state affiliation.

Thrones as Paraphernalia of the Royal Court

Louis XIV. The throne in European courts became synonymous with the office itself. When the ruler sat upon this special royal seat he personified all the traits of his office: god, leader, head of the judiciary, diplomat, and supporter of the church.[3] In a period painting of Louis on his throne at Versailles, receiving ambassadors from Asia, there is shown a scene that can be nearly duplicated in principle from the paintings on Maya vessels of the Classic period. The throne is a symbolic seat of office representing the pinnacle of the royal court. When the king was on his throne, he was displaying his most godlike role. The throne was the major emblem of power.

Inka: In Inka society the throne has at least two variations. There was a small stool of office which was used by the Inka to receive visitors or to dispense justice from the formal rooms of his *kancha.* In this instance, the important feature was the seating of the ruler per se, rather than the impressiveness of the seat itself. There is said to have been a royal throne of gold and silver that was captured by the conquistadores, which was either lost at sea or melted down, and thus it remains in the realm of myth.

On the other hand, there were stone-carved seats known as *ushnu* (Hyslop 1990: 99–101) that did serve as state symbols. These were elaborate and large carved stone or masonry platforms upon which, it is said, the Inka sat when he was visiting conquered lands. Such stone platforms were places of public appearance, not of private reception or judgment. While one is reported from the plaza of Cuzco, all others were found in the provinces, suggesting a distinction between functions in these two forms of seating—the stool and the *ushnu*—for the ruler-deity.

Lowland Classic Maya. Thrones of the Maya are found in the form of stone and masonry benches located inside the complex structures called palaces. While these benches occur in many shapes and sizes, we can be guided by the frequently occurring representations on painted vessels of throne scenes. Typically, the ruler, wearing his headdress livery, is seated cross-legged upon a bench of varying decorative complexity and opulence. The presence of animal skins and textiles, in the form of cushions and hangings, embellish and soften the severity of the basic masonry construct. Archaeologically, at Tikal these benches occur in certain rooms within the royal palaces of the Central Acropolis, as well as in all the other previously mentioned palace groups at Tikal. The most complex bench has masonry sidearms and is accompanied by holes in the surrounding walls that suggest the support system for textiles hung both as frontal curtains and backdrops of the throne-bench. These more complex benches have been interpreted as thrones (Harrison 1970) based on a variety of factors and reinforced by the painted scenes on vessels. These scenes show a variety of activity: reception of visitors, acceptance of gifts, which may be tax, tribute, or booty, apparent judgment scenes, and receiving of prisoners. The use of the bench-throne by the Maya as a device to elevate the ruler to a position of power, physically and symbolically, parallels the use of such devices in the courts of Louis XIV and the Inka, as well as other societies.

Summary. The throne is a device used in royal courts to formally raise the ruler to a position above the visitor-supplicant and to symbolize his power. Its use by the Inka was most closely paralleled in other cultures by the stone *ushnu*. The Maya throne was interior and formal, as was that of Louis XIV. There are suggestions of outdoor platform-terraces among the Maya that may parallel architecturally the use of the Inka *ushnu*. Examples have been described at Copan, and similar terraces occur in the Great Plaza at Tikal in public, rather than private, places. The differences in locale and architectural structure likely indicate equal differences in their functions.

The purpose of this brief cross-cultural exercise was to establish the existence of a royal court in the case of lowland Classic Maya civilization. Comparison with two other cultures indicates that uniformity outweighs the differences. Where differences do exist, such as the case of the Inka *kancha*, a new interpretation is offered for certain palace groupings at Tikal that may indeed reflect this type of configuration, although not the permanency of the individual's court, as was the case for the Inka. Rather, it is suggested that two types of court existed at Tikal: one exemplified by the Central Acropolis that grew by accretion over a long period of time (five hundred years); and another, exemplified by Groups F and G, in which quadrangular compounds are suspected of having been constructed specifically as royal houses. This latter interpretation remains in the realm of speculation.

Royal courts are based upon family power, asserted divinity, and warfare and are expressed in physical ideological symbols such as livery, thrones, and architectural structures as residences. The conclusion of this part of this chapter is that royal courts are demonstrated to have existed for the lowland Classic Maya and that they were in conformity with similar royal courts in other cultures.

Other Forms of Evidence for the Maya Royal Court

Epigraphy: Court Titles

In recent years, the translation of hieroglyphic texts has accelerated under the impetus of several scholars. The annual gatherings under the aegis of Linda Schele at Austin, Texas, served as a stimulus to many individuals, including Nikolai Grube, Simon Martin, Stephen Houston, David Stuart, Barbara MacLeod, and Peter Mathews, to name a few. The list of recognized titles of office is increasing monthly under the study of these scholars. The following selected examples indicate the presence of political stratification as well as offices which served roles within a court structure. These are:

kalomte: High emperor. The exact meaning is not yet known, but the indications are that this individual held power over a territory that was larger in scope than was the case for the next-lower title in rank. This title appears to have been introduced late in the development of Tikal and likely is a reflection of the growing complexity of the society, as well as the city. Texts at a number of cities have yielded this title.

ajaw (or *ahau, ahaw*): This term is variously interpreted as "lord," "king," and "ruler." It pertained at the time of its earliest appearance in the Early Classic period at Tikal to the overseer of a city, and then later, to part of a city, such that a very large population center like Tikal could conceivably have supported more than one *ajaw.*

sajal: An underlord, usually subservient to an *ajaw.* Occurrences of this title indicate a ranking of sites, in which the *sajal* controls a smaller site within the realm of power of an *ajaw,* and ultimately of a *kalomte.*

ah tz'ihb: This is the name of the office of scribe, in the sense of the act of writing. The contexts of references to this term suggest that holders of the office were members of the royal family.

ah ch'ul hun: A term that denotes the position of office of a scribe, as opposed to the act of writing. It is also interpreted as "Keeper of the Holy Books." This term is closely associated with *ajaw*, suggesting that an *ajaw* always also held the office of *ah ch'ul hun* (Coe and Kerr 1998).

As Coe and Kerr (1998) have demonstrated, the king is frequently shown on painted vessels in the role of scribe, wearing pens or paintbrushes in his hair or headdress as if they were a part of his livery, at least upon certain occasions or in certain roles. Literacy on the part of the king and the role of supplementary scribes are features of the royal court.

There are other words in the texts which further reflect the functions of courtly activities. These include a possessive with reference to the title *ajaw*—a further indication of a more subtle stratification. An "owned" *ajaw* is at a higher level than a *sajal,* suggesting a patronage system in which one king installs another, creating a chain of allegiance (Martin and Grube 1995). Certain verbs—to seize (*chuk*); to burn (*pulyi*); to accede to office (*ch'am k'awil* [literally, to seize or take the *k'awil,* the staff of office]); to arrive (*hul-I* [literally, to seize or accept rule]); friend (*yokum* [companion])— are all indications of the militaristic functions of the royal court in its external relations with its neighboring and distant fellow city-states.[4] This list is a mere sample of the growing lexicon of words in the texts that support the concept and functions of a royal court for the ancient Maya.

Iconography

Besides epigraphy, another source of data about the existence and functions of a royal court has appeared in the publication of the *Maya Vase Book* series (volumes 1–6) by Justin Kerr (1989–2000). While many of these vessels are unprovenienced, the wealth of information that they contain, especially with reference to scenes of formal reception, is prodigious. In these painted scenes are found enough details to identify architecture with doorways and exterior platforms, so that their association with palaces is virtually unquestionable. Details of luxury goods made of perishable materials, such as curtains and draperies, cushions, and the costumes of the players, fill in the blank walls and stark benches that are found archaeologically.

While the Central Acropolis was certainly one seat of the royal court at Tikal, evidence from other parts of the city suggest that the court had not one single permanent location, but rather shifted physically from place to place over time. We do not have sufficient hard evidence to trace this movement throughout time, but there is sufficient evidence to suggest at least an outline of the history of this facet of royal life at Tikal.

Definition of the Maya Royal Court

The above considerations can allow us to forge a definition of what a royal court meant for the ancient Maya at Tikal—a definition which includes the court's functions as well as its architectural setting.

A royal court was a place or series of places with a complex architectural setting, where a group of people met to affirm the tenets of their society. These tenets included the managing of both internal and external affairs of that society. The proceedings of management were cloaked in ritual. The participants of these meetings were formalized and called courtiers. They performed a range of specific functions and represented a range of social classes, all of whom honored their leader, usually called a king or some similar title denoting high power. The king himself was often a limited prisoner of his office, in the sense that he was tied to the conventions of the society and the necessity of the presence of the courtiers. The internal affairs governed by the court included the business of the immediate community, usually of city-sized dimensions, and its rituals. In societies where the ruler's power was closely allied to the state religion, these rituals were essential to maintenance of that power. The external functions dealt with the centripetal and centrifugal forces of relationships within the greater state. The physical location of the court could be moved from its usual architectural setting, as long as the courtiers who validated it moved with it. For example, the king could be carried on a portable throne away from his permanent architectural setting and perform courtly functions outside of that setting.[5]

The physical setting has been associated with structures that are called palaces, but these structures have no fixed form, and range from very simple to highly complex. Functions of the court were military, judicial, ritual, governmental, and residential. A single structure could embody all, or only one, of these functions. The location of the court could change over time, likely for political reasons.

Conclusions

Following the above discussion, several conclusions are warranted. (1) The institution of a royal court did exist for the ancient Maya in general and for Tikal in particular, on the basis of comparison with the seventeenth-century court of Louis XIV and the eighteenth-century court of the Inka empire. Specific features of both courts compare favorably with the features of Maya of the seventh through tenth century. (2) The functions of such a royal court included military, judicial, governmental, ritual, and residential functions. (3) The palaces which supported the court as an architectural locale were complex, with a wide range of simplicity to complexity both in their floor plans and their contained functions; at Tikal there are several loci of the royal court, of which the most comprehensively investigated has been the Central Acropolis, which by interpretation fulfills all of the described functions. (4) The site specific of the royal court was subject to movement, and while the Central Acropolis remained one such site for five centuries, there were other loci at Tikal, some of which are designated only by formal speculation (for example, Groups F and G and the Bat Palace). (5) The function of residence of the royal family is definitely a prominent feature of royal court complexes, a function which is verified by Structure 5D-46 at Tikal in the Central Acropolis, a building that survived five hundred years of occupation despite conquests from outside. (6) The definition of a royal court for the ancient Maya is couched in terms of the political and ritual functions that characterize other societies which support this type of complex institution, which apparently also defines what anthropologists have acknowledged previously as "high civilization."

NOTES

1. Between November 1996 and November 1998, no less than four symposia were conducted in a variety of venues with the subject of Maya palaces and their role in a royal court. The first and last of these were related, in that the earliest symposium served as a trial run for a more formal presentation two years later with publication as the intent. These four symposia were chronologically:

(1) "The Royal Courts of the Classic Maya: An Anthropological Perspective," organized by Stephen Houston and Takeshi Inomata for the ninety-fifth annual meeting of the American Anthropological Association, San Francisco, November 20–24, 1996.
(2) "Maya Palaces and Elite Residences," organized by Jessica Christie for the sixty-third annual meeting of the Society for American Archaeology, Seattle, March 25–29, 1998.
(3) "Ancient Palaces of the New World: Form, Function and Meaning," organized and chaired by Susan Toby Evans and Joanne Pillsbury, as a Pre-Columbian symposium for Dumbarton Oaks, Washington, D.C., October 10–11, 1998.
(4) "Royal Courts of the Ancient Maya," a symposium organized by Takeshi Inomata and Stephen Houston, held at Yale University, November 7–8, 1998.

As a contributing participant in all four of these symposia, and drawing from the same data set at Tikal, I have attempted to focus upon different aspects of the analysis of palaces as a structure type, as well as their role in a posited royal court. Three of the symposia are resulting in expected publication. Therefore, I have selected the following methods of dealing with my data, in what is intended to be an increasingly narrowing focus of topic. In this chapter, which is the chronologically earliest paper, I draw upon materials presented in the AAA Symposium of 1996 as well as in the SAA Symposium of 1998. The goal is to examine the variation in palace form and function and to establish the reality of a royal court for Tikal. The second paper that I will publish, coauthored with E. Wyllys Andrews for Dumbarton Oaks, focuses on the topic of the elite residence and its evidence and meaning for a royal court. The third paper to be published focuses even more narrowly upon the topic of throne rooms and thrones as a signifier of courtly functions. Of necessity, there is some overlap in these three publications, which I have attempted to minimize while expressing the variety of palace form and function and the reality of the Royal Court at Tikal.

2. Organized by Stephen Houston and Takeshi Inomata, with six contributed papers and two discussants, November, 1996, San Francisco.

3. The ultimate western example of this concept would be that when the Pope, as leader of the Holy Roman Catholic Church, speaks officially from his throne, ex cathedra, the pronouncement is considered infallible.

4. I am indebted to Steve Houston for providing the Maya words for these terms by personal communication.

5. Although forged by this author, this definition resulted from participation in a symposium at Yale University, November 7–8, 1998, titled "Royal Courts of the Ancient Maya."

REFERENCES

Brundage, Burr Cartwright
1967 *Lords of Cuzco: A History and Description of the Inca People in Their Final Days.* Norman: University of Oklahoma Press.
Coe, Michael D., and Justin Kerr
1998 *The Art of the Maya Scribe.* New York: Harry N. Abrams.
Harrison, Peter D.
1970 *The Central Acropolis, Tikal, Guatemala: A Preliminary Study of the Functions of Its Structural Components during the Late Classic Period.* Ph.D. dissertation, University of Pennsylvania. Ann Arbor: University Microfilms.
1996 Court of Courts: Ceremonial, Legal and Hierarchical Functions in Maya Elite Society at Tikal. Paper presented in the symposium "The Royal Courts of the Classic Maya: An Anthropological Perspective," organized by Stephen Houston and Takeshi Inomata for the ninety-fifth annual meeting of the American Anthropological Association, San Francisco, November 20–24.
1999 *The Lords of Tikal: Rulers of an Ancient Maya City.* London: Thames and Hudson.
Houston, Stephen, and David Stuart
1996 Of Gods, Glyphs and Kings: Divinity and Rulership among the Classic Maya. *Antiquity* 70: 289–312.
1998 (with Karl Taube) Folk Classification of Classic Maya Pottery. *American Anthropologist* 91 (3): 720–726.
Hyslop, John
1990 *Inka Settlement Planning.* Austin: University of Texas Press.

Kerr, Justin, et al.
1989–2000   *The Maya Vase Book*, vols. 1–6. New York: Kerr Associates.
Laporte, Juan Pedro, and Vilma Fialko C.
1990   New Perspectives on Old Problems: Dynastic References for the Early Clas-
       sic at Tikal. In *Vision and Revision in Maya Studies*, edited by Flora S. Clancy
       and Peter D. Harrison, 33–66. Albuquerque: University of New Mexico Press.
Marcus, Joyce
1992   *Mesoamerican Writing Systems, Propaganda, Myth, and History in Four An-
       cient Civilizations.* Princeton: Princeton University Press.
Martin, Simon, and Nikolai Grube
1995   Maya Superstates. *Archaeology Magazine* 48 (6): 41–46.
Mitford, Nancy
1966   *The Sun King.* London: Hamish Hamilton.
Orrego, Miguel C., and Rudy Larios V.
1983   *Reporte de las investigaciones arqueológicas en el Grupo 5E-II, Tikal.* Guate-
       mala: Instituto de Antropología e Historia de Guatemala.
Proskouriakoff, Tatiana
1950   *A Study of Classic Maya Sculpture.* Carnegie Institution of Washington Pub-
       lication 593. Washington, D.C.

CHAPTER FIVE

The Political Acquisition of Sacred Geography

THE MURCIÉLAGOS COMPLEX AT DOS PILAS

Arthur Demarest, Kim Morgan, Claudia Wolley, and Héctor Escobedo

Many recent studies have emphasized the role of ideology and cosmology in pre-Columbian site planning and perception (e.g., Benson 1981; Aveni and Hartung 1986; Ashmore 1986, 1989, 1991; Berlo 1993; Carlson 1981; Freidel and Schele 1988a; Freidel 1986; Miller 1988; Sugiyama 1993). Contemporary ethnography (e.g., Vogt 1981) and ancient epigraphy (e.g., Stuart and Houston 1994) confirm that worldview and cosmology structured Maya perceptions of space, settlement, and architecture in ways that do not necessarily correspond to Western concepts of geography. These aspects of Maya architecture and settlement patterns cannot be effectively studied by objective analysis of demographic distributions, economic efficiency, defensibility, or other geographic parameters. Only with an understanding of what the ancient Maya themselves considered to be critical geographical features can we begin to comprehend the placement and distribution of their architecture, particularly their public and elite architecture. Insights into emic geography and cosmology drawn from ethnography, iconography, and epigraphy can be applied to interpret the nature and placement of individual ceremonial structures and elite residential groups (e.g., Ashmore 1986, 1989, 1991; Freidel 1986; Miller 1988; Schele 1981).

Recent symposia and studies have also stressed that palaces bridge the categories of public versus residential architecture (e.g., Evans and Pillsbury in press; Christie and Sarro n.d.). Palaces, especially royal palaces, had special significance in societies in which rulers were regarded as both secular and sacred in their nature and their duties. In the ancient Maya civilization, *ajaws* were just such holy lords; they were divine rulers with many sacred and ritual duties. Yet they were also competing political leaders in a landscape of war, economic pursuits, alliances, and intrigue. It follows that Maya palaces were places of residence but were also sacred loci of public and elite rituals. In some cases, as with temples, palaces could dominate

and define aspects of ancient sites—drawing upon sacred geography to enhance royal power and to physically structure relationships between rulers,
subordinates, and other groups in society.

Dos Pilas and Its Hegemony

The subject of this chapter is one such example of careful political use
of sacred geography in palace form and placement, which was recovered
by the recent Vanderbilt Petexbatun Regional Archaeological Project at
the site of Dos Pilas. Seven years of excavations, survey, and paleoecologi-
cal studies by the Petexbatun project explored all aspects of Classic Maya
civilization in that region (Figure 5.1). The theoretical focus of the project
was the problem of the decline or collapse of the Classic Maya kingdoms
there (Demarest 1997; Demarest and Valdés 1995a, 1995b). Extensive excavations, specialized studies, and cave surveys at the site of Dos Pilas recovered an unusually detailed record of the public architecture, residential
settlement, and ecological and economic nature of that capital center of
the Petexbatun kingdom.

As summarized elsewhere (e.g., Demarest 1997: 218–223), the kingdom
of Dos Pilas was a late entry in the Maya world, established by Tikal lords
in the seventh century. In the late seventh and early eighth centuries, the
Dos Pilas lords embarked upon an unrelenting campaign of expansionism. They used warfare and political alliance to dominate the more ancient local centers of Tamarindito, Arroyo de Piedra, Aguateca, and Punta
de Chimino—controlling the entire Petexbatun region. Subsequent cam-
paigns and alliances led to Dos Pilas' conquest of Seibal and control of most
of the Pasión River valley, a critical highland-to-lowland trade artery of the
Classic period. In A.D. 761, the century of Dos Pilas' success and expansionism ended with a military defeat, subsequent cessation of public construction and monument erection at that site, and a rapid decline in its population. There followed from A.D. 761 to 830 an epoch of intensive endemic
warfare between the vying centers of the disintegrated Dos Pilas hegemony.

During its brief trajectory of expansionism, the Petexbatun dynasty
came to control a vast and strategically situated region. For that reason one
would expect the temples and palaces of the principal seat of the dynasty,
Dos Pilas, to have impressive examples of lowland Classic Maya architecture like those of the dynasty's relatives and rivals at Tikal. Yet the founding
and construction of the center of Dos Pilas occurred late and suddenly in
Peten history, and its architecture reflects that fact. Upon its founding in
the seventh century, the major acropoli of Dos Pilas were rapidly thrown

FIGURE 5.1. Map of the western Peten showing the Petexbatun sites.

together. Natural hills and terraces were enhanced by terrace walls so as to present them as artificial constructions. Thin veneers of masonry and plaster covered unstable loose rubble cores, quickly creating great architectural masses that imitated the more ancient acropoli at sites such as Tikal, where substructure masses had accumulated from many centuries of successive constructions (Valdés 1991; Valdés and Suasnávar 1992).

Principal Architectural Groups of Dos Pilas

Such massive but shoddy temple structures characterized the temples and palaces of the Western Plaza Group and the eastern El Duende complex of Dos Pilas (Figure 5.2). Identified by distinctive hieroglyphic toponyms, these two complexes—about a kilometer apart—were the principal foci for public rituals (Valdés 1991; Escobedo 1992, 1995; Escobedo et al. 1990; Escobedo, Robles, and Wright 1992; Palka 1990, 1995; Houston and Stuart 1990; Stuart and Houston 1994).

The eastern El Duende complex was built over a natural, eroded limestone hill. A megalithic stairway and several terraces were built along the contour lines of the hill, topped by a massive temple rising to 70 m in height (Escobedo 1992, 1995; Escobedo et al. 1990; Escobedo, Robles, and Wright 1992). On the terraces to the north of El Duende, carved stelae 3 to 5 m in height recorded the ceremonies held before the great hilltop complex.

The Western Plaza Group was the principal public epicenter of Dos Pilas —and indeed of the entire Petexbatun kingdom that was under its sway. The hieroglyphic stairways, great plaza, temples, shrines, ballcourt, and palaces of the Dos Pilas Plaza Group were excavated by the Petexbatun project (Demarest 1997; Palka 1997; Demarest, Valdés, and Escobedo 1992; Palka 1990, 1995; Palka and Foias 1991; Palka Moscoso, and Demarest 1992; Symonds, Arroyo, and Houston 1990; Valdés and Suasnávar 1992; Wolley and Wright 1990). There, inscribed stelae, altars, panels, and stairways recorded ceremonies ranging from royal bloodlettings to captive sacrifices. Some of these rituals also were staged or restaged at the El Duende complex a kilometer to the east, probably after (or before) a procession between these two principal ceremonial complexes of Dos Pilas (Figure 5.2). The identi-

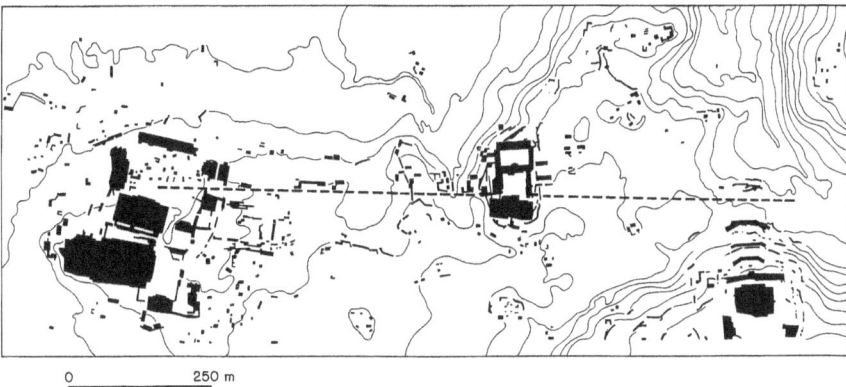

0   250 m

FIGURE 5.2. Schematic map of Dos Pilas showing the location of the three major architecture complexes (left to right: Plaza Group, Murciélagos, and Duende) and the probable procession route between them.

fication of each of these complexes by a specific toponym allows placement of specific rituals or events (Stuart and Houston 1994; Houston and Stuart 1990).

A third toponym found on Dos Pilas monuments cannot yet be linked to a specific architectural complex or site feature. It could perhaps refer to the massive Murciélagos complex, the subject of this chapter, which is located between the eastern El Duende and Western Plaza Group temple and monument complexes. This third major architectural group sits atop a natural hill with a spring in it, the most sacred possible location. The east-west procession route between the plaza group and the first megalithic stairway and terrace of the El Duende complex would have passed over the southern end of this hill. The Murciélagos complex, built upon this central hill in the eighth century, included small funerary temples, residential and presentation palaces, throne rooms, and plain and carved stone monuments. In the 1990s the area was covered by a beautiful stand of old-growth mahogany and cedar rain forest that obscured the architecture and displaced many structure lines.

The 1994 Investigations

Daunted by the complexity and importance of the Murciélagos complex, we waited until the sixth season of the Petexbatun project in 1994 to remap and extensively explore this palace group and its setting (Demarest 1995a). Mapping by Robert Wheat, Jeff Hooper, Matt O'Mansky, and José Suasnávar produced the final map (Figure 5.3), which reveals the way in which the palace was placed to incorporate the contours of the hill and its natural limestone terraces and outcrops.

In 1994 the complex was completely excavated by Arthur Demarest, Kim Morgan, Claudia Wolley, Héctor Escobedo, Irma Rodas, and Erin Sears (Demarest 1995a; Demarest, Valdés, and Escobedo 1995). Excavation and interpretation were complicated by the poor quality of construction fills (typical of the Petexbatun), by the natural complexity of the hill itself, and by damage and displacement of structure lines by the heavy forest growth. In order to understand individual structures, their relationship, and the overall nature of the complex, the horizontal extent of excavation was increased throughout the 1994 field season. Fortunately, the shallow depth of occupation allowed for such continuous extensions. In the end, over 800 m² of the complex were exposed, allowing a detailed understanding of its form and planning. These extensive operations now allow us to draw a number of conclusions about the natural and sacred geography of the Murciélagos

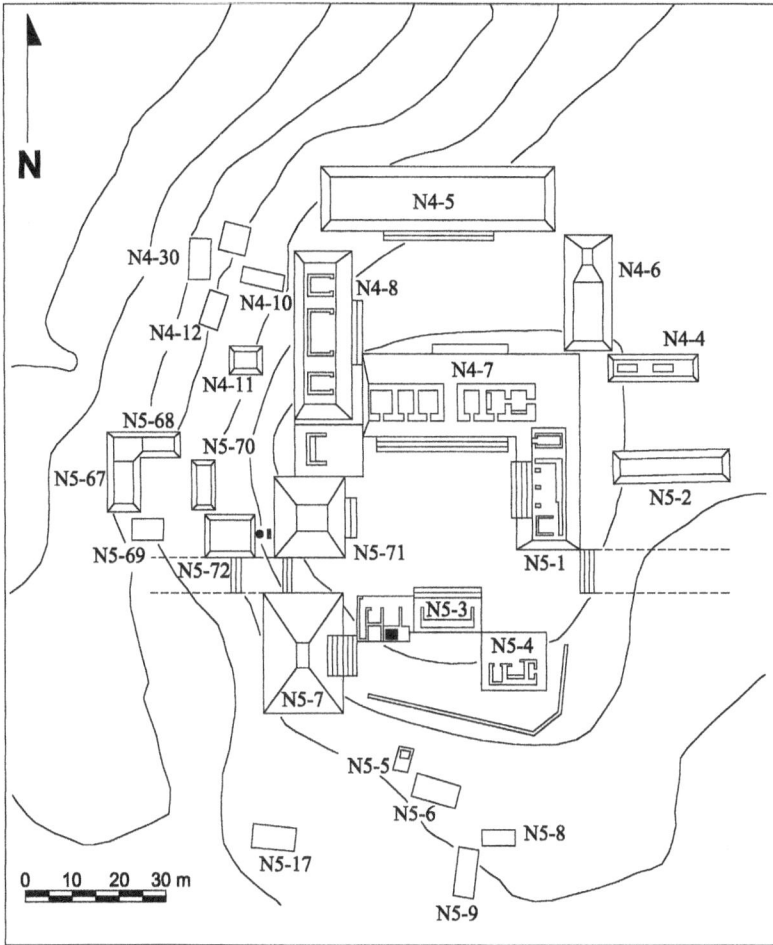

FIGURE 5.3. Map of the Murciélagos complex showing numbered structures of the northern and southern plazas. (Map by Robert Wheat, José Suasnávar, Matt O'Mansky, and Jeff Hooper)

complex, the function of its individual structures, and the role of the palace in the Late Classic politics, ritual, and ideology of Dos Pilas.

Palace Placement

Looking first at its location, the very placement of the palace was a daring political act. The Murciélagos hill has a gushing spring at its base emerging from the extensive Dos Pilas cavern system (Brady 1991, 1997). In all regions and periods of Mesoamerican civilization, such a location was supremely sacred. Hills with caves and springs were generally seen as the womb of the earth from which people, gods, and sacred waters emerged—a belief which persists even today (e.g., Heyden 1981; Vogt 1981). Studies throughout Mesoamerica have found close relationships between sacred architecture and cave and spring systems (Heyden 1973, 1975; Manzanilla et al. 1994). Indeed, years of epigraphic study by Stuart, Schele, Freidel, and others have shown that the *witz*, the sacred mountain with cave, was the metaphor and model for the Maya temple complex and for sacred places in general (MacLeod and Puleston 1979; Coe 1988; Schele and Freidel 1990: 427; Freidel, Schele, and Parker 1993: 139, 432). Brady has even shown that in the Maya highlands the presence of caves became almost a required feature of sacred epicenters and temples. At Utatlan and other sites, artificial caves were carved beneath epicenters that lacked them (Brady 1991).

The Murciélagos hill is situated astride the east-west axis of the subterranean universe of Dos Pilas. In their years of survey, Brady and his team of cave archaeologists (Brady 1997; Brady et al. 1997) have mapped and excavated miles of interconnected caverns beneath Dos Pilas and its various epicenters. The east-west component of the cavern system passes beneath the great eastern El Duende complex and the Western Plaza Group, with springs emerging in both locations. The Murciélagos hill and its cave and spring sit midway between the El Duende cave and Dos Pilas springs directly over the cavern system. The subterranean and sacred universe of the underworld was consciously mirrored in the surface architecture groups (Brady 1997; Brady et al. 1997). Both the surface and subterranean east-west axes on which the hill sat also were, of course, parallel to the course of the sun itself.

The ideologically strategic position of the Murciélagos complex in the geography of Dos Pilas was further enhanced by its position astride the east-west procession route between the two principal areas of public ritual, the Western Plaza Group and the monumental complex on the north side of the El Duende Group. Processions between these groups would have passed over this hill and later, after its construction, such processions would actually have passed through the Murciélagos palace itself (see below).

The surprising fact about the Murciélagos hill is that, unlike the two other major sacred loci of the site, it was not dominated by temple complexes and areas for public ritual. Instead, it was only occupied late in the history of the region with this elite—almost certainly royal—residential complex. The artifacts, monument fragments, and sequence of architectural construction recovered by our excavations all indicate that most of

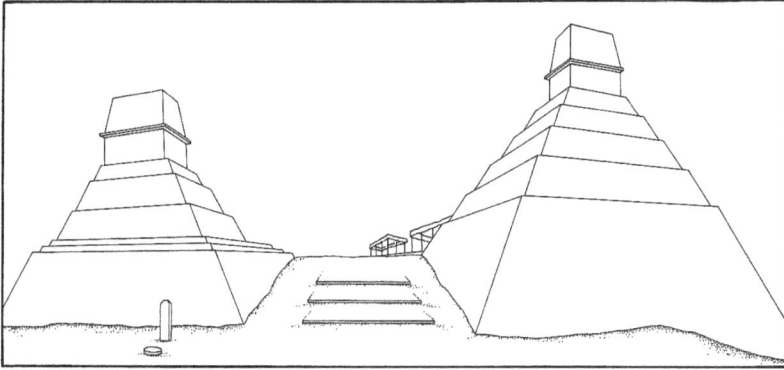

FIGURE 5.4. Reconstruction of the west entry into the palace.

this sacred hill was not occupied until the eighth century. We can speculate that perhaps this locus was initially considered to be too sacred for individual occupation. Yet in the eighth century the overreaching royal family of Dos Pilas covered the entire hilltop with its palace. As we shall see, every building was strategically placed to draw from this hallowed setting every drop of its sacred prestige and to apply it to the legitimization of the *ajaw* and the royal family.

The Principal Palace Group, the Southern Complex

Turning to the architecture itself, the principal structures of the Murciélagos complex were placed on two natural terraces that define the top of the hill. The principal courtyard group sat atop the crest of the hill surrounding the southern plaza, as defined by Structures N5-71, N4-8A, N5-7, N5-3A, N5-3, N5-4, N5-1, N5-1A, and N4-7 (Figure 5.3). All elements of the palace have an east-west directionality. Reflecting (and generating) social distance, the complex is completely closed atop the hill, with access limited to two very formal entrances (Demarest 1995b).

The western entrance was a graveled, and probably plastered, ramp with two terrace steps rising between the two western funerary shrines, Structures N5-71 and N5-7 (Figure 5.3). This imposing entry (Figure 5.4) led the procession path from the Western Plaza Group into the heart of the palace between the oratories of deceased royalty and directly in front of the throne room, N5-3A, and presentation palace, N5-3 (Figure 5.5). Auxiliary structures (N5-69, N5-72, etc.) paralleled the entranceway. A plain stela and altar to the west of the entranceway (Figures 5.4, 5.5) may have provided a stop-

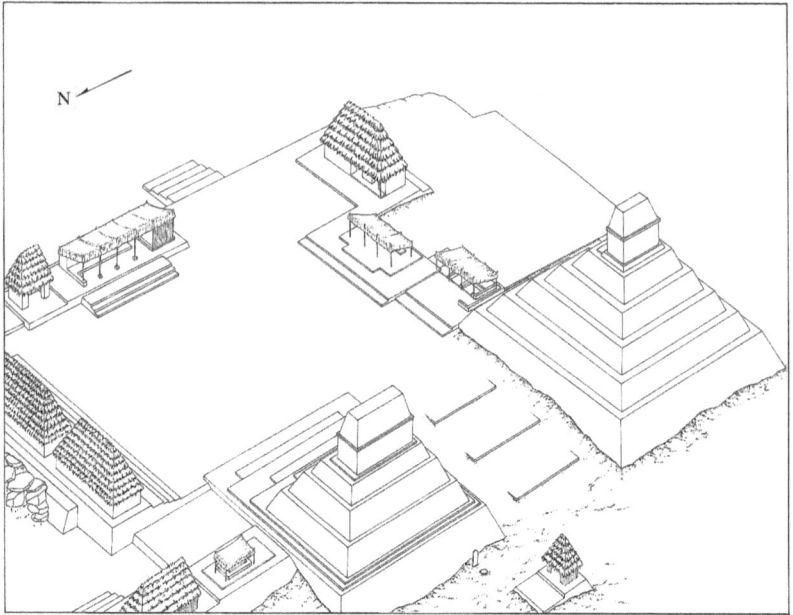

FIGURE 5.5. Perspective view of the Southern Plaza Group, entries, and procession way through Murciélagos.

ping point for processions, with only the most elite participants proceeding into the palace itself.

Ancestral Shrine Temple and Throne Room

As one entered the complex from the west, the first structure to the right was one of the two funerary temples, the highest and first structure built on the hill, N5-7 (Figures 5.3, 5.5, 5.6). This small temple was constructed in a style unusual for Petexbatun architecture. It was steeply inclined with a true corbeled-vaulted temple atop it and fine-fitted masonry over its entire surface. On its front (eastern) side the N5-7 temple had a very precipitous, almost vertical, front stairway (Figure 5.6) leading to the vaulted temple above. Later this stairway abutted the sidewall of Structure N5-3A (Figure 5.7; Wolley 1995, fig. 31.6). Careful horizontal excavations by Claudia Wolley (1995) revealed that the throne room, N5-3A, was built over the bottom levels of Temple N5-7. In turn, the substructure platform of the presentation palace structure, N5-3, overlaps and therefore postdates the throne room, N5-3A (Figure 5.7).

Thus the N5-7 temple appears to be the first structure of the principal

Southern Plaza Group of Murciélagos. It may be that this 10 m high funerary shrine was for a time the only structure on the Murciélagos hill. Its
steep form and fine masonry are reminiscent of the great Tikal temples of
the late seventh and early eighth centuries. Given the Tikal origins of the
Dos Pilas dynasty, we may speculate that N5-7 may have been a mid-to-
late-seventh-century shrine to one of the earlier Tikal-born members of the
royal family. It may have subsequently become a legitimizing monument,
literally towering over the throne room of a later Petexbatun ruler, probably
Ruler 4, his family, and his patrons. Such a reconstruction remains only
speculation, since N5-7 was one of the few structures of the Murciélagos
complex not completely excavated by the project. It is a small, beautiful,
and reconstructible temple that should be carefully excavated and restored
in the future.

The throne room, Structure N5-3A (Figures 5.6, 5.7), was excavated
by Claudia Wolley (Wolley 1995). The upper part of the structure appears
to have been made of perishable materials, probably wood with a cloth
canopy, as often portrayed in ceramic art. The lower portion of the structure, however, was well preserved, with whole vessels placed on the throne
room floor. Also on the floor were three long, unbroken obsidian blades
next to a banner stone tilted on its sides. Yet the throne slab, originally almost 4 m in length, had been flipped over and broken into over a dozen fragments (Figure 5.7). The fragmented slab with offerings of vessels, obsidian,

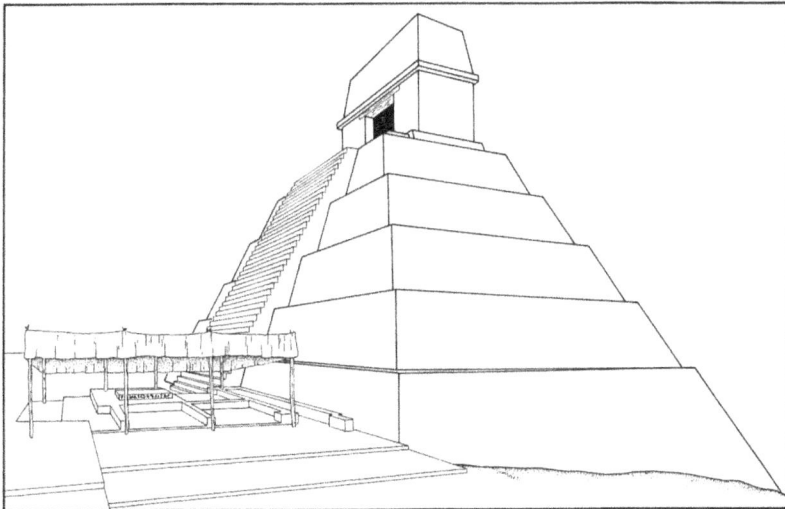

FIGURE 5.6. Structure N5-7 temple and N5-3A throne room.

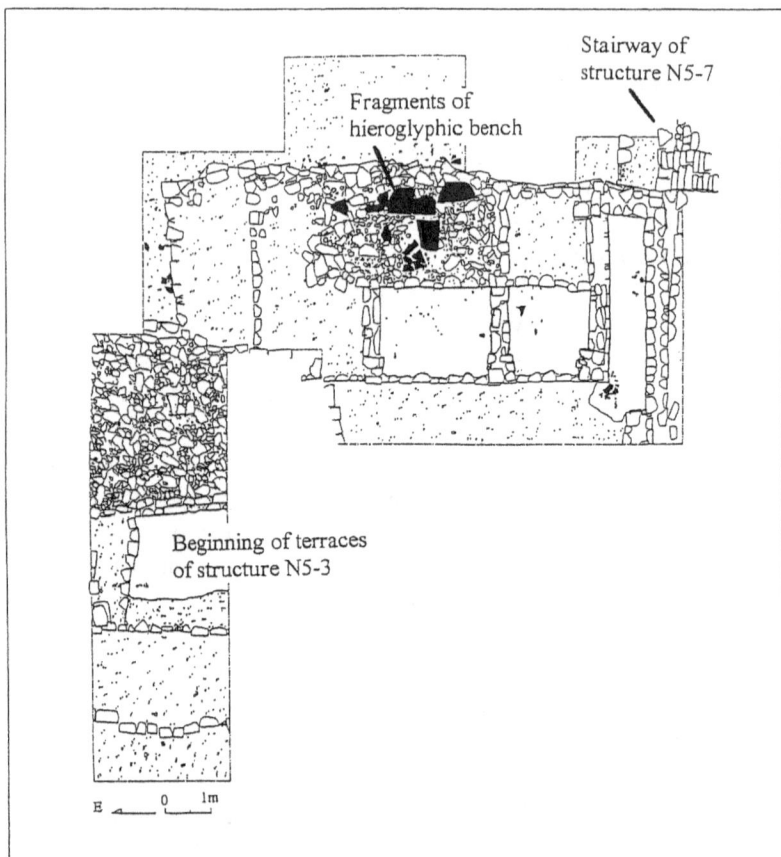

FIGURE 5.7. Plan of excavations of N5-3A (center), portion of N5-3 (left), and stairway of N5-7 (right), with hieroglyphic throne fragments shown in black.

and the overturned banner laid before it appear to represent a careful ritual act of destruction.

The literal and symbolic overturning of the throne and toppling of the banner before it, as well as the fragmentation and partial defacing of the throne and its inscription, appear to be a classic example of a Maya termination ritual. As documented at many sites by Freidel, Schele, and others (e.g., Freidel and Schele 1989; Freidel, Schele, and Parker 1993; Suhler and Freidel 1998; Mock 1998), such systematic destruction of monuments was often the conclusion of a military or political defeat. The throne and banners of a ruler were the preeminent symbols of sovereignty and would be the first targets of destruction or defacement.

It is possible that the termination of the Murciélagos throne room occurred at the time of that center's military defeat in A.D. 761. At that time Ruler 4, the last Dos Pilas lord, was defeated and the dominance of the Petexbatun hierarchy became contested between several centers (Houston and Mathews 1985; Houston 1987; Houston and Stuart 1990). The Petexbatun project investigations have shown that all public architecture and monuments ceased at Dos Pilas after this date. The subsequent decades witnessed a rapid decline in population at Dos Pilas and a period of endemic, highly destructive, siege and fortification warfare throughout the region (Demarest 1997; Demarest et al. 1997; Palka 1995, 1997). Recovered artifacts and stratigraphy suggest that the Murciélagos palace was the principal royal residence in the time of Rulers 3 and 4, so it is likely that the ritual destruction of the hieroglyphic bench in Structure N5-3A corresponds to the dramatic end of the political supremacy of Dos Pilas and the defeat of Ruler 4.

Unfortunately, the destruction of the throne itself was sufficiently effective to obscure the inscription, with some portions completely obliterated (Figure 5.8). Other glyphs are unusual and are yet undeciphered. None-

FIGURE 5.8. Fragments of the bench or royal throne of Murciélagos Structure N5-3A with glyphic inscriptions or traces of inscriptions. Note probable Dos Pilas emblem glyph ("holy lord") variant (top left).

theless, one glyph has been identified as a possible Dos Pilas *ajaw* title (H. Escobedo, personal communication 1996; F. Fahsen, personal communication 1999). Another set of glyphs appears to refer to a Calakmul lord (S. Martin, personal communication 1999). The style of the inscription is that of the period of the last Dos Pilas regent, Ruler 4 (D. Stuart, personal communication 1998). There is no occupation in the palace group from the postdynastic period of Dos Pilas, the late facet of the Nacimiento phase (A.D. 760–830), or from the Terminal Classic—although there were small, scattered occupations elsewhere in Dos Pilas from those periods. The ritual destruction of the N5-3 throne room and its hieroglyphic bench appears, then, to have been the last of many rituals held in the Murciélagos palace during the Classic period.

Presentation Palaces and Residences

The adjacent structure, N5-3, and the plaza before it would have been the setting for earlier, more felicitous, palace rituals of the eighth century. This long platform structure has a heavy masonry wall and a wider earth and rubble bench, which forms the closed back of the structure (Demarest, Wolley, Morgan, and Rodas 1995). The open front faced northward into the main plaza of the Murciélagos complex, with two low, wide terraces stepping down into the plaza itself (Figures 5.5, 5.9). This presentation palace faced directly onto the east-west procession path between the only two entrances of the Murciélagos complex. With a canopy over the back bench and porch, N5-3 would have provided for ideal royal viewing of processions, rituals, and ceremonies in the southern plaza of the palace. Unlike presentation palaces at some sites, this open, porched structure had a perishable roof, but that is typical of almost all Dos Pilas elite architecture. With its two restricted and imposing formal entrances, its two temple shrines, throne room, and presentation structures, the southern courtyard formed a compact dramatic theater for ceremonies, probably restricted to Dos Pilas nobles and visiting elites.

To the east of the presentation palace, also facing north toward the plaza, was a small well-constructed residential structure, N5-4 (Morgan, Demarest, and Wolley 1995). Its central room had a large bench with a cache containing vessel offerings. The plaster floors and fine, lower-course masonry of N5-4 identify it as an elite residence. Small chambers on either side of the central room contained large quantities of utilitarian ceramics, especially striated vessels for water storage. Deep middens behind Structure N5-4 confirmed its residential function and eighth-century date.

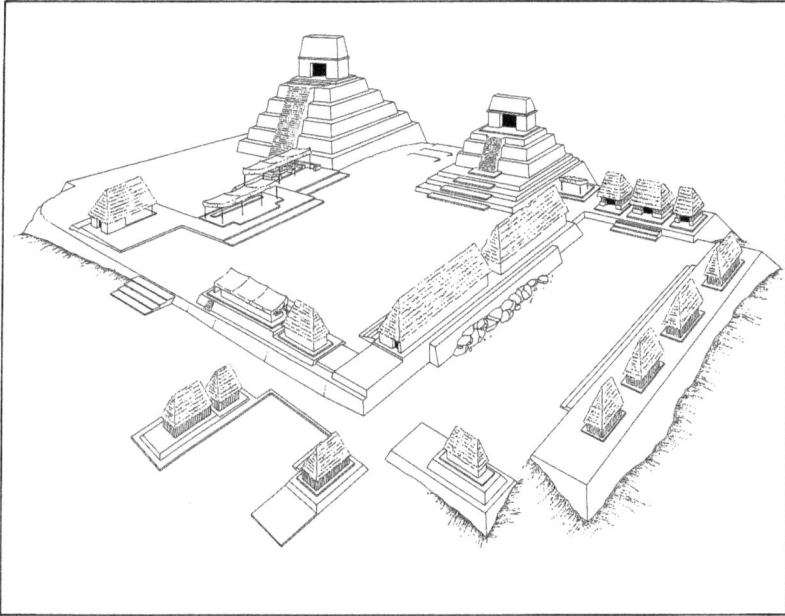

FIGURE 5.9. Overall reconstructed view of the Northern and Southern Plaza Groups and outbuildings of the Murciélagos palace.

To the north of this small residence was the eastern entrance to the compound (Figures 5.3, 5.5, 5.9), a formal stairway of four tiers of massive blocks (Demarest 1995b). North of the stairway, forming the eastern side of the palace courtyard, Structures N5-1 and N5-1A defined another presentation palace (Figures 5.9, 5.10) and associated residential structure. Facing west onto the southern courtyard, Structure N5-1 was fronted by a wide, low stairway of large blocks rising in three tiers to the heavily plastered platform surface. Excavation of N5-1 by Kim Morgan (Morgan, Demarest, and Wolley 1995) uncovered low pedestals of masonry that were probably bases for wooden posts to support a canopy or perishable roof (Figure 5.10). A wide back bench would have provided seating and viewing for receptions and court ritual. A more closed room on the south end of the platform and a masonry structure on a lower terrace to the north may have been residential or sleeping rooms. Both contain wide benches. Caches in the floor of the N5-1 open platform yielded several ceramic effigy censers (Figure 5.11).

On the north side of the southern plaza, the platform of N4-7 supported the largest residential block of rooms in the palace (Figures 5.3, 5.9, 5.10). Excavation uncovered six well-defined rooms with doorways facing

FIGURE 5.10. Structure N5-1, a presentation palace, and adjacent audience/residential Structure N5-1A (left).

south into the Southern (principal) Plaza Group (Morgan 1995). Benches of single massive slabs were found in two of the three excavated rooms (Figure 5.12). Extremely thick plaster floors, fine masonry, and a dedicatory burial attest to the status of the occupants. The six-step front (south) access to these rooms was constructed in typical Petexbatun style, with two tiers of finely cut stone masonry but with the rest of the steps formed by rough-cut small stones, clay, and rubble. The large habitation rooms had lower walls of stone and plaster masonry but cooler roofs of perishable materials. The habitation rooms were somewhat unusual for the Petexbatun in that they had thick plaster floors and wide plaster-covered stone slab sleeping benches, as in central Peten architecture. Side and back entrances gave private access to the more secluded Northern Courtyard Group, where kitchens and additional residences were located (Figures 5.9, 5.10). The rooms of N4-7 afforded fairly comfortable living areas for the royal family, and had a view of courtyard ceremonies and easy access across the plaza to the presentation and audience structures where they performed their daily political and religious duties.

Second Shrine and Audience Chamber

The southern plaza was closed on the west side by another pairing of an audience room with bench, N4-8A, and a temple shrine, N5-71. The audience room had been demolished by tree growth, and its walls and slab bench were fragmented. While also damaged by trees, the adjacent temple was still intact. The 7 m high N5-71 temple was paired with the more impressive N5-7 to flank the western ramp entrance into the palace with two royal burial shrines, forming an intimidating (and thus politically effective) approach to the throne room, audience chambers, and presentation structures of the southern plaza (Figures 5.3, 5.4, 5.5). Unlike the Tikal-style

N5-7, however, N5-71 was built in characteristic Petexbatun style: some thin lines of fine masonry and plaster veneers covered rough masonry and poorly compacted loose rubble cores. The plain stela and altar behind the temple to the west would have allowed offerings outside of the palace (Figures 5.4, 5.5). The Murciélagos occupants and elites themselves could approach the front of the shrine from inside the courtyard through a stairway of wide steps with alternating courses of fine and rough facing stones (Figure 5.13).

The N5-71 shrine was excavated by Demarest and Héctor Escobedo (Demarest and Escobedo 1995). This funerary temple, in typical Petexbatun style, contained a burial chamber also in the style associated with the royal burials in this region at Dos Pilas, Arroyo de Piedra, and Tamarindito. Despite the partially collapsed state of the tomb chamber, Escobedo succeeded in excavating over half of the burial and grave goods (Escobedo 1998). The style of the chamber and burial followed the pattern of royal burials of the Tikal dynasty and the Tikal-related lineage that ruled Dos Pilas. In a poorly executed imitation of Tikal burial chambers, the Petexbatun royal tombs had coverings of clay filled with thousands of obsidian and chert fragments.

FIGURE 5.11. One of the effigy censers found in N5-1.

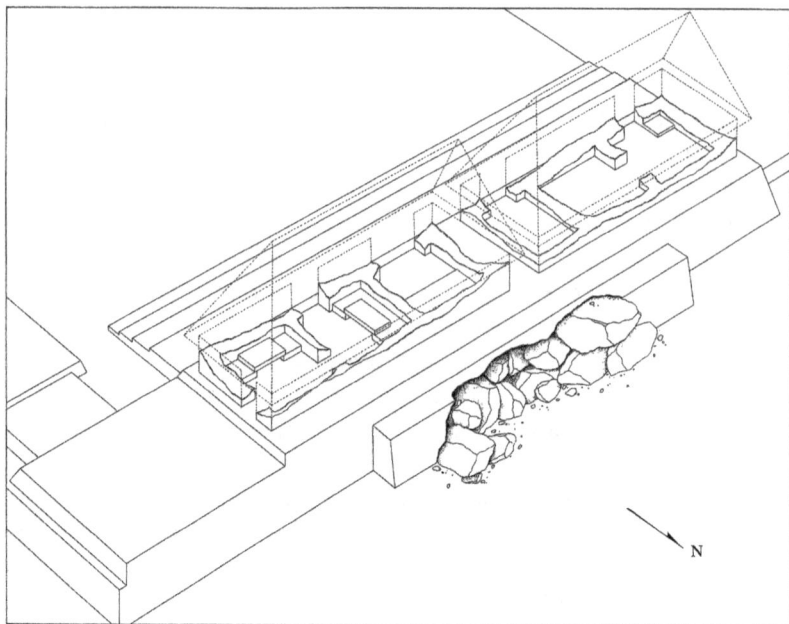

FIGURE 5.12. Structure N4-7, an elite residence, showing internal benches, corridors to the north plaza, and terrace facade over bedrock outcrop (viewed from behind, i.e., from the northern plaza).

The Petexbatun versions, however, have stacked rough-cut blocks loosely fitted together to form a small vault. From the N5-71 chamber, Escobedo recovered the upper portion of the burial, including the skull and upper torso.

Grave goods recovered confirm the high status of the individual entombed, though sex could not be determined from the crushed and partial skeleton (Escobedo 1998). These grave goods included a *Spondylus* shell, conch earspools, jade beads and earpieces, and an anthropomorphic jade pendant (again, all features of the highest status). The form, placement, lithic coating, grave goods, and painted stucco fragments in the chamber were all consistent in style with Petexbatun royal burials. The placement of the tomb and shrine in the west side of the plaza, however, suggests that this was not the burial of a ruler or *k'uhul ajaw*, who were generally buried under east side shrines (Escobedo 1998).

Function of the Southern Plaza Group

After reviewing each structure of this Southern Courtyard Group of the Murciélagos complex, we can conclude that this well-planned architectural ensemble served more ideological and political than residential functions. Placed atop the crest of this sacred hill and aligned with the site's procession path and subterranean cave system, this complex of structures displays an internal order in which each structure was located and constructed for dramatic effect. The two structures on the west (N5-71 and N4-8A) and the two on the east (N5-1 and N5-1A) mirror the four structures along the southern procession way itself, each with a temple and throne room (N5-7 and N5-3A) and an adjacent presentation palace and residence/reception structure (N5-3 and N5-4).

The Southern Plaza Group formed a small dramatic arena, literally an intimate stage, in which the rulers of the Petexbatun theater-state could perform for an elite audience. Less privileged participants in site processions probably would have waited outside before the monuments and imposing entrances of the palace. The rituals and audiences carried out would have been regarded with even greater awe due to their restricted access.

The Northern Plaza Group

The Northern Plaza Group of the Murciélagos complex (Figure 5.3) was more private and residential in form and function. The only access was

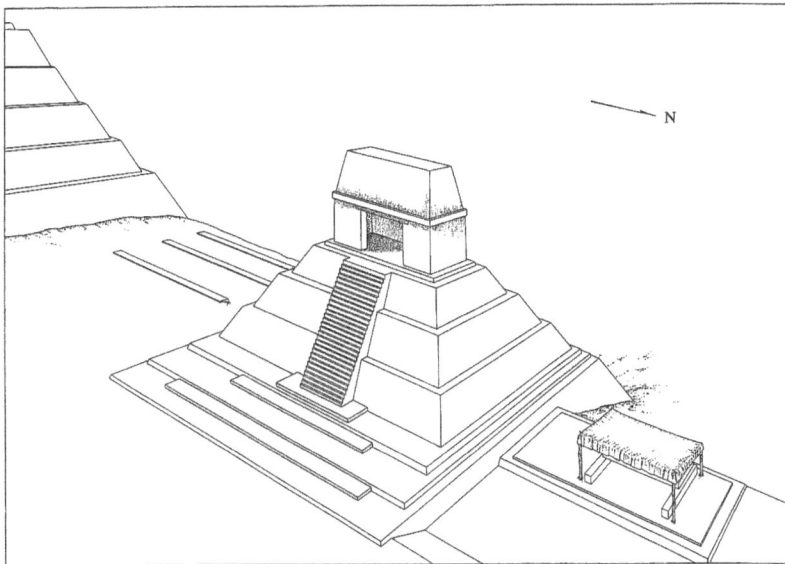

FIGURE 5.13. Structure N5-71, a funerary shrine.

from the southern courtyard and passed through one of two corridors between the rooms of the N4-7 royal residential complex (Figures 5.3, 5.10, 5.12). The fine masonry walls of the back of this royal residence defined the southern side of the Northern Plaza Group. An artificial terrace extended out from the platform to cover partially the irregular rock outcrop of the higher natural hill of the southern group (Figure 5.12). This modification was one of a number of terrace and leveling operations that redefined the natural rock hilltop under the southern plaza as a human construction. The northern plaza was pure bedrock that had been cleared to expose a clean white expanse of limestone. A large natural crevice in the plaza floor led eastward under Structure N4-6. Apparently this cleft was left open to enhance the symbolic significance of this eastern shrine, as discussed below.

These residences atop Structure N4-8 closed the western side of this private northern courtyard. The wide platform of N4-5 on the northern side of the plaza had low rough walls, burned areas, and massive kitchen debris in a deep midden behind it to the north (Wolley and Rodas 1995). These structures, N4-7 and outlier platforms, defined the truly residential and private nature of the northern group of the palace.

The Entombment of Xibalba

The only structure in the Northern Courtyard Group of ceremonial nature was N4-6, a surprising and unique shrine. The tall mound on the east side of the courtyard was too steep and narrow to have a residential function and was easily identified as an ancestor shrine in the typical Plaza Plan 2 form characteristic of Tikal and the Central Peten and also often found elsewhere. Demarest excavated this structure (Demarest, Rodas, and Morgan 1995) expecting to find a rich cyst or tomb of a revered ancestor at its base. Indeed, just above bedrock a large slab was encountered, sealing what promised to be the opening of a tomb. Lifting the slab we discovered the typical burial assemblage of three vessels—a polychrome vase, bowl, and plate in Tepeu 2 styles, along with burnt animal bone offerings. But instead of a burial, we found a wide crevice in the bedrock blocked with an artificial fill of black earth, stones, and eroded ceramics (Figure 5.14). Clearing of the earth revealed a narrow natural tunnel which led downward and to the west.

At this point it was clear that we had found a sealed natural entrance to the east-west corridor of caves that ran for several kilometers beneath Dos Pilas and directly below the Murciélagos complex. The Petexbatun Regional Cave Survey team, directed by James Brady, was called upon for assistance. Cave archaeologist Irma Rodas completed the excavation of the

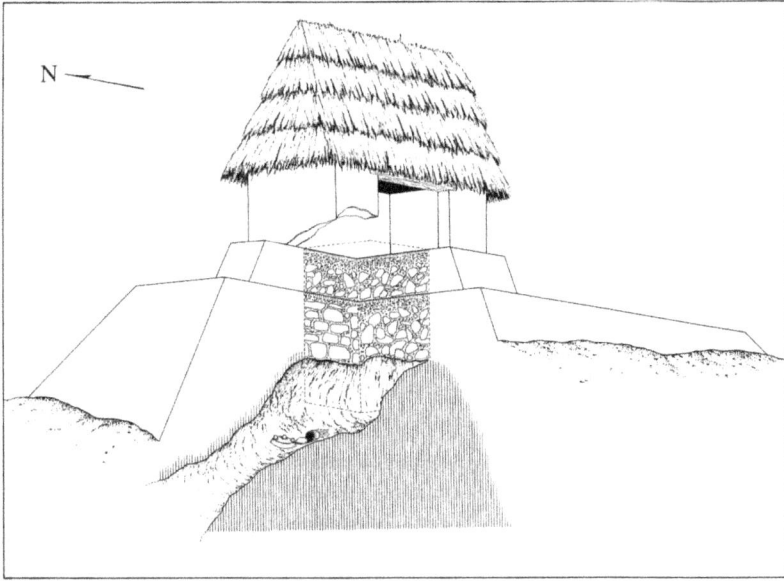

FIGURE 5.14. Structure N4-6, an oratory and entombed cave entrance.

offerings and crevice, which led for 6 m down and west before narrowing to an impassable crawl space that turned downward into the cave system (Demarest, Rodas, and Morgan 1995).

The N4-6 Plaza Plan 2 shrine was indeed a sacred tomb structure. It symbolically and physically entombed the entrance to Xibalba, the entrance to the underworld itself. Many years of study by the Petexbatun Regional Cave Survey team had led to the proposition that much of the region's surface architecture was placed and aligned in accordance with the location and the orientation of the Petexbatun network of caves (Brady 1997; Brady et al. 1997). The subterranean linear passages in the eroded limestone escarpment also held most of these kingdoms' religious offerings of whole vessels, artifacts, and even sacrificial victims (Brady 1994, 1990). The N4-6 shrine provided an unexpected and powerful vindication of these hypotheses regarding the importance of subterranean geology to the Maya and to the planning of their surface architecture (cf. Brady 1997; Brady et al. 1997).

The Murciélagos Palace and the Capture of Sacred Power

In its placement, general alignments, component structures, and even architectural details, the Murciélagos complex was a clear and elegant example of the role of sacred geography and cosmology in Maya site planning. Sacred geography does not refer to a fixed set of elements in the landscape to which Maya lords adapted their architecture. Rather, it was a flexible combination of natural features and cosmological understandings that guided construction, but also could be manipulated by rulers and elites to legitimate and enhance their power. We would argue that the very heavy reliance of Maya rulers on such instruments of ideological and cosmological legitimation was one of the characteristic features of state power among the Maya lords.

Archaeologists, iconographers, and epigraphers have struggled for a century to understand the complex nature of royal power among the Maya (Coe 1981; Rathje 1977; Sanders and Webster 1988; Webster 1993). Despite recent breakthroughs in epigraphy and more theoretically oriented archaeological research designs, there is still no consensus about the functions of Maya leadership (Ball and Taschek 1991; Chase and Chase 1992; Fash 1988; Freidel 1981, 1986; Marcus 1983; Schele and Miller 1986; Webster 1993). The degree of state involvement in infrastructure or economic relations is still unclear, although the preponderance of evidence indicates that in most regions the ruler's control of economic or subsistence activities was limited (but see Aoyama 1999, Kovacevich et al. 2000, and Demarest and Barrientos 2000 for some notable exceptions). Instead, most Maya kings may have maintained their tenuous hold on power through a complex mix of redistribution of exotics, leadership in warfare, and, above all, a central role in state ritual and religion (e.g., Ball 1993; Demarest 1992; Freidel 1992; Freidel and Schele 1988a, 1988b; Marcus 1993; Mathews and Willey 1990; Sabloff 1986; Schele and Freidel 1990; Schele and Mathews 1990).

Elsewhere, Demarest (1992) has argued at length that aspects of the Maya statecraft are strikingly similar to the "galactic polity" or "theater state" models that have been applied to the kingdoms of Southeast Asia (Bentley 1986; Geertz 1980; Gesick 1983; Tambiah 1976, 1982, 1984). Like the Maya, the historical kingdoms of Southeast Asia were tenuously held together through warfare, redistribution of foreign goods, and state pageantry and ritual. Such events generated public support, as well as compliance from nobles and elites. We also would argue that, like the Negara of Southeast Asia, Maya polities were, to some degree, "ideologically dependent" (Demarest 1992). The ruler exercised power, not so much by the type of managerial functions which we often assume to have existed, but rather through performance in rite, ritual, and ceremony, as well as in self-aggrandizing interelite warfare and alliance. Control over satellite centers was due "not so much by the real exercise of power as by devices and mechanisms which have a performative validity" (Tambiah 1976: 125). While not "segmentary" in the sense of being true lineage-based states, Maya kingdoms, like their "galactic" Asian counterparts, were certainly structurally segmentary, since they were composed of functionally redundant centers that could easily break away or even join other states or hegemonies (Stuart 1995; Schele and Mathews 1990; Marcus 1993; Martin and Grube 1995). Much of the power of the regent, not just the legitimation of that power, was generated by the awesome spectacles themselves: the processions, rites, and ceremonies beautifully orchestrated "to make inequality enchant" (Geertz 1980: 123).

Even if one assumes that Maya rulers had some economic roles (e.g., Aoyama 1999; Kovacevich et al. 2000), there can be little doubt that the ideological component of state power was extremely great. The vast and dazzling corpus of Classic Maya art, iconography, monuments, and architecture is largely devoted to the cult of the *ajaw*, to the aggrandizement of the ruler, his divine ancestry, and his sacred duties (Freidel 1992; Freidel and Schele 1988a; Schele and Miller 1986; Miller 1996). Classic period energies and resources were lavishly expended on this monumental display, on the props and stages of royal ritual performance.

This ideological dependency of Maya leadership is evident in the case of Dos Pilas and the construction and use of the Murciélagos complex. The Dos Pilas dynasty that ruled the sprawling Petexbatun kingdom was newly arrived in the sixth century, probably from Tikal (Houston and Mathews 1985). They could not draw as easily on a deep local ancestry and revered ancient architecture. For prestige they relied on tenuous claims to the throne of the distant center of Tikal. To a greater degree than many states, the Dos Pilas hegemony expanded through direct conquest or political alliance, seizing control of the critical Pasión River trade artery, the conduit into the lowlands for exotic jades, quetzal feathers, and other adornments critical to state ritual performance (Demarest 1997; Demarest and Valdés 1995a, 1995b; Demarest and Barrientos 2000). Given this late and somewhat secular history, one would expect the dynasty of Dos Pilas to use primarily displays of military force to reinforce their power. Most of their stelae and hieroglyphic stairways do, in fact, portray the military triumphs of strutting Dos Pilas lords and the humiliation of conquered rulers. Yet the kings of even this bellicose polity had to rely upon "devices and mechanisms which have a performative validity," in Tambiah's (1976: 125) terms.

For the Maya of Dos Pilas, such performances and public rituals were staged in architectural complexes like that of the El Duende temple and its terraces and the Plaza Group courtyard with its altars, monuments, ballcourt, and the spacious dramatic arena formed by its temples. In such architectural theaters, the Maya kings presided over public spectacles of divination, sacrifice, initiation, coronation, and celebration of high points of the calendric and astrological cycles. In addition to major propitiatory rituals on behalf of the populace, rulers also generated, legitimated, and reinforced their power through events limited to local leaders and to visiting dignitaries, including royal visits, marriage alliances, interelite warfare, gift exchanges, and sacrificial rites (see, for example, Culbert 1988; Fash and Stuart 1990; Freidel 1986; Marcus 1993; Mathews and Willey 1990; Sabloff 1986; Schele and Mathews 1990; Stuart 1995).

The Murciélagos compound was designed to aid in both public and private ritual and ceremony. The most public of the rituals at the colossal El Duende and Plaza Group temples also involved processions between these complexes. Events and rites were repeated according to the ancient Maya canons of movement and ritual reenactment, the physical tracing of the Maya cosmogram (Carlson 1981; Freidel and Schele 1988a, 1988b; Vogt 1981). This grammar of ritual movement and the definition of the sacred center through such movements have deep circum-Pacific roots in shared shamanistic concepts with later ecclesiastical elaborations (Eliade 1954, 1961). The motion of all such pageants, processions, and rituals and the cosmic pattern that they emulated rotated around the "sacred center." In Maya political, cosmological, and ritual performance, as in the Negara of Southeast Asia, the ruler appropriated for himself that position in the sacred center, embodying and becoming the axis of the universe (e.g., Freidel, Schele, and Parker 1993; Freidel and Schele 1988a, 1988b; Schele 1981; Schele and Freidel 1990; Schele and Miller 1986).

The placement and architecture of Murciélagos, the abode of the regent, were skillfully chosen to define the ruler and his family as the center of the east-west ceremonial axis of Dos Pilas (Figure 5.15). The ruler sat atop the sacred mountain, cave, and spring—a holy place through which processions would pass. As we have seen, this position as the pivot of ritual was enhanced by the placement along the procession corridor of restricted imposing entrances, ancestor shrines, presentation palaces, and the throne room. The ruler and his palace literally sat astride the site's axis, which also corresponded with the east-west axis of the subterranean cave system and, of course, the east-west movement of the sun itself. Even the populace, which was probably excluded from entry into the palace during processions, would have been aware of events within and the central location of the palace in the sacred order of the site.

Meanwhile, the interior arrangements and details of the palace were

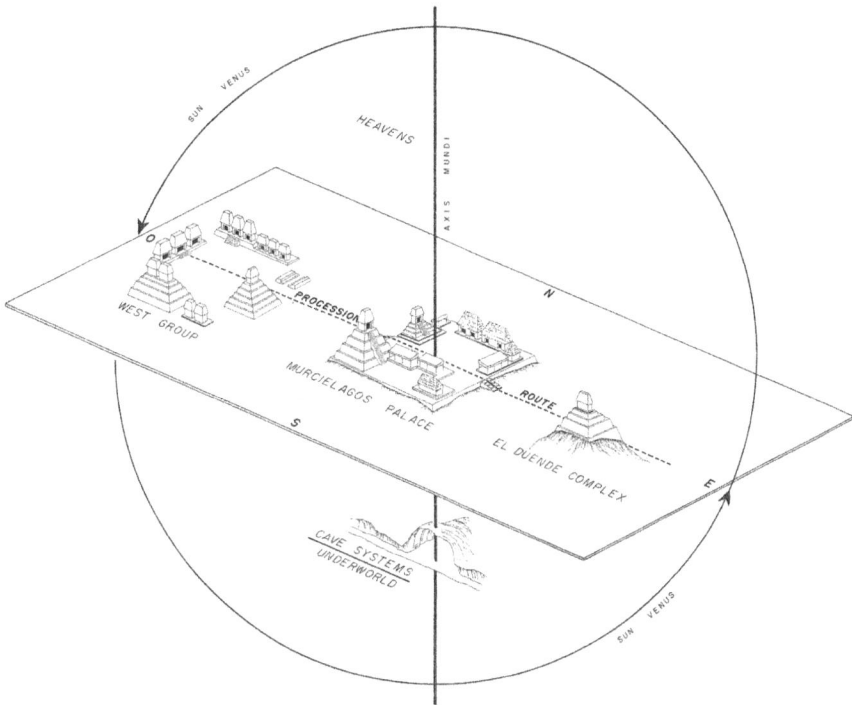

FIGURE 5.15. Schematic representation of the position of the Murciélagos palace and its *k'uhul ajaw* in the physical layout of the ritual center, procession route, and caves, and possibly in the ancient Maya conceptualization of the cosmos.

constructed for their use in the private rituals, visitations, and elite cere-monies that were equally critical to the maintenance of royal power. In the intimate, yet imposing, settings of the Southern Courtyard Group, gift exchange, receipt of tribute, feasting, bloodletting, and dynastic ancestor veneration took place in chambers and temples designed for those func-tions. Nearby the royal family resided in the comfortable rooms of N4-7 and the secluded Northern Plaza Group. The elite interactions that took place in the Southern Plaza Group were part of the network of ties that held together the Maya world (Freidel 1986; Marcus 1993; Sabloff 1986; Schele and Mathews 1990). These shared experiences and rituals unified the canons of politics and ideology of the Maya lords and helped to define the alliances that united them into a system of collaborating and compet-ing peer polities, larger loose alliances, or far-flung warring hegemonies (cf. Mathews and Willey 1990; Marcus 1993; Martin and Grube 1995, 2000: 68–83).

In the case of Dos Pilas, we know that such receptions and rituals with visiting rulers and their emissaries were particularly crucial in the mid-eighth century. The Murciélagos palace was probably constructed during the last decade of the period in which the Dos Pilas dynasty dominated over most of the Pasión River Valley. Dos Pilas alliances, rites, and sacrifices involved lords of Cancuen, far to the south at the base of the highlands, and even more distant Calakmul to the north. Ruler 4, the last Dos Pilas regent, struggled to maintain his overextended hegemony by conducting rituals involving his vassals and allies at sites along the Pasión Valley (Fahsen and Demarest 2000; Houston 1987; Houston and Mathews 1985; Houston and Stuart 1990; Martin and Grube 2000). The sacred prestige of Murciélagos and its dramatic architectural settings may have aided these—ultimately futile—efforts to reinforce the last ruler's prestige and power.

The final symbolic flourish of the Murciélagos compound was its relationship to the cave system and the enshrinement of that entrance to the underworld. Aligning architecture to the caves and incorporating a cave entry into the palace completed the process of identifying the ruler and the dynasty as the sacred center and axis of the universe of Dos Pilas. The east-west cave system, the procession path, and the Murciélagos corridor of entries and presentation structures all paralleled and represented the east-west movement of the sun itself. Just as Itzamnaaj moved across the earth's surface by day, so did his incarnation as the Night Jaguar move through the underworld at night. Both the solar and the subterranean levels of this circuit had been captured at Murciélagos and tied physically and symbolically to the ruler and his family.

Thus, in the final decades of their rule, the royal family had established the Murciélagos palace in the site's most sacred place as a final instrument of their overreaching royal power. They refined that instrument to establish a unique setting for the enhancement of authority through the political acquisition of the power of sacred geography. The Plaza Plan 2 shrine on the east side of the north courtyard of this palace, the royal family's true residence, was the most powerful possible statement. Sitting astride the axis of the universe, the regent and his family revered as an ancestral shrine this entrance to the subterranean passageway of Itzamnaaj's nightly journey through the underworld. Not content to capture the surface circuit of the sun in the Southern Plaza Group, the lords of Murciélagos had also enshrined its nocturnal path and incorporated it into the royal compound. In their personal family shrine in the Northern Plaza Group, they thus declared their revered ancestor to be the sun himself. Architecture and ritual were configured so as to confound the identity of the holy lord of Dos Pilas with that of Itzamnaaj.

With plaster and stone they had harnessed the power of the sacred mountain to the ends of the state.

ACKNOWLEDGMENTS

All figures are by Luis Fernando Luin, courtesy of Vanderbilt University Press and the Vanderbilt Petexbatun Regional Archaeological Project. The research described in this chapter was supported by the National Geographic Society, the H. F. Guggenheim Foundation, the Swedish International Development Authority, and Alimentos Kern, S.A.

REFERENCES

Aoyama, Kazuo
1999   *Ancient Maya State, Urbanism, Exchange, and Craft Specialization: Chipped Stone Evidence of the Copan Valley and the La Entrada Region, Honduras.* University of Pittsburgh Memoirs in Latin American Archaeology 12. Pittsburgh: University of Pittsburgh Press.
Ashmore, Wendy
1986   Peten Cosmology in the Maya Southeast: An Analysis of Architecture and Settlement Patterns at Classic Quiriguá. In *The Southeast Maya Periphery*, edited by Patricia Ann Urban and Edward Mark Schortman, 35–49. Austin: University of Texas Press.
1989   Construction and Cosmology: Politics and Ideology in Lowland Maya Settlement Patterns. In *Word and Image in Maya Culture: Explorations in Language, Writing, and Representation*, edited by William Hanks and Don Rice, 272–286. Salt Lake City: University of Utah Press.
1991   Site-Planning Principles and Concepts of Directionality among the Ancient Maya. *Latin American Antiquity* 2 (3): 199–226.
Aveni, Anthony F., and Horst Hartung
1986   *Maya City Planning and the Calendar.* Transactions of the American Philosophical Society, vol. 76, pt. 7. Philadelphia: American Philosophical Society.
Ball, Joseph W.
1993   Pottery, Potters, Palaces, and Polities: Some Socioeconomic and Political Implications of the Late Classic Maya Ceramic Industries. In *Lowland Maya Civilization in the Eighth Century A.D.*, edited by Jeremy A. Sabloff and John S. Henderson, 243–272. Washington, D.C.: Dumbarton Oaks Research Library and Collection.
Ball, Joseph W., and Jennifer T. Taschek
1991   Late Classic Lowland Maya Political Organization and Central-Place Analysis: New Insights from the Upper Belize Valley. *Ancient Mesoamerica* 2 (2): 149–165.
Benson, Elizabeth P. (ed.)
1981   *Mesoamerican Sites and World-Views.* Washington, D.C.: Dumbarton Oaks Research Library and Collection.

Bentley, G. Carter
1986   Indigenous States of Southeast Asia. *Annual Review of Anthropology* 15: 275–305.

Berlo, Janet Catherine (ed.)
1993   *Art, Ideology, and the City of Teotihuacan.* Washington, D.C.: Dumbarton Oaks Research Library and Collection.

Brady, James E.
1990   Investigaciones en la cueva de "El Duende." In *Proyecto Arqueológico Regional Petexbatún: Informe preliminar #2, segunda temporada,* edited by Arthur A. Demarest and Stephen D. Houston, 334–352. Guatemala: Instituto de Antropología e Historia; Nashville: Department of Anthropology, Vanderbilt University.
1991   The Petexbatún Regional Cave Survey: Ritual and Regional Cave Survey. Paper presented at the 47th International Congress of Americanists, Tulane University, New Orleans.
1994   El impacto del ritual en la economía maya. In *VII Simposio de Arqueología Guatemalteca, 1993,* edited by Juan Pedro Laporte and Héctor Escobedo, 87–91. Guatemala: Museo Nacional de Antropología y Etnología.
1997   Settlement, Architecture and Cosmology: The Role of Caves in Determining the Placement of Architecture at Dos Pilas. *American Anthropologist* 99: 602–681.

Brady, James E., Ann Scott, Allan Cobb, Irma Rodas, John Fogarty, and Mónica Urquizú
1997   Glimpses of the Dark Side of the Petexbatun Project: The Petexbatun Regional Cave Survey. *Ancient Mesoamerica* 8 (2): 353–364.

Carlson, John B.
1981   A Geomantic Model for the Interpretation of Mesoamerican Sites: An Essay in Cross-Cultural Comparison. In *Mesoamerican Sites and World-Views,* edited by Elizabeth P. Benson, 143–215. Washington, D.C.: Dumbarton Oaks Research Library and Collection.

Chase, Arlen F., and Diane Z. Chase (eds.)
1992   *Mesoamerican Elites: An Archaeological Assessment.* Norman: University of Oklahoma Press.

Christie, Jessica, and Patricia Sarro (eds.)
n.d.   *Ancient American Elite Residences: The Context of Political Power.* Ms. submitted to UCLA Cotsen Institute of Archaeology.

Coe, Michael D.
1981   Religion and the Rise of Mesoamerican States. In *The Transition to Statehood in the New World,* edited by Grant D. Jones and Robert R. Kautz, 157–171. Cambridge: Cambridge University Press.
1988   Ideology of the Maya Tomb. In *Maya Iconography,* edited by Elizabeth Benson and Gillett Griffin, 222–235. Princeton: Princeton University Press.

Culbert, T. Patrick
1988   Political History and the Decipherment of Maya Glyphs. *Antiquity* 62: 135–152.

Demarest, Arthur A.
1992   Ideology in Ancient Maya Cultural Evolution: The Dynamics of Galactic Polities. In *Ideology and Pre-Columbian Civilization,* edited by Arthur A. Demarest and Geoffrey W. Conrad, 135–157. Albuquerque: University of New Mexico Press.
1995a   Investigaciones en el complejo Murciélagos: Objetivos, metodología y opera-

ciones de mapeo. In *Proyecto Arqueológico Regional Petexbatún: Informe preliminar #6, tercera temporada 1994*, edited by Arthur A. Demarest, Juan Antonio Valdés, and Héctor Escobedo, 287–295. Guatemala: Instituto de Antropología e Historia; Nashville: Department of Anthropology, Vanderbilt University.

1995b Excavación y limpieza de las entradas formales del complejo Murciélagos Suboperación DP39D. In *Proyecto Arqueológico Regional Petexbatún: Informe preliminar #6, tercera temporada 1994*, edited by Arthur A. Demarest, Juan Antonio Valdés, and Héctor Escobedo, 319–324. Guatemala: Instituto de Antropología e Historia; Nashville: Department of Anthropology, Vanderbilt University.

1997 The Vanderbilt Petexbatun Regional Archaeological Project, 1989–1994: Overview, History, and Major Results of a Multi-disciplinary Study of the Classic Maya Collapse. *Ancient Mesoamerica* 8 (2): 209–227.

Demarest, Arthur A., and Tomás Barrientos (eds.)
2000 *Proyecto Arqueológico Cancuen: Informe preliminar #2, segunda temporada.* Guatemala: Instituto de Antropología e Historia; Nashville: Department of Anthropology, Vanderbilt University.

Demarest, Arthur A., and Héctor Escobedo A.
1995 Operaciones de rescate en un santuario ancestral en el Grupo Murciélagos: Suboperación DP39B. In *Proyecto Arqueológico Regional Petexbatún: Informe preliminar #6, tercera temporada 1994*, edited by Arthur A. Demarest, Juan Antonio Valdés, and Héctor Escobedo, 349–356. Guatemala: Instituto de Antropología e Historia; Nashville: Department of Anthropology, Vanderbilt University.

Demarest, Arthur A., Matt O'Mansky, Claudia Wolley, Dirk Van Tuerenhout, Takeshi Inomata, Joel Palka, and Héctor Escobedo
1997 Classic Maya Defensive Systems and Warfare in the Petexbatun Region: Archaeological Evidence and Interpretations. *Ancient Mesoamerica* 8 (2): 229–253.

Demarest, Arthur A., Irma Rodas, and Kim Morgan
1995 Investigación de Estructura N4-6, una estructura oratorio en el Grupo Murciélagos: Suboperación DP39F. In *Proyecto Arqueológico Regional Petexbatún: Informe preliminar #6, tercera temporada 1994*, edited by Arthur A. Demarest, Juan Antonio Valdés, and Héctor Escobedo, 357–361. Guatemala: Instituto de Antropología e Historia; Nashville: Department of Anthropology, Vanderbilt University.

Demarest, Arthur A., and Juan Antonio Valdés
1995a Guerra, regresión política y el colapso de la civilización maya clásica en la región Petexbatún. In *VIII Simposio de Investigaciones Arqueológicas en Guatemala, 1994*, edited by Juan Pedro Laporte and Héctor L. Escobedo, 777–781. Museo Nacional de Arqueología y Etnología, Guatemala.

1995b Nuevos análisis e interpretaciones del colapso de la civilización maya en la región de Petexbatún. In *IX Simposio de Investigaciones Arqueológicas en Guatemala, 1995*, edited by Juan Pedro Laporte and Héctor L. Escobedo, 207–212. Museo Nacional de Arqueología y Etnología, Guatemala.

Demarest, Arthur A., Juan Antonio Valdés, and Héctor Escobedo
1992 Una tumba real en el centro ceremonial de Dos Pilas: Excavación e implicaciones. In *V Simposio de Arqueología Guatemalteca, 1991*, edited by Juan Pedro Laporte, Héctor Escobedo, and Sandra Villagrán de Brady, 301–316. Museo Nacional de Arqueología y Etnología, Guatemala.

Demarest, Arthur A., Juan Antonio Valdés, and Héctor Escobedo (eds.)
1995   Proyecto Arqueológico Regional Petexbatún: *Informe preliminar #6, sexta temporada 1994.* Guatemala: Instituto de Antropología e Historia; Nashville: Department of Anthropology, Vanderbilt University.

Demarest, Arthur A., Claudia Wolley, Kim Morgan, and Irma Rodas
1995   Limpieza y excavación del palacio de presentación en el Grupo Murciélagos Suboperación DP39E. In *Proyecto Arqueológico Regional Petexbatún: Informe preliminar #6, sexta temporada 1994,* edited by Arthur A. Demarest, Juan Antonio Valdés, and Héctor Escobedo, 325–330. Guatemala: Instituto de Antropología e Historia; Nashville: Department of Anthropology, Vanderbilt University.

Eliade, Mircea
1954   *The Myth of the Eternal Return.* New York: Pantheon.
1961   *Image and Symbols.* London: Harvill Press.

Escobedo A., Héctor L.
1992   Operación DP38: Excavaciones en la terraza 5 de El Duende. In *Proyecto Arqueológico Regional Petexbatún: Informe preliminar #4, cuarta temporada 1992,* edited by Arthur A. Demarest, Takeshi Inomata, and Héctor Escobedo, 166–184. Guatemala: Instituto de Antropología e Historia; Nashville: Department of Anthropology, Vanderbilt University.
1995   DP 40A: Rescate arqueológico en la Estructura P6-1 de El Duende, Dos Pilas. In *Proyecto Arqueológico Regional Petexbatún: Informe preliminar #6, sexta temporada 1994,* edited by Arthur A. Demarest, Juan Antonio Valdés, and Héctor Escobedo, 262–267. Guatemala: Instituto de Antropología e Historia; Nashville: Department of Anthropology, Vanderbilt University.
1998   Notas sobre la excavación del entierro 54: Una tumba en el Grupo Murciélagos de Dos Pilas. Manuscript. Department of Archaeology, Universidad del Valle, Guatemala.

Escobedo, Héctor L., María Teresa Robles, and Lori Wright
1992   El Duende: Excavaciones en un sector ceremonial y habitacional de Dos Pilas. In *IV Simposio de Arqueología Guatemalteca, 1990,* edited by Juan Pedro Laporte, Héctor Escobedo, and Sandra Villagrán de Brady, 131–138. Museo Nacional de Arqueología y Etnología, Guatemala.

Escobedo, Héctor, Lori Wright, Oswaldo Chinchilla, Stacey Symonds, and María Teresa Robles
1990   Operación DP8: Investigaciones en "El Duende." In *Proyecto Arqueológico Regional Petexbatún: Informe preliminar #2, segunda temporada,* edited by Arthur A. Demarest and Stephen D. Houston, 277–333. Guatemala: Instituto de Antropología e Historia; Nashville: Department of Anthropology, Vanderbilt University.

Evans, Susan Toby, and Joanne Pillsbury (eds.)
in press   *Ancient Palaces of the New World: Form, Function, and Meaning.* Washington, D.C.: Precolumbian Studies, Dumbarton Oaks.

Fahsen, Federico, and Arthur Demarest
2000   El papel del reino de Cancuén en la historia de las tierras bajas mayas: Nuevos datos epigráficos. In *XIV Simposio de Investigaciones Arqueológicas en Guatemala,* edited by Juan Pedro Laporte and Héctor Escobedo. Guatemala: Museo Nacional de Arqueología y Etnografía.

Fash, William L., Jr.
1988   A New Look at Maya Statecraft from Copan, Honduras. *Antiquity* 62: 157–169.

Fash, William L., Jr., and David Stuart
1990 Dynastic History and Cultural Evolution at Copán, Honduras. In *Classic Maya Political History: Hieroglyphic and Archaeological Evidence,* edited by T. Patrick Culbert, 147–179. Cambridge: Cambridge University Press.
Freidel, David A.
1981 Civilization as a State of Mind: The Cultural Evolution of the Lowland Maya. In *The Transition to Statehood in the New World,* edited by Grant D. Jones and Robert R. Kautz, 188–227. Cambridge: Cambridge University Press.
1986 Terminal Classic Lowland Maya Successes, Failures and Aftermaths. In *Late Lowland Maya Civilization,* edited by Jeremy A. Sabloff and E. Wyllys Andrews V, 409–430. Albuquerque: University of New Mexico Press.
1992 The Trees of Life: Ahau as Idea and Artifact in Classic Lowland Maya Civilization. In *Ideology and Pre-Columbian Civilization,* edited by Arthur A. Demarest and Geoffrey W. Conrad, 114–133. Albuquerque: University of New Mexico Press.
Freidel, David A., and Linda Schele
1988a Kingship in the Late Preclassic Maya Lowlands: The Instruments and Places of Ritual Power. *American Anthropologist* 90 (3): 547–567.
1988b Symbol and Power: A History of the Lowland Maya Cosmogram. In *Maya Iconography,* edited by Elizabeth Benson and Gillette Griffin, 44–93. Princeton: Princeton University Press.
1989 Dead Kings and Living Temples: Dedication and Termination Rituals among the Ancient Maya. In *Word and Image in Maya Culture: Explorations in Language, Writing, and Representation,* edited by William Hanks and Don Rice, 233–243. Salt Lake City: University of Utah Press.
Freidel, David A., Linda Schele, and Joy Parker
1993 *Maya Cosmos: Three Thousand Years on the Shaman's Path.* New York: William Morrow.
Geertz, Clifford
1980 *Negara: The Theater State in Nineteenth-Century Bali.* Princeton: Princeton University Press.
Gesick, Loraine (ed.)
1983 *Centers, Symbols, and Hierarchies: Essays on the Classical States of Southeast Asia.* Southeast Asia Studies Monograph Series, no. 26. New Haven: Yale University.
Heyden, Doris
1973 ¿Un Chicomostoc en Teotihuacán? La cueva bajo de la Pirámide del Sol. *Boletín del Instituto Nacional de Antropología e Historia* 6: 3–18.
1975 An Interpretation of the Cave beneath the Pyramid of the Sun at Teotihuacan, Mexico. *American Antiquity* 40: 131–147.
1981 Caves, Gods, and Myths: World-View and Planning in Teotihuacan. In *Mesoamerican Sites and World Views,* edited by Elizabeth P. Benson, 1–39. Washington, D.C.: Dumbarton Oaks Research Library and Collection.
Houston, Stephen D.
1987 The Inscriptions and Monumental Art of Dos Pilas, Guatemala: A Study of Classic Maya History and Politics. Ph.D. dissertation, Yale University.
1993 *Hieroglyphs and History at Dos Pilas: Dynastic Politics of the Classic Maya.* Austin: University of Texas Press.
Houston, Stephen D., and Peter Mathews
1985 *The Dynastic Sequence of Dos Pilas, Guatemala.* Monograph 1. San Francisco: Pre-Columbian Art Research Institute.

Houston, Stephen D., and David Stuart
1990   Resultados generales de los estudios epigráficos del Proyecto Petexbatún. In *Proyecto Arqueológico Regional Petexbatún: Informe preliminar #2, segunda temporada, 1990*, edited by Arthur A. Demarest and Stephen D. Houston, 568–577. Guatemala: Instituto de Antropología e Historia; Nashville: Department of Anthropology, Vanderbilt University.

Kovacevich, Brigitte, Tomás Barrientos, Arthur Demarest, Michael Callaghan, Cassandra Bill, Erin Sears, and Lucia Moran
2000   Producción e intercambio en el reinado de Cancuen. In *XIV Simposio de Arqueología Guatemalteca*, edited by Juan Pedro Laporte and Héctor Escobedo. Guatemala: Museo Nacional de Antropología y Etnología.

MacLeod, Barbara, and Dennis Edward Puleston
1979   Pathways into Darkness: The Search for the Road to Xibalba. In *Third Palenque Round Table, 1978*, part 1, edited by Merle Greene Robertson, pp. 71–79. Austin: University of Texas Press.

Manzanilla, L. L. Barba, R. Chávez, A. Tejero, C. Cifuentes, and N. Peralta
1994   Caves and Geophysics: An Approximation to the Underworld of Teotihuacan, Mexico. *Archaeometry* 36: 141–157.

Marcus, Joyce
1983   On the Nature of the Mesoamerican City. In *Prehistoric Settlement Patterns: Essays in Honor of Gordon R. Willey*, edited by Evon Z. Vogt and Richard M. Leventhal, 195–242. Albuquerque: University of New Mexico Press.
1993   Ancient Maya Political Organization. In *Lowland Maya Civilization in the Eighth Century A.D.*, edited by Jeremy A. Sabloff and John S. Henderson, 111–183. Washington, D.C.: Dumbarton Oaks Research Library and Collection.

Martin, Simon, and Nikolai Grube
1995   Maya Superstates: How a Few Powerful Kingdoms Vied for Control of the Maya Lowlands during the Classic Period (A.D. 300–900). *Archaeology* 48 (6): 41–46.
2000   *Chronicle of the Maya Kings and Queens: Deciphering the Dynasties of the Ancient Maya.* London: Thames and Hudson.

Mathews, Peter, and Gordon R. Willey
1990   Prehistoric Polities of the Pasión Region: Hieroglyphic Texts and Their Archaeological Settings. In *Classic Maya Political History: Hieroglyphic and Archaeological Evidence*, edited by T. Patrick Culbert, 30–71. Cambridge: Cambridge University Press.

Miller, Mary Ellen
1988   The Meaning and Function of the Main Acropolis, Copan. In *The Southeast Classic Maya Zone*, edited by Elizabeth Boone and Gordon R. Willey, 149–194. Washington, D.C.: Dumbarton Oaks Research Library and Collection.
1996   *The Art of Mesoamerica: From Olmec to Aztec*, rev. ed. New York: Thames and Hudson.

Mock, Shirley (ed.)
1998   *The Sowing and the Dawning: Termination, Dedication, and Transformation in the Archaeological and Ethnographic Record of Mesoamerica.* Albuquerque: University of New Mexico Press.

Morgan, Kim
1995   Suboperación DP39A: Excavaciones en una residencia de elite. In *Proyecto Arqueológico Regional Petexbatún: Informe preliminar #6, sexta temporada 1994*, edited by Arthur A. Demarest, Juan Antonio Valdés, and Héctor Escobedo, 296–309. Guatemala: Instituto de Antropología e Historia; Nashville: Department of Anthropology, Vanderbilt University.

Morgan, Kim, Arthur A. Demarest, and Claudia Wolley
1995   Excavaciones de una estructura elite: Suboperación DP39G. In *Proyecto Arqueológico Regional Petexbatún: Informe preliminar #6, sexta temporada 1994*, edited by Arthur A. Demarest, Juan Antonio Valdés, and Héctor Escobedo, 342–348. Guatemala: Instituto de Antropología e Historia; Nashville: Department of Anthropology, Vanderbilt University.

Palka, Joel
1990   Operación DP10: Excavaciones en la Estructura L5-49 de Dos Pilas. In *Proyecto Arqueológico Regional Petexbatún: Informe preliminar #2, segunda temporada, 1990*, edited by Arthur A. Demarest and Stephen D. Houston, 225–234. Guatemala: Instituto de Antropología e Historia; Nashville: Department of Anthropology, Vanderbilt University.
1995   Classic Maya Social Inequality and the Collapse at Dos Pilas, Peten, Guatemala. Ph.D. dissertation, Vanderbilt University.
1997   Reconstructing Classic Maya Socioeconomic Differentiation and the Collapse at Dos Pilas, Peten, Guatemala. *Ancient Mesoamerica* 8 (2): 293–306.

Palka, Joel, and Antonia Foias
1991   Operación DP2: Excavaciones en la Plaza Mayor de Dos Pilas. In *Proyecto Arqueológico Regional Petexbatun: Informe preliminar #3, tercera temporada 1993*, edited by Arthur A. Demarest, Takeshi Inomata, Héctor Escobedo, and Joel Palka, 12–36. Guatemala: Instituto de Antropología e Historia; Nashville: Department of Anthropology, Vanderbilt University.

Palka, Joel, Fernando Moscoso, and Arthur A. Demarest
1992   La consolidación y reconstrucción del Templo L5-1 de la Plaza Principal de Dos Pilas. In *Proyecto Arqueológico Regional Petexbatún: Informe preliminar #4, cuarta temporada 1992*, edited by Arthur A. Demarest, Takeshi Inomata, and Héctor Escobedo, 243–249. Guatemala: Instituto de Antropología e Historia; Nashville: Department of Anthropology, Vanderbilt University.

Rathje, William J.
1977   The Tikal Connection. In *The Origins of Maya Civilization*, edited by Richard E. W. Adams, 373–382. Albuquerque: University of New Mexico Press.

Sabloff, Jeremy A.
1986   Interaction among Classic Maya Polities: A Preliminary Examination. In *Peer Polity Interaction and Socio-Political Change*, edited by Colin Renfrew and John F. Cherry, 109–116. Cambridge: Cambridge University Press.

Sanders, William T., and David Webster
1988   The Mesoamerican Urban Tradition. *American Anthropologist* 80: 521–546.

Schele, Linda
1981   Sacred Site and World-View at Palenque. In *Mesoamerican Sites and World-Views*, edited by Elizabeth P. Boone, 87–117. Washington, D.C.: Dumbarton Oaks Research Library and Collection.

Schele, Linda, and David Freidel
1990   *A Forest of Kings: The Untold Story of the Ancient Maya*. New York: William Morrow.

Schele, Linda, and Peter Mathews
1990   Royal Visits along the Usumacinta. In *Classic Maya Political History: Hieroglyphic and Archaeological Evidence*, edited by T. Patrick Culbert, 226–253. Cambridge: Cambridge University Press.

Schele, Linda, and Mary Ellen Miller
1986   *The Blood of Kings: Dynasty and Ritual in Maya Art*. New York: George Braziller.

Stuart, David

1984   Royal Auto-Sacrifice among the Maya: A Study of Image and Meaning. *RES: Anthropology and Aesthetics* 7/8: 6–20.

1988   Blood Symbolism in Maya Iconography. In *Maya Iconography*, edited by Elizabeth Benson and Gillett Griffin, 175–221. Princeton: Princeton University Press.

1995   A Study of Maya Inscriptions. Ph.D. dissertation, Department of Anthropology, Vanderbilt University.

Stuart, David, and Stephen D. Houston

1994   *Classic Maya Place Names.* Studies in Pre-Columbian Art and Archaeology, no. 33. Washington, D.C.: Dumbarton Oaks Research Library and Collection.

Sugiyama, Saburo

1993   Worldview Materialized in Teotihuacan, Mexico. *Latin American Antiquity* 4 (2): 103–129.

Suhler, Charles, and David Freidel

1998   Life and Death in a Maya War Zone. *Archaeology* 51 (3): 28–34.

Symonds, Stacey, Bárbara Arroyo, and Stephen D. Houston

1990   Operación DP11: Investigaciones en el palacio de Dos Pilas. In *Proyecto Arqueológico Regional Petexbatún: Informe preliminar #2, segunda temporada, 1990*, edited by Arthur A. Demarest and Stephen D. Houston, 235–276. Guatemala: Instituto de Antropología e Historia; Nashville: Department of Anthropology, Vanderbilt University.

Tambiah, Stanley J.

1976   *World Conqueror and World Renouncer.* Cambridge: Cambridge University Press.

1982   Famous Buddha Images and the Legitimation of Kings. *RES: Anthropology and Aesthetics* 4: 5–20.

1984   *The Buddhist Saints of the Forest and the Cult of Amulets: A Study in Charisma, Hagiography, Sectarianism, and Millennial Buddhism.* Cambridge: Cambridge University Press.

Valdés, Juan Antonio

1991   Arquitectura regional de los sitios cercanos a la Laguna de Petexbatún, Petén, Guatemala. Paper presented at the 47th International Congress of Americanists, Tulane University, New Orleans.

Valdés, Juan Antonio, and José S. Suasnávar

1991   Estudio preliminar de la arquitectura en la región de Petexbatún. In *Proyecto Arqueológico Regional Petexbatún: Informe preliminar #3, tercera temporada*, edited by Arthur A. Demarest, Takeshi Inomata, Héctor Escobedo, and Joel Palka, 785–806. Guatemala: Instituto de Antropología e Historia; Nashville: Department of Anthropology, Vanderbilt University.

Vogt, Evon Z., Jr.

1981   Some Aspects of the Sacred Geography of Highland Chiapas. In *Mesoamerican Sites and World Views*, edited by Elizabeth P. Benson, 119–142. Washington, D.C.: Dumbarton Oaks Research Library and Collection.

Webster, David

1993   The Study of Maya Warfare: What It Tells Us about the Maya and What It Tells Us about Maya Archaeology. In *Lowland Maya Civilization in the Eighth Century A.D.*, edited by Jeremy A. Sabloff and John S. Henderson, 415–444. Washington, D.C.: Dumbarton Oaks Research Library and Collection.

Wolley, Claudia

1995   Investigaciones en la Estructura N5-3A del Grupo Murciélagos. In *Proyecto*

Arqueológico Regional Petexbatún: Informe preliminar #6, tercera temporada 1994, edited by Arthur A. Demarest, Juan Antonio Valdés, and Héctor Escobedo, 331–341. Guatemala: Instituto de Antropología e Historia; Nashville: Department of Anthropology, Vanderbilt University.

Wolley, Claudia, and Irma Rodas
1995   Suboperaciones DP39L, DP39M, DP39N, DP39O y DP39P. In *Proyecto Arqueológico Regional Petexbatún: Informe preliminar #6, tercera temporada 1994,* edited by Arthur A. Demarest, Juan Antonio Valdés, and Héctor Escobedo, 362–366. Guatemala: Instituto de Antropología e Historia; Nashville: Department of Anthropology, Vanderbilt University.

Wolley, Claudia, and Lori E. Wright
1990   Operación DP7: Investigaciones en el Grupo L4-4. In *Proyecto Arqueológico Regional Petexbatún: Informe preliminar #2, segunda temporada, 1990,* edited by Arthur A. Demarest and Stephen D. Houston, 44–65. Guatemala: Instituto de Antropología e Historia; Nashville: Department of Anthropology, Vanderbilt University.

CHAPTER SIX

Where Did Elites Live?

IDENTIFYING ELITE RESIDENCES AT AGUATECA, GUATEMALA

Takeshi Inomata and Daniela Triadan

Architecture is one of the most important sources of information for archaeologists about social organization, lifestyle, and worldviews. In particular, residences of elites provide critical data concerning the nature of social stratification, administrative mechanisms, and dominant ideologies. Our understanding of Maya elite residences, however, is still limited. Above all, we are not able to identify elite residences with reasonable certainty (Tourtellot 1993: 230–232). Inquiries into this issue is further hampered by the ambiguity of the concept of elite. In this chapter we first review the related concepts of palace, elite, and elite residence. We then examine problems related to the identification of elite residences, using data from the center of Aguateca, Guatemala. Aguateca, where rapidly abandoned buildings in its epicenter contain rich assemblages of de facto refuse, presents an exceptionally favorable condition for the study of elite residences. The identification of elite residences in general, however, still remains problematic.

Maya Palaces and Elite Residences

Palaces

An important term related to elite residence is "palace," which is commonly used by Mayanists. The use and concept of this word are rather problematic. One problem originates in the European bias inherent in the use of this term. Another, which derives partly from the first problem, is the conflation of morphological descriptions and functional inferences. The history of the concept of palace in Maya archaeology traced by Webster (1998; Webster and Inomata 1998) illuminates this point. Spaniards in the colonial period and the early explorer John Lloyd Stephens ([1841] 1949: 243–244) used the words "palacios" and "palaces," through European analogies, to refer to presumed residences of lords and nobles (Kowalski 1987: 76). As the theocratic model of Classic Maya society became dominant, Mayanists came to use the word "palace" as a purely descriptive term (Webster and Inomata 1998; see Satterthwaite 1935). "Palace" in this sense generally refers to a large and long structure with multiple rooms or long galleries, usually built on relatively low platforms (G. F. Andrews 1975: 43–46). This type of building is contrasted with "temples," which consist of relatively small superstructures with one or few rooms on high pyramidal bases. Only after the demise of the theocratic model and the introduction of modern scientific excavation methods—most notably the study of the Tikal Central Acropolis by Peter Harrison (1970)—did it become clear that some of the palace-type structures were indeed residences of rulers and other privileged individuals (Adams 1970: 492, 1974; Haviland 1981). It is, however, necessary to remember that not all palace-type buildings were residences, and that some royal residences may have been placed on large pyramid-shaped bases (Chase and Chase 2001; Folan, Gunn, and Domínguez 2001; Harrison 1970). For analytical purposes, morphological definitions and functional ones need to be distinguished clearly. The correlation between morphology and functions should not be presumed a priori but should be demonstrated through empirical research.

The Concept of Elite

As terms referring to the functions of the building and the status of its residents, Mayanists commonly use "elite residential structures" and "elite residences." The definition of these terms also remains vague. The problem is that the concept of "elite" is not clearly defined, and the term "elite" is often used uncritically by Mayanists (Chase and Chase 1992: 3; Houston and Stuart 2001; Marcus 1983a: 7). In a broad sense, elites may mean individuals who enjoy significantly higher power, wealth, or prestige than other members of society, and the term has been used interchangeably with the upper class, the wealthy, or the privileged (Chase and Chase 1992: 3; Marcus 1983a: 34, 1983b: 3). In most societies, different dimensions of social inequality, such as power, wealth, and prestige, do not always correlate with each other (Dumont 1970; Fallers 1973; McGuire 1983; Palka 1995; Paynter 1989). The relation between these variables and the elaborateness of residences is equally complex. In Edo period Japan, many nobles of the emperor's court, who maintained a certain level of prestige and status but had lost political power to the samurai class, lived in dilapidated structures. On the other hand, some merchants, who were near the bottom of the class system, enjoyed considerable economic wealth. In Ming dynasty

China, disrespected eunuchs, who originated in the lower classes, lived in the residential compound of the emperor and sometimes enjoyed political power greater than state ministers through their closeness to the sovereign (Mitamura 1970). The elite in a broad sense, then, encompasses individuals of diverse social positions whose residences may vary significantly in size and elaborateness. It follows that palaces and elite residences are not synonymous, not only in that some of so-called palaces may not be residences, but also in that elite residences are not always buildings of palatial scale.

In the social sciences, the concept of the elite is generally used in a more specific way (for a discussion of the concept of the elite in Maya archaeology, see Chase and Chase 1992; Houston and Stuart 2001). Marcus (1983a: 10–13; see also Mills 1956: 3–15) lists three broad qualities of elites. First, elites are agents that bring about effects, shaping events for others. Second, elites are exclusive. Third, elites control social institutions that organize the general population. In other words, the elite can be defined as a minority of powerful people who, through their control of social institutions, bring about effects of broad significance for society at large (Giddens 1974: 4; Schneider and Schneider 1983: 159). Marcus (1992) also warns that elite theory has developed in the specific historical context of the modern Western world, where it has focused on the human counterparts of developing bureaucracy and other institutions of a rather impersonal nature. In traditional societies, the relation between elites and social institutions may be less clear-cut than in the modern West and elites may depend more on informal personal relations (Inomata and Houston 2001). In any case, elites in this definition are associated more closely with power, particularly *power over others* in relations of domination, than other dimensions such as wealth and prestige. While this definition is more specific, elites are not easy to identify through the material remains that archaeologists rely on (Chase and Chase 1992: 3). This leads some scholars to question the utility of the concept of elite in the analysis of archaeological data (Kowalewski, Feinman, and Finsten 1992; Marcus 1992).

Although it is beyond us to identify and describe elites archaeologically with the clarity and certainty of ethnography, we still believe that important insights can be gained through the analysis of material remains. In this regard, the strategies laid out by Cowgill (1992) are suggestive. First, the exclusivity of elites may be expressed or defined by certain lifestyles or subcultures, which may lead to recognizable material residues (see Marcus 1983c: 34; Schneider and Schneider 1983). Second, critical institutional positions in traditional societies are often associated with specific iconographic or material symbols. In the study of the pre-Hispanic Maya, researchers can take advantage of the epigraphic record. For example, titles examined by Houston and Stuart (2001) provide important clues to the elites constituting the royal court. Cowgill (1992) also reminds us that the lifestyle and symbols related to elites should be distinguished clearly from generalized wealth. In addition, we need to keep in mind that some elites may not leave any distinguishable material residues.[1]

Elite Residences

Architecture has often been used as one of the primary indicators of elite status by archaeologists (Chase and Chase 1992; Haviland and Moholy-Nagy 1992; Pendergast 1992). In other words, the practice of archaeological research of elite residences generally does not start with the identification of the elites, leading to the examination of their dwellings. Instead, it usually begins with the identification of large and elaborate buildings with residential functions on the ground, which, often in combination with other types of data, leads to the assumption that their residents were elites. Thus, archaeological inquiries concerning elites and their residences are always in danger of falling into circular arguments: Elites are those who lived in presumed elite residences, and elite residences are buildings occupied by elites. It is necessary to consider the possibility that there might have been elites who did not live in large buildings and that some large and elaborate buildings might have reflected generalized wealth or resulted from inheritance rather than the power of the residents (see Kowalewski, Feinman, and Finsten 1992: 263).

Despite these potential problems, architectural analysis still serves as one of the most powerful tools archaeologists have to address elites. In addition, with the development of architectural studies, scholars have come to see architecture itself as an important subject of inquiry, not simply as an indicator of the social status of the residents (Houston 1998; Kent 1990; Parker Pearson and Richards 1994). Such a study may focus on elaborate architecture as an expression of power or of exclusive lifestyles, rather than on elite residences in general that potentially include modest houses. Since the scale and elaborateness of architecture closely reflect the amount of labor investment (Abrams 1994; Inomata and Aoyama 1996), large buildings, the construction of which requires the labor of individuals other than the residents, often reasonably reflect the power of the residents or owners. In this regard, Landa noted that the houses of lords in contact-period Yucatan were built with the labor of commoners (Tozzer 1941: 87). The power and exclusiveness of elites may also be expressed in more subtle ways, such as location, spatial arrangements, and the use of specific icons. These buildings as expressions of power may serve to distinguish elites from the rest of society and to facilitate their exclusive lifestyle. On the other hand, elites in some societies may be expected, whether they like it or not, to live in appropriate elite residences, and this noblesse oblige may sometimes strain them economically, as seen in pre-revolution France (Elias 1983). It is, again, necessary to remember that some elites may choose not to use their power for the construction of large residences or their power may be restricted in terms of issues it can be applied to (see below). With these problems in mind, we now turn to data from Aguateca.

Aguateca

Aguateca is located in the Petexbatun region in the tropical lowlands of the southwestern Peten, Guatemala. It is a relatively small center, and its epicenter includes the Palace Group, which was probably a residential complex of the royal family, the Main Plaza where carved monuments lie, and the Causeway that connects the Palace Group and the Main Plaza (Figure 6.1). The area along the Causeway was a densely occupied residential area. Previous studies at Aguateca by Ian Graham (1967) and by Stephen Houston (1987, 1992b, 1993; Houston and Mathews 1985) focused on recording inscribed monuments and mapping the site center. Houston's epigraphic decipherment demonstrated that Aguateca was the twin capital of Dos Pilas, governed by the same dynasty.

Inomata and his colleagues conducted more systematic archaeological investigations from 1990 to 1993 as a subproject of the Petexbatun Regional Archaeological Project, directed by Arthur Demarest, and from 1996 to 1999 as the Aguateca Archaeological Project (Inomata 1995, 1997; Inomata et al. 1996, 1997, 1998; Inomata, Ponciano, and Triadan 1997; Inomata, Triadan, and Ponciano 1998). Excavation data indicated that most structures visible on the surface were occupied during the Late Classic period. Extensive defensive walls were constructed in a hasty manner toward the end of this period, most likely as a response to the intensification of warfare in the region. Excavations in the residential area along the Causeway revealed an extraordinary amount of complete and reconstructible artifacts in and around structures. Furthermore, all the excavated structures in this area showed evidence of burning, such as pieces of carbon, heat-damaged chert objects, and burned ceramics, bones, and shell. Inomata has hypothesized that Aguateca was attacked by enemies and its central part was burned. The inhabitants in the epicenter probably fled or were taken away, leaving most of their belongings behind. Areas outside the epicenter were probably deserted soon after this event. These areas were abandoned gradually enough that the residents could carry away most of their be-

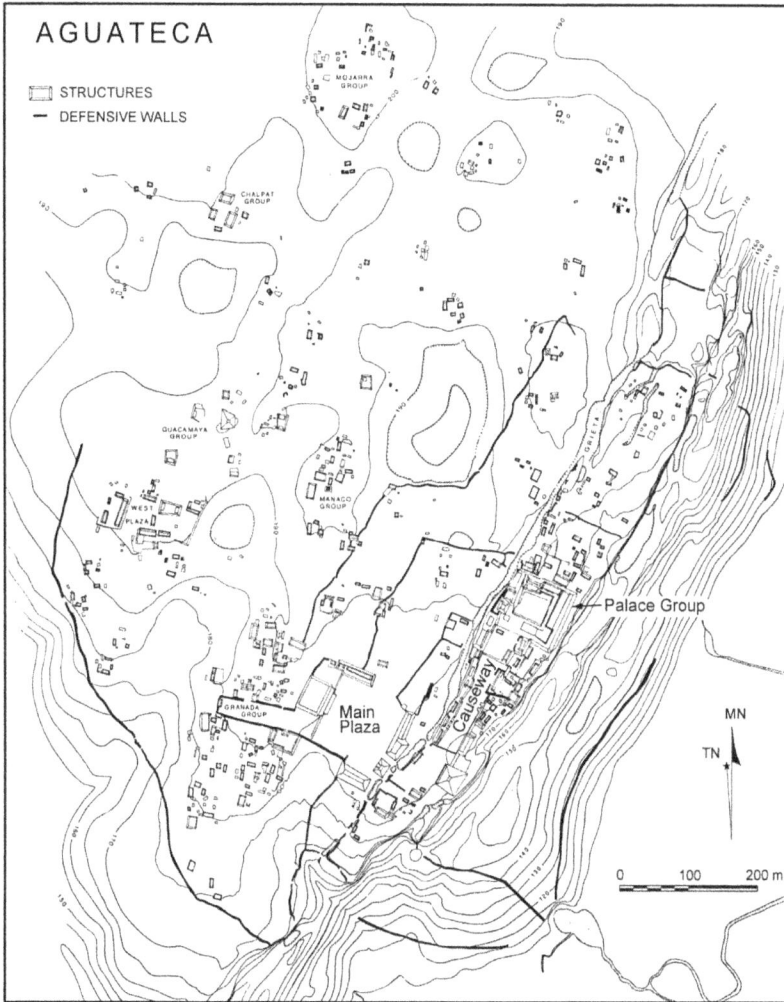

FIGURE 6.1. Map of Aguateca showing the location of the Palace Group, Causeway, and Main Plaza.

longings (Demarest et al. 1997; Inomata 1995, 1997, in press; Inomata and Stiver 1998).

Among the 704 structures mapped at the Aguateca center, we estimate that 622 are possible Late Classic domestic structures, that is, residences, kitchens, family shrines, and other buildings related to domestic life. The terms "residences" and "dwellings" are used in a narrower sense, meaning structures where people slept and spent a significant amount of pri-

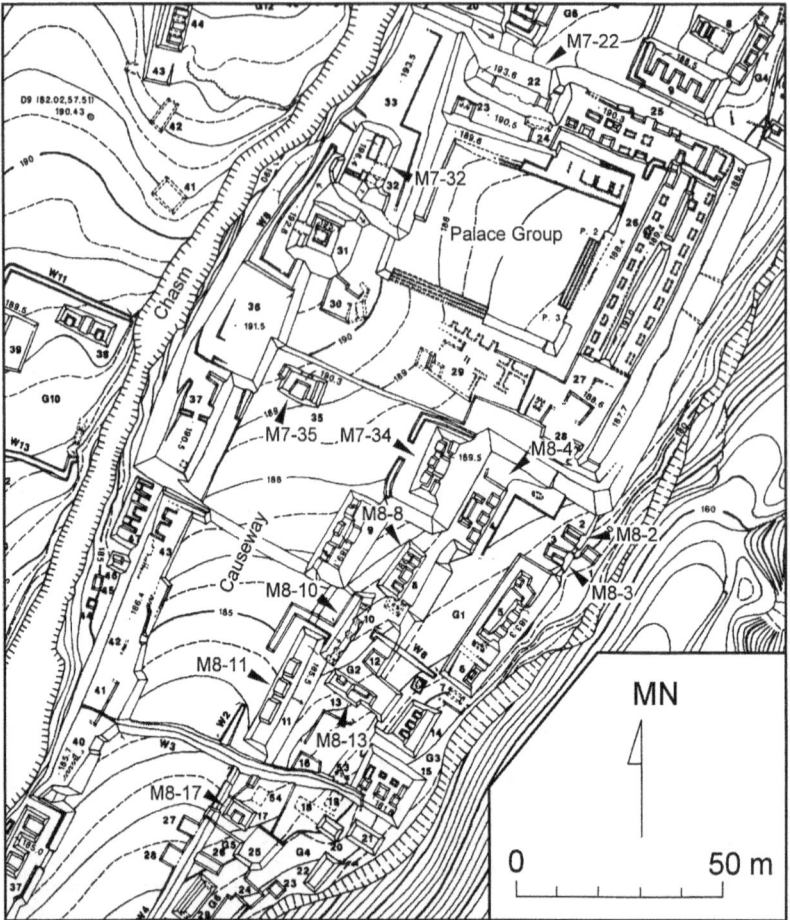

FIGURE 6.2. Map of the Palace Group and the area along the Causeway, with the location of extensively excavated buildings.

vate time. Another concept mentioned in the following discussion is residential unit, which refers to a spatial aggregation of domestic structures, usually surrounding a patio. Extensively excavated structures in the area around the Causeway include Structures M7-22 and M7-32, probable royal residences; Structures M7-35, M8-4, M8-8, and M8-10, which were most likely elite residential structures; Structure M8-13, a residence occupied by a household of relatively low status; Structures M7-34 and M8-11, which may have been communal houses; Structure M8-17, a probable shrine; and Structures M8-2 and M8-3, which may have been buildings used for manufacturing activities (Figure 6.2).

Aguateca provides unique information for the study of Maya elite residences in two respects. The first point is that the peak occupation of Aguateca lasted for a relatively short time. Occupation in the early part of the Late Classic period was relatively light. Aguateca as the twin capital of Dos Pilas was established probably in the late-seventh or early-eighth century. The center appears to have been attacked and deserted at the beginning of the ninth century. Many buildings and plazas seem to have been constructed rapidly and have had only one major construction phase. Thus, the settlement data of Aguateca may reflect the social and political organization at a given time more closely than the data of other centers with longer occupations, where such patterns are blurred by numerous episodes of construction and modification. The second point concerns the rapid abandonment of Aguateca. Rich assemblages of on-floor artifacts found in burned buildings present an unprecedented opportunity to examine the use, function, and meaning of these structures (Inomata and Sheets 2000). In the following section, we first examine Aguateca's elites through data other than architecture. Because of the nature of our data set, the discussion focuses on the royal family that probably lived in the Palace Group and on possible elites that occupied the area along the Causeway. These groups are compared with the less well known population in other parts of the center. We then analyze the scale and elaborateness of structures, as well as their functions and spatial arrangements. By examining the conformity and discrepancy between architectural and nonarchitectural data, we assess the possibility of identifying elite residences.

Elite Status Viewed through Nonarchitectural Data

Royal Family

In addition to the large scale of its architecture, the following facts imply that the Palace Group was the royal residential complex of this center. First, defensive walls were placed in a roughly concentric pattern, with the Palace Group located at its center (Figure 6.1). In other words, this architectural complex was the most heavily defended part of Aguateca. This suggests that the residents of this compound were politically or symbolically the most important. Second, the Causeway, a well-defined street, directly led to the plaza of the Palace Group (Figures 6.1, 6.2). Many other possible elite structures are found along this street. The other end of the Causeway connected to the Main Plaza, which was the primary public ceremonial space of this center. This location indicates that the Palace Group was the most important residential group at this center.

FIGURE 6.3. The easternmost, east, and center rooms of Structure M7-22, viewed from the north (left to right).

Third, the Palace Group was abandoned in a unique manner (Inomata in press). In 1998 and 1999, Erick Ponciano, Estela Pinto, and Inomata excavated Structures M7-22 and M7-32, the probable main living quarters of the royal family. Most other buildings in the Palace Group appear to have had administrative or ceremonial functions (see below). Structure M7-22 had five main rooms and probably two small front rooms (Figure 6.3), whereas Structure M7-32 consisted of three main rooms and a wide front room. Although most rooms were clean of artifacts, the easternmost room of Structure M7-22 contained numerous reconstructible objects and its entrance was sealed. It appears that the residents evacuated the Palace Group before the final fall of Aguateca, strongly sensing the threat of an imminent attack by enemies. They cleaned their living rooms and stored some of their possessions in the easternmost room of Structure M7-22, hoping to come back later. This pattern of abandonment has not been found outside the Palace Group. The uniqueness of this abandonment process is probably related to the special status of the residents. It is likely that only the royal family and their close attendants left the center, while most of the population, including the majority of nobles, remained until the bitter end.

Fourth, the artifact assemblage stored in the easternmost room of Structure M7-22 points to the royal status of the occupants of this compound.

It is possible that the fleeing royal family took the most important re-galia with them and that the enemy who attacked Aguateca plundered this building. Still, the remaining objects are spectacular. They include a carved shell and bone with glyphic texts, pyrite mosaic mirrors, a greenstone celt, and two thin-walled ceramic masks made of layers of clay-saturated tex-tiles (Beaubien and Kaplan 2000; Inomata et al. 1998). Fifth, the enemies who attacked Aguateca appear to have conducted termination rituals in the Palace Group (Inomata in press). Dense deposits of broken sherds, mixed with jade, shell, bone, and pyrite, were found around Structure M7-22 and in the center room of Structure M7-32. Excavators did not find compa-rable deposits outside the Palace Group. These materials were probably de-posited during termination rituals, in which the buildings were deliber-ately destroyed (see Mock 1998). If this interpretation is correct, such ritual behavior most likely reflected the unique symbolic value of this architec-tural compound.

Other Elites

Data concerning other elites derive mostly from the excavation of burned structures in the area along the Causeway (Figures 6.1, 6.2). This location appears to have been suitable for an elite residential zone. It is situated be-tween the royal residential compound and the Main Plaza, as well as being next to the Causeway, which was probably an important public and cere-monial space. In addition, the area is well defended by the escarpment, the chasm, and defensive walls. Even more suggestive is its abandonment pat-tern. So far, only this area has been confirmed to have been burned and abandoned rapidly. There is a slight possibility that the residential area to the north of the Palace Group was also burned, but data from small test pits are not sufficient to determine its abandonment processes. The rest of the center was clearly deserted gradually. Together with the aforemen-tioned defensive strategy, these patterns indicate that the primary target of the enemy attack was the epicenter, particularly the area along the Cause-way. It is reasonable to assume that those who lived in this area possessed prominent political power.

Artifactual data also imply the elite status of the inhabitants of this area. Particularly relevant are data from Structures M7-35, M8-4, M8-8, and M8-10, excavated by Triadan and Inomata. These buildings were most likely residential structures. Floor assemblages found in these buildings include finely carved shell ornaments, greenstone beads, and high-quality poly-chrome ceramics. In particular, Structure M8-10 contained a human skull carved with a glyphic text referring to an accession ceremony accompanied by the Aguateca ruler. Also found in this building was a finely carved shell with a text mentioning a personal name, titles, the Aguateca emblem glyph, and a scribal title (Inomata 1995; Inomata and Stiver 1998). It is likely that Structure M8-10 was occupied by a noble scribe who enjoyed a close relationship with the ruler.

Despite these rich data, uncertainty remains. A problem derives from the difficulty of evaluating the *eliteness* reflected in these material possessions in comparative terms, because of the completely different abandonment patterns in other parts of Aguateca. Although these materials of high value (long-distance-trade goods and labor-intensive products) have not been found outside the epicenter, one needs to consider the possibility that similar objects were possessed by numerous other households of Aguateca but were simply not left behind in gradually abandoned structures. Burial data are suggestive in this regard. An extended male burial unearthed under the center room of Structure M8-10 probably belongs to a former household head, but it was rather poor, containing only one ceramic bowl of mediocre quality. The number of excavated burials at Aguateca is small, possibly reflecting the short duration of occupation, but a few burials found in structures of similar sizes outside the epicenter contained one to three vessels. It is probable that burials in the Petexbatun region are generally poor, possibly due to the late establishment of the Dos Pilas/Aguateca dynasty. Even the alleged royal tombs excavated at Dos Pilas are not as spectacular as tombs found in the central Peten and other areas (Demarest 1997). Still, the burial at Structure M8-10 seems rather unimpressive. The contents of the midden associated with Structure M8-10 were also largely similar to those found in other parts of the center, except that a few fragments of shell ornaments, elaborate figurines, and fine ceramic vessels hinted at the elevated status of the inhabitants.

Despite these ambiguities, the residents of Structures M7-35, M8-4, M8-8, and M8-10 were certainly better off than the average, which is demonstrated by the excavation results from Structure M8-13. Structure M8-13 is a relatively small building, forming a residential unit with Structure M8-10 (Figure 6.2). The assemblage of utilitarian objects from Structure M8-13, including storage and cooking vessels, grinding stones, and chipped stone tools, was similar to those from Structures M7-35, M8-8, and M8-10. This indicates that Structure M8-13 was a residence of a separate coresidential group, not an ancillary building of Structure M8-10 (Inomata, Ponciano, and Triadan 1996, 1997). Structure M8-13, however, was virtually devoid of objects of high value, such as shell ornaments and greenstone pieces. These data show that, within the residential area along the Causeway, the inhabitants were internally differentiated. While the residents of Structures M7-35, M8-4, M8-8, and M8-10 belonged to the upper social layer, Structure M8-13 appears to represent the middle or lower stratum.

Scale and Elaborateness of Buildings

Palace Group

In terms of the scale of the buildings, the Palace Group, a probable royal residential complex, is significantly more elaborate and larger than any of the other residential compounds at Aguateca (Figure 6.4a). In this complex, Structures M7-22 and M7-32 appear to have been the main residential quarters of the royal family (see below). So far they are the only buildings at Aguateca that have been confirmed as having had vaulted roofs. The exterior masonry of Structures M7-22 and M7-32 was well executed (Figure 6.5). In particular, finely cut stones of complex shapes have been found to date only in Structure M7-22. The stucco floors also were thicker and better made than those in other excavated structures. In other words, the prominent scale and elaborateness of the Palace Group accords well with the aforementioned nonarchitectural data, which indicate that the residents of this compound were royalty. The Palace Group of Aguateca, however, is not particularly impressive compared to large buildings of other centers. The interior masonry was relatively rough, using slabs of irregular shapes (Figure 6.6). In addition, excavation did not reveal any stone sculptures in these buildings. This stands in contrast to Dos Pilas, where hieroglyphic benches and other sculptures have been found in possible royal residences and other structures (Demarest 1997). A reason for this difference is probably that Aguateca, as the secondary capital, was less important for the dynasty than Dos Pilas.

Buildings in the Causeway Area

Differences among other structures are subtler. Figure 6.4b shows that some residential complexes are substantially larger than others, but differences are not as clearly marked as in the case of the royal residence. Structures M7-35, M8-4, M8-8, and M8-10, discussed above, belong to the top 10 to 15 percent of Aguatecan domestic structures in terms of construction volume (Inomata 1995). In particular, Structures M8-4 and M8-8, together with Structures M8-5 and M8-6 (Figure 6.2), form one of the largest residential units after the Palace Group in terms of the average construction volume (Unit M8-1 in Figure 6.4b). Nevertheless, it is necessary to note that buildings of similar sizes are also found in various parts outside the

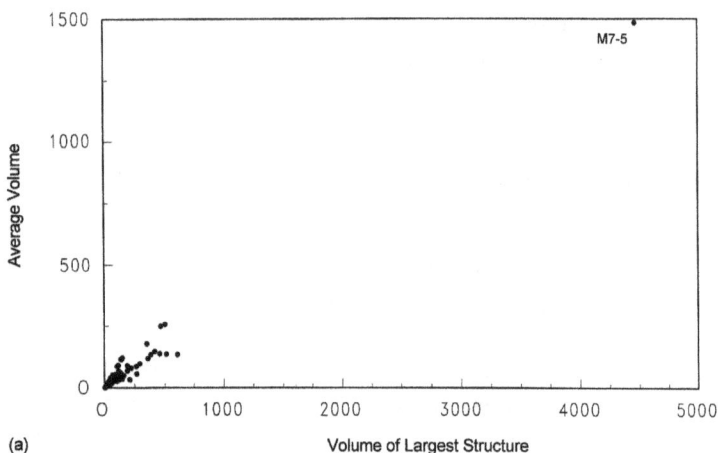

(a)

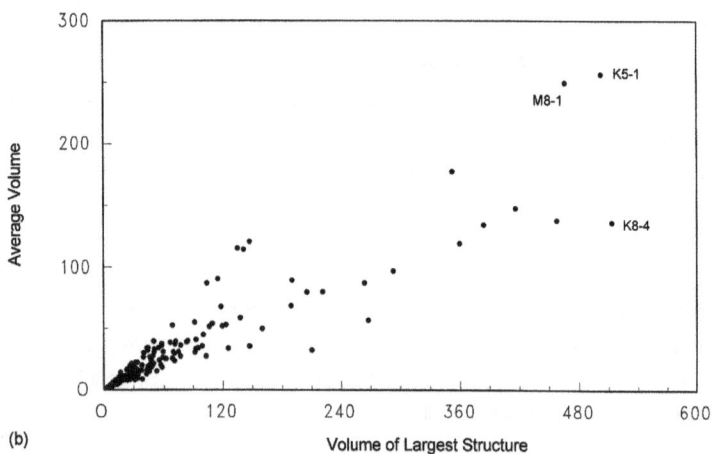

(b)

FIGURE 6.4. Plots of average volume and the volume of the largest structures of domestic units. (a) Plot with all domestic units, including Unit M7-5 (Palace Group). (b) Plot excluding Unit M7-5 (Palace Group).

epicenter, as well as in another residential zone in the epicenter, namely, the Granada Group to the west of the Main Plaza. Structures M7-35, M8-8, and M8-10 may have been slightly more elaborately built than buildings of comparable sizes in other parts of Aguateca. Their walls consisted of nicely cut stones, and floor stucco was, albeit thin, relatively well preserved (Figure 6.7). Seven structures of similar or slightly smaller sizes have been excavated outside the Causeway area, but excavators did not find recognizable stucco floors in any of these buildings. It appears that the floors of these structures were made of dirt, or that the stucco was so thin and so poorly made that it did not preserve. In addition, the masonry of these buildings was slightly coarser. Among Aguateca buildings, which are poorly built in general, those in the Causeway area seem to have comparatively better quality of construction. At the same time, as seen in nonarchitectural data, internal differentiation within the Causeway area is also recognizable in terms of the scale and elaborateness of buildings. Structure M8-13, with poorer assemblages, was smaller, and its walls consisted mostly of roughly shaped stones.

Building Functions and Spatial Arrangements

Residential Structures

Excavations of Structures M7-35, M8-4, M8-8, and M8-10 provided the most valuable information on the use of space in residential structures. These data have been discussed elsewhere in more detail (Inomata 1995; Inomata and Stiver 1998; Inomata et al. 1998; Webster and Inomata 1998), and here we summarize them briefly. They are multichambered structures with three main rooms and two to three small annexes or back rooms

FIGURE 6.5. Exterior masonry of Structure M7-22 of the Palace Group. Note finely cut stones of complex shape.

FIGURE 6.6. Interior masonry of Structure M7-22.

(Figure 6.8). The center rooms had a relatively small number of objects and were probably used for the work of the household heads, as well as for gatherings and receiving visitors. Other main rooms flanking the center rooms appear to have been related to various domestic activities and craft production. One of these rooms in each structure housed numerous objects, including large storage jars, and was probably associated with storage and food preparation. The other main room, with a smaller quantity of artifacts, may have been a place for living and sleeping. Smaller annexes and back rooms usually did not have benches, and were probably used for storage, food preparation, and craft production.

These data indicate that the use patterns of space in these buildings were fairly consistent. Similar patterns probably apply to other multiroom buildings, including Structures M7-22 and M7-32 of the Palace Group. Because of their abandonment process, discussed above, the distribution of artifacts does not reflect the original arrangement of activity areas. Their architectural features, however, point to a pattern of space use essentially comparable to those of the rapidly abandoned subroyal residences. The center rooms were larger than the others that had a spacious bench, and appear to have been appropriate for use by the ruler or a high-status individual in official business. The two adjacent main rooms of Structure M7-22 were originally connected with the center room through narrow passages in the room divisions. The doorway between the center and east rooms was later sealed. It is possible that the west room, which remained connected with the center room, served as a private chamber for the ruler or a high-status individual, while the east room was used by other members of the royal family (see Sanders 1989 and Webster 1989 for similar interpretations of Copan buildings). Likewise, the north room of Structure M7-32 was connected with the center room and appears to have been used by the ruler, whereas the south room with a separate entrance may have been occupied by other individuals. Although the function of the easternmost room of Structure M7-22 is not clear, the fact that it was sealed with numerous objects inside may reflect its original storage function.

Multichambered structures similar to Structures M7-35, M8-4, M8-8, and M8-10 are relatively common throughout Aguateca. Among 610 possible Late Classic domestic structures, excluding the Palace Group, 63 were identified as buildings with three or more rooms, and 32 as two-room structures. Since buildings with three or more rooms can be easily misidentified as one- or two-chamber structures if they have not been excavated, the actual number of structures with more than three rooms should be substantially higher than 63. In addition, the 610 structures labeled as domestic probably include numerous small ancillary buildings with functions other than use as dwellings. Thus, we estimate that a considerable portion

FIGURE 6.7. The northern part of Structure M8-8 after excavation.

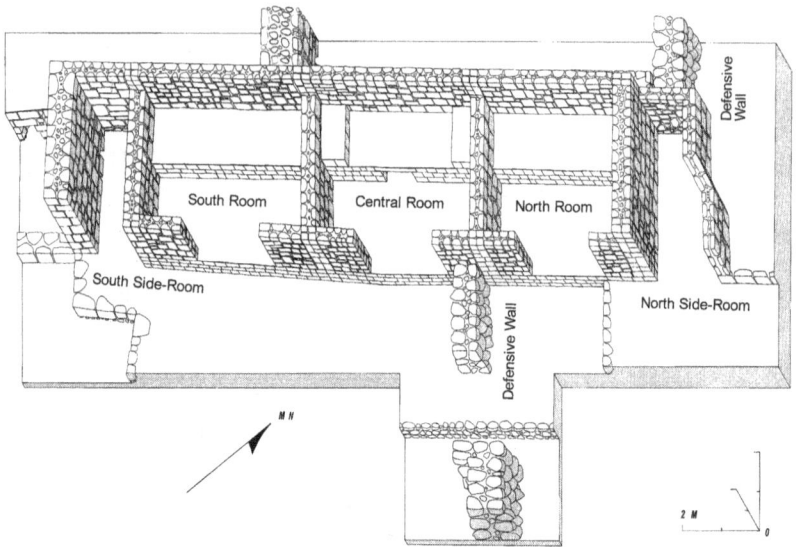

FIGURE 6.8. Axonometric drawing of Structure M8-10.

of the Late Classic residences—probably more than 20 percent—was made up of buildings with three or more rooms. It is likely that these multichambered buildings were used in manners similar to Structures M7-35, M8-4, M8-8, and M8-10.

Residential Units and Zones

We now turn to spatial arrangements in residential units and zones that encompass more than one residence, as well as to structures with other functions. In the area along the Causeway, many buildings lie parallel to this street and escarpment. This stands in contrast to many residential units in other parts of the center, which, like those at many other Maya centers, usually surround a square-shaped patio (Figures 6.1, 6.2). This uniqueness is most likely due to the spatial limitations in the small area demarcated by the chasm and escarpment, and the parallel layout as opposed to a square one probably does not have important social implications. Yet the crowded occupation in the Causeway area may have another significance. Outside the epicenter, most residential units have open spaces around them, which might have been used for intensive gardening (see Drennan 1988; Killion et al. 1989). In the Causeway area, on the other hand, all buildings were placed close to each other. Moreover, test excavations have shown that in most open spaces along the Causeway the solid bedrock was exposed, serving as patio or exterior floors. Thus, there was no room for substantial cultivation in the Causeway area. Tourtellot (1993: 231) has noted that in many Maya centers so-called palaces lack house lots for cultivation around them, and has suggested two alternative interpretations: Either these structures were not residences or the inhabitants were supplied food through some form of tribute. In the case of the Causeway area of Aguateca, at least some buildings were clearly residences, as discussed above. The residents of this area were most likely not food producers. Considering their proximity to the royal residence and textual information, we suspect that they engaged primarily in courtly activities and polity administration. This lends additional support to the assumption that some inhabitants of the Causeway area were elites.

While many buildings in the area along the Causeway were probably residences, there were also buildings with other functions. For example, Structure M8-17 (Figure 6.2) was most likely a shrine. This was a square-shaped building, with its inner space divided by thin walls running parallel to the front wall. The number of on-floor artifacts was small, but they included two complete stingray spines, figurine pieces, and a large fragment of an *incensario* (Inomata 1995; Inomata and Stiver 1998). Structure M8-54, a small platform to the north of Structure M8-17, was probably a kitchen. Structures M8-2 and M8-3, small one-room buildings, may have been used for manufacturing activities. These nonresidential domestic structures, together with the dwellings, formed residential units. The composition of residential units in this area appears to be essentially the same as that in other parts of the center, despite the difference in their layouts.

A potential difference between the Causeway area and other parts may be seen in Structure M7-34, excavated by Erick Ponciano and Estela Pinto. This large, multiroom building may have been a communal house. Its floor plan was somewhat different from those of the aforementioned residences in that room partitions were found only in the rear part of the building and the front areas were divided by thin walls running parallel to the front walls. There were at least eleven large metates for grinding corn associated with Structure M7-34, while Structures M7-35, M8-4, M8-8, and M8-10 had only one or two grinding stones of this type. In addition, excavators unearthed an elaborate *incensario* in front of Structure M7-34, whereas no artifacts of this type have been found associated with the excavated residences. This possible communal house faced the Causeway, and does not appear to have formed a residential unit with other buildings. It is not clear whether there were such buildings in other residential zones.

The Palace Group had a well-defined square shape surrounding a plaza. In this sense, its general layout is comparable to many residential units. In terms of function, however, the Palace Group appears to have been geared more heavily toward ceremonial and public use than other residential complexes. Structures M7-22 and M7-32, discussed above, may have been the only residential structures in this compound. Structure M7-31, on the western side of the group, sat on a pyramid-shaped base and may have been a temple or shrine. Structures M7-25 and M7-26, which occupied the northeastern and eastern parts of the complex, had a series of pillarlike front walls and long galleries. It appears that these structures were used for ceremonies and gatherings. It is not clear whether Structures M7-27, M7-28, M7-29, and M7-33, which probably had perishable superstructures, served residential functions. Some smaller structures around the Palace Group appear to have had other domestic functions related to this complex. In a test pit placed to the east of Structure M7-9, excavators unearthed several large fragments of manos, which were larger than most of the manos found associated with other residential structures. It is possible that Structure M7-9 or a nearby building served as a kitchen for the royal compound.

An Evaluation of the Aguateca Data

Multiple lines of evidence indicate that the Palace Group was a residence of the royal family. In terms of architectural scale, elaborateness, and spatial arrangement, the clearest difference among residential groups at Aguateca can be seen between this royal compound and the rest of them. The Palace Group is significantly larger than any other residential complex. Moreover, because it has open-gallery structures (Structures M7-25 and M7-26) and a temple (Structure M7-31), the ratio of its nondwelling structures to dwellings is higher than that of most other residential units.

These differences carry three important implications. First, in the case of Aguateca, rulers were capable of commanding the labor force not only for the construction of this imposing architectural compound but also to build the concentric stone-and-timber walls for its defense. Second, the prominent scale and elaborateness of the Palace Group may have served to stress its difference from the rest of the center and to represent its unique symbolic meaning. In many traditional complex societies, royal palaces are loaded with symbolic meanings (Inomata and Houston 2001). They are often representations of cosmology, and their difference and distance from the rest of society are emphasized. At present, we know little about the symbolic meanings of Classic Maya royal residences, although promising data are being obtained at Copan (E. W. Andrews V et al., this volume; E. W. Andrews V and Fash 1992; see also Kowalski 1987). Yet we do know that iconographic representations of Maya rulers are often surrounded by numerous cosmological symbols. It is probable that architectural complexes where rulers lived also represented cosmological views. Third, the Palace Group appears to have been more geared toward administrative and ceremonial functions than other residential units. The temple and the open-gallery structures were probably related to religious ceremonies and public gatherings. It is also possible that the royal compound was an important focus in diplomatic events, in which the Aguatecans received rulers and emissaries from other centers.

We, however, do not wish to overemphasize the morphological and functional gap between the Palace Group and other residential complexes. Although the Palace Group is significantly larger than the others, its arrangement—surrounding a courtyard—is essentially the same as that of other domestic compounds. In particular, the architectural plans of the main living quarters (Structures M7-22 and M7-32) are similar to those of the dwellings excavated in the Causeway area. Moreover, public functions were not features unique to the Palace Group but were shared with many other residential units. Excavation data suggest that nobles conducted a significant portion of their administrative duties and received visitors in their own residences (Inomata 1995, 2001a, 2001b; Inomata and Stiver 1998; Inomata and Triadan 2000; Webster and Inomata 1998).

Identifying subroyal elite residences and extracting the unique attributes of such buildings are more problematic. Various data, including the proximity to the royal compound, rich material possessions, and glyphic texts, suggest that the residents of Structures M7-35, M8-4, M8-8, and M8-10 in the Causeway area were important members of the Aguateca royal court and can be called elites. Questions remain concerning the nature of the Causeway area as a residential zone in relation to other parts of the center. Was it the only elite residential zone or the residential area of the highest level of elites? Or were there more elites of comparable power dispersed in other parts of the center (see Chase and Chase 1992, 2001)? Some data may imply the dispersion of the elite population throughout the center and consequently the less prominent position of the Causeway area. In particular, buildings of a similar size with three or more rooms are relatively common, not only in the area along the Causeway, but throughout the Aguateca center. Some of the largest residential units are found outside the epicenter. It is also possible that there were elite residences of smaller sizes and with different appearances that we simply cannot recognize. Some other lines of evidence, however, may suggest otherwise. The area along the Causeway might have been the only sector in the center where there were no house lots for intensive gardening. In addition, it is possible that the superiority of buildings in the Causeway area is marked by rather subtle indications, such as better masonry, stucco floors, and a small number of high-value objects in middens. Power and status may also have been signaled by features that did not preserve well, such as a finer finish on exterior walls (see Tozzer 1941: 87).

We also need to consider the practice of multiple residences. Since Aguateca and Dos Pilas were twin capitals, some courtiers may have periodically moved between the two centers (see Ball and Taschek 2001; Houston 1993). In addition, some elites may have possessed residences both in areas near the royal compound and in peripheral areas closer to their own subjects, kin groups, or agricultural lands (see Tourtellot 1993). Such a practice of multiple residences among elites is common in traditional complex societies.

Discussion

A small group of elites by definition possesses disproportionally strong power over the rest of the population. The study of such groups provides critical insights into the organization and processes of a society. For a better understanding of Maya elites, future research needs to be based on theoretically informed strategies. Giddens (1974) has laid out three important dimensions to which researchers should pay attention in such studies (see also Houston and Stuart 2001; Marcus 1983a; Mills 1956). The first dimension is the recruitment of elites—whether they come from small closed groups, such as a hereditary noble class, or from a broader social pool. The second is the social and moral integration of the elite—the nature of the social contacts and relationships among elites, and the degree to which elites share common ideas and a common ethos. The third dimension is how power is diffused in society. With regard to this question, Giddens has set two parameters. One is centralization, which refers to the degree that power is centralized in the hands of elites, or the degree to which elite power is limited by constraints imposed from below. The other is issue-strength, which concerns the range of issues on which elites can exercise their power.

The analysis of elite residences can be an effective tool in such studies of elite groups. For example, if a significant portion of Classic Maya elites lived in similar houses that were significantly larger than other residences and that had long histories of occupation, it might mean that elites were recruited primarily from a closed hereditary class, that they were closely integrated, and that their power could be applied to a wide range of issues, including the construction of their dwellings. The elite might well correspond to the top layer of a horizontally stratified, pyramid-shaped social structure, to use a simplified model. But if some elites lived in large houses while others occupied small domiciles, it might suggest that not all elites shared the same value systems—at least not about their dwellings—or that the power of some elites was rather restricted in terms of issue-strength and they could not exercise their power effectively in the construction of their houses. In this case, the social structure cannot be described as a layered-cake-like pattern even in the most simplified metaphor (McGuire 1983), and the elite group itself may have been internally diverse.

In the archaeological investigation of elite residences, researchers face two questions of different scopes. The first question, with a limited scope derived from easily observable archaeological data, is whether large, imposing buildings that are clearly recognizable on the surface were elite residences. The second question, with a broader scope based on theoretical inquiry, is whether archaeologists can identify all or most types of elite residences, potentially including both large and small houses. As to the first question, an increasing amount of data indicate that many of these buildings indeed accommodated those who may be called elites. Imposing architectural remains are particularly visible at medium-to large-sized centers with long occupation histories, such as Tikal, Caracol, and Copan. The results of excavations at these centers are providing multiple lines of evidence, including artifacts, burials, hieroglyphic texts, and iconographic data, which point to the elite status of the residents of such buildings (Chase and Chase 2001; Harrison 1970, this volume; Harrison and W. Andrews 1998; Haviland 1981). In particular, the extensive excavation program at Copan, aided by rich epigraphic and iconographic evidence, has demonstrated that such imposing buildings functioned as an expression of power and served to distinguish the privileged from the rest of the population (Ashmore 1991; E. W. Andrews V and Fash 1992; Fash 1991; Webster 1989; Webster et al. 1998).

With regard to the second question, our understanding is much more limited. Settlement patterns at small to medium-sized centers with shorter occupations are particularly important in addressing this question. Tourtellot (1993; Tourtellot, Sabloff, and Carmean 1992) found that the masonry buildings, many of them vaulted, at Sayil were too numerous for all to be elite residences, whereas masonry structures at Seibal were too few to accommodate all elites. He warned that elite residences are not readily recognizable on the ground. The settlement pattern at Aguateca may be understood to be between those at Sayil and Seibal. Although there are only a few vaulted buildings, structures with stone walls are relatively common. From the surface map alone, it is not easy to distinguish elite residences. Although, thanks to rapid abandonment, we could confirm that some of the masonry buildings at Aguateca were elite residences, we are still not certain whether all of them were. Moreover, at present Maya archaeologists do not have an effective means to identify elites who may have lived in less impressive structures.

The inability to identify elites who may have lived in modest residences significantly hampers the attempt to examine the aforementioned different dimensions of Classic Maya elite groups. An educated guess derived from archaeological data, epigraphic evidence, and ethnohistorical analogy is that a significant portion of Classic Maya elites may have come from the hereditary noble class. Still, one needs to consider the possibility that there existed different types of elites. Dwarfs and hunchbacks, who may have been recruited from various sectors of society, apparently occupied important positions in Maya royal courts (Chase and Chase 1994; Houston 1992a; Inomata 2001a; Miller 1985). These individuals had the potential of gaining significant power through the favor of the ruler. It is also possible that Classic Maya society had elected officials, comparable to the *nacom* in contact-period Yucatan described by Landa (Tozzer 1941: 112–113, 122–123). In addition, some religious specialists may have had strong power in relation to a rather restricted range of issues and may have lived in modest houses.

Since we now know with reasonable certainty that some of the most imposing buildings at large centers were occupied by elites, more research on potential elite residences at such sites as Aguateca, Seibal, and Sayil, where they cannot be clearly distinguished on the surface, seems to be a critical key to better understanding the nature of Maya elite groups. More data from these buildings may also provide important insights into the residents of medium-sized structures at large centers and their relations to those who lived in the most imposing houses. Although we may never be able to distinguish elites who occupied modest structures, data from less-imposing elite residences at small-to-medium-sized centers may hint at what one should look for in addressing this issue. For these purposes, contextual data obtained through extensive horizontal excavations will be indispensable (Webster et al. 1998; Webster and Inomata 1998). Some of the successful results of such extensive excavations carry important implications related to the foregoing research questions. For example, the most ambitious excavation program at Copan has been revealing commonalities and differences between various elite residences and their inhabitants (E. W. Andrews et al., this volume; Webster 1989; Webster et al. 1998). At Caracol, Chase and Chase (1994) have detected architectural features possibly related to dwarfs. Investigations into Maya elite residences, in which researchers can take advantage of rich epigraphic and iconographic evidence and the relatively good visibility of architectural remains on the surface, have a potential of making important contributions not only to an understanding of Maya society but to the archaeological study of elites in general.

ACKNOWLEDGMENTS

We are grateful to Dr. Juan Antonio Valdés and other personnel of the Instituto de Antropología e Historia de Guatemala for the permit to work at Aguateca and for their help. The Aguateca Archaeological Project has been supported by grants from Yale University, the National Science Foundation, the National Geographic Society, the Foundation for the Advancement of Mesoamerican Studies, Inc., the H. John Heinz III Charitable Trust, and the Mitsubishi Foundation.

NOTE

1. Questions related to the issue of elites are those of the royalty and nobles. Although the royalty and nobles may constitute a significant portion of the elite in certain societies, they are not synonymous with elites. Their definitions and criteria are emic and made in each society, and it would be misleading to establish specific a priori definitions for such categories. In this chapter, "the royalty" rather vaguely refers to the ruler and to individuals closely related to him or her through real or fictive kinship. In most cases, archaeologically recognizable royalty is limited to the immediate family members of the ruler who shared the same architectural compound. By "nobles," we mean individuals of a hereditary class associated with certain privileges, including the right to membership in the royal court. We do not intend to make a clear distinction between the royalty and nobles, and nobles and subroyal elites in our usage may include close offspring and relatives of the ruler. We do not necessarily expect that these operational definitions correspond closely with the emic notions held by the Classic Maya.

REFERENCES

Abrams, Elliot
1994   *How the Maya Built Their World: Energetics and Ancient Architecture.*
       Austin: University of Texas Press.
Adams, R. E. W.
1970   Suggested Classic Period Occupational Specialization in the Southern Maya
       Lowlands. In *Monographs and Papers in Maya Archaeology*, edited by

William R. Bullard, Jr., 487–498. Papers of the Peabody Museum of Archaeology and Ethnology, vol. 61. Cambridge, Mass.: Harvard University.

1974   A Trial Estimation of Classic Maya Palace Populations at Uaxactun. In *Mesoamerican Archaeology: New Approaches*, edited by Norman Hammond, 285–296. London: Duckworth.

Andrews, E. Wyllys, V, and Barbara Fash

1992   Continuity and Change in a Royal Maya Residential Complex at Copán. *Ancient Mesoamerica* 3: 63–88.

Andrews, George F.

1975   *Maya Cities: Placemaking and Urbanization.* Norman: University of Oklahoma Press.

Ashmore, Wendy

1991   Site-Planning Principles and Concepts of Directionality among the Ancient Maya. *Latin American Antiquity* 2: 199–226.

Ball, Joseph W., and Jennifer T. Taschek

2001   The Buenavista–Cahal Pech Royal Court: A Multi-Palace Court Mobility and Usage in a Petty Lowland Maya Kingdom. In *Royal Courts of the Ancient Maya*, vol. 2: *Data and Case Studies*, edited by Takeshi Inomata and Stephen D. Houston, 165–200. Boulder: Westview.

Beaubien, Harriet F., and Emily Kaplan

2000   A Textile-Clay Composite from the Ancient Maya World: A Previously Unreported Artifact Material. Paper presented at the 32nd International Symposium on Archaeometry, Mexico City.

Chase, Arlen F., and Diane Z. Chase

1992   Mesoamerican Elites: Assumptions, Definitions, and Models. In *Mesoamerican Elites: An Archaeological Assessment*, edited by Diane Z. Chase and Arlen F. Chase, 3–17. Norman: University of Oklahoma Press.

1994   Maya Veneration of the Dead at Caracol, Belize. In *Seventh Palenque Round Table, 1989*, edited by Virginia M. Fields, 53–60. San Francisco: Pre-Columbian Art Research Institute.

2001   The Royal Court of Caracol, Belize: Its Palaces and People. In *Royal Courts of the Ancient Maya*, vol. 2: *Data and Case Studies*, edited by Takeshi Inomata and Stephen D. Houston. Boulder: Westview Press.

Cowgill, George L.

1992   Social Differentiation at Teotihuacan. In *Mesoamerican Elites: An Archaeological Assessment*, edited by Diane Z. Chase and Arlen F. Chase, 206–220. Norman: University of Oklahoma Press.

Demarest, Arthur A.

1997   The Vanderbilt Petexbatun Regional Archaeological Project, 1989–1994: Overview, History, and Major Results of a Multidisciplinary Study of the Classic Maya Collapse. *Ancient Mesoamerica* 8: 209–227.

Demarest, Arthur, Matt O'Mansky, Claudia Wolley, Dirk Van Tuerenhout, Takeshi Inomata, Joel Palka, and Héctor Escobedo

1997   Classic Maya Defensive Systems and Warfare in the Petexbatún Region: Archaeological Evidence and Interpretations. *Ancient Mesoamerica* 8 (2): 229–254.

Drennan, Robert D.

1988   Household Location and Compact versus Dispersed Settlement in Prehispanic Mesoamerica. In *Household and Community in the Mesoamerican Past*, edited by Richard R. Wilk and Wendy Ashmore, 273–294. Albuquerque: University of New Mexico Press.

WHERE DID ELITES LIVE? **179**

Dumont, Louis
1970   *Homo Hierarchicus: An Essay on the Caste System.* Translated by Mark Sains-
       bury. Chicago: University of Chicago Press.
Elias, Norbert
1983   *The Court Society [Die Höfische Gesellschaf, 1969].* Translated by Edmund
       Jephcott. New York: Pantheon.
Fallers, Lloyd A.
1973   *Inequality: Social Stratification Reconsidered.* Chicago: University of Chi-
       cago Press.
Fash, William L., Jr.
1991   *Scribes, Warriors, and Kings: The City of Copán and the Ancient Maya.* Lon-
       don: Thames and Hudson.
Folan, William J., Joel D. Gunn, and María del Rosario Domínguez Carrasco
2001   Triadic Temples, Central Plazas and Dynastic Palaces: A Diachronic Analysis
       of the Royal Court Complex, Calakmul, Campeche, Mexico. In *Royal Courts
       of the Ancient Maya*, vol. 2: *Data and Case Studies*, edited by Takeshi Inomata
       and Stephen D. Houston. Boulder: Westview.
Giddens, Anthony
1974   Elites in the British Class Structure. In *Elites and Power in British Society*,
       edited by Philip Stanworth and Anthony Giddens, 1–21. London: Cambridge
       University Press.
Graham, Ian
1967   *Archaeological Explorations in El Peten, Guatemala.* Middle American Re-
       search Institute Publication 33. New Orleans: Tulane University.
Harrison, Peter D.
1970   The Central Acropolis, Tikal, Guatemala: A Preliminary Study of the Func-
       tions of Its Structural Components during the Late Classic Period. Ph.D. dis-
       sertation, University of Pennsylvania.
Harrison, Peter D., and Wyllys Andrews
1998   The Palaces of Tikal and Copán. Paper presented at the Dumbarton Oaks sym-
       posium "Ancient Palaces of the New World: Form, Function, and Meaning,"
       organized by Susan Toby Evans and Joanne Pillsbury.
Haviland, William A.
1981   Dower Houses and Minor Centers at Tikal, Guatemala: An Investigation into
       the Identification of Valid Units in Settlement Hierarchies. In *Lowland Maya
       Settlement Patterns*, edited by Wendy Ashmore, 89–117. Albuquerque: Uni-
       versity of New Mexico Press.
Haviland, William A., and Hattula Moholy-Nagy
1992   Distinguishing the High and Mighty from the Hoi Polloi at Tikal, Guatemala.
       In *Mesoamerican Elites: An Archaeological Assessment*, edited by Diane Z.
       Chase and Arlen F. Chase, 50–60. Norman: University of Oklahoma Press.
Houston, Stephen D.
1987   The Inscriptions and Monumental Art of Dos Pilas, Guatemala: A Study of
       Classic Maya History and Politics. Ph.D. dissertation, Yale University.
1992a A Name Glyph for Classic Maya Dwarfs. In *The Maya Vase Book*, vol. 3,
       edited by Justin Kerr, 526–531. New York: Kerr Associates.
1992b Classic Maya History and Politics at Dos Pilas, Guatemala. In *Epigraphy*,
       edited by Victoria R. Bricker, 110–127. *Supplement to the Handbook of Middle
       American Indians*, vol. 5, Victoria R. Bricker, general editor. Austin: Univer-
       sity of Texas Press.
1993   *Hieroglyphs and History at Dos Pilas: Dynastic Politics of the Classic Maya.*
       Austin: University of Texas Press.

Houston, Stephen D. (ed.)

1998 *Function and Meaning in Classic Maya Architecture.* Washington, D.C.: Dumbarton Oaks Research Library and Collection.

Houston, Stephen D., and Peter Mathews

1985 *The Dynastic Sequence of Dos Pilas, Guatemala.* Precolumbian Art Research Institute Monograph 1. San Francisco.

Houston, Stephen D., and David Stuart

2001 Peopling the Classic Maya Court. In *Royal Courts of the Ancient Maya,* vol. 1: *Theory, Comparison, and Synthesis,* edited by Takeshi Inomata and Stephen D. Houston, 54–83. Boulder: Westview.

Inomata, Takeshi

1995 Archaeological Investigations at the Fortified Center of Aguateca, El Petén, Guatemala: Implications for the Study of the Classic Maya Collapse. Ph.D. dissertation, Vanderbilt University.

1997 The Last Day of a Fortified Classic Maya Center: Archaeological Investigations at Aguateca, Guatemala. *Ancient Mesoamerica* 8 (2): 337–351.

2001a King's People: Classic Maya Royal Courtiers in a Comparative Perspective. In *Royal Courts of the Ancient Maya,* vol. 1: *Theory, Comparison, and Synthesis,* edited by Takeshi Inomata and Stephen D. Houston, 27–53. Boulder: Westview Press.

2001b The Power and Ideology of Artistic Creation: Elite Craft Specialists in Classic Maya Society. *Current Anthropology* 42 (3): 321–349.

in press War, Destruction, and Abandonment: The Fall of the Classic Maya Center of Aguateca, Guatemala. In *Abandonment of Centers and Villages in Prehispanic Middle America,* edited by Takeshi Inomata and Ronald Webb. Boulder: Westview Press.

Inomata, Takeshi, and Kazuo Aoyama

1996 Central Place Analyses in the La Entrada Region, Honduras: Implications for Understanding the Classic Maya Political and Economic Systems. *Latin American Antiquity* 7 (4): 291–312.

Inomata, Takeshi, and Stephen D. Houston

2001 Introduction. In *Royal Courts of the Ancient Maya,* vol. 1: *Theory, Comparison, and Synthesis,* edited by Takeshi Inomata and Stephen Houston, 3–23. Boulder: Westview Press.

Inomata, Takeshi, Erick Ponciano, and Daniela Triadan

1997 *Informe preliminar del Proyecto Arqueológico Aguateca: La temporada de 1997.* Report presented to the Instituto de Antropología e Historia de Guatemala.

Inomata, Takeshi, Erick Ponciano, and Daniela Triadan

1996 *Informe preliminar del Proyecto Arqueológico Aguateca: La temporada de 1996.* Report presented to the Instituto de Antropología e Historia de Guatemala.

Inomata, Takeshi, Erick Ponciano, Daniela Triadan, Bruce Bachand, Shannon Coyston, and Byron Castellanos

1997 Proyecto Arqueológico Aguateca: La temporada de 1996. In *X Simposio de Investigaciones Arqueológicas en Guatemala, 1996, Museo Nacional de Arqueología y Etnología,* edited by Juan Pedro Laporte and Héctor L. Escobedo, 403–416. Guatemala: Ministerio de Cultura y Deportes, Instituto de Antropología e Historia, and Asociación Tikal.

Inomata, Takeshi, and Payson Sheets

2000 Mesoamerican Households Viewed from Rapidly Abandoned Sites: An Introduction. In *Mesoamerican Households Viewed from Rapidly Abandoned Sites* (special issue), edited by Takeshi Inomata and Payson Sheets. *Mayab* 13: 5–10.

Inomata, Takeshi, and Laura Stiver

1998 Floor Assemblages from Burned Structures at Aguateca, Guatemala: A Study of Classic Maya Households. *Journal of Field Archaeology* 25 (4): 431–452.

Inomata, Takeshi, and Daniela Triadan

2000 Craft Production by Classic Maya Elites in Domestic Settings: Data from Rapidly Abandoned Structures at Aguateca, Guatemala. In *Mesoamerican Households Viewed from Rapidly Abandoned Sites* (special issue), edited by Takeshi Inomata and Payson Sheets. *Mayab* 13: 57–66.

Inomata, Takeshi, Daniela Triadan, and Erick Ponciano (eds.)

1998 *Informe del Proyecto Arqueológico Aguateca: La temporada de 1998.* Report presented to the Instituto de Antropología e Historia de Guatemala.

Inomata, Takeshi, Daniela Triadan, Erick Ponciano, Richard Terry, Harriet Beaubien, Estela Pinto, and Shannon Coyston

1998 Residencias de la familia real y de la élite en Aguateca, Guatemala. *Mayab* 11: 23–39.

Kent, Susan (ed.)

1990 *Domestic Architecture and the Use of Space: An Interdisciplinary Cross-Cultural Study.* Cambridge: Cambridge University Press.

Killion, Thomas W., Jeremy Sabloff, Gair Tourtellot, and Nicholas Dunning

1989 Intensive Surface Collection of Residential Clusters at Terminal Classic Sayil, Yucatán, Mexico. *Journal of Field Archaeology* 18: 273–294.

Kowalski, Jeffrey

1987 *The House of the Governor.* Norman: University of Oklahoma Press.

Kowalewski, A. Stephen, Gary M. Feinman, and Laura Finsten

1992 The Elite and Assessment of Social Stratification in Mesoamerican Archaeology. In *Mesoamerican Elites: An Archaeological Assessment*, edited by Diane Z. Chase and Arlen F. Chase, 259–277. Norman: University of Oklahoma Press.

Marcus, George E.

1983a "Elite" as a Concept, Theory, and Research Tradition. In *Elites: Ethnographic Issues*, edited by George E. Marcus, 7–27. Albuquerque: University of New Mexico Press.

1983b Introduction. In *Elites: Ethnographic Issues*, edited by George E. Marcus, 3–6. Albuquerque: University of New Mexico Press.

1983c A Review of Ethnographic Research on Elites in Complex Societies. In *Elites: Ethnographic Issues*, edited by George E. Marcus, 29–39. Albuquerque: University of New Mexico Press.

1992 The Concern with Elites in Archaeological Reconstructions: Mesoamerican Materials. In *Mesoamerican Elites: An Archaeological Assessment*, edited by Diane Z. Chase and Arlen F. Chase, 292–302. Norman: University of Oklahoma Press.

McGuire, Randall H.

1983 Breaking Down Cultural Complexity: Inequality and Heterogeneity. In *Advances in Archaeological Method and Theory*, vol. 6, edited by Michael Schiffer, 91–141. New York: Academic Press.

Miller, Virginia E.

1985 The Dwarf Motif in Classic Maya Art. In *Fourth Palenque Round Table, 1980*, edited by Elizabeth P. Benson, 141–153. San Francisco: Pre-Columbian Art Research Institute.

Mills, C. Wright
1956 *The Power Elite.* New York: Oxford University Press.
Mitamura, Taisuke
1970 *Chinese Eunuchs; the Structure of Intimate Politics* [Kangan]. Translated by Charles A. Pomeroy. Rutland, Vt.: C. E. Tuttle.
Mock, Shirley B. (ed.)
1998 *The Sowing and the Dawning: Termination, Dedication, and Transformation in the Archaeological and Ethnographic Record of Mesoamerica.* Albuquerque: University of New Mexico Press.
Palka, Joel
1995 Classic Maya Social Inequality and the Collapse at Dos Pilas, Peten, Guatemala. Ph.D. dissertation, Vanderbilt University.
Parker Pearson, Michael, and Colin Richards (eds.)
1994 *Architecture and Order: Approaches to Social Space.* London: Routledge.
Paynter, Robert
1989 The Archaeology of Equality and Inequality. *Annual Review of Anthropology* 18: 369–399.
Pendergast, David M.
1992 Noblesse Oblige: The Elites of Altun Ha and Lamanai, Belize. In *Mesoamerican Elites: An Archaeological Assessment,* edited by Diane Z. Chase and Arlen F. Chase, 61–79. Norman: University of Oklahoma Press.
Sanders, William T.
1989 Household, Lineage, and State at Eighth-Century Copan, Honduras. In *The House of the Bacabs, Copan, Honduras,* edited by David Webster, 89–105. Studies in Pre-Columbian Art & Archaeology, no. 29. Washington, D.C.: Dumbarton Oaks Research Library and Collection.
Satterthwaite, Linton, Jr.
1935 *Palace Structures J-2 and J-6, with Notes on Structure J-6-2nd and Other Buried Structures in Court 1.* Piedras Negras Preliminary Papers, no. 3. Philadelphia: University Museum, University of Pennsylvania.
Schneider, Jane, and Peter Schneider
1983 The Reproduction of the Ruling Class in Latifundist Sicily. In *Elites: Ethnographic Issues,* edited by George E. Marcus, 141–168. Albuquerque: University of New Mexico Press.
Stephens, John Lloyd
[1841] 1949 *Incidents of Travel in Central America, Chiapas, and Yucatán.* New Brunswick: Rutgers University Press.
Tourtellot, Gair, III
1993 A View of Ancient Maya Settlements in the Eighth Century. In *Lowland Maya Civilization in the Eighth Century A.D.,* edited by Jeremy A. Sabloff and John S. Henderson, 219–242. Washington, D.C.: Dumbarton Oaks Research Library and Collection.
Tourtellot, Gair, III, Jeremy A. Sabloff, and Kelli Carmean
1992 Will the Real Elites Please Stand Up? An Archaeological Assessment of Maya Elite Behavior in the Terminal Classic Period. In *Mesoamerican Elites: An Archaeological Assessment,* edited by Diane Chase and Arlen Chase, 80–98. Norman: University of Oklahoma Press.
Tozzer, Alfred M.
1941 *Landa's Relación de las Cosas de Yucatán: A Translation.* Papers of the Peabody Museum of American Archaeology and Ethnology, vol. 18. Cambridge, Mass.: Harvard University.

Webster, David

1989   The House of the Bacabs: Its Social Context. In *The House of Bacabs, Copan, Honduras*, edited by David Webster, 5–40. Studies in Pre-Columbian Art & Archaeology, no. 29. Washington, D.C.: Dumbarton Oaks Research Library and Collection.

1998   Spatial Dimensions of Maya Courtly Life: Problems and Issues. Paper presented at the Yale symposium "Royal Courts of the Ancient Maya," organized by Takeshi Inomata and Stephen Houston.

Webster, David, Barbara Fash, Randolph Widmer, and Scott Zeleznik

1998   The Skyband Group: Investigation of a Classic Maya Elite Residential Complex at Copán, Honduras. *Journal of Field Archaeology* 25: 319–343.

Webster, David, and Takeshi Inomata

1998   Identifying Sub-Royal Elite Palaces at Copán and Aguateca. Paper presented at the Dumbarton Oaks symposium "Ancient Palaces of the New World: Form, Function, and Meaning," organized by Susan Toby Evans and Joanne Pillsbury.

CHAPTER SEVEN

Access Patterns in Maya Royal Precincts

Rodrigo Liendo Stuardo

Introduction

This chapter examines the notion that architectural space is more than a mere representation of society; it is one of the primary means through which society is constituted. Following this idea, I try to highlight some aspects of social control in Classic Maya society by applying an analysis of access patterns (Hillier and Hanson 1984; Foster 1989; Moore 1992; Ferguson 1996; Blanton 1995) to a sample of prehispanic Maya royal compounds. The Palace at Palenque, the Central Acropolis at Tikal, and the Acropolis at Uaxactun are contrasted with similar data from Uxmal, Labna, Kabah, and Sayil. The study of access patterns is here believed to provide important indicators of how space was used, contributing a slightly different perspective on the cultural uses of space.

Built Environment and Anthropological Thought

Among architects and scholars who study the built environment, there is little agreement on many fundamental issues, including the nature of the medium itself, the basic units of organization, the meanings and functions of architectonic objects, and the relationships of built environments with symbolic systems. However, studies that focus on relations between social behavior and spatial organization are frequently surpassed by architectural analysis centering on aesthetic concerns relating to surfaces rather than context (Hillier and Hanson 1984). A corollary to this approach is the evaluation of social organization in normative terms. An example of this line of reasoning is exemplified by Lang's contention that "at any given time, the built environment reflects past and present concepts of normative patterns of behavior. We thus have a circular relationship in which social organization leads to patterns of built form and then social organizations, as they change, have to adapt to the affordances of the built environment and in their efforts to adapt they change the built world" (Lang 1987: 177).

The importance of architectural analysis in anthropological and archaeological research is undisputedly recognized, while an explicit anthropological theory pertaining to the built environment has only recently begun emerging (Blanton 1995; Ferguson 1996).

One of these recent attempts is McGuire and Schiffer's theory aimed at explaining the design of vernacular architecture. With this goal in mind, they define architectural design as a "process whereby social groups make choices concerning recurrent sets of activities" (1983: 278), and relate this process to the emergence of social inequalities, as reflected by a differential access to the resources used in the construction of architecture. They do not address the problem of how architecture itself becomes a resource used in the structuring of the social interaction that reproduces society. In this regard, McGuire and Schiffer do not deal directly with the more fundamental issue of how architecture affects society in an objective, material sense.

In conceptualizing the relationship between architecture and society, some researchers subscribe to a theoretical perspective in which the built environment reflects rather than constitutes society (Lang 1987: 166–177). According to this view, the built environment and the society responsible for its construction and maintenance reflect and are shaped by cultural templates that approximate cognitive models held by people in that society (Rapoport 1980: 287–289). Anthropologists who subscribe to this theory consider architecture to be a form of communication in which the primary meaning of architecture is cultural rather than behavioral. Current trends in Maya archaeology have stressed this perspective, looking for such templates (Ashmore 1986), and with improvements in ancient Maya text decipherment, buildings have been used as a metaphor for experiencing the ancient past of myth in the present (Schele and Friedel 1990).

In general terms, semiotic analysis of architecture envisions the built environment as an important medium through which a society conveys a symbolic message. Nevertheless, within the same approach there are several attitudes regarding the interaction of the built environment and society. Preziosi (1979: 77) considers the material structure of the built environment as partly architectonic in origin and partly cultural, and he suggests that the architectonic system metaphorically mediates between the cognitive environment and the physical environment. On the other hand, Ankerl (1981) favors a different semiotic approach, in which the sociological meaning of architecture is brought about by its capacity to structure face-to-face communication. Ankerl in this way focuses on how architectural space conditions, stimulates, and affects the network of communications. Accordingly, the built environment has to be studied in terms of the framework it provides for social activities.

The study of how architectural space conditions social interaction has triggered the development of a set of techniques using graph analysis as a universal frame of reference. These graphs are concerned with the description of space in a very abstract way (March and Steadman 1971; Scott 1971; Friedman 1975; Tabor 1976; Earl 1980; Baglivo and Graver 1983; Mitchell 1990; for applications in archaeology see Ferguson 1996; Moore 1992; and Foster 1989).

Schematically, a graph consists of a set of points called nodes that are connected by lines. In an architectural analysis, each architectural space is represented by a node and the routes of movement between spaces are represented by lines. One of the most useful properties of an analysis like this lies in its ability to provide a means of visual representation and a method of structuring spatial organization for the comparative analysis of architecture from historically and culturally varied contexts.

A Graphic Method for Architectural Analysis

There are several graphic methods available for architectural analysis (Hillier and Hanson 1984; Foster 1989; Hopkins 1987). In this study, two different analyses will be applied: gamma analysis (Foster 1989; Hillier and Hanson 1984) and an alternative approach measuring the interconnectedness of access within a structure based on the number of rooms and the number of connections among them (network graphs) (Moore: 1992).

Gamma maps are an analytical approach that reduce a set of interconnected rooms to standardized drawings (gamma maps) in which the rooms are represented by dots and their connections by linking lines (Foster 1989). The network of dots and connecting lines forms an access map of the structure under study:

> This map can be justified, in this case from an outsider's perspective (the carrier), the stance of the stranger, although it could have been from any point in the building. By justification it is meant that all points of a certain depth (that is the minimum number of steps taken to reach them from the carrier) have been positioned on the same horizontal line, subsequent depth values or lines parallel to the first. Given the rules of construction, any line will either connect with points on the same level of depth, or two levels separated by only one level of depth. (Foster 1989: 42)

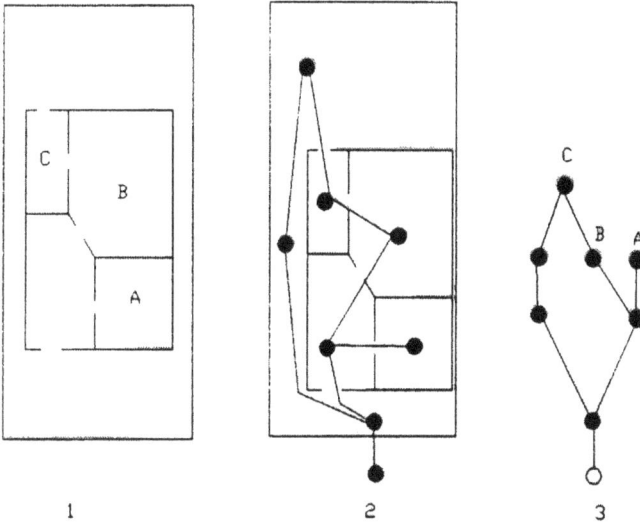

FIGURE 7.1. Justified and unjustified gamma maps: (1) plan view of modern house; (2) unjustified gamma maps; (3) justified access map.

This analysis could further be combined with a quantitative measure of interconnectedness of access within a structure based on the number of rooms (called vertices or V in network graphs) and the number of connections (edges or E). The maximum of interconnectedness is expressed by formulas that describe relations between the number of rooms (V) and the number of connections between rooms (E) (Moore 1992).

One possibility is that each room opens onto one and only one other room; then there will be one less connection than the number of rooms, a relation expressed by the equation $E = V - 1$; the result is a chain of rooms and a very restricted access plan (Moore 1992).

In an ideal network, unlimited by structural considerations, a full linked network is expressed by the slope of $E = 3V - 6$. In reality, the actual maximum slope will be less than $E = 3V - 6$, but values approaching $E = 3V - 6$ are closer to a pattern of unrestricted access.

Besides graphic representation, access patterns can be represented by a series of indexes, each having a slightly different property and measuring minor differences in a network. The simplest index is the beta index, $b = E/V$, which measures the overall complexity of the graph. Treelike and disconnected graphs tend to have beta indexes of less than 1.0; when the number of connections increases, the value approaches a maximum of 3.0. Networks may be composed of distinct subgraphs. The cyclomatic number (N) is used to characterize the overall complexity of the equation; as the num-

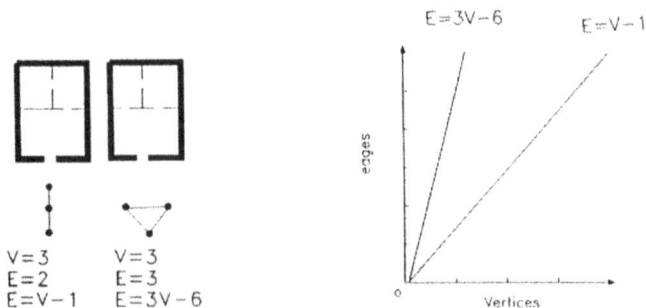

FIGURE 7.2. Graphic network representation.

Beta index: measures the overall complexity of a graph. B = E/V

The cyclomatic number (N) is used to characterize the overall complexity of a graph. E = the number of edges; V = the number of vertices; G = the number of subgraphs. N = E − V + G

ber of connections and the complexity of a graph increase, the cyclomatic number increases also. The cyclomatic number is given by the following equation:

$$N = E - V + G$$

where N is the cyclomatic number, E the number of edges, V the number of vertices, and G the number of subgraphs.

Contrary to the definition of space in archaeology (the distance between two points measured in two or three dimensions), connectivity maps treat space in terms of its formal and relational properties rather than its dimensional attributes (Hillier et al. 1976: 151–153).

According to this logic, spaces within buildings have different values depending on the distance from the "carrier" (or different degree of accessibility). Spaces are represented by circles and permeability by lines, and all spaces at the same depth are arranged horizontally above the carrier and connected with lines representing direct permeability.

Access Patterns in a Sample of Royal Compounds

A sample of several royal compounds were selected. They represent what one might expect to be the most restricted (in terms of access) sectors in any ancient Maya city. The sample consists of seven palace structures: one each in Palenque, Tikal, and Uaxactun, and four in the Yucatan Peninsula (at Sayil, Labna, Kabah, and Uxmal). They also account for two different periods: Classic (A.D. 250–950), the former, and Early Postclassic (A.D. 950–1250), the latter. Both samples were contrasted using graph analysis in order to answer two related questions regarding the nature of palace structures in the Maya area:

1. Could royal compounds have functioned as residential areas for the ruling elite?
2. Did access patterns change through time, responding perhaps to broader changes in political organization?

Palace Architectural Change in the Maya Lowlands

Several years ago, Kubler (1975: 152) made the interesting observation regarding northern Yucatan architecture that innovations which took place during the Late Classic and Early Postclassic might reflect major changes in Maya social organization. Although Kubler seemed to be comfortable with the idea that palaces in northern Yucatan served as permanent residences for the ruling elite, he was unwilling to assess a specific function for certain palace groups like the Nunnery Quadrangle at Uxmal, whose buildings he believed may have been palace groups or institutional dwellings—or even mere concourse centers with surrounding chambers for official ceremonies and storage (Kowalski 1987: 79).

The following graphic analysis supports Kubler's previous ideas about social change as reflected by change in architectural layout.

Table 7.1 shows a tendency to cluster in two different subgroups. Beta indexes for the structures analyzed tend to cluster around 1 with the exception of the Palace of Palenque (beta index = 1.80) and the Acropolis of Uaxactun (beta index = 1.16).

When the slope of the equation is close to $E = V - 1$, the result is a very restricted access plan. However, $E = 3V - 6$ expresses a very unrestricted one.

The depth of the gamma graphs also tends to cluster in two subgroups, with a depth very similar for the Palace in Palenque ($N = 17$), the Central Acropolis at Tikal ($N = 17$), the Acropolis at Uaxactun ($N = 12$), and the Nunnery complex at Uxmal ($N = 13$). The depth in the gamma graphs indicates the degree of accessibility of a building. It is interesting to note that although the overall complexity in the plan of the Central Acropolis at Tikal is much higher than that at Palenque or Uaxactun (reflecting a much longer period of construction), the depth in the gamma maps shows a very regular pattern among the three. This is in part due to the existence of more subsystems operating at the Central Acropolis at Tikal ($G = 28$) than in any other compound.

Table 7.1. *Differences in Accessibility between Palaces*

Structure Name	No. Rooms	No. Connections	Graph Depth	Access Ratio (Beta Index)
CLASSIC PERIOD				
Palace, Palenque	66	119	17	1.80
Central Acropolis, Tikal	159	174	17	1.09
Acropolis, Uaxactun	53	62	12	1.16
POSTCLASSIC PERIOD				
Nunnery Complex, Uxmal	105	105	13	1.00
Palace, Labna	70	64	8	0.91
Kodz Pop, Kabah	79	88	5	1.10
Palace, Sayil	114	116	5	1.01

When compared to southern lowland Maya buildings, the Early Post-classic structures of northern Yucatan show a much simpler access pattern. This is true for the Nunnery complex at Uxmal (N = 13), the Palace at Labna (N = 8), the Kodz Pop at Kabah (N = 5), and the Palace at Sayil (N = 5). Nevertheless, the beta index for all of them indicates a much more restricted access pattern.

In general terms, the apparent contradiction between beta indexes (B) and depth in levels of access (N) is the product of the existence in northern lowland structures of a very different building layout. In all the Yucatan cases, buildings are generally composed of long structures with several entrances in the front leading to rear rooms. These buildings commonly face open plazas, forming a compound. In several cases (Sayil, Labna, and Kabah), the main building in the compound is a two- or three-floor building, with different stories connected by a main staircase. This layout favored a use of space different from that characteristic of the royal compounds in the southern Maya lowlands.

This change in the general layout of Postclassic Maya royal compounds could be related to other changes in the visual arts as well as to major changes taking place in the political sphere. For example, stylistic differences in architecture and ceramics compared to the Classic period, such as the introduction of veneer masonry, the use of facades decorated with stone mosaic designs, the growing employment of columns in place of doors and vaults to open up rooms, and the demise of polychrome paintings on ceramics in favor of much simpler decorations. Before the end of Terminal Classic times, the carving of hieroglyphic inscriptions on monuments had completely died out (Sabloff 1990: 123).

Classic Maya political organization emphasized named rulers, ancestor veneration, the politics of warfare and marriage alliances, and trade and craft specialization (Blanton et al. 1996: 12). The development of a Maya lowland concept of kingship gave rulers a central place with respect to the political system.

For Postclassic times, there is a growing corpus of evidence suggesting a clear departure from Classic forms of rulership, especially with reference to the functions of the paramount ruler: "The dissolution of the kingship into a council of nobles . . . was . . . a fundamentally new and revolutionary definition of power and government for a people who had acknowledged sacred kings for a thousand years" (Schele and Friedel 1990: 361). At the time of the Spanish conquest, this form of rulership was designated as *multepal,* joint or confederate government.

From Classic to Postclassic times we see a gradual tendency for an emerging upper class to become more wealthy and powerful. "The accelerated construction of palaces may mean that this group was taking on greater bureaucratic functions, including the organization of larger labor forces and the management of food procurement and distribution for the increasing numbers of urban laborers" (Sabloff 1990: 142; see also Chapter 1, this volume).

Representation of particular rulers is scant, despite the considerable amount of iconography at many sites in northern Yucatan. Architectonic

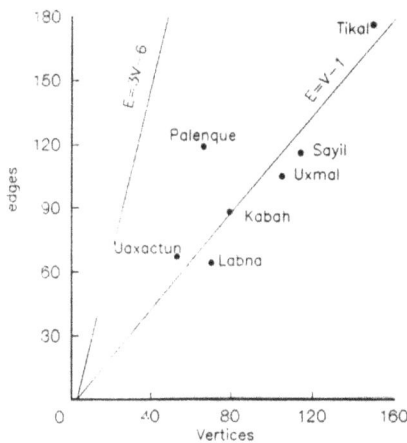

FIGURE 7.3. Palace structures. Plot of edges by vertices.

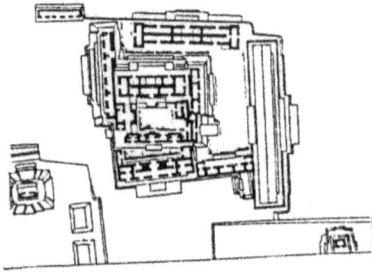

The Acropolis, Uaxactun.　　　　　　　　Gamma Map

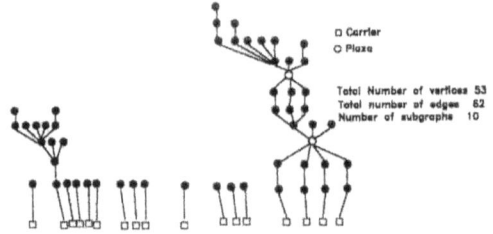

The Palace, Palenque　　　　　　　　Gamma Map

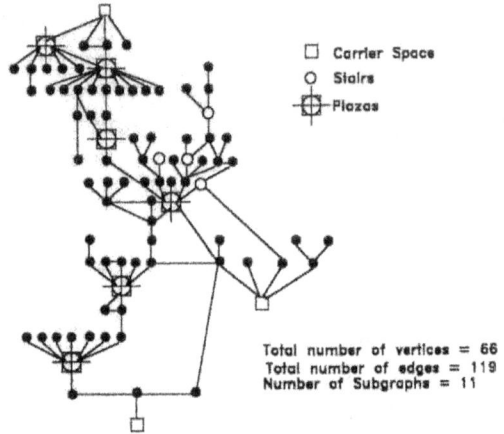

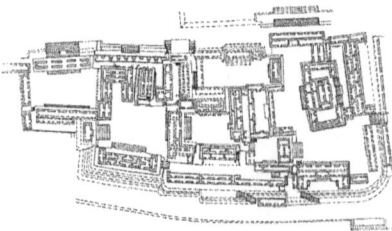

The Acropolis, Tikal　　　　　　　　Gamma Map

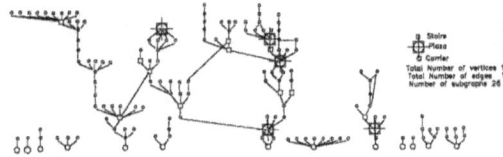

FIGURE 7.4. Gamma maps showing access patterns in a sample of Classic period Maya palaces.

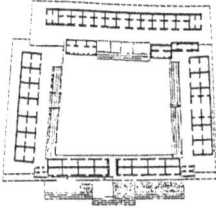

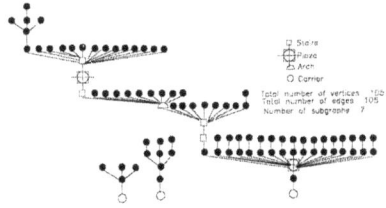

The Nunnery Complex, Uxmal   Gamma Map

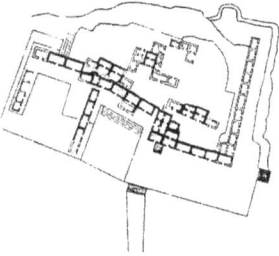

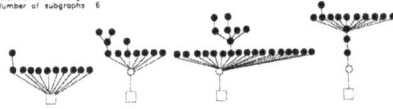

The Palace, Labna   Gamma Map

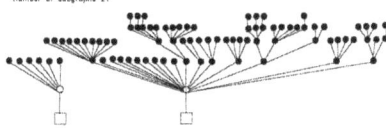

The Kodz Pop, Kabah   Gamma Map

FIGURE 7.5. Gamma maps showing access patterns in a sample of Postclassic period Maya palaces.

modification also testifies to a change in the political organization of Post-classic centers. Main plazas are larger and more open than previous Classic layouts. Moreover, the open colonnaded buildings on the main plazas suggest wider participation in ritual events.

Figure 7.4 shows that the Palace at Palenque, the Central Acropolis at Tikal, and the Acropolis at Uaxactun tend to have a more accessible and often a more complex layout in terms of the number of subgraphs, when compared to Postclassic buildings.

One of the major changes in the design of Maya royal compounds is, I believe, a change in the residential functions of Classic Maya palaces. During Classic times, the evidence seems to indicate an association of residential and other functions within palace structures. During the Postclassic period, these functions tended to be dissociated, which might indicate a shift in political organization as well—a shift from a society described by Webster (1989) as "court centered" to one evidencing the growth of a formal bureaucracy associated with the state.

Were Maya Palaces Elite Residence Compounds?

Although the use of the term "palace" is widely accepted for descriptive purposes, the disagreement concerning its function is a lingering problem in Maya archaeology today. Value-neutral terms, which refer to form rather than function, have been proposed to account for such buildings ("range-type structures," "multiroom buildings," etc.). The source of the confusion goes back to the sixteenth century, when Spanish writers described certain Maya structures as *palacios* because of their notable size and decoration. No clear definitional criteria have been used for the denotation of palaces. The term has been applied indiscriminately to a wide range of building types whose major feature in common is that they are distinguished from temples (see Introduction, this volume).

Pollock offered a widely accepted definition of the distinction between palaces and temples: "temples and shrines in their most typical forms, because of the restricted interior arrangements and exalted location of the former and the diminutive size of the latter, seem fairly certainly to have housed the esoteric rites of a selected priesthood. . . . whereas the term palace is used primarily for multiroom structures that most often rest on relatively low substructures" (Pollock 1965: 409–411).

Among researchers of pre-Hispanic Maya society, ideas about the functions of palace structures remain somewhat polarized. Some scholars hold that the palaces were not used as residences. Instead, it is argued, they were important public buildings which may have been used for administrative purposes, for storage of ritual objects, and perhaps from time to time as temporary quarters for priests and novitiates (Thompson 1954: 57–58). Satterthwaite (1935: 20) argues that because of the general discomfort of the interiors and the difficulties implied in transporting drinking water from the Usumacinta River, Piedras Negras palaces could hardly have been used on a permanent basis for housing the nobility of the site.

Evon Z. Vogt, using a rather different line of reasoning, arrived at a similar conclusion regarding palaces as permanent residences of the Maya elite. Based on ethnographic analogy, he opposed the idea that the central masonry buildings were used on a permanent basis. For Vogt, the lowland Maya settlement pattern, as defined by Bullard and Willey, could be interpreted in the same terms as the pattern in highland Chiapas, where a ceremonial center or vacant town is surrounded by outlying hamlets whose inhabitants engage in a cyclical delegation of religious administrative duties according to a system known as the *cargo* (burden of office) (Vogt 1964: 23–30). To fulfill their official burdens or responsibilities, they reside temporarily in the ceremonial center.

Some of the arguments for the unlikely use of palace structures as permanent residences of the Maya nobility seem currently controversial. Their judgments concerning the comfort of the palaces have been criticized as being ethnocentric, and it has been pointed out that other social considerations, such as a desire for prestige, could have outweighed the value of comfort in the design of elite dwellings (Kowalski 1987: 79). On the other hand, recent epigraphic research revealing the dynastic history of several Maya sites and the burst of settlement pattern projects in the lowland Maya area in the last twenty years have cast doubts (to say the least) on the validity of Vogt's use of contemporary highland Maya analogies to explain the structure of pre-Hispanic Maya settlement patterns (Price 1974: 461).

A. M. Tozzer could be considered one of the earliest scholars to propose a residential function for palaces. He explicitly recognized a residential function for all the buildings in the Central Acropolis of Tikal (Tozzer 1911: 85). Tozzer based his argument on the clear differences between temples (for which ritual functions had long been established) and multiroom structures that indicated some form of residential function. Herbert Spinden also embraced the idea of palaces as residences for nobles but suggested, at the same time, the inherent difficulties of trying to delimit specific residential, as opposed to ritual, functions for palaces. For Spinden, there was a clear merging of ritual and secular functions in palace buildings (Spinden 1913: 98). Following Spinden, Kubler (1975: 152) and Pollock (1965: 409–411) have mentioned the extreme difficulty of dividing ancient Maya buildings into separate classes (see Introduction, this volume).

By use of direct archaeological evidence, several authors have tried to pin down the functional character of palace compounds in the Maya area. The evidence reported by A. L. Smith at Uaxactun (1950) allowed the author to suggest that palaces were mainly residential dwellings for the ruling elite. He acknowledges, however, the difficulties of making absolute distinctions between temples and palaces. Pollock (1965), using the same information, makes the case for a variety of functions for different palaces structures in the lowlands. At Uaxactun, he suggests, some palaces might have had a domiciliary as well as religious function, whereas at Piedras Negras the same type of buildings apparently might have been meeting places or audience halls rather than residences.

According to W. R. Bullard (1960), the ruling elite in Maya sites "lived in the often enormous palace-type buildings which occur near the center of such sites" (p. 60), as evidenced by the settlement pattern structure in the northeastern Peten.

One of the most thorough attempts to identify the possible function of palace-like structures in the Maya area is Peter Harrison's (1970) study of the Central Acropolis of Tikal. Harrison notes that the Central Acropolis was used as a continuous residence for a very long sequence of Tikal history. The spatial layout of buildings consisting of large numbers of well-lit and well-ventilated rooms could strongly support the notion that the buildings were suitable for permanent living. The long sequence of occupation is further attested to by the numerous alterations to the original plan made through the addition of new rooms, patios, and corridors in order to accommodate continuous growth in the number of dwellers. Harrison calculated that about two hundred people may have occupied the Central Acropolis on a full-time basis at the end of the Late Classic period (A.D. 750).

The basic similarity of plan between the houses of the poor and the houses of the nobility suggests, according to Kowalski (1987: 82), the residential function of palace structures.

Using several graphical methods available for architectural analysis, this study supports the notion of palace structures as residential loci for the ruling elite in ancient Maya society. The discussion of new archaeological data from the Palace at Palenque will further strengthen this position.

The Palace at Palenque

In the Palace at Palenque, the depth of different levels of access provides an interesting case. One of the subgroups in the gamma map represents the southern section of the Palace (Figure 7.6).

The main access to the southeastern section is from the south. The sec-

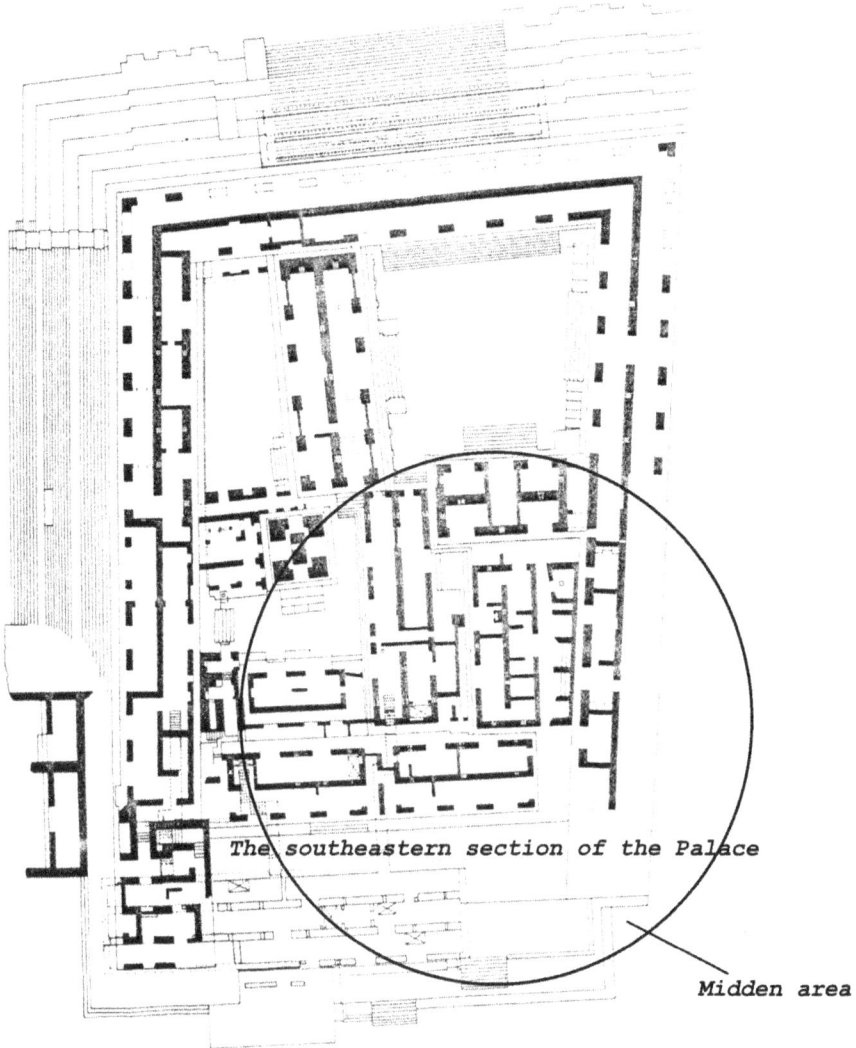

The southeastern section of the Palace

Midden area

FIGURE 7.6. The southeastern section of the Palace at Palenque.

tion is isolated from the three other courts composing the Palace. The East Court is the main access to the Palace and probably served as public space for official performances (Robertson 1985; Ruz 1954). The access from here to the other sections (West Court, Tower Court, and the southeastern quarters) was highly controlled, as attested by the graph analysis. This difference in the internal architectural layout of the Palace leads us to think that this section had a more private character.

The southeastern section was the one that presented the "deepest" pat-

Table 7.2. *Ceramic Form Types Found at the Palace at Palenque*

Ceramic Form Type	Frequency	% of Total
Unslipped basins and jars	949	17.4
Slipped basins and jars	3,447	63.2
Vases	418	7.7
Bowls	556	10.2
Unidentified	83	1.5
Total	5,453	100.0

Table 7.3. *Lithic Material Found at the Palace at Palenque*

Type	Frequency	% of Total
Prismatic blade	1,339	97
Prismatic core	16	1
Flake	33	2
Total	1,388	100

tern if the carrier was coming from the north or west. In this regard, it represents an unusually segregated space within the compound. Access to the East Court and West Court was possible only through one point of entrance.

Several authors (Robertson 1985; Ruz 1962) have argued that this section might indeed have been the ruler's living quarters. There are several archaeological indicators that support this conclusion: the existence of a complex sewer system framing this area, the abundant utilitarian wares found in the corridors and floors of several structures forming the compound, and the existence of a sizable midden area in the southeast corner of the Palace containing several serving vessels, jars, figurines, needles, bone awls, obsidian blades, jade beads, and macrobotanical remains. The content of the assemblage is quite similar to what we would expect to find in association with household contexts. This evidence plus the segregated subsystems shown by the gamma maps might suggest a possible residential function for this area.

It is highly debatable that this inference could be extrapolated to the Central Acropolis of Tikal or the Acropolis at Uaxactun, but the similarities in access patterns and general layout in these three buildings suggest a similar function for some of the subsystems.

The most striking differences appear when the Classic palace buildings are compared to Postclassic ones. The results of graph analysis cast some doubts about the possibility of assigning residential functions to certain palace-like structures in Postclassic Yucatan. Two facts are particularly relevant in this regard. First, the evidence at Uxmal and other sites in northern Yucatan indicates that the surrounding residential zone appears to stop several hundred meters short of the perimeter wall around the central precincts (Tourtellot 1993). This situation is very different at Tikal, Copan, Palenque, and Uaxactun, where regal-ritual plaza precincts are situated at the center of densely occupied areas. Second, the shallowness of the graphs, which testifies to the existence of fewer subsystems for each building, indicates an apparent functional specialization among buildings.

Final Comments

Although graph analysis represents an important tool for emphasizing the similarities and differences among buildings, it does not yield any information about the meaning and use of specific spaces. This situation has

Table 7.4. *Faunal Remains Found at the Palace at Palenque*

Faunal Remains	Frequency (total counts)	% of Total
Unionidae	276	17.70
Unio digitatus	7	0.40
Unio cuprinus	81	5.20
Euglandina	2	0.10
Arca zebra	1	0.06
Anadara transversa	1	0.06
Carditamera floridana	1	0.06
Anomalocardia brasiliana	37	2.37
Oliva scripta	1	0.06
Pinctada mazatlanica	1	0.06
Spondylus princeps	1	0.06
Chama echinata	1	0.06
Morum tuberculosum	1	0.06
Agriocharis ocellata	3	0.19
Orthogeomys hispidus	213	13.68
Agouti paca	1	0.06
Canis familiaris	48	3.08
Odocoileus virginianus	37	2.37
Not identified	843	54.17
Total	1,556	100.00

led some to believe that graph analysis cannot fully work unless something is already known of the relevant social structure and the observed patterns in spatial arrangement can be related to known social structures in retrospect (Leach 1978). However, the combination of graph analysis with more conventional archaeological procedures can be used as an additional tool for developing new research questions and methods for pattern recognition.

The use of graph analysis and its applicability to the study of architectural features from an archaeological point of view can be justified for two principal reasons. First, the simplicity of the model makes it quite utile; it requires only the recognition of closed and open architectural spaces for its application. This is an important point for an archaeological application of the model, mainly because the identification of architectural functions is generally a difficult archaeological procedure. Second, the applicability of the method for archaeological purposes is enhanced by the variety of sources of information that can be used for diachronic and comparative analysis, rather than its being limited to archaeological excavations. Descriptions of houses that can be found in historical documents such as diaries, as well as the crude plans occasionally included in general ethnographic accounts, are also amenable to graph analysis. The method can be further improved with the addition of different sets of data, including, for example, room dimensions, room functions, decoration, and building materials (Blanton 1995: 26).

Although Hillier (1989) emphasizes the role of Durkheimian concepts of social integration in the social logic of space, the application of the method and techniques of graph analysis do not necessarily need to be subsumed under a concrete social model. For archaeological proposes, the simplicity of the model makes it a valuable tool for the empirical evaluation of social interaction.

In the above investigation of palace structures, much of the analysis consisted of verifying existing information about palace functions. Nevertheless, the application of graph analysis also revealed new patterns that deserve to be pursued in more detail. Hence, more empirical work is needed to develop a research program in which new data are collected.

REFERENCES

Abrams, Elliot M.
1987 Economic Specialization and Construction Personnel in Classic Period Copan, Honduras. *American Antiquity* 52: 485–499.

Andrews, George
1975 *Maya Cities, Placemaking and Urbanization.* Norman: University of Oklahoma Press.
Ankerl, Guy
1981 *Experimental Sociology of Architecture.* The Hague: Mouton.
Ashmore, Wendy
1986 Peten Cosmology in the Maya Southeast: An Analysis of Architecture and Settlement Patterns at Classic Quiriguá. In *The Southeast Maya Periphery,* edited by Patricia A. Urban and Edward M. Schortman, 35–49. Austin: University of Texas Press.
Baglivo, Jenny A., and Jack E. Graver
1983 *Incidence and Symmetry in Design and Architecture.* Cambridge: Cambridge University Press.
Blanton, Richard E.
1995 *Houses and Households. A Comparative Study.* New York: Plenum Press.
Blanton, Richard E., Gary M. Feinman, Stephen A. Kowalewski, and Peter N. Peregrine
1996 A Dual-Processual Theory for the Evolution of Mesoamerican Civilization. *Current Anthropology* 37 (1): 1–14.
Bullard, W. R., Jr.
1960 Maya Settlement Patterns in Northeastern Peten, Guatemala. *American Antiquity* 25: 355–372.
Coggins, Clemency C.
1975 Painting and Drawing Styles at Tikal: An Historical and Iconographic Reconstruction. Ph.D. dissertation, Harvard University.
Earl, C. F.
1980 Rectangular Shapes. *Environment and Planning* 7: 311–342.
Erasmus, Charles J.
1965 Monument Building: Some Field Experiments. *Southwestern Journal of Anthropology* 21 (4): 277–301.
Ferguson, T. J.
1996 *Historic Zuni Architecture and Society. An Archaeological Application of Space Syntax.* Anthropological Papers of the University of Arizona, no. 60. Tucson: University of Arizona Press.
Foster, Sally M.
1989 Analysis of Spatial Patterns in Buildings (Access Analysis) as an Insight into Social Structure: Examples from the Scottish Atlantic Iron Age. *Antiquity* 63: 40–50.
Friedel, David A., and Linda Schele
1988 Kingship in the Late Preclassic Maya Lowlands: The Instruments and Places of Ritual Power. *American Anthropologist* (3): 547–567.
Friedman, Yona
1975 *Toward a Scientific Architecture.* Cambridge, Mass.: MIT Press.
Harrison, Peter D.
1970 The Central Acropolis, Tikal, Guatemala: A Preliminary Study of the Functions of Its Structural Components during the Late Classic Period. Ph.D. dissertation, University of Pennsylvania.
Hillier, Bill
1989 The Architecture of the Urban Object. *Ekistics* 334/335: 5–21.
Hillier, Bill, and Julienne Hanson
1984 *The Social Logic of Space.* Cambridge: Cambridge University Press.

Hillier, Bill, Adrian Leaman, P. Stansall, and M. Bedford
1976   Space Syntax. *Environment and Planning* 3: 147–185.
Hopkins, M. R.
1987   Network Analysis of the Plans of Some Teotihuacán Apartment Compounds. *Environment and Planning* 14: 387–406.
Kowalski, Jeff K.
1987   *The House of the Governor. A Maya Palace at Uxmal, Yucatan, Mexico.* Norman: University of Oklahoma Press.
Kubler, George
1975   *The Art and Architecture of Ancient America.* 2d ed. Harmondsworth, England: Penguin.
Lang, Jon
1987   *Creating Architectural Theory: The Role of the Behavioral Sciences in Environmental Design.* New York: Van Nostrand Reinhold.
Leach, Edmund R.
1978   Does Space Syntax Really "Constitute the Social"? In *Organization and Settlement: Contributions from Anthropology,* edited by David R. Green, Colin Haselgrove, and Mathew Spriggs, 385–401. British Archaeological Reports, International Series 471. Oxford.
March, Lionel, and Philip Steadman
1971   *The Geometry of Environment.* London: RIBA Publications.
McGuire, Randall H., and Michael B. Schiffer
1983   A Theory of Architectural Design. *Journal of Anthropological Archaeology* 2: 277–303.
Mitchell, William J.
1990   *The Logic of Architecture: Design, Computation, and Cognition.* Cambridge, Mass.: MIT Press.
Moore, Jerry D.
1992   Pattern and Meaning in Prehistoric Peruvian Architecture: The Architecture of Social Control in the Chimu State. *Latin American Antiquity* 3 (2): 95–113.
Pollock, H. E. D.
1965   Architecture of the Maya Lowlands. In *Handbook of Middle American Indians.* Vol. 2, *Archaeology of Southern Mesoamerica,* edited by G. R. Willey, 378–440. Austin: University of Texas Press.
Preziosi, Donald
1979   *The Semiotic of the Built Environment: An Introduction to Architectonic Analysis.* Bloomington: Indiana University Press.
Price, B. J.
1974   The Burden of Cargo: Ethnographical Models and Archaeological Inference. In *Mesoamerican Archaeology: New Approaches,* edited by Norman Hammond, 445–465. Austin: University of Texas Press.
Rapoport, Amos
1980   Vernacular Architecture and the Cultural Determinants of Forms. In *Buildings and Society,* edited by Anthony D. King, 283–305. London: Routledge and Kegan Paul.
Robertson, Merle G.
1985   *The Sculpture of Palenque: The Late Buildings of the Palace.* Vol. 3. Princeton: Princeton University Press.
Ruz Lhuillier, A.
1954   Exploraciones en Palenque: 1952. In *Anales del Instituto Nacional de Antropología e Historia* 6 (34): 79–112. Mexico City: Secretaría de Educación Pública.

1962 Exploraciones arqueológicos en Palenque, 1957. In *Anales del Instituto Nacional de Antropología e Historia* 14: 35–90.
Sabloff, Jeremy A.
1990 *The New Archaeology and the Ancient Maya.* Scientific American Library. New York: W. H. Freeman.
Satterthwaite, Linton, Jr.
1935 *Palace Structures J-2 and J-6.* Piedras Negras Preliminary Papers, no. 3. Philadelphia: University Museum, University of Pennsylvania.
Schele, Linda, and David Friedel
1990 *A Forest of Kings.* New York: William Morrow.
Scott, Allen
1971 *Combinatorial Programming, Spatial Analysis and Planning.* London: Methuen.
Smith, A. Ledyard
1950 *Uaxactun, Guatemala: Excavations of 1931–1937.* Carnegie Institution of Washington Publication 588. Washington, D.C.
Spinden, Herbert J.
1913 *A Study of Maya Art.* Memoirs of the Peabody Museum of American Archaeology and Ethnology, vol. 6. Cambridge, Mass.: Harvard University.
Tabor, Philip
1976 Analyzing Route Patterns. In *The Architecture of Form*, edited by Lionel March, 352–378. Cambridge: Cambridge University Press.
Thompson, J. E. S.
1954 *A Presumed Residence of the Nobility at Mayapan.* Current Report 19. Carnegie Institution of Washington. Cambridge, Mass.: Department of Archaeology.
Tourtellot, Gair
1993 A View of Ancient Maya Settlements in the Eighth Century. In *Lowland Maya Civilization in the Eighth Century A.D.*, edited by Jeremy A. Sabloff and John S. Henderson, 219–243. Washington, D.C.: Dumbarton Oaks.
Tozzer, Alfred M.
1911 *A Preliminary Study of the Ruins of Tikal, Guatemala.* Memoirs of the Peabody Museum of American Archaeology and Ethnology, vol. 5, no. 2. Cambridge, Mass.: Harvard University.
Vogt, Evon Z.
1964 Some Implications of Zinacantan Social Structure for the Study of the Ancient Maya. *Actas y Memorias del 35° Congreso Internacional de Americanistas* 1: 307–319. Mexico City.
Webster, David
1989 *The House of the Bacabs.* Studies in Pre-Columbian Art and Archaeology 29. Washington, D.C.: Dumbarton Oaks.

CHAPTER EIGHT

Evidence for the Functions and Meanings of Some Northern Maya Palaces

Jeff Karl Kowalski

In Maya studies, a long-lived distinction has been made between "palaces," which are typically defined as large, range-type, vaulted masonry multi-room structures, or as architectural groups composed of several such multi-room structures surrounding small plazas or patios, and "temples," which are smaller structures with more restricted interior space constructed in more inaccessible locations atop high pyramidal substructures (Satterth-waite 1943; Pollock 1965; G. F. Andrews 1975). In their discussion of courtly life, Schele and Miller (1986: 133) suggest that the Maya palace was a place where the sophistication and social complexity of ancient Maya society was perhaps most evident. The large scale and spatial complexity of these buildings, their associated architectural sculpture and mural paintings, as well as the remaining furnishings within, including niches, benches, thrones, and cordholders for the tying of fabrics and mattings, suggest that many Maya palaces were multiuse structures which simultaneously served as elite residences, administrative centers, and settings for dramatic rituals.[1] In other words, like most chiefly royal residences throughout the world, they housed a myriad of important people involved in a spectrum of both personal and official bureaucratic state-level activities, as well as specialized rituals of rulership. In this chapter I discuss evidence regarding the possible uses, symbolic significance, and sociocultural roles of palace architecture at several sites in the northern Maya area.

Palace Groups in the Western Puuc Region

A regional variant of early Puuc architecture occurs at a number of western Puuc sites located in southwestern Yucatan state and Campeche. At Xcalumkin, Xculoc, Xcocha, and other sites, buildings associated with eighth-century dates display a blend of early and late Puuc traits (Pollock

1980; Gendrop 1983; G. F. Andrews 1986).[2] At Xcalumkin the distribution and layout of palace groups, as well as references to several individuals bearing the title of *sajal* (a regional governor or subordinate lord), suggest that the site may have had an early form of conciliar government known as *multepal* (joint or crowd rule) (Grube 1994: 319–323).

Xcalumkin consists of a compact central sector, known as the Main Group, surrounded by "a semicircle of buildings located on natural rises" (Pollock 1980: 419).[3] Pollock (1980: 419–420, figs. 702–703) describes the Main Group, which includes the vaulted palace known as the Initial Series Building and Initial Series Court, as "a tightly packed arrangement of contiguous and connecting courts and plazas, from which radiate more isolated buildings and groups of buildings, often located on hilltops." Many of the masonry buildings have several vaulted rooms. In some cases, the exterior doorways are divided by circular columns. Such columns, along with doorjambs, lintels, and wall panels, were areas used for relief sculpture and hieroglyphic inscriptions. The Hieroglyphic Group, located some 400–500 m south of the Main Group, features several multiroom vaulted structures defining a northern and southern court (Figure 8.1). Judging from inscriptions surrounding the inner doorway of the south building, as well as from a figural panel (no. 5) flanking the door, a lineage lord named Kit Pa occupying this group held the *sajal* title (Pollock 1980: fig. 748; Grube 1994: 319–321, fig. 5).

Those who dwelt in the courtyard groups of masonry buildings were probably members of higher-ranking and more influential lineages at the site, perhaps along with various retainers. Their permanent stone houses contrast with the "numerous remains of what presumably were simple dwellings" that Pollock (1980: 419) observed in the savanna and on the surrounding hillsides, but which were not recorded on his sketch map.

Recent settlement pattern studies carried out in the vicinity of Xculoc (Becquelin 1994) have increased knowledge about the construction and spatial organization of palace groups in midsize western Puuc Maya centers, including Xcochkax, Chunhuhub, and Xculoc. Xcochkax occupies a central area of 8 hectares and consists of three principal architectural groups; it also includes an additional 6 hectares of area extending to the northeast. The entire site includes some 93 structures, 43 of which are vaulted. Xculoc is located in the middle of a small valley surrounded by hills. The site center covers an area of 5 hectares and contains 80 structures, some 43 of which are vaulted. Chunhuhub was built on the southern edge of a valley ringed by a series of hills, two of which are occupied by satellite architectural groups (Maler's Castillos 1 and 2). The site center covers some

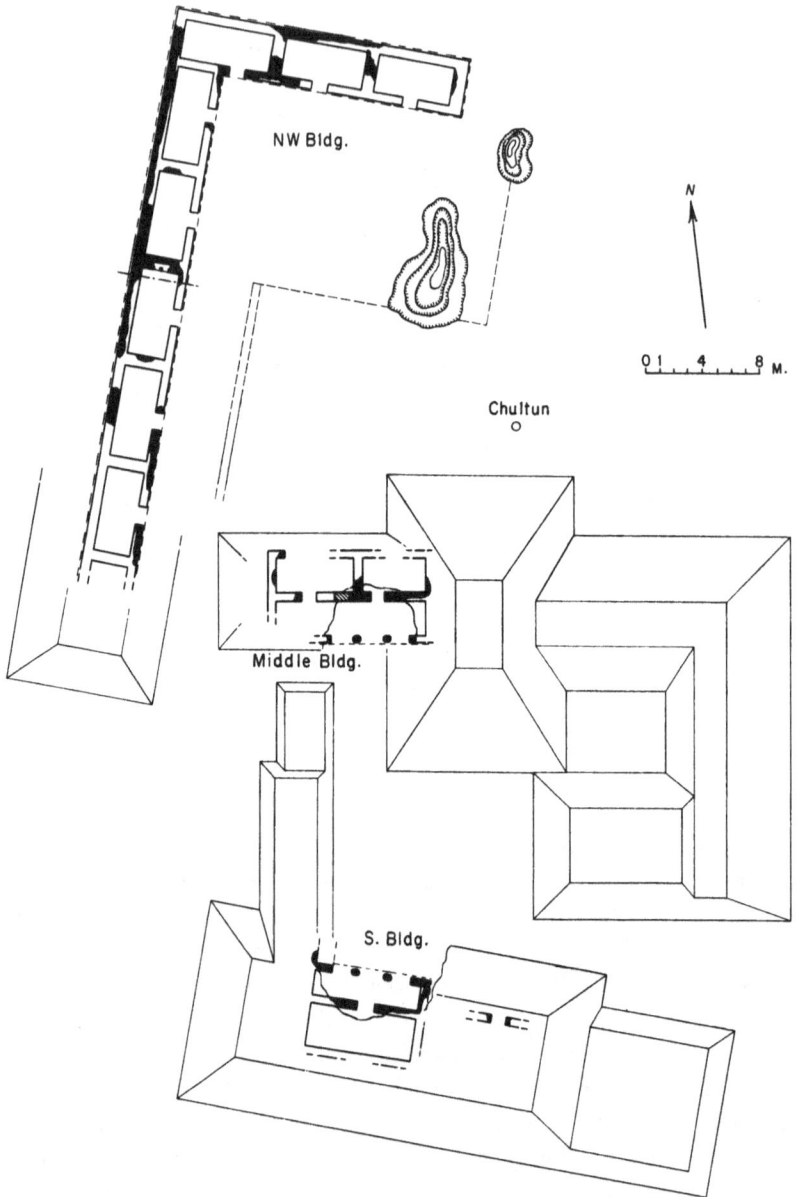

NW Bldg.

N

Chultun
○

0 1   4   8 M.

Middle Bldg.

S. Bldg.

FIGURE 8.1. Plan of the Hieroglyphic Group at Xcalumkin, Yucatan. (Figure 735 from H. E. D. Pollock, *The Puuc: An Architectural Survey of the Hill Country of Yucatan and Northern Campeche, Mexico,* Memoirs of the Peabody Museum, vol. 19, Copyright 1980 by the President and Fellows of Harvard College)

5 hectares with structures constructed on several platform surfaces and on the slope of a hill converted into three or four terraces. Some 78 structures have been recorded, of which 32 are vaulted. If room numbers are considered, then the ratio of vaulted to unvaulted structures actually is reversed at Xcochkax center, Chunhuhub, and Xculoc center. On this basis, as well as the fact that many of the groups containing vaulted buildings also contain associated perishable structures, *chultuns*, and *pilas* (basinlike water containers), Becquelin (1994: 62) argues that the majority of vaulted buildings were residential structures, although he also suggests that some of the larger vaulted buildings with more complex plans may have had other functions.

The excavation of E4-southwest at Xcochkax provides a good indication of the functions of various structures in such residential groups (Figure 8.2). This group, comprising a plazuela group consisting of both vaulted masonry and perishable structures built on a rather broad supporting platform containing three *chultuns*, was built up over time, but in its final phase it contained structures interpreted as residences (Structures 13, 12N, 9S), kitchens (Structures 12C, 9N), and a possible shrine or oratory (Structure 11). Based on the holding capacity of the *chultuns*, it is estimated that some twenty-one people lived in this complex (Becquelin 1994: 66–67), perhaps with an extended family of higher rank in the southern area and another, less important (or perhaps a son taking up patrilocal residence?) in the north.

According to Becquelin (1994: 70), the simultaneous existence during the Terminal Classic period of three important, comparable centers suggests that the political organization of the Puuc region may have been more complex than has been imagined previously. In the region comprising these sites, political organization may have differed from that of the northeast (i.e., the eastern Puuc or Santa Elena district), where there existed several prominent centers (e.g., Uxmal, Kabah, Nohpat, etc.) that could have controlled fairly extensive territories.

Palace Structures at Dzibilchaltun

The site of Dzibilchaltun, located in the flat plain north of present-day Mérida, was an extensive urban center with several hundred vaulted masonry or palace-type buildings (E. W. Andrews IV and E. W. Andrews V 1980; Kurjack 1974). After an occupational hiatus during the Early Classic period, Dzibilchaltun began to increase in population, to expand in size, and to undertake monumental construction projects once again during the

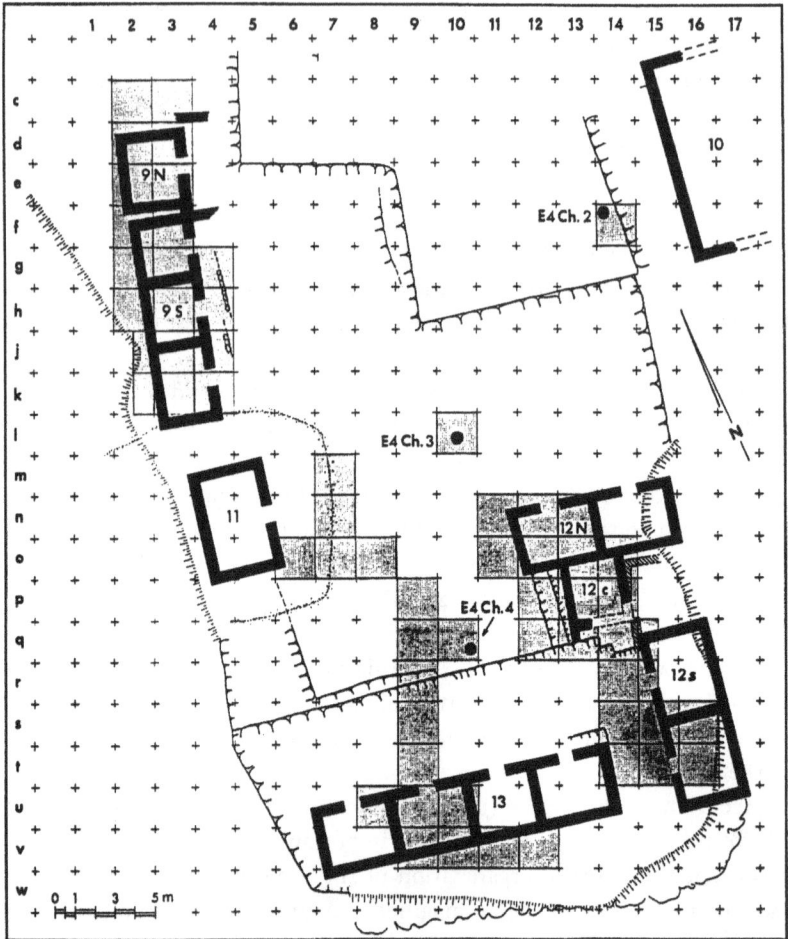

FIGURE 8.2. Group E-4 Southwest. Location of excavations and interpretation of the structures. (After Becquelin 1994: fig. 5)

seventh century and throughout the Late and Terminal Classic periods (ca. A.D. 650–950). Coggins (1983) has pointed out that Dzibilchaltun's city plan, which was apparently laid out during the seventh century, was influenced by the ancient Mayas' view of their cosmos (Figure 8.3). At the site, a prominent east-west causeway system that culminates in the east at the Temple of the Seven Dolls complex is bisected by shorter north-south causeways, so as to divide the site into four sections, thereby producing an approximation of the quadripartite arrangement of the world. These two axes converge at the center of the site, marked by a large plaza, a 134 m (ca. 425 ft.) long and 26 m wide palace building known as Structure 44 (E. W. Andrews IV and E. W. Andrews V 1980: 13; Maldonado C. 1994: 28), and the Cenote Xlacah, a natural sinkhole and spring which constitutes a kind of pivot in the planning scheme, and which undoubtedly was considered to be a passage to the underworld.[4]

Structure 44 is one of the longest range-type palace structures in the Maya world.[5] It surmounts a terraced platform with a broad, monumental stairway on the north leading to the principal facade (Figure 8.4). The front of the building featured some thirty-five doorways. Unlike many Maya palaces, in which such doors conducted to multiple separate rooms, those at Structure 44 led to only three extraordinarily long, single-vaulted corridor-like rooms. Its centralized location and prominent placement in the overall site layout suggest that Structure 44 must have been a particularly important edifice and probably had a significant public administrative, rather than purely private residential, function. What we know of Dzibilchaltun's sociopolitical organization, which can be gleaned from studies of its monumental art tradition and its settlement pattern, can assist with an interpretation of Structure 44's function.

Dzibilchaltun's monumental sculpture, such as Stela 19 or Stela 9 (E. W. Andrews IV 1965: fig. 14; E. W. Andrews IV and E. W. Andrews V 1980: 187–190; E. W. Andrews V 1978: figs. 8–10), depicts single, elaborately dressed

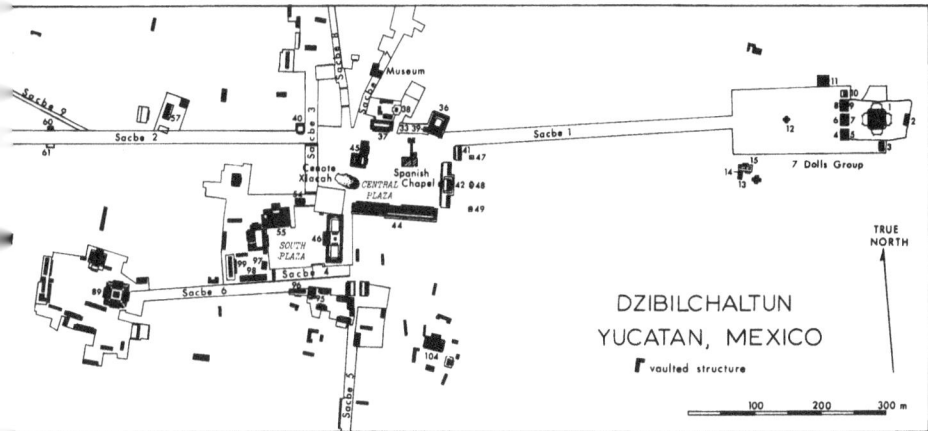

FIGURE 8.3. Map of the central portion of Dzibilchaltun, showing Sacbe 1 leading to the Temple of the Seven Dolls (Structure 1-sub) and the location of the major palace, Structure 44 on the south side of the Central Plaza. (After E. W. Andrews IV and E. W. Andrews V 1980: fig. 2. Courtesy of the Middle American Research Institute, Tulane University.)

FIGURE 8.4. View of Structure 44 and its monumental stairway, from the north. (Photograph by Jeff Kowalski)

individual rulers holding shields and carrying local versions of God K manikin scepters. These variations on the "Classic Motif" (image of a single elite personage; Proskouriakoff 1950) imply that Dzibilchaltun's political system was dominated by a paramount ruler, or *k'uhul ajaw*, during the site's Late Classic florescence. In fact, a king called U K'uy Kan is specifically referred to by a *k'uhul ajaw* title on Stela 19 (Schele, Grube, and Boot 1997; Schele and Mathews 1998). On the other hand, Edward Kurjack's (1974) study of the Dzibilchaltun settlement pattern demonstrates that there were some 240 examples of vaulted masonry structures at the site. In most cases, these structures form parts of interrelated compounds, termed platform-terrace complexes by Kurjack (1974: 92–93), sharing a common raised platform and centralized courtyard or courtyards, suggesting that they are the residential quarters for a series of local, prominent extended families or lineages. In several cases these elite house groups are physically connected to the site center by means of secondary *sacbes* (artificial roadways). In addition, these residential complexes "vary substantially in quantity and quality of constituent architecture." Some, like the complex comprising the Pure Florescent Structures 95, 95A, and 96, form part of larger residential courtyard groups, while others, like the late Early Period Structure 57 (the Standing Temple), are more modest in scale, form part of smaller groups, and were probably occupied by lower-ranked and less politically influential lineages

(E. W. Andrews IV and E. W. Andrews V 1980: 190–204, 207–232; see also fig. 2).

Based on what we now know about the sociopolitical organization of other southern Maya centers such as Copan (Webster 1989; W. Fash 1991: 130–137, 153–172; Abrams 1994), Yaxchilan (Schele and Freidel 1990: chap. 7), and Palenque (Schele 1991), where there is clear evidence for intra-site social hierarchy and for the presence of a variety of subsidiary political statuses occupied by the heads of high-ranking but nonroyal lineages (Villela 1993), it seems reasonable to assume that the lineage heads from the larger and more prominent of these various compounds would have formed some sort of advisory council to the *k'uhul ajaw* and that some sort of power-sharing arrangements existed. Perhaps Structure 44, with its central location and extraordinary plan featuring multiple doorways but only three long public chambers, would have constituted a kind of Popol Nah, or community administrative center, for the Dzibilchaltun polity.[6] Its location overlooking and dominating a spacious central courtyard suitable for large group meetings, receptions, and performances also supports this interpretation (Ringle and Bey [2001] provide a recent discussion of such courtyards as important foci for social, political, economic, and ritual activities connected with Maya royal courts; also see the discussion of the Nunnery Quadrangle at Uxmal in this chapter). The incorporation of all of Dzibilchaltun's residential assemblages within a fairly comprehensive, cosmically structured site plan suggests that such spaces, and the rituals and other activities which took place within them, provided an important mechanism for binding the polity together despite hierarchical and dynastic differences in wealth, power, and authority.

Palaces, Cosmic Charters, and Political Authority: Uxmal and the Puuc Region

Several of the most grandiose, sculpturally embellished, and iconographically rich palaces in the northern Maya region are located at Uxmal, which experienced its apogee during the Terminal Classic period from about A.D. 750 to 950 (E. W. Andrews V 1979; Kowalski 1987) (Figure 8.5). Uxmal emerged as the largest city in, and probably became the regional capital of, the eastern Puuc or Santa Elena district during the late ninth–early tenth century reign of its energetic ruler, "Lord Chaak" or Chan Chak K'aknal Ahaw (Dunning 1992; Dunning and Kowalski 1994; Kowalski and Dunning 1999; Schele and Mathews 1998).

The single most imposing palace building at Uxmal is the House of the

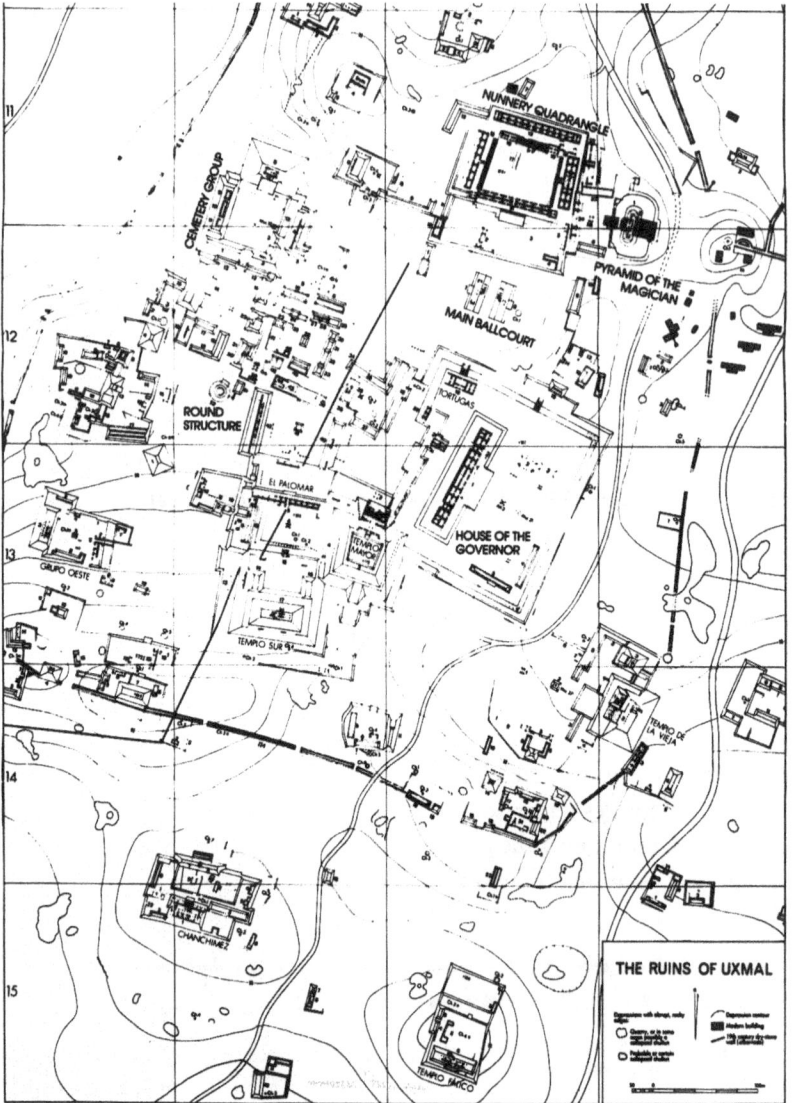

FIGURE 8.5. Plan of the civic-ceremonial center of Uxmal. (Adapted from Graham 1992, vol. 4: 83)

FIGURE 8.6. The House of the Governor at Uxmal, showing the radial platform supporting the two-headed jaguar throne in the foreground. (Photograph by Jeff Kowalski)

Governor (Figure 8.6). Uxmal Stela 14 shows Lord Chaak standing on a two-headed jaguar throne like that located on a small radial platform in front of the House of the Governor, suggesting that this grandiose palace building was probably constructed during this king's reign as a testament to his power and a symbol of his authority (Kowalski 1987; Graham 1992, vol. 4: 107, 108). The House of the Governor rests on a primary platform some 25–40 ft. (7–11.8 m) high and 540 ft. (160 m) long by 450 ft. (133 m) wide, one of the largest such basal platforms constructed in northern Yucatan.[7] The upper facade of this massive 99 m (ca. 328 ft.) long palace is covered by a complex array of architectural sculpture featuring latticework, step frets, and long-snouted Chaak masks (Foncerrada 1965; Kowalski 1987). Human figures of different sizes are shown seated along the eastern front of the building, culminating above the central doorway in the depiction of a dominant individual who wears a mat-weave medallion and a towering feather headdress (Kowalski 1987: chap. 10) (Figure 8.7). I have suggested that this is a portrait of Lord Chaak himself, who may have commissioned the House of the Governor as a royal residence or as an administrative center, or both (Kowalski 1987: chaps. 6, 10).

The extraordinary length, multiple doorways, and centralized location of the House of the Governor are reminiscent of Structure 44 at Dzibil-chaltun. In previous discussions, I have argued that the multiroom plan of

FIGURE 8.7. The figural sculpture above the central doorway of the House of the Governor, probably a portrait of the ruler known as Lord Chaak. (Photograph by Jeff Kowalski)

the House of the Governor, and the existence of several collapsed *chultuns* on its terrace, support the idea that some of its chambers were occupied by members of the royal family on a continuous basis. However, it should also be noted that the scale and formality of the structure, coupled with its placement on a broad platform that could have accommodated thousands of people, would support the idea that it had a predominantly public, nonresidential function. An argument can be made that the building also may have been a local version of a Popol Nah, where the ruler met in council with his subordinate lords to discuss affairs of state and plan community festivals (B. Fash et al. 1992: 438; Kowalski and Dunning 1999: 295). The symmetrical and hierarchical distribution of human figures of varying sizes suggests the concept of a paramount king, represented by the central figure of Lord Chaak, flanked and accompanied by other individuals of *ajaw* status, either local lineage heads or regional governors, or both, who formed his council of advisors. This arrangement of subsidiary personages accompanying a larger, centralized image of the king also appears, albeit in a slightly different composition, on Structure 22-A at Copan, a palace-type structure which has been most convincingly interpreted as a Classic version of a Popol Nah to date (B. Fash et al. 1992). At the House of the Governor, a two-headed jaguar throne is located in front of the sculpture of Lord Chaak, while at Copan the image of the ruler "Smoke-Monkey" was shown seated on a jaguar throne at the center of the roof comb. The presence of the two-headed jaguar throne at the House of the Governor also relates it to House E of the Palace at Palenque, another structure which has been identified as a *nikte' il nah* (white flower house), a version of a Popol Nah (Schele 1998: 499–500).[8]

The House of the Governor is also aligned so that its central doorway faces the horizon where Venus rises at its most southern extreme (Aveni 1980: 275; H. M. Bricker and V. R. Bricker 1996). The spectacle of Venus emerging from the underworld above the jaguar throne in front of the House of the Governor may have been calculated to connect the historical king with cosmic acts of creation (Kowalski, in H. M. Bricker and V. R. Bricker 1996).

Another of the most imposing architectural groups at Uxmal is the Nunnery Quadrangle, constructed around A.D. 890 to 910 during the reign of Lord Chaak (Figures 8.5, 8.8). In its plan and architectural sculpture program, the Nunnery Quadrangle embodies fundamental Maya cosmological concepts to convey the idea that Uxmal identified itself as the principal religious center and political capital of the eastern Puuc region. The quadrangular layout and approximate correspondence of the principal buildings to the cardinal points represents an effort to replicate the quadripartite horizontal organization of the Maya cosmos, with east and west associated with the rising and setting sun, and with north and south corresponding to the upperworld and underworld. Further, much of the iconography of the quadrangle can be associated with Maya creation mythology, which served as a divine charter for kingship and functioned periodically to ritually renew the bonds between the ruler, the gods, the ancestors, and the living community (see Kowalski 1994a; Dunning and Kowalski 1994; Kowalski and Dunning 1999). Here we will only mention a few of these cosmological motifs to convey their general significance.

The West Structure features the aged turtle-man earth deity God N. This

FIGURE 8.8. View of the Nunnery Quadrangle at Uxmal, seen from Temple IV of the Pyramid of the Magician. (Photograph by Jeff Kowalski)

deity, also known as Bacab or Pawahtun, is the Maya world sustainer, an earth- and sky-bearer who is associated with the partitioning of the world and who plays an important role in Maya creation myth (Schele and Miller 1986: 4, 61; Taube 1992a). As a Bacab, he is associated with the great flood that preceded the formation of the present world and with the raising of the Trees of Abundance at the quadrants of the world. He is also associated with the establishment of a world axis by the raising of the Yaxcheelcab, the First Tree of the World (Tozzer 1941: 135–137).

Small miniature Maya huts crowned by reptilian masks and sprouting vegetation scrolls appear above the doorways of the South Structure of the Nunnery (Dunning and Kowalski 1994: 84). These images recall the maize plant rising from a reptilian earth monster on the Tablet of the Foliated Cross at Palenque (Maudslay 1889–1902, vol. 4: pl. 81), as well as a related depiction of a leafy maize god emerging from a cleft with a monster/turtle carapace on the sculpted pillars of the Lower Temple of the Jaguars at Chichen Itza (Seler [1902–1923] 1960, vol. 5: fig. 162). Other emergence or resurrection scenes on Late Classic polychrome vases suggest that the young maize god rising from a turtle carapace is a variant of Hun Hunahpu, the first father of the Hero Twins in the Popol Vuh and a solar-maize deity who is reborn annually in the underworld (Taube 1985). The maize-sprouting masks of the South Structure of the Nunnery seem to pertain to this mythic complex, referring to the regeneration of the maize/sun god within the earth.

A massive cylindrical stone column stood at the conceptual center of the Nunnery Quadrangle. This column embodied the Yaxcheel Cab, the gigantic ceiba tree that formed the central axis of the cosmos (Roys [1933] 1967: 161; Kowalski 1994a: 110–111). The erection of this tree was the action that separated the sky from the earth at the time of creation, which was associated with the "partitioning" of the world and which preceded the creation of a new humanity and the subsequent establishment of legitimate political order (Freidel, Schele, and Parker 1993: 66–68). In this connection, Ringle and Bey (2001: 270) have pointed out that a fairly rare term, *tzucub te*, which appears in the Chilam Balam of Tizimin, seems to be associated with various cities (e.g., Mayapan, Chetumal) that functioned as "cycle seats" and perhaps metaphorically identifies them as capitals connected with the world tree.

A single-headed jaguar throne originally stood on a low platform near the central stone column/world tree monument (Ruz Lhuillier 1959: 14; Kowalski 1994a: 112). Such jaguar seats function as royal thrones in Classic Maya art (Kowalski 1987: chap. 14), and apparently represent one of the three "throne-stones" which were occupied by deities at the time of creation (Freidel, Schele, and Parker 1993: 65–67). At Uxmal the link between the jaguar throne and the columnar world tree apparently associated the ruler with primordial acts of world creation and served as a divine charter for kingship. Many of the other sculptural motifs at the Nunnery, such as feathered serpent sculptures, Tlaloc masks, and captive figures, although not as clearly associated with Maya creation myth, also can be interpreted as symbols of rulership and political authority (Kowalski 1994b).

Recently Schele and Mathews (1998: 269) have described the complex lattice on the North Building of the Nunnery as a "flower lattice" and suggested that it "replicates a kind of flower-laden scaffolding once used in Maya ritual," as well as marking the structure as a variant of a *nikte' il nah* (flower house), another name for the community house corresponding to the Popol Nah type of building mentioned earlier. As noted, the Popol Nah is described as a building where the council members also met to practice dancing and to plan public festivals. This aspect of the North Structure may be supported by the presence of several musicians among the figural facade sculptures. Schele and Mathews (1998: 271–272) have also identified the uppermost masks placed above the small thatched roof hut models above doorways 3 and 5 as personified versions of the *ch'ok* ("sprout" or "young person") glyph in the inscriptions. Noting that at Copan and several other Classic sites the word for lineage was *ch'ok-te-nah* (sprout-tree-house), they further argue that these masks identify the North Building as a lineage house. In addition, the lower masks of the stacked mask towers are identified as variants of Itzam Yeh on the basis of their flower headdresses, thus indicating that the North Building served as a conjuring house, a "place of sorcery and magic" (Schele and Mathews 1998: 275). While these interpretations are not certain, they indicate the complex, multivocal symbolism evident on these structures.

An association between the Nunnery Quadrangle and the dynastic founder of Uxmal may appear in the architectural sculpture of the East Structure. I have previously suggested that the distinctive reticulated owl sculptures located at the center of the tiered serpent bar arrangements above East Structure's doorways pertain to a Teotihuacan-related cult of war and sacrifice connected with Venus and the emergence of the Sun from the underworld (Kowalski 1994a: 108–110; Dunning and Kowalski 1994: 84–85) (Figure 8.9). Classic Maya art often features owls coupled with other prominent Teotihuacan-derived costume elements and iconographic motifs in contexts associated with warfare and captive or personal sacrifice (Stone 1989; Schele and Freidel 1990: 156–164, 443–444, n. 45). Taube (1992b: 2, 37) has related the reticulated appearance of the Uxmal owls to the appearance of the "war serpent" creatures, which alternate with feathered serpent heads on the Old Temple of Quetzalcoatl at Teotihuacan and which also occur as a basic component of the Teotihuacan warrior complex in Classic Maya art. He suggests that such Teotihuacan iconographic elements may have been connected with a cult of sacred warfare associated with "cosmogonic acts of creation," particularly the creation of the Sun at Teotihuacan. Thus, the Uxmal owl sculptures could pertain to a martial complex connected with the birth (and cyclical rebirth) of the Sun and Venus. In addition, the East Structure's "owl-and-weapons" symbol might also be an iconographic reference to the ethnohistorically documented "founder" of Uxmal, Ah Kuy Tok Tutul Xiu (he of the owl flint Tutul Xiu?).[9]

In his chapter in this volume, Edward Kurjack rightly points out that many Maya masonry buildings are arranged around one or more common courtyards, and that in many instances the presence of metates, *chultuns*, or other domestic artifacts supports the idea that they functioned as a communal residential compound (see the discussion of such courtyard groups at Xcalumkin, Chunhuhub, and Dzibilchaltun Structures 95, 95A, and 96 in this chapter). However, the exceptionally formal character of the Nunnery

FIGURE 8.9. View of one of the owl masks above the doorways of the East Structure of the Nunnery at Uxmal. (Photograph by Jeff Kowalski)

Quadrangle, the abundance of its architectural sculpture, and the fact that no *chultuns* have been located within or nearby support the idea that this was a nonresidential courtyard rather than a house compound writ large. Ringle and Bey (2001: 275) recently have cited passages from the Chronicle of Calkini in which a location referred to as the *tancabal*, quite possibly such a formal courtyard, appears to be the place where subordinate governors or *batab'ob*, ward leaders or *ah cuchcab'ob*, and other minor officials gather together with their overlord to consult on community affairs and/or receive tribute.[10] One of these passages specifically links the presentation of tribute with the *popolna*, or council house:

> bitun u cah u chic u banal u cuchteel tu tancabal tu chi yotoch to poplnaob. ca hop'u mulcanob. ti ca tal u paabaob ca likiob ca talob

> there occurred the assembling of the subjects in the patio at the doors of the council houses. then began the public consultation. then came their breaking up and they departed and came to . . . (Calkini f. 14 [cited in Ringle and Bey 2001: 275–276]; see Barrera Vásquez 1957)

The association between the Nunnery Quadrangle and tribute is suggested by the prominent display of both warriors and captives on the upper facades of the West and North Structures, since an outcome of warfare was the gaining of territory, labor, and tribute. Moreover, the participation of the ruler in outdoor state ceremonies, reception of dignitaries, etc., is suggested by the prominent placement of a jaguar throne near the center of the quadrangle courtyard, and by the location of another glyphic throne (Stela 17) at the base of the stairway of the North Structure.[11] Based on such evidence, I would concur with Ringle and Bey (2001: 281), who write:

> We identify the Monjas [Nunnery Quadrangle] as the primary meeting place for the Uxmal court; by extension, certain quadrangles probably played a similar function at other sites (e.g., Tiho). This is supported by the general lack of domestic features in such quadrangles, their placement relative to other "civic" structures such as pyramids and sacbeob, and, perhaps most important, by formally defined entries.

In an earlier discussion of Uxmal's architecture, art, iconography, and epigraphy, I stressed the importance of Lord Chaak as the head of a "more traditional dynastic ruler-centric" polity (Kowalski 1994a: 118). I would like to modify my interpretation, however, by noting that at Uxmal, as in other Classic Maya polities, the king's authority depended on the support of other high-ranking lineages (McAnany 1995; Villela 1993). One source of evidence regarding the king's relationship to other influential members of the community is the columnar monument known as Altar 10 (Pollock 1980: 275; Graham 1992, vol. 4: 115).

Interestingly, according to information from Ian Graham (cited by Grube 1994: 323), Altar 10 may originally have been located in front of the building that Frans Blom (1934) designated as Structure 16, an outlying group southeast of the Uxmal site center.[12] Graham (1992, vol. 4: 79) identifies Group 16 as the large hilltop architectural complex in quadrant 17L of his Uxmal map (see Figure 8.10, this volume). This consists of a series of some four courtyards located on platforms that ascend from the north to the south. The courtyards are bounded by platforms which undoubtedly represent the remains of multiroom range-type palaces (indications of a series of vaulted rooms appear as Structure 17-L-6 on the Graham map). The presence of several *chultuns* indicates that this was a residential palace compound, but a substantial pyramid temple structure on the west side of the largest courtyard indicates that the elite family living there probably also maintained a separate lineage temple or ancestral shrine.

In addition to mentioning Lord Chaak, who is designated by a *k'uhul ajaw* title, Altar 10 also mentions four other individuals. Three of these—

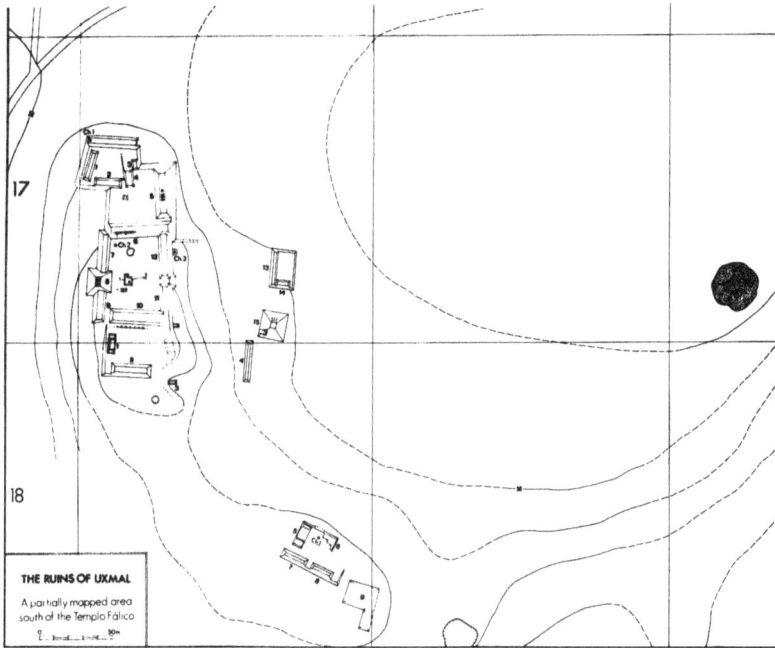

FIGURE 8.10. Plan of Group 16 (quadrants 17 and 18), probable location of Uxmal Altar 10. (After Graham 1992 4: 84)

Lord Chaak, an individual named E-Wits-Ahau (E-Wits-Ajaw), and an individual whose name begins with the syllable *ko* and who also has *ajaw* status—are linked with one another by the *y-itah* glyph, identifying such individuals either as Lord Chaak's "siblings" or "companions" (Grube 1994: 323–324), or as persons who witnessed or saw something in his presence (Stuart 2000). The text around the upper edge of Altar 10 again refers to E-Wits-Ahau, who is referred to as a "ch'ok" (sprout, a young royal offspring), to his mother, and probably to his father. Grube (1994: 324) notes that this indicates that Altar 10 "focuses on E-Wits-Ahau and his family," and further suggests that "Structure 16 may have been the residence of the family of E-Wits-Ahau, who was an important companion of Lord Chaak. By placing Altar 10 in front of Structure 16, E-Wits-Ahau publicly displays his ancestry and his close ties to Lord Chaak, Uxmal's most powerful individual."[13]

Recent mapping and excavations at the medium-sized site of Xkipche, located about 10 km southwest of Uxmal, suggest that Xkipche may have become a dependency of the larger center, although the exact nature of the political relationship remains to be clarified. This site has been ranked as a

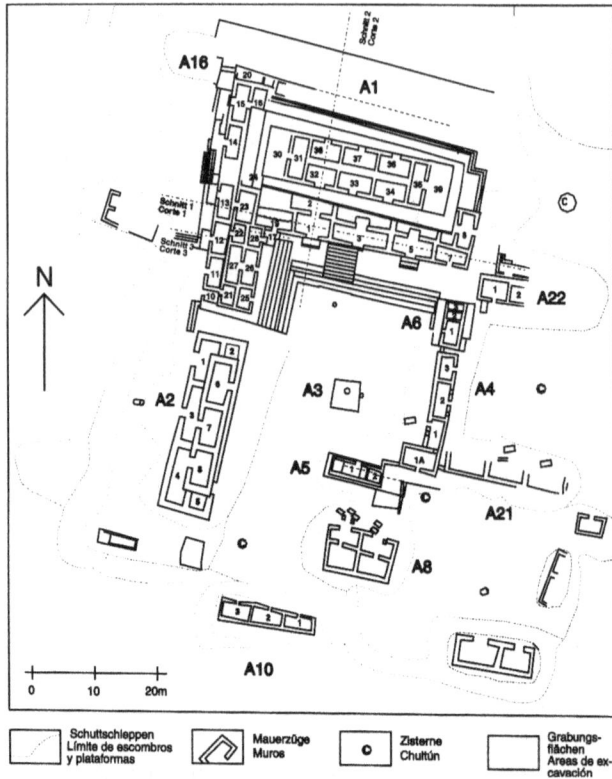

FIGURE 8.11. Xkipche, plan of Structure A-1 and associated structures. (After Reindel 1997: abb 5)

Class 3 site (G. F. Andrews [1992?]), which puts it in the same class as Chunhuhub, Kiuic, and Xculoc. However, it is distinguished by the presence of a particularly large palace-type building, Structure A-1, which contains a total of thirty-eight rooms on two levels (G. F. Andrews [1992?]: 1; see also Reindel 1997) (Figures 8.11, 8.12). According to G. F. Andrews ([1992?]: 1):

In terms of its size, Structure A-1 at Xkipche appears to be the third largest building in the entire Puuc region since it is exceeded by only two other buildings; Structure 1 (Palace) at Labna with 63 rooms and Structure 2B1 at Sayil (Three-Story Palace) with 94 rooms in all. Structure 2C3 at Kabah is about the same size, with 36 rooms on two levels. Like its counterparts at Labna and Sayil, Structure A-1 at Xkipche is the result of a series of additions and alterations over time, but just how much time is still an open question.[14]

Noting the fact that Xkipche is located only some 10 km southwest of Uxmal, a proximity which suggests "some kind of interdependence," Andrews ([1992?]: 2) points out that "architecturally the two sites have little in common." In particular, he observes that there are no stylistic counterparts for the monumental Late Uxmal structures such as the House of the Governor or the Nunnery Quadrangle at Xkipche, although there are several structures at Uxmal which feature sloping upper facades related to that of the East Wing of Structure A-1 at Xkipche. Although the function of Structure A-1 is uncertain, its somewhat irregular plan and prolonged, additive building sequence support the idea that it served as an elite residence. Contrasting with Structure A-1 is Group D, which "consists of a single great but quite destroyed edifice located on a very high and quite extensive platform." The isolated nature and greater formality of this palace-style building suggests that it may have served a more public, administrative function at the site (Reindel 1997).

Uxmal, the sole rank 1 site in Nicholas Dunning's (1992) settlement hierarchy for the eastern Puuc region, is connected to two other rank 2 Puuc cities, Kabah and Nohpat, by means of an artificial roadway or *sacbe* that extends over some 18 km (Carrasco Vargas 1993).

Although only portions of Kabah or Nohpat have been adequately

FIGURE 8.12. Xkipche, south facade of the Structure A-1 palace after consolidation. (After Reindel 1997: pl. 9)

mapped, the scale and diversity of their monumental architecture and the presence of many carved monuments indicate their regional political importance (Pollock 1980). At Kabah, for example, the massive range-type palace structure known as the Codz Poop features an impressive array of hundreds of stacked Chaak masks covering virtually its entire west facade. A recent archaeological project at Kabah has revealed that the upper eastern facade of the Codz Poop supported a series of gigantic stone warrior sculptures. Each wears a similar distinctive headdress and has raised facial scarification patterns like those seen on a previously documented Kabah sculpture (known as the "King of Kabah") and seen on dancing warrior figures that appear on the "panel style" carved jambs of the palace's central doorway (Carrasco and Pérez 1996).

The most comprehensive mapping project at a Puuc city has been carried out at Sayil, whose areal extent and structural remains were mapped in the 1980s (Sabloff and Tourtellot 1991, 1992; Tourtellot and Sabloff 1994) (Figure 8.13). Although smaller than Uxmal, Sayil also is a major site, where about ten thousand people occupied an urban core covering some 4.5 km². Some seven thousand additional people lived in a larger surrounding area. They probably provided the city's rulers with a source of tribute in goods and labor. The Sayil mapping project showed that the site center was organized about a 1.2 km long north-south internal *sacbe*. At the northern end of this causeway was Structure 2B1, the massive Great Palace (or Three-Story Palace), believed to have been a palatial residence for the site's paramount lineage (Figure 8.14). Structure 2B1 contains ninety-four rooms, arranged in three setback terraces linked by a grand southern stairway (Pollock 1980: 89–105, figs. 173–175). At the southern end of the *sacbe* were more public structures, including a ballcourt, stela platform, and a multistory palace, Structure 4B2 (Pollock 1980: 124–129, figs. 258–259), which may have served as an administrative center[15] or may have been the residence of a secondary powerful family at the site. The latter interpretation is that of Ringle and Bey (2001: 284), who view the contiguous courtyards and temple of the Mirador Group, located on the *sacbe* between the two palace groups (and appearing at the bottom of the partial Sayil map in Figure 8.13) as a more likely formal ceremonial and administrative courtyard space.

A recent study of the distribution of vaulted masonry (i.e., "palace") architecture at Sayil, coupled with a complementary analysis of two artifact types—Puuc columnar altars and Oxkutzcab Appliqué censers—by Carmean (1998: 259–270), suggests the presence of a number of residential compounds that served as elite households occupied by local lineage heads

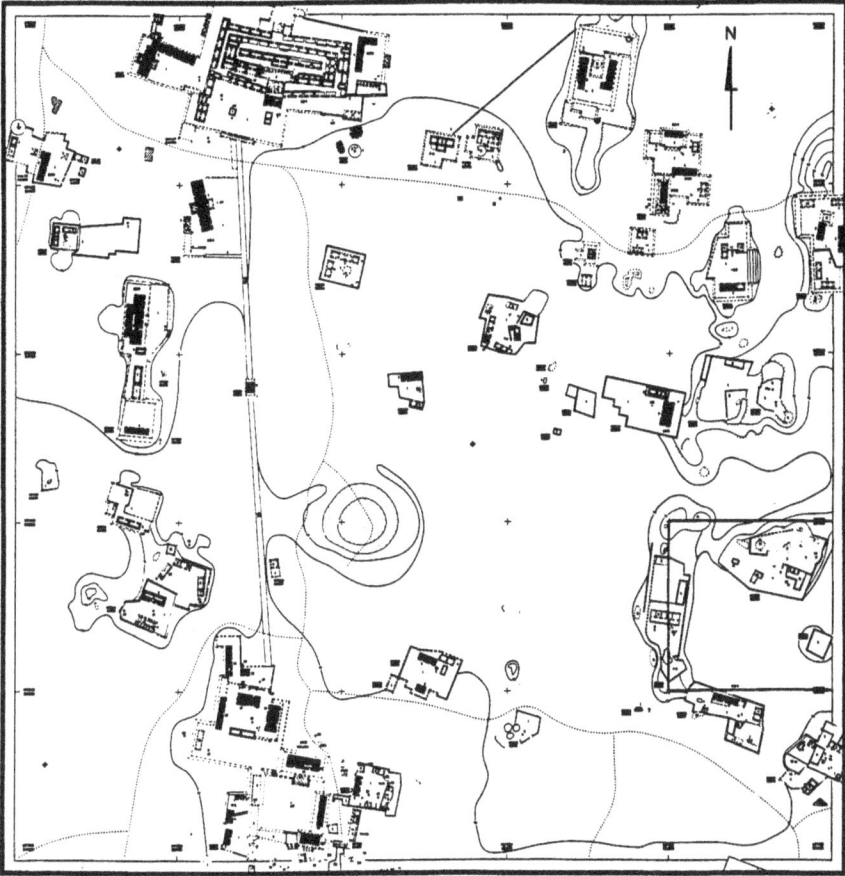

FIGURE 8.13. Map of the northern portion (hectare Miguel T.) of the central civic-ceremonial core of Sayil, Yucatan, showing the location of the great Three-Story Palace (Structure 2B1) at the northern end of the north-south *sacbe*. (After Tourtellot and Sabloff 1994: fig. 4)

and their families. Although the impressive size and number of rooms of the Great Palace suggest that it was the royal palace, Carmean notes that the dispersed placement of columnar altars (which Carmean [1998: 259] uses as an indicator of "supernaturally sanctified political leadership within the community"; cf. the previous discussion of the world tree columnar altar in the Nunnery Quadrangle, and of Altar 10 in Group 16 at Uxmal) and the widespread occurrence of the specialized censers (which she interprets as evidence of the practice of lineage-oriented religious activities) support the idea that political power at Sayil was shared out among

FIGURE 8.14. Reconstruction painting of the Three-Story Palace (Structure 2B1) at Sayil, Yucatan. (After Proskouriakoff 1963 [1946]: 57)

a wide range of ranked lineages. The approximate wealth and rough ranking of these corporate kin groups can be estimated by the size, the amount of vaulted space, and the sculptural embellishment of the residential compounds featuring masonry structures. On this basis, the Sayil "palaces" are subdivided into three ranks, with all rank 1 compounds located in the central core of the site and not far from the north-south *sacbe* system.

According to Dunning's (1992) analysis, Sayil is a rank 2 site, suggesting that it was a local political capital that relied on both a surrounding system of satellite centers and scattered agricultural populations, as well as on the inhabitants in its immediate site confines, to support its local elites. The nature of the political relationship between the elite occupants of the Great Palace and those located at other nearby centers is still difficult to clarify. This is illustrated by the case of sites such as Chac (or Chac II) and Xcavil de Yaxche (located, according to Pollock [1980: 138–139], some 4 km north-northwest and 4 km southwest of Sayil, respectively; according to Smyth et al. [1998: 234], Chac II is located some 1.7 km north of the North Palace at Sayil). Chac II is a small site (rank 4 in *Atlas arqueológico del estado de Yucatán*, Garza T. and Kurjack 1980) but features several architectural groups with range-type structures, including a fairly substantial three-story masonry palace containing at least twenty-two rooms located on top of a hill (Hissink 1934: 50–51; Pollock 1980: 138; Smyth et al. 1998: 237; a some-what similar two-story palace also occurs at Xcavil de Yaxche, see Pollock 1980: 138, fig. 280). My brief investigations at this hilltop structure in 1977 revealed the presence of several *pilas* (tublike stone water containers) on or around a low platform (kitchen area?) and remnants of subsidiary vaulted structures on the large primary platform supporting the palace (see Smyth et al. 1998: fig. 5). The presence of water containers and a possible kitchen support the idea that at least some of the rooms in the three-story edifice were used for residential purposes. By analogy with the similar, but sub-stantially larger, three-story palace at Sayil, it seems reasonable to suppose that the two-story palaces at Chac II and Xcavil de Yaxche were occupied by prosperous and politically influential local lineage groups. The proximity of Chac II and Xcavil de Yaxche to the larger site suggests the possibility that their lineage leaders would have been responsible for both the collec-tion of tribute and the arrangement of labor from local farming inhabitants, and supplying such goods and services to the lordly family(ies) at Sayil; in addition, physical separation from the Sayil site center suggests the local lineage heads would have maintained some degree of political autonomy and independence, perhaps participating periodically as royal councilors or advisors. According to Smyth et al. (1998: 233), however, a recent site sur-vey and excavation at Chac II indicate that the site was founded during the Early Classic period and continued to be occupied during the Late Classic period, but was largely separate in time and space from Sayil and "was not a satellite of its nearby neighbor." It is possible, of course, that the site was autonomous for an early period of occupation but came under Sayil's in-fluence during the period after about A.D. 700–750, as is suggested by the presence of a *sacbe* linking Sayil to the smaller center and a radiocarbon date of A.D. 850 ± 60 from a crossbeam in the Chac Palace (Smyth et al. 1998: 244; Smyth and Dore 1992).

Labna, another Puuc site that has recently been excavated and restored, is an intermediate-size elite center with a multilevel residential palace con-nected to a southern pyramid-temple and monumental arch by a short *sacbe* (Thompson 1897; Pollock 1980: 7–52; see Gallareta Negron et al. 1992 for a summary of recent excavations) (Figure 8.15). Pollock (1980: 7–8) in-dicates that there are at least sixty-seven rooms in the Labna palace at the north end of the causeway. Some seventeen of these rooms form part of eight multiroom units. It has been estimated that some 116 adults, or 58 nuclear family units, could have lived in this palace (Kurjack 1994: 314). The group of structures known as the Mirador complex located at the south end of the sacbe includes at least twenty-two rooms in various range-type vaulted buildings, and Kurjack (1994: 314) suggests that "the rubble from collapsed structures represents at least 18 additional vaulted chambers and ruins in the forest south of the cleared area may also be part of the group." Kurjack (1994: 313) has suggested that the *sacbe* at Labna is as symbolic as functional, since it signified "the enduring tie between two groups of kinsmen . . . by the road physically joining their houses." This is debatable, however, since the Mirador Group includes a specialized temple structure (the Mirador proper) and a specialized portal arch. The presence of a columnar altar bearing a relief carving of dancing Chaak impersonators suggests that part of this area may have had a more ritualistic rather than residential function. Ringle and Bey (2001: 283–284) contrast the more rambling and additive plan of the northern palace, which they suggest was the residence of a single important group, with the more formal courtyard spaces to the east and west of, and linked by, the Arch in the south. These more formal courtyards they interpret as more public and ceremonial spaces, comparable in general function if not in scale to the Nunnery Quadrangle at Uxmal, where members of a smaller, more localized court met.

Located only some 1.5 km north of Labna is the site called Chuncatzim (Pollock 1980: 53). Chuncatzim consists of a small civic and religious center located on the top of a low hill surmounted by a terraced platform supporting several structures (Blom 1935). The principal masonry structure is a multiroom, two-story palace known as Structure 1, Canel Cruz, or Xcanalcruz (Figure 8.16). The presence of probable collapsed *chultuns* (Pollock 1980: 53) suggests that the Xcanalcruz palace was an elite residence. Another small group of multiroom palace buildings exists at the site of Xlabpak (Maler 1902: 204–205; Saenz 1968; Pollock 1980: 60), located some 3 km west of Labna and Chuncatzim. The two best-documented buildings, Structures 1 and 2, form a common courtyard with buildings on two sides. Structure 1, the best-preserved building, contained nine rooms in its final form and displays elaborate geometric stone mosaic sculpture featuring step-fret designs and long-snouted Puuc mask panels in the upper facade. The presence of perishable dwellings and a large number of *chultuns* nearby suggests that Structure 1 formed part of a residential compound. According to Pollock (1980: 60), "At least six house platforms with chultuns" are located in the vicinity of Structures 1 and 2. In his chapter in this volume, Kurjack rightly notes that outlying palace groups such as that at Chuncatzim should be considered part of the larger political territory administered from Labna. He interprets the presence of several substantial palace structures as making it "difficult to point out one building that was the regal residence." While I believe he is correct to suggest that the distribution of a number

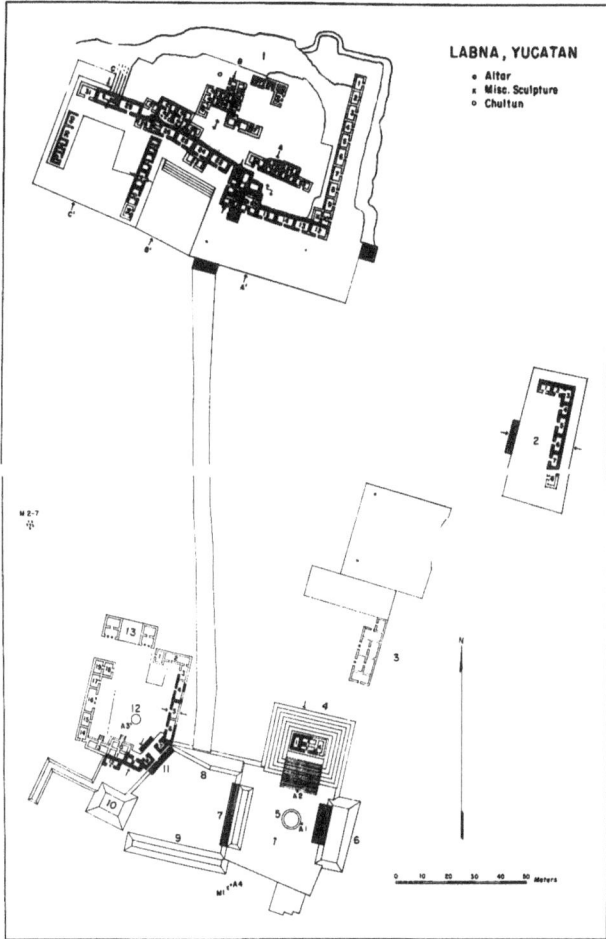

FIGURE 8.15. Plan of the central section of Labna, Yucatan. (Figure 3 from H. E. D. Pollock, *The Puuc: An Architectural Survey of the Hill Country of Yucatan and Northern Campeche, Mexico*, Memoirs of the Peabody Museum, vol. 19, Copyright 1980 by the President and Fellows of Harvard College)

of multiroom vaulted masonry palace-style structures within Labna and at sites nearby indicates the presence of several highly ranked and politically influential families, I would agree with Ringle and Bey that the Labna Palace was most likely the residence of the most powerful group (perhaps consisting of an extended family and their retainers) at the site. However, given Labna's designation as a rank 3 site (Dunning 1992: 89–90, table 5-2, fig. 5.2), one should probably think of this as the palace not of the king

FIGURE 8.16. Structure 1 at Chuncatzim, looking south. (Figure 107 from H. E. D. Pollock, *The Puuc: An Architectural Survey of the Hill Country of Yucatan and Northern Campeche, Mexico*. Memoirs of the Peabody Museum, vol. 19, Copyright 1980 by the President and Fellows of Harvard College)

of a fully autonomous polity, but the sumptuous dwelling of a regional governor equivalent to a *batab*, perhaps owing allegiance to the ruler of the nearby rank 2 site of Sayil, whose "kingly" household was centered in the Great Palace and whose "royal" status is suggested by depictions of the single, ornately costumed individuals on Sayil's stelae (Proskouriakoff 1950: 162–163, figs. 81a, 89).

The site plan of Chacmultun (Pollock 1980: 363–368), mapped by Edward Thompson (1904), suggests that the political organization of this intermediate size city in the eastern Puuc region might have involved the collaboration of at least three principal lineages or extended families. The site features three principal platforms/palace groups (known as the Chacmultun, Cabal Pak, and Xeth Pool groups) located on natural eminences between 100 to 200 m apart (Marquina 1964: 739–745, pl. 225). These structures contain forty, thirty-six, and sixteen vaulted rooms, respectively, some of which may have been used for storage, but many of which surely were living and sleeping quarters (Kurjack 1994: 313). According to Kurjack, "The core of the settlement . . . consisted of three compact residential kin groups, two of these containing approximately a hundred adults each while a third elite family may have been only about half that size." Recent excavation and restoration carried out by Carlos Pérez Alvarez and associates has revealed the presence of a ballcourt and a paved plaza area southeast of the Chacmultun group,[16] which contains the greatest number of vaulted rooms on the largest artificial platform at the site, supporting the idea that the family living here may have been the highest-ranked lineage at the site or that the main palace here may have served as a Council House, as well as the idea that the plaza and ballcourt area may have marked the location of rituals and festivals (like those depicted in the mural paintings in Building C of the Chacmultun group) that integrated the larger community (Thompson 1904).

The variations in site size, architectural volume, and associated political symbols outlined in this chapter and documented more completely by Pollock (1980), Gendrop (1983), G. F. Andrews (1986), Dunning (1992), and others implies a corresponding, although imperfectly understood, sociopolitical hierarchy among and within the various centers. It is known that a prominent type of political organization in northern Yucatan at the time of the conquest concentrated political power in a head town (*hol cah*) that was the capital city of a political territory known as a *cuchcabal.* The head town and the larger *cuchcabal* were governed by a *halach uinic* who was owed allegiance and tribute by regional governors, or *batab'ob*, and local town leaders of various ranks (Roys 1943; Marcus 1993; see Ringle and Bey 2001 for a recent review of the political organization of northern Maya courts). It seems likely that many of the smaller centers in the vicinity of a larger city such as Uxmal, Kabah, or Sayil would have been under its control or owed it allegiance, perhaps administered by subordinate governors who had kinship or other political ties to the ruling family at the principal center. The spatial distribution and monumental art and architecture at major sites (rank 1 or 2) suggest that they may have been the head towns of autonomous polities, although some larger cities probably dominated others at particular times. In this regard, it has been argued that Kabah and Nohpat were politically independent during the eighth and early part of the ninth century, but that during the later ninth century they were incorporated in a political/military alliance in which Uxmal was the leading partner (Dunning and Kowalski 1994). By the same token, a rank 2 center such as Sayil might have exerted political control over a smaller, nearby rank 3 center such as Labna. Within sites we find distributions of vaulted, multiroom structures ranging from a series of relatively comparable, semi-isolated palace groups (as at Xcalumkin, Xculoc, or Chacmultun) to evidence for more dominant "royal" palaces accompanied by a range of related but smaller elite residential groups (as at Uxmal or Sayil). Both patterns are consistent with models which stress the importance of ranked lineages and their households as a basis for ancient Maya sociopolitical organization (cf. McAnany 1995) and which interpret Maya polities as variants of the "segmentary state" (Ball and Taschek 1991; Demarest 1992; Houston 1993).

Transformations of the Palace at Chichen Itza

The traditional Maya palace underwent significant change at the Terminal Classic to Early Postclassic site of Chichen Itza. Due to the rapid rise of this site and accompanying profound changes in political organization, Chichen Itza's rulers deliberately sought to deemphasize the cult of the single divine king that had dominated Maya art of the preceding centuries (see Krochock 1988; Schele and Freidel 1990; Wren and Schmidt 1991; Grube 1994). At Chichen Itza there are not as many clear-cut counterparts for the extensive, multiroom range-type palaces that abound in the Puuc region sites previously discussed, although Tozzer (1957, vol. 1: 23, citing Ruppert 1952) describes several variants of such buildings (e.g., Structure 7B3 Temple of the Three Lintels; Structure 7B2; Structure 5B7; Structure 5B25; Structure 3C9 Casa Colorada; Structure 5C14 House of the Phalli; and Structure 4C1 first phase of the Monjas). For this reason, investigators have been less certain about what types of structures constitute the residential remains of the elite occupants of the site.

The single most imposing palace building at Chichen Itza is the Monjas, which consisted of an eastern range of rooms (part of which represents the earliest phase of construction) encased by a high, massive platform supporting a second-story range (whose hieroglyphic lintels date it to A.D. 880), on whose roof was located a smaller, shoddier late building (Figures 8.17, 8.18). Based on its plan, its "Chichen-Maya" Puuc-related architectural style, and its hieroglyphic lintels, Tozzer included the Monjas among his examples of Chichen-Maya buildings which were considered to predate the Toltec-Maya structures clustered on the massive northern platform known as the Gran Nivelación (Tozzer 1957, 23–24). The work of Charles Lincoln (1986, 1990), however, challenged the traditional sequential view of Chichen Itza by demonstrating that so-called Maya and Toltec type buildings frequently appear in the same architectural group, and by arguing that the differences in plan, architectural style, and associated iconography among such structures reflect differences in function rather than chronological sequence or ethnic identity. Studies of the hieroglyphic lintels spanning the doorways of the second story suggest that its rooms may have served as a place where dedication ceremonies by various high-ranking individuals took place in A.D. 880 (Krochock 1988, Schele and Freidel 1990, Grube 1994). Aside from such ritual associations, its function is not certain, although Lincoln (1990: 608) suggests that the height of the second story, reached by means of a monumental stairway, and the structure's location at the south side of a broad public plaza support the idea that it was a "dis-

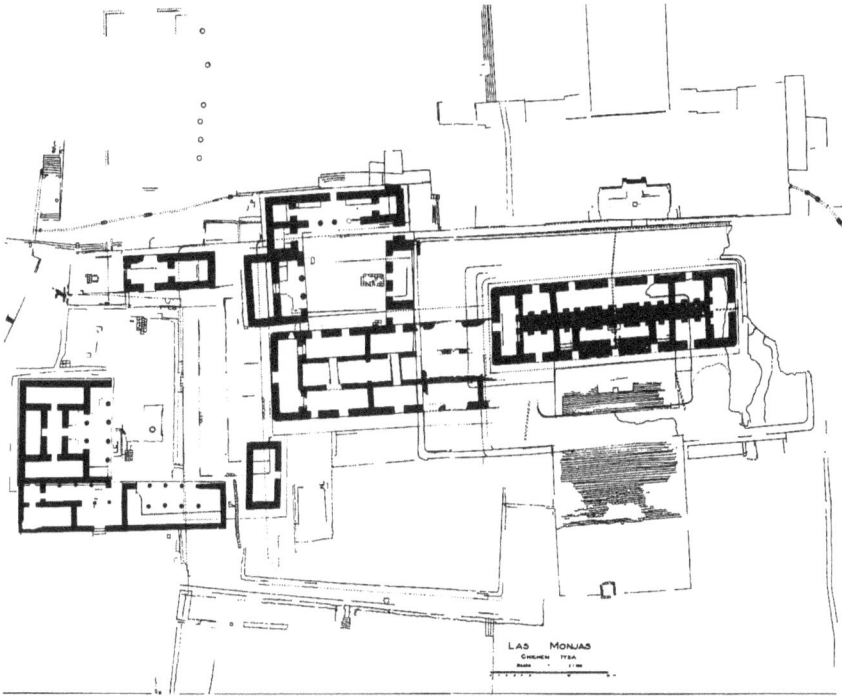

FIGURE 8.17. Plan of the Monjas and associated structures. (After Bolles 1977: 40)

tinctive type of temple for mass-display, in which priests might have lived at most part-time (compare Harrison 1970)."

More recently, Headrick (1995) has argued that Las Monjas served as a "founder's house" at Chichen Itza. She bases this argument on the prominent use of the simple latticework pattern that covers much of the lower walls of the first story of the building, as well as on the prominence given to the long-snouted mask panels in the upper facade. Headrick terms the latticework a "net motif," and compares it to the net patterns that enclose the various warrior figures in the murals at the Atetelco apartment compound at Teotihuacan. I do not believe that the formal similarities are strong enough to demonstrate that these two motifs are identical. However, the simple lattice's strand-over-strand composition makes it clear that it represents a woven mat, long recognized as a symbol of rulership among the Maya (Kowalski 1987: chap. 12). Headrick (1995: 6) also identifies the seated human figure above the central doorway of the East Wing of the Monjas as an ancestor and as "the founder of the Chichen dynasty."[17]

Another argument for identifying Las Monjas as a founder's house is the

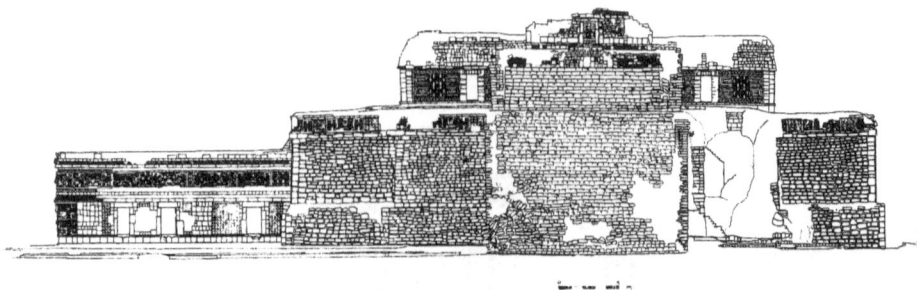

FIGURE 8.18. North elevation of the Monjas. (After Bolles 1977: 33)

presence of a sculpture of a spotted jaguar at the foot of the stairway to the second story. Headrick (1995: 7) points out the relationship between this jaguar throne and the one at the House of the Governor at Uxmal, and to the one depicted on the Oval Palace Tablet at Palenque. The Oval Palace Tablet is particularly associated with accession, a royal ritual which was apparently long associated with House E of the Palace, which the Maya referred to as the Sak Nik Naah (White Flower House). On the basis of these similarities, Headrick (1995: 8) concludes that "The consistent pattern of residential palace structures associated with jaguar thrones suggests that the Monjas functioned not only as the living quarters of the king but also as the location of accession."

Although I find several (though not all) of Headrick's iconographic comparisons persuasive, I would like to suggest the possibility that the Monjas may have functioned as a Popol Nah structure rather than a royal residence. The prominent use of the mat-weave lattice pattern on the lower story and the presence of the jaguar throne, associated with Structure 22-A at Copan, the House of the Governor at Uxmal, and House E at Palenque, support this interpretation. Further, the references on the hieroglyphic lintels to multiple individuals bearing the *ajaw* title and involved in similar dedicatory rituals, as well as the more prominent role given to K'ak'upacal (probably the contemporary ruler who had inherited the ancestral title of kingship represented by the sun disk figures in Chichen Itza's iconography), would be consistent with the use of the structure as a place where a group of "equals" in the conciliar *multepal* government of Chichen Itza assembled under the direction of a principal lord or paramount ruler (cf. Grube 1994: 329; Kowalski 2000a,b).

Another prominent palace-type structure at Chichen Itza is the Akab Dzib. This edifice, located a short distance east of the Monjas, consists of tandem ranges of vaulted rooms surrounding a massive, solid masonry platform. The plan of the Akab Dzib, with this central platform, resembles those of various multilevel palace structures in the Puuc region referred to earlier (e.g., the Great Palace at Sayil, the Xcanalcruz at Chuncatzim near Labna, etc.), suggesting that it may have been an elite residence (cf. Lincoln 1990: 606–607). If so, it may have housed a branch of the powerful Cocom family, since the sculpted lintel above the doorway in the southern rooms depicts a seated individual who is identified as a *k'uhul kokom* (divine Cocom) (Schele and Freidel 1990: 361–363; Grube 1994: 327–328).

Noting the widespread and fairly regular distribution of the so-called gallery-patio structural type at Chichen Itza (Figure 8.19), David Freidel (1981: 321) argues that it may have replaced the elongated multidoor palace building as the characteristic upper-class dwelling at Chichen Itza.[18] He cogently challenges Ruppert's (1943: 230) suggestion that such buildings were market courts or markets. There are problems with Freidel's residential interpretation, however. One problem is the lack of any suitable enclosed private space within such structures that could be used either for sleeping or storage. I would argue that the elongated multicolumn vestibules or "galleries" (often equipped with benches and daises) which front several of these structures, as well as the spacious interior patio and veranda on the interior, seem more appropriate for large gatherings, that is, for use as council or meeting houses. Freidel notes the presence of metates and "fireboxes" in the Mercado complex, and suggests that "the presence of metates and hearths in primary context has traditionally been seen as strong evidence for a domestic function for the structure in which they are found (Haviland 1963; Willey et al. 1965: 17)." There is a problem, however, with identifying the large, formal sunken "fireboxes" in the Mercado as domestic hearths, which typically are located in small, ancillary kitchen structures and consist of the three-stone *koben* (hearth). More likely, the firepits in the gallery-patio structures were used in conjunction with fire rituals conducted by a corporate group or groups that used such buildings as meeting places. The nature of these rituals is alluded to on the *talud* of the carved dais of the Mercado (Figure 8.20), where files of bound "Toltec" warriors flank a central eagle warrior (accompanied by a feathered serpent) possibly engaged in sacrificial ritual. Above this scene, on the projecting *tablero*, are feathered serpents with star or Venus signs among the undulating folds of their bodies. Such scenes of communal martial ritual suggest that the gallery-patio structures are more comparable to the large rooms of the Burnt Palace at Tula (Diehl 1983: 64–66, pls. 6, 11; Kristan-Graham 1989), or to the colonnaded space with bench reliefs in the Eagle House of the Aztec Templo Mayor (Klein 1987), than to domestic residential buildings.

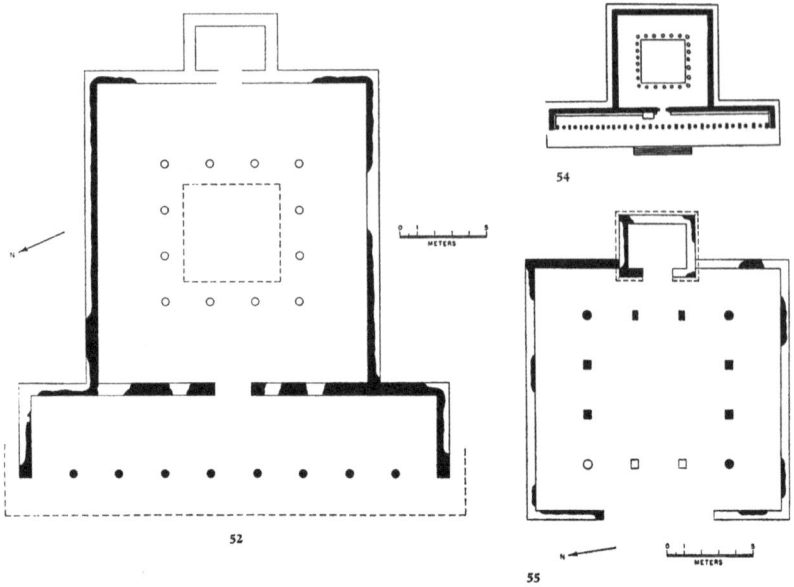

FIGURE 8.19. Plans of gallery-patio and patio-quad structures at Chichen Itza. (After Tozzer 1957, 12: figs 52 [Structure 3B8], 54 [Structure 3D11, the Mercado], and 55 [Structure 3C13])

In plan, the Chichen Itza gallery-patio is more closely related to, and probably served as an antecedent for, the large colonnaded halls distributed throughout the later Postclassic city of Mayapan.[19] Proskouriakoff (1962: 89) identified such edifices as the possible "living quarters for unmarried boys being trained in the arts of war and ritual." According to Proskouriakoff (1962: 90), there were thirteen colonnaded halls in the Main Group and at least four outside it that were considered to be "major independent units." On this basis, she notes that "the number of such independently located halls is close to what Roys [1957] has estimated as the number of provinces under the hegemony of Mayapan. . . . it is possible that each of these halls served the nobility of a specific province." Building on this identification, Ringle and Bey (2001: 276) argue that "given the overwhelming dominance of censers in the pottery assemblages of these structures, colonnaded halls are unlikely to have been residences and instead were almost certainly *popol nas.*"[20]

Why was the older range-type palace less common, less prominent, and less grandiose at Chichen Itza? Clearly, there are some recognizable counterparts of Classic multiroom palaces at Chichen Itza, but, with the exception of the Monjas,[21] none vie with the House of the Governor at

Uxmal or the Central Acropolis at Tikal in scale, sumptuousness, or sculptural elaboration. Edward Kurjack (1994: 315) has suggested that each of the larger palace complexes at Classic Maya sites represented the residence of an extended family or kinship group, and that these lineages, representing "strong local political, economic and military power, were the essential components of lowland government." More recently, Patricia McAnany (1995) has argued for the central importance of such kinship affiliations among the Maya, pointing out that reckoning of descent from founding ancestors provided various lineages, from lower to higher ranking, as well as the royal house itself, with strong claims to hereditary rights and privileges. One major difference between Chichen Itza and various other Classic centers could hinge on the fact that its relatively late foundation and rapid rise to economic, political, and military power involved the coming together (voluntary in some cases, forcible in others, but always with opportunities for contested power relationships) of a number of powerful lineages both from the southern lowlands, southwestern part of the peninsula, and northern Yucatan, all of which had previously enjoyed greater political independence and autonomy as lords of their own domains. If this was indeed the case, then new forms of architecture and art were needed to create the impression of unity and to forge a sense of "nationhood" (Wren and Schmidt 1991). In this case, Kurjack (1994: 315) may be correct in asserting that "new principles of military and governmental organization exemplified by the huge colonnades at Chichen Itza were formulated and the institution of the Palace was superseded." Additionally, no major palace-type structures are located in the major civic-ceremonial heart of Chichen Itza, the Gran Nivelación or northern platform. Like the absence of stelae and dynastic inscriptions in this part of the site, this can perhaps be taken as additional confirmation that the institution of divine kingship, although

FIGURE 8.20. The sculpted dais from the Mercado (Structure 3D11) at Chichen Itza. (After Tozzer 1957, 12: fig. 598)

probably surviving in some form, underwent a significant structural transformation at Chichen Itza.

Conclusions

Vaulted masonry architectural "palace" structures reflecting a wide variety
of plans and having different degrees of finish and sculptural elaboration
existed at both larger cities and smaller towns throughout the northern
Maya region. When they are considered in the context of wider aspects of
regional settlement patterns and individual site plans, and are interpreted
based on indigenous sources of information such as hieroglyphic inscriptions, ethnohistorical sources, and artistic iconography, such substantial
masonry structures provide important insights regarding the nature of political and social organization at such communities, and evidence regarding how such organization differed over space and time. In addition, careful
attention to the specialized form and sculptural adornment of individual
palace buildings has shed light on their possible individualized functions
and uses, and has clarified some ways in which religious and cosmological
symbolism supported the power of the elite individuals who either lived
in, planned, or performed rituals at, and/or administered their cities and
territories from, such sumptuous structures.

At Xcalumkin the somewhat isolated distribution of vaulted masonry
residential courtyard groups—no one of which stands out as that site's royal
palace—as well as references to several individuals bearing the title of *sajal*
(a regional governor or subordinate lord), suggests that this site, as well as
other sites in the region such as Xculoc, Chunhuhub, and Xcochcax, may
have had less centralized conciliar forms of local government. Perhaps centers in this region featured an earlier variant of the form of conciliar government known as *multepal*, although there is now some question regarding the extent to which such *multepal* government at later centers such as
Mayapan or Chichen Itza was truly decentralized.

At Dzibilchaltun, Uxmal, and Sayil, the identification of centralized
palaces of impressive size, coupled with the focus on powerful, elaborately
costumed individuals on the stelae at these sites, suggests that such cities
possessed more centralized forms of rulership in which the political system
was dominated by a paramount ruler who bore the Ch'ul Ajaw (holy lord)
title, similar to that used by the divine kings of southern Maya cities such
as Tikal, Palenque, and Copan. At Dzibilchaltun, the largest single palace
building, Structure 44, has a centralized placement and formal plan, which
suggests it had a more public and administrative, rather than residential,

function. It may have served as the local Popol Nah or Council House. At Uxmal the House of the Governor, though possessing more individual rooms and possibly used as a dwelling in part, is also centrally located on a prominent public platform and has a program of sculpture on its upper facade featuring a mat-weave lattice design and a hierarchical distribution of lordly individuals, which supports its identification as another version of a Popol Nah. The Nunnery Quadrangle, consisting of the four-part radial arrangement of multiroom range structures around a common courtyard with a central columnlike monument, seems to be a deliberate evocation of the quadripartite layout of the Maya cosmos, perhaps designed to indicate and affirm Uxmal's status as the capital of a regional state in the eastern Puuc district at around A.D. 900. Furthermore, the exceptionally formal character of the Nunnery Quadrangle, the subject matter of its architectural sculpture, and the fact that no *chultuns* have been located within or nearby support the idea that it was a nonresidential courtyard, perhaps corresponding to the location referred to in the Chronicle de Calkini as the *tancabal,* a place where the king gathered together with subordinate governors (*batab'ob*), ward leaders (*ah cuchcab'ob*), and other minor officials to consult on community affairs and/or receive tribute. Other palace buildings located farther from the site center at Uxmal, such as those which form parts of the elevated courtyard of Group 16, are more likely candidates for residences and other mixed-use buildings forming the households of high-ranking and influential lineages at the site.

Other sites in the eastern Puuc district, such as Sayil and Labna, have plans in which large, multiroom palaces (the Great Palace or Three-Story Palace at Sayil, the Main Palace at Labna) were probably residences for extended elite families and their retainers, while other multiroom vaulted buildings (the South Palace at Sayil, the courtyard west of the Portal Arch at Labna) may have served more public administrative purposes or been meeting places for local councils. At Sayil, although the tremendous size and number of rooms of the Great Palace suggest that it was a royal residence, the distribution of smaller courtyard groups of vaulted masonry palace architecture, coupled with the analysis of the distribution of Puuc columnar altars and Oxkutzcab Appliqué censers, suggests that these were residential compounds that served as households for ranked elite lineages that shared economic wealth and political power at the site to some degree.

Though more work remains to be done to analyze the form and location of different types of vaulted architecture at sites in the Puuc region, a preliminary examination of the spatial distribution and sculptural iconography of palace architecture at a major rank 1 site (Uxmal) and at rank 2 sites (Kabah, Nohpat, Sayil) suggests that they may have been the head towns of autonomous polities, although some larger cities such as Uxmal probably dominated others (e.g., Kabah and Nohpat) during relatively short periods of political centralization and state formation. In a similar fashion, rank 2 centers such as Sayil may have exerted political control over a smaller, nearby rank 3 center such as Labna. Within sites we find distributions of vaulted, multiroom structures ranging from a series of relatively comparable, semi-isolated palace groups (as at Xcalumkin, Xculoc, and Chacmultun) to evidence of more dominant "royal" palaces accompanied by a range of related but smaller elite residential groups (as at Uxmal or Sayil). Both patterns are consistent with models that stress the importance of ranked lineages, supported by their clients or retainers, as a basis for ancient Maya sociopolitical organization.

At Chichen Itza during the transition from the Terminal Classic to the Early Postclassic period, the traditional Maya palace underwent significant transformations in form and distribution that seem to correspond to changes in political organization, changes that are reflected in that site's public art programs and hieroglyphic texts, which deemphasized the Classic Maya cult of the single divine king. Fewer clear-cut examples of the extensive, multiroom range-type palaces that abound in the Puuc region exist at Chichen Itza, although a few larger structures of this type (e.g., the Monjas, the Akab Dzib, the House of the Phalli) apparently were built during the late-ninth century. Aspects of the sculptural iconography (mat-weave lattice designs on the lower story and the presence of a jaguar throne) and the content of the inscriptions on its carved lintels (referring to multiple individuals of comparable rank involved in dedicatory rituals) suggest that the Monjas might have been a Popol Nah type of structure where a group of high-ranking lineage heads who were "equals" in the conciliar government of Chichen Itza assembled under the direction of a principal lord (perhaps K'ak'upakal). The Akab Dzib, with its glyphic references to the Cocom lineage, and the House of the Phalli, which forms part of an architectural compound some distance from the site center, are better candidates for elite residences for leading families. Although some have proposed that gallery patio structures, such as the Mercado and its kin, replaced the multiroom range-type palace as an elite residence at Chichen Itza, the lack of suitable sleeping space, kitchen areas, and other domestic artifacts in large quantities supports the idea that both the colonnaded galleries and the broader interior courtyards of such buildings housed rituals conducted by a corporate group or groups which used such buildings as meeting places. The gallery-patio structures of Chichen Itza seem closer in form to, and probably served as models for, the large Colonnaded Halls at the later Postclassic city of Mayapan. The notable absence of any major or clearly paramount multiroom or multiple-story palace structure on the North Terrace at Chichen Itza seems consistent with the deemphasis of the image of the single ruler in the site's public art programs and seems to support the idea that the institution of divine kingship, though apparently continuing to exist in some form, underwent an important transformation.

NOTES

1. General discussions of arguments concerning the form and function of Maya palace structures are found in Harrison (1970), Adams (1970), and Kowalski (1987: chap. 6).

2. Becquelin (1994) notes that both Xculoc and Xcochkax have a few palace buildings displaying stylistic features associated with Early Puuc architecture (ca. 670–770) and others of Classic Puuc style, while Chunhuhub and Xpostanil have only buildings of the Classic Puuc style (after A.D. 770).

3. According to Pollock (1980: 419), "Strung out across the savanna to the south for a distance of nearly 2 km are isolated buildings and groups of buildings resting on low outcrops, on somewhat higher eminences, or on hilltops. Approximately 0.5 km north of the central area are building remains that continue north or northeast for another 0.5 km or so, where there is a large group of ruins comprising possibly ten courtyards surrounded by fallen buildings . . . the so-called North Group."

4. Cenotes were sacred to the ancient Maya of northern Yucatan. They provided access to the waters and the spirits of the underworld. Coggins (1983: 61) suggests that "cenotes represented an opening to the underworld, and in northern Yucatan those waters were also thought to be continuous with the waters of the surrounding sea."

5. The multidoorway palace Structure U8-3, at Edzna, Campeche, is over 450 ft. long (G. F. Andrews 1969: 95). Structure D at Nakum, Guatemala, is "more than 400 feet long and only 30 feet wide, with about 44 rooms, opening north or south by narrow doorways" (Kubler 1958: 520).

6. The most convincing interpretation of a Classic Maya vaulted palace structure as a Popol Nah is the case of Structure 22-A at Copan (B. Fash et al. 1992)

7. The platform of the K'inich K'akmo pyramid at Izamal is comparable (Barrera Rubio 1991).

8. The House of the Governor also may be compared formally, and perhaps functionally, to the highland Quiché Maya palace structures known as Nim Ja. In addition to the multipurpose and more rambling palaces, the Quiché capital city, Gumarcaaj or Utatlan, also contained several long, horizontal structures that were entered through multiple doorways and that were set on prominent platforms reached by stairways. These apparently correspond to the structures known as Nim Ja, meaning "Big House," which are described in Ximénez's account of Utatlan. According to Carmack (1981: 288):

> The long structures revealed by the archaeology are clearly the "big houses" of the documentary sources. Apparently, their "bigness" referred to their horizontal size rather than to their height. The multiple stairways and entrances of these structures were functionally related to the long benches against the back walls,

where the ruling lords met to set public policy. It would have been important to have both visual and physical access to all those sitting in council. The burials underneath the bench, especially the impressive one near the central "altar"—or perhaps "throne"—reminds us of Lopez Medel's claim that just rulers were buried underneath the place where they sat in judgment. . . .

The main-plaza big houses are not directly connected to residential buildings, which supports the argument that they were primarily administrative centers for the major lineages.

A possible alternative interpretation of the secondary figures on the facade of the House of the Governor has been proposed by Annabeth Headrick (1995: 5). She likewise identifies them as human rulers, based on their naturalistic rendition, elaborate feathered headdresses, and mat-thrones, but suggests that the open-mawed serpent heads beneath their thrones are "vision serpents," identifying the figures as "the ruling lineage's ancestors." In addition, she has proposed that the celestial location of the central figure, indicated by the two-headed serpent bands surrounding him, "marks him as the founder, the most ancient king in a long line of descent."

9. An argument for the identification of the owl motif on the East Structure of the Nunnery as a reference to the founder of Uxmal, Ah Kuy Tok Tutul Xiu, appears in the paper "Seats of Power and Cycles of Creation: Continuities and Changes in Political Iconography and Political Organization at Dzibilchaltun, Uxmal, Chichen Itza, and Mayapan," coauthored by Jeff Kowalski, Rhonda Silverstein, and Mya Follansbee and presented at the 1997 International Congress of Americanists in Quito, Ecuador. The paper has been forwarded to session organizers Hanns Prem and Pierre Becquelin for publication by the Centro de Estudios Mayas (UNAM), Mexico, in the Estudios de Cultura Maya Series.

10. Ringle and Bey (2001: 275) note that "both passages establish the tancabal, literally 'In the middle of the town/region,' as the locus of tribute presentation and noble congregation," but they also note that the passages do not "clarify whether this was an indoor or outdoor area." Roys (1929) translates *tancabal* as a "reception hall," but Barrera Vásquez prefers a translation as "cortile," "yard," or "patio." *U tancabil yotoch ku* is the patio of a church in the Cordemex dictionary (Barrera Vásquez 1980: 773). An excellent recent review of the political organization and types of activities associated with northern Maya courts, and of their possible association with particular types of buildings and spaces, is provided in Ringle and Bey's chapter.

11. Elsewhere, Kowalski (2000a,b) has noted that Uxmal Stela 13 may depict an encounter between an armed emissary from Chichen Itza and the king, Lord Chaak, who is shown seated on a throne similar to that at the foot of the North Structure stairway.

12. Holmes (1895–1897: 96) states that the altar was discovered by E. H. Thompson "half a mile south and a little east of the Governor's Palace." According to Seler (1917: 153–154), the monument was located in the center of a court in a small architectural complex south of the House of the Old Woman.

13. Grube (1994: 324) also notes: "The inscription on Altar 10 nicely confirms that high-ranking nobles played an important role in the inscriptions of Uxmal as companions of the king, but their role was not much different than in the royal dynasties of other southern lowland sites. Though the recorded history of Uxmal is very late, it is more deeply embedded in Classical Tradition than the history of most of the surrounding sites, an observation which also finds support in Uxmal's 'individual supported' art style (Greene Robertson 1990) which contrasts strongly with the grand mass scenes of Chichen Itza and the equally portrayed nobles of Xcalumkin."

Group 16 is not the only elite palace group at Uxmal. Group 17, a "small group of buildings," is located some 400 m southwest of the Chanchimez structure and "consists of a southern court that is raised above, and faces on, a somewhat larger northern court" (Pollock 1980: 262). The well-preserved West Building has a multi-room plan with three frontal rooms and a central rear chamber. The masonry quality of this structure is superb, and of late Puuc date, and the preserved section of the facade above the southern room features groups of three engaged colonnettes and tiers of long-snouted mosaic mask panels which interrupt the cornice molding and appear to have formed mask crenellations like those of the North Structure of the Nunnery (Pollock 1980: 263). The remains of a palace structure in the northern court also display an elaborate and extremely well carved mosaic facade which Pollock (1980: 263) likens to the sculpture on the Outer West Building of the House of the Magician. A small square platform was located at the center of the southern court-yard, and two identical altars, nos. 8 and 9, were found in front of the East and West Buildings. These altars stand about 1.1 m high and have an upper molding consist-ing of intertwined bands and a ruff of feathers. These altars resemble Altar 10 in basic form, but are not as high and lack hieroglyphic inscriptions. Coupled with the smaller size of the palace compound itself, this suggests that the corporate group who occupied Group 17 held a social and political rank lower than that of the family of E-Wits-Ahau in Group 16.

14. Structure A-1 was constructed using two different architectural styles, indi-cated by the use of plain, sloping upper facades with no medial molding on the lower level of the East Wing (which is of earlier date), while rooms on both levels of the West Wing (constructed later) have plain vertical upper facades, with two-member medial moldings and three-member cornices.

15. According to Carmean (1998: 265), "Although the amount of vaulted area present in the Great Palace is extremely high, relatively few altars occur there. This fact may point to the possibility that the Great Palace was more a residential than a political center for the ruling elite. Indeed, more chultuns also occur in association with the Great Palace, suggesting that activities there may have been more domes-tic in nature when compared to the South Palace, which has few chultuns but many altars and the ballcourt nearby. Thus, this southern area may have been a locus for political decision making at Sayil."

16. Personal information from Carlos Pérez Alvarez, March 2001, and Alfredo Barrera Rubio, April 2001. See also Barrera Rubio 2000.

17. This argument is based on the fact that he sits on a skyband, and on the fact that he is surrounded by a radiating *mandorla* or nimbus. Headrick identifies this framing device as "a variation of the circular shape often referred to as a sun disk." Based on the identification of this form as a sun disk, she further asserts that "the sun disk with its associated seated figure presides over the battles depicted in the Upper Temple of the Jaguars" (Headrick 1995: 7). Schele and Freidel (1990: 393) have argued that "this Captain Sun disk is the Itza version of the ancestral king. By placing the same mytho-historical figure on the Monjas, the kings of Chichen Itza recalled the glory and conquests of this founding ancestor."

18. Freidel (1981: 321) describes the gallery-patio structures as an "Early Postclas-sic structure type possessing sufficient interior space to be a candidate for an elite residential function."

19. Proskouriakoff (1962: 90) notes that such colonnaded halls typically consist of "a long room with an open colonnade on the facade and a second longitudinal row of columns on the interior. . . . A bench along the end rear walls is interrupted in the center by a slightly narrower and higher altar."

20. Ringle and Bey (2001: 276) further suggest that the raised shrines which face the midline of the colonnade in ceremonial groups might have been "places from

which leaders either addressed the members of their cuchcabal/cuchteel, or received tribute." Such a function could have been fulfilled by the dais in the Mercado structure at Chichen Itza. The Mayapan colonnaded halls also could correspond to the so-called Nim Ja or big house type of structure known from the Quiché Maya capital of Utatlan. These Nim Ja are long, horizontal structures which were entered through multiple doorways, and which were set on prominent platforms reached by stairways. According to Carmack (1981: 288), "The main-plaza big houses are not directly connected to residential buildings, which supports the argument that they were primarily administrative centers for the major lineages. . . ."

The Mayapan colonnaded halls differ from the other major palace-type structures at the site, which A. L. Smith (1962: 218) calls "dwellings of the wealthy or important"; typically such noble dwellings are arranged in groups and most are located near the main ceremonial center of the site. There are only around fifty structures which fall into this category. One of the most elaborate of these groups is the palace-like quadrangle composed of Structures R-85 to 90. Smith (1962: 218) notes that "this is a truly palatial assemblage worthy of housing the powerful Cocom family." This quadrangular group consists of four masonry buildings with beam-and-mortar roofs and with colonnaded frontal facades and a center wall leading to several enclosed rear chambers. In addition, the enclosed courtyard contains three small masonry shrine structures (R-85a, R-89, R-90). Two of the palace buildings, R-86 and R-87, contain altar shrines against the rear wall of their central rear room (which projects back from the rear wall of the building in Structure R-87). In addition, Structure R-86a, which forms a contiguous corner space linking Structures R-86 and R-87, is one of the few indisputable kitchen spaces containing two hearths (Smith 1962: 219). Except for a few other examples (cf. Smith 1962: 219–220), there is no absolute artifactual evidence indicating the presence of kitchens, although Smith points out that "all groups at Mayapan must have had at least one kitchen"; he proposes that they consisted of perishable buildings located either on lower platforms attached to residential groups or on separate small platforms forming part of such a group.

21. Lincoln (1990: 607) notes, however, that "there exists, at Chichen Itza, yet another palace complex, the 'East Group' described by Karl Ruppert (1952: 150) and today known locally as 'Las Cinco Bovedas.' Archaeological survey has yet to reach the East Group (but see Schmidt 1981: fig. 6). . . . The East Group Palace stands on a low platform at the east end of Sacbe 6 from the Court of the Thousand Columns."

REFERENCES

Abrams, Elliot M.
1994 *How the Maya Built Their World: Energetics and Ancient Architecture.* Austin: University of Texas Press.
Adams, R. E. W.
1970 Suggested Classic Period Occupational Specialization in the Southern Maya Lowlands. *Monographs and Papers in Maya Archaeology*, edited by W. R. Bullard. Papers of the Peabody Museum of Archaeology and Ethnology, vol. 61. Cambridge, Mass.: Harvard University.
Andrews, E. Wyllys, IV
1965 Archaeology and Prehistory in the Northern Maya Lowlands: An Introduction. In *Handbook of Middle American Indians*, vol. 3, edited by Gordon R. Willey, 288–330. Austin: University of Texas Press.
Andrews, E. Wyllys, IV, and E. Wyllys Andrews V
1980 *Excavations at Dzibilchaltun, Yucatan, Mexico.* Middle American Research Institute Publication 48. New Orleans: Tulane University.

Andrews, E. Wyllys, V
1978   *Dzibilchaltun: Official Guide.* Mexico City: Instituto Nacional de Antropología e Historia.
1979   Some Comments on Puuc Architecture of the Northern Yucatan Peninsula. In *The Puuc: New Perspectives,* edited by Lawrence Mills, 1–17. Scholarly Studies in the Liberal Arts, no. 1. Pella, Iowa: Central College.
Andrews, George F.
1969   *Edzna, Campeche, Mexico: Settlement Patterns and Monumental Architecture.* Eugene: University of Oregon.
1975   *Maya Cities: Placemaking and Urbanization.* Norman: University of Oklahoma Press.
1986   *Los estilos arquitectónicos del Puuc: Una nueva apreciación.* Mexico City: Instituto Nacional de Antropología e Historia.
[1992?]   Architecture at Xkipché. Report in the Archive of the Centro Regional de Yucatán del I.N.A.H., Mérida, Yucatán.
Aveni, Anthony F.
1980   *Skywatchers of Ancient Mexico.* Austin: University of Texas Press.
Ball, Joseph W., and Jennifer T. Taschek
1991   Late Classic Lowland Maya Political Organization and Central-Place Analysis. *Ancient Mesoamerica* 2: 149–165.
Barrera Rubio, Alfredo
1991   La gran plataforma del palacio del gobernador de Uxmal. *Cuadernos de Arquitectura Mesoamericana* 12: 41–56.
[2000]   La arqueología en Yucatán en la última década del siglo. Paper presented at the Second Maler Symposium on the Archaeology of Northwestern Yucatan, organized by Hanns J. Prem, Bonn, Germany, July 3–8, 2000.
Barrera Vásquez, Alfredo (ed.)
1957   *Códice de Calkini.* Campeche, Mexico: Talleres Gráficos del Estado.
Barrera Vásquez, Alfredo, et al.
1980   *Diccionario maya Cordemex.* Mérida: Ediciones Cordemex.
Becquelin, Pierre
1994   La civilización Puuc vista desde la región de Xculoc. In *Hidden among the Hills: Maya Archaeology of the Northwest Yucatan Peninsula,* edited by Hanns J. Prem, 58–70. Acta Mesoamericana 7. Mockmuhl, Germany: Verlag Von Flemming.
Blom, Frans
1934   Short Summary of Recent Explorations in the Ruins of Uxmal, Yucatan. In *Proceedings of the 24th International Congress of Americanists,* 55–59. Hamburg.
1935   A Hitherto Unrecorded Building at Labna. *Maya Research* (New York) 2: 189–190.
Bolles, John S.
1977   *Las Monjas: A Major Pre-Mexican Architectural Complex at Chichen Itza,* with introduction by John H. Jennings and new contributions by J. E. S. Thompson and Ian Graham. Norman: University of Oklahoma Press.
Bricker, Harvey M., and Victoria R. Bricker
1996   Astronomical References in the Throne Inscriptions of the Palace of the Governor at Uxmal. *Cambridge Archaeological Journal* 6 (2): 191–229.
Carmack, Robert M.
1981   *The Quiché Mayas of Utatlan: The Evolution of a Highland Guatemala Kingdom.* Norman: University of Oklahoma Press.

Carmean, Kelli
1998　Leadership at Sayil: A Study of Political and Religious Decentralization. *Ancient Mesoamerica* 9 (2): 259–270.
Carrasco Vargas, Ramón
1993　Formación sociopolítica en el Puuc: El sacbe Uxmal-Nohpat-Kabah. In *Perspectivas antropológicas en el mundo maya*, edited by M. J. Iglesias Ponce de León and F. Ligorred P., 199–212. Sociedad Española de Estudios Mayas.
Carrasco Vargas, Ramón, and Eduardo Pérez de Heredia Puente.
1996　Los últimos gobernantes de Kabah. In *Palenque Round Table 1993*, edited by Martha Macri and Jan McHargue, vol. 10, pp. 297–307. San Francisco: Pre-Columbian Art Research Institute.
Coggins, Clemency C.
1983　*The Stucco Decoration and Architectural Assemblage of Structure 1-sub, Dzibilchaltun, Yucatan, Mexico.* Middle American Research Institute Publication 49. New Orleans: Tulane University.
Demarest, Arthur A.
1992　Ideology in Ancient Maya Cultural Evolution: The Dynamics of Galactic Polities. In *Ideology and Pre-Columbian Civilizations*, edited by Arthur A. Demarest and Geoffrey Conrad, 135–158. Santa Fe: School of American Research Press.
Diehl, Richard A.
1983　*Tula: The Toltec Capital of Ancient Mexico.* New York: Thames and Hudson.
Dunning, Nicholas P.
1988　The Yaxhom Conurbation. *Mexicon* 10 (1): 16–19.
1992　*Lords of the Hills: Ancient Maya Settlement in the Puuc Region, Yucatan, Mexico.* Monographs in World Archaeology 15. Madison: Prehistory Press.
Dunning, Nicholas P., and Jeff K. Kowalski
1994　Lords of the Hills: Classic Maya Settlement Patterns and Political Iconography in the Puuc Region, Mexico. *Ancient Mesoamerica* 5: 63–95.
Fash, Barbara W., William L. Fash, Sheree Lane, Rudy Larios, Linda Schele, Jeffrey Stomper, and David Stuart
1992　Investigations of a Classic Maya Council House at Copan, Honduras. *Journal of Field Archaeology* 19 (4): 419–442.
Fash, William L.
1991　*Scribes, Warriors, and Kings: The City of Copan and the Ancient Maya.* London: Thames and Hudson.
Foncerrada de Molina, Marta
1965　*La escultura arquitectónica de Uxmal.* Mexico City: Universidad Nacional Autónoma de México.
Freidel, David
1981　Continuity and Disjunction: Late Postclassic Settlement Patterns in Northern Yucatan. In *Lowland Maya Settlement Patterns*, edited by Wendy Ashmore, 311–332. School of American Research Series. Albuquerque: University of New Mexico Press.
Freidel, David A., Linda Schele, and Joy Parker
1993　*Maya Cosmos: Three Thousand Years on the Shaman's Path.* New York: William Morrow.
Gallareta Negron, Tomás, José Huchim Herrera, Carlos Peraza Lope, Carlos Pérez Alvarez, Lourdes Toscano Hernández
1992　*Restauración e investigaciones arqueológicas en Labna: La temporada de campo de 1991.* Preliminary report presented to the Consejo Nacional de Arqueología del INAH, Mérida, Yucatan, April 1992.

Garza Tarazona de González, Sylvia, and Edward B. Kurjack
1980   Atlas arqueológico del estado de Yucatán. Mexico City: Instituto Nacional de Antropología e Historia.
Gendrop, Paul
1983   *Los estilos Río Bec, Chenes y Puuc en la arquitectura maya.* Mexico City: Universidad Nacional Autónoma de México.
Graham, Ian
1992   *Corpus of Maya Hieroglyphic Inscriptions.* Vol. 4, part 2, *Uxmal.* Peabody Museum of Archaeology and Ethnology. Cambridge, Mass.: Harvard University.
Grube, Nikolai
1994   Hieroglyphic Sources for the History of Northwest Yucatan. In *Hidden among the Hills: Maya Archaeology of the Northwest Yucatan Peninsula,* edited by Hanns J. Prem, 316–358. Acta mesoamericana 7. Mockmuhl, Germany: Verlag Von Flemming.
Harrison, Peter D.
1970   *The Central Acropolis, Tikal, Guatemala: A Preliminary Study of the Functions of Its Structural Components during the Late Classic Period.* Ph.D. dissertation, University of Pennsylvania. Ann Arbor: University Microfilms.
Haviland, William A.
1963   *Excavation of Small Structures in the Northeast Quadrant of Tikal, Guatemala.* Ph.D. dissertation, University of Pennsylvania. Ann Arbor: University Microfilms.
Headrick, Annabeth
1995   Las Monjas and the Tradition of Founder's Houses. Paper presented at "The XIth Texas Symposium: The Maya Meetings at Texas," Austin, March 10, 1995.
Hissink, Karin
1934   Masken als Fassadenschmuck, untersucht an alten Bauten der Halbinsel Yukatán. Akademische Abhandlungen zur Kulturgeschichte. Strassburg: Sammlung Heitz.
Holmes, William H.
1895–1897   *Archaeological Studies among the Ancient Cities of Mexico.* Chicago: Field Museum of Natural History.
Houston, Stephen D.
1993   *Hieroglyphs and History at Dos Pilas: Dynastic Politics of the Classic Maya.* Austin: University of Texas Press.
Klein, Cecelia F.
1987   *The Ideology of Autosacrifice at the Templo Mayor: The Aztec Templo Mayor,* edited by Elizabeth H. Boone, 293–370. Washington, D.C.: Dumbarton Oaks Research Library and Collection.
Kowalski, Jeff K.
1987   *The House of the Governor: A Maya Palace at Uxmal, Yucatan, Mexico.* Norman: University of Oklahoma Press.
1994a   The Puuc as Seen from Uxmal. In *Hidden among the Hills: Maya Archaeology of the Northwest Yucatan Peninsula,* edited by Hanns J. Prem, 93–120. Acta Mesoamericana 7. Mockmuhl, Germany: Verlag Von Flemming.
1994b   Los mascarones de Tlaloc del cuadrángulo de Las Monjas, Uxmal: Formas teotihuacanas como símbolos "toltecas." *Memorias del Primer Congreso Internacional de Mayistas* 3: 104–156. Mexico City: Universidad Nacional Autónoma de México.
2000a   Collaboration and Conflict: An Interpretation of the Relationship between

Uxmal and Chichen Itza during the Terminal Classic/Early Postclassic Periods. Paper presented at the Second Maler Symposium on the Archaeology of Northwestern Yucatan, organized by Hanns J. Prem, Bonn, Germany, July 3–8, 2000.

2000B   What's Toltec and What's Maya at Uxmal and Chichén Itzá? Merging Mayan and Mesoamerican Worldviews and World Systems in Terminal Classic/Early Postclassic Yucatán. Paper presented at the colloquium "Rethinking Chichén Itzá, Tula, and Tollan," organized by Cynthia Kristan-Graham and Jeff K. Kowalski. Dumbarton Oaks Research Library and Collections, Washington, D.C., February 19–20, 2000.

Kowalski, Jeff K., Alfredo Barrera Rubio, Heber Ojeda Mas, and Jose Huchim Herrera
1996   Archaeological Excavations of a Round Temple at Uxmal: Summary Discussion and Implications for Northern Maya Culture History. In *Eighth Palenque Round Table, 1993*, Merle Greene Robertson, general editor, Martha J. Macri and Jan McHargue, volume editors, 281–296. San Francisco: Pre-Columbian Art Research Institute.

Kowalski, Jeff Karl, and Nicholas P. Dunning
1999   The Architecture of Uxmal: The Symbolics of Statemaking at a Puuc Maya Regional Capital. In *Mesoamerican Architecture as a Cultural Symbol*, edited by Jeff Karl Kowalski, 274–297.

Kristan-Graham, Cynthia
1989   Art, Rulership, and the Mesoamerican Body Politic at Tula and Chichen Itza. Ph.D. dissertation, Department of Art History, University of California at Los Angeles.

Krochock, Ruth
1988   The Hieroglyphic Inscriptions and Iconography of the Temple of the Four Lintels and Related Monuments, Chichen Itza, Yucatan, Mexico. Master's thesis, Department of Anthropology, University of Texas at Austin.

Kubler, George
1958   The Design of Space in Maya Architecture. In *Miscellanea Paul Rivet, Octogenario Dictata*, 515–531. Universidad Nacional Autónoma de México, Instituto de Historia, 1st series, no. 50. Mexico City.

Kurjack, Edward B.
1974   *Prehistoric Lowland Maya Community and Social Organization: A Case Study at Dzibilchaltun, Yucatan, Mexico.* Middle American Research Institute Publication 38. New Orleans: Tulane University.
1994   The Political Geography of the Puuc Hill Country. In *Hidden among the Hills: Maya Archaeology of the Northwest Yucatan Peninsula*, edited by Hanns J. Prem, 308–315. Acta Mesoamericana 7. Mockmuhl, Germany: Verlag Von Flemming.

Lincoln, Charles
1986   The Chronology of Chichen Itza: A Review of the Literature. In *Late Lowland Maya Civilization: Classic to Postclassic*, edited by Jeremy A. Sabloff and E. Wyllys Andrews V, 141–196. Albuquerque: University of New Mexico Press.
1990   *Ethnicity and Social Organization at Chichen Itza, Yucatan, Mexico.* Ph.D. dissertation, Department of Anthropology, Harvard University. Ann Arbor: University Microfilms.

Maldonado Cardenas, Rubén
1994   Dzibilchaltún. *Arqueología Mexicana* 2 (10): 26–28.

Maler, Teobert
1902   Yukatekische Forschungen. *Globus* (Braunschweig) 82: 197–230.
1994   Political Geography of the Yucatecan Hill Country. In *Hidden among the*

Hills: Maya Archaeology of the Northwest Yucatan Peninsula, edited by Hanns J. Prem, 308–315. Acta Mesoamericana 7. Mockmuhl, Germany: Verlag Von Flemming.

Marcus, Joyce
1993 Ancient Maya Political Organization. In *Lowland Maya Civilization in the Eighth Century A.D.,* edited by Jeremy A. Sabloff and John S. Henderson, 111–183. Washington, D.C.: Dumbarton Oaks Research Library and Collection.

Marquina, Ignacio
1964 *Arquitectura prehispánica.* 2d ed. Mexico City: Instituto Nacional de Antropología e Historia.

Maudslay, Alfred P.
1889–1902 *Archaeology.* 4 vols. Biologia Centrali-Americana. London: R. H. Porter and Dulau.

McAnany, Patricia A.
1995 *Living with the Ancestors: Kinship and Kingship in Ancient Maya Society.* Austin: University of Texas Press.

Pollock, H. E. D.
1965 Architecture of the Maya Lowlands. In *Handbook of Middle American Indians,* vol. 2, edited by Robert Wauchope and Gordon R. Willey, pp. 378–440. Austin: University of Texas Press.

1980 *The Puuc: An Architectural Survey of the Hill Country of Yucatan and Northern Campeche, Mexico.* Memoirs of the Peabody Museum of Archaeology and Ethnology, vol. 19. Cambridge, Mass.: Harvard University.

Prem, Hanns J., and Peter J. Schmidt
1993 El Proyecto Arqueológico Xkipche. Report in the archive of the Centro Regional de Yucatán del INAH, Mérida, Yucatan.

Proskouriakoff, Tatiana
1950 *A Study of Classic Maya Sculpture.* Carnegie Institution of Washington Publication 593. Washington, D.C.

1962 Civic and Religious Structures of Mayapan. In *Mayapan, Yucatan, Mexico,* by Harry E. D. Pollock, Ralph E. Roys, Tatiana Proskouriakoff, and A. Ledyard Smith, 87–164. Carnegie Institution of Washington Publication 619. Washington, D.C.

[1946] 1963 An *Album of Maya Architecture.* Originally Carnegie Institution of Washington Publication 558. Reprint, Norman: University of Oklahoma Press.

Reindel, Markus
1997 *Xkipche: Eine Maya-Siedlung im nordlichen Yucatan, Mexiko/Un asentamiento maya en el norte de Yucatan, Mexico.* KAVA, Sonderdruck aus Beitrage zur Allgemeinen und Vergleichenden Archäologie, Band 17. Mainz am Rhein: Verlag Philip von Zabern.

Ringle, William M., and George J. Bey III
2001 Postclassic and Terminal Classic Courts of the Northern Maya Lowlands. In *Royal Courts of the Ancient Maya,* vol. 2, edited by Takeshi Inomata and Stephen Houston, 266–307. Boulder: Westview Press.

Roys, Ralph L.
1929 Crónica de Calkini. Unpublished manuscript in the Latin American Library, Tulane University (cited in Ringle and Bey 2001: 275–276).

1943 The Indian Background of Colonial Yucatan. Carnegie Institution of Washington Publication 548. Washington, D.C.

[1933] 1957 The Political Geography of the Yucatan Maya. Carnegie Institution of Washington Publication 613. Washington, D.C.

[1933] 1967   *The Chilam Balam of Chumayel.* Originally published by Carnegie Institution of Washington. Reprint, Norman: University of Oklahoma Press.

Ruppert, Karl

1943   *The Mercado, Chichen Itza, Yucatan.* Carnegie Institution of Washington Publication 546; Contributions to American Anthropology and History, no. 43. Washington, D.C.

1952   *Chichen Itza: Architectural Notes and Plans.* Carnegie Institution of Washington Publication 595. Washington, D.C.

Ruz Lhuillier, Alberto

1959   *Guía oficial de Uxmal.* Mexico, D.F.: Instituto Nacional de Antropología e Historia.

Sabloff, Jeremy A, and Gair Tourtellot

1991   *The Ancient Maya City of Sayil: The Mapping of a Puuc Region Center.* Middle American Research Institute Publication 60. New Orleans: Tulane University.

1992   Beyond Temples and Palaces: Recent Settlement Pattern Research at the Ancient Maya City of Sayil (1983–1985). In *New Theories on the Ancient Maya,* edited by Elin C. Danien and Robert J. Sharer, 155–160. University Museum Monograph 77. Philadelphia: University of Pennsylvania.

Saenz, César A.

1968   Exploraciones y restauraciones en Yucatán. *Boletín* (Instituto Nacional de Antropología e Historia, Mexico) 31: 17–23.

Satterthwaite, Linton

1943   Piedras Negras Archaeology: Architecture. Part 2, no. 1, Introduction. Philadelphia: University Museum, University of Pennsylvania.

Schele, Linda

1991   The Demotion of Chac-Zutz': Lineage Compounds and Subsidiary Lords at Palenque. In *Sixth Palenque Round Table, 1986,* Merle Greene Robertson, general editor, Virginia M. Fields, volume editor, 151–166. Norman: University of Oklahoma Press.

1998   The Iconography of Maya Architectural Facades during the Late Classic Period. In *Function and Meaning in Classic Maya Architecture,* edited by Stephen D. Houston, 479–517. Washington, D.C.: Dumbarton Oaks Research Library and Collection.

Schele, Linda, and David Freidel

1990   *A Forest of Kings: The Untold Story of the Ancient Maya.* New York: William Morrow.

Schele, Linda, Nikolai Grube, and Erik Boot

n.d.   Some Suggestions on the K'atun Prophecies in the Books of Chilam Balam in Light of Classic-Period History. Texas Notes, Center for the History and Art of Ancient American Culture (CHAAAC), Department of Art, University of Texas at Austin [1997].

Schele, Linda, and Peter Mathews

1998   *The Code of Kings: The Language of Seven Sacred Maya Temples and Tombs.* New York: Scribner.

Schele, Linda, and Mary Ellen Miller

1986   *The Blood of Kings: Ritual and Dynasty in Maya Art.* New York: George Braziller, in association with the Kimbell Art Museum, Fort Worth.

Schmidt, Peter J.

1981   Chichén Itzá: Apuntes para el estudio del patrón de asentamiento. In *Memoria del Congreso Interno 1979, Centro Regional del Sureste (Mérida),* 55–70. Mexico City: Instituto Nacional de Antropología e Historia.

Seler, Eduard

1917 *Die Ruinen von Uxmal.* Abhandlungen der Königlich Preussischen Akademie für Wissenschaften, Philosophisch-Historische Klasse 2. Berlin.

[1902-1923] 1960 *Gesammelte Abhandlungen zur amerikanischen Sprach- und Alterthumskunde.* 5 vols. Graz, Austria: Akademische Druck-und Verlagsanstalt.

Smith, Augustus Ledyard

1962 Residential and Associated Structures at Mayapan. In *Mayapan, Yucatan, Mexico,* by Harry E. D. Pollock, Ralph E. Roys, Tatiana Proskouriakoff, and A. Ledyard Smith. Carnegie Institution of Washington Publication 619. Washington, D.C.

Smyth, Michael P., and Christopher D. Dore

1992 Large Site Archaeology at Sayil, Yucatan, Mexico: A Preliminary Report. *Mexicon* 14: 52-56.

Smyth, Michael P., José Ligorred Perramon, David Ortegón Zapata, and Pat Farrell

1998 An Early Classic Center in the Puuc Region: New Data from Chac II, Yucatan, Mexico. *Ancient Mesoamerica* 9 (2): 233-257.

Stone, Andrea

1989 Disconnection, Foreign Insignia, and Political Expansion: Teotihuacan and the Warrior Stelae of Piedras Negras. In *Mesoamerica after the Decline of Teotihuacan,* A.D. *700-900,* edited by Richard A. Diehl and Janet C. Berlo, 153-172. Washington, D.C.: Dumbarton Oaks Research Library and Collection.

Stuart, David

2000 The Arrival of Strangers: Teotihuacan and Tollan in Classic Maya History. *Mesoamerica's Classic Heritage: From Teotihuacan to the Aztecs,* edited by Davíd Carrasco, Lindsay Jones, and Scott Sessions, 465-513. Boulder: University Press of Colorado.

Taube, Karl A.

1985 The Classic Maya Maize God: A Reappraisal. In *Fifth Palenque Round Table, 1983,* edited by Merle Greene Robertson and Virginia M. Fields, 171-182. San Francisco: Pre-Columbian Art Research Institute.

1992a *The Major Gods of Ancient Yucatan.* Studies in Pre-Columbian Art and Archaeology 32. Washington, D.C.: Dumbarton Oaks Research Library and Collection.

1992b The Temple of Quetzalcoatl and the Cult of Sacred War at Teotihuacan. *RES: Anthropology and Aesthetics* 21: 53-87.

Thompson, Edward H.

1897 *The Chultuns of Labna.* Memoirs of the Peabody Museum of American Archaeology and Ethnology, vol. 1, no. 2. Cambridge, Mass.: Harvard University.

1904 *Archaeological Researches in Yucatan.* Memoirs of the Peabody Museum of American Archaeology and Ethnology, vol. 3, no. 1. Cambridge, Mass.: Harvard University.

Tourtellot, Gair, and Jeremy A. Sabloff

1994 Community Structure at Sayil: A Case Study of Puuc Settlement. In *Hidden among the Hills: Maya Archaeology of the Northwest Yucatan Peninsula,* edited by Hanns J. Prem, 71-92. Acta Mesoamericana 7. Mockmuhl, Germany: Verlag Von Flemming.

Tozzer, Alfred M.

1941 *Landa's Relación de las Cosas de Yucatán: A Translation.* Papers of the Peabody Museum of American Archaeology and Ethnology, vol. 18. Cambridge: Harvard University. (See Diego de Landa.)

1957   *Chichen Itza and Its Cenote of Sacrifice.* Memoirs of the Peabody Museum of Archaeology and Ethnology, vols. 11, 12. Cambridge: Harvard University.

Villela, Khristaan D.

1993   The Classic Maya Secondary Tier: Power and Prestige at Three Polities. M. A. thesis, University of Texas at Austin.

Webster, David (ed.)

1989   *The House of the Bacabs.* Washington, D.C.: Dumbarton Oaks Research Library and Collection.

Willey, Gordon R.

1965   Artifacts. In *Prehistoric Maya Settlements in the Belize Valley,* by G. R. Willey, W. R. Bullard, Jr., J. B. Glass, and J. C. Gifford. Papers of the Peabody Museum of Archaeology, vol. 54. Cambridge, Mass.: Harvard University.

Wren, Linnea, and Peter J. Schmidt

1991   Elite Interaction during the Terminal Classic Period: New Evidence from Chichen Itza. In *Classic Maya Political History: Hieroglyphic and Archaeological Evidence,* edited by T. Patrick Culbert, 199–225. School of American Research Series. Cambridge: Cambridge University Press.

CHAPTER NINE

The Function of a Maya Palace at Yaxuna

A CONTEXTUAL APPROACH

James N. Ambrosino

In the study of archaeological materials, we commonly find it necessary to classify objects according to similar attributes in order to manage the massive amounts of data available to us. Classification has been fundamental to archaeology since the beginning of the discipline. While classification can be quite useful in organizing information, there remains the nagging question of the meaning or significance behind the resulting classes or types. That is, do the classification schemes imposed on the data by the researcher reflect real phenomena in the past? These schemes tend to be based on formal characteristics of the objects being studied, since this is what is visible to us given the static nature of the archaeological record. However, we must first be assured that variability within these formal characteristics directly relates to variability within the past cultural system in which they were manifested in order to say something meaningful about the dynamic cultural past.

Within Maya archaeology, the classification of monumental architecture presents particular problems. Maya archaeologists typically classify buildings according to a widely held set of criteria based on form, but sometimes there is no attempt to get at the cultural meanings behind these forms. More often, the cultural meanings that are attributed to various building classes are treated in a noncritical fashion. Such has been the case with the class of Maya buildings known as palaces. This is a major reason for the publication of the current volume, and hopefully the various studies herein will partly rectify this situation.

Over thirty years ago in a review of Maya architecture, Pollock (1965: 411) remarked that "the least satisfactory class of buildings, both from the point of view of type and of function, is the so-called palace." Unfortunately, the argument can be made that this still holds true today. As it is used in Maya archaeology, the term "palace" generally refers to multiroom structures that are organized according to layouts that stress horizontal rather than vertical dimensions. It frequently becomes a sort of catchall category for monumental architecture that is clearly different from buildings that would normally be considered part of the temple-pyramid class—that is, buildings in which the vertical aspect dominates. Further problems arise when considering structures that appear to be amalgams in which both horizontal and vertical aspects are equally stressed, for example, whether such structures should be considered elaborate palaces or elaborate temples. It is likely that the many structures lumped together within the class of palace served a variety of different functions. Moreover, a single palace may have been used in a number of ways at a given time and may have changed functions over time.

The essential question, then, is, How can we gain an understanding of the functions of particular Maya palaces? There are two major ways in which this can be done. One is through an examination of the formal characteristics of a given structure. These include such things as the layout of space within interiors, the form of the exteriors including decorative and/or iconographic elements, and the spatial positioning within the surrounding site, especially as this relates to other types of buildings. The other way in which we can hope to discern function is through an examination of the cultural deposits associated with Maya palaces. It is usually through a combination of the two that functions can be ascribed.

Although interpretations of formal characteristics of Maya architecture often are advanced through very sophisticated study, the analysis of associated archaeological deposits are sometimes lacking. This is an unfortunate circumstance, especially since this is the heart and soul of archaeological research throughout most of the world, where large, conspicuous remains are not the norm. It would seem that this situation would severely limit the extent to which Maya archaeology both incorporates and contributes to advances in general archaeological method and theory.

However, care must be taken in the interpretation of the cultural deposits associated with Maya palaces. It is crucial that we pay strict attention to the organization of these deposits. We must especially consider the formation processes that have created them. To overlook the patterns within these deposits or, even more dangerous, to render those patterns irretrievable through low-resolution excavation techniques would be to run the risk of arriving at false conclusions concerning the functions of these buildings.

A case study involving a particular Maya palace from the site of Yaxuna will be used to demonstrate the importance of a contextual approach to the archaeological record. This particular palace will be examined with an eye toward identifying its function through the analysis of both the formal characteristics of the structure and the cultural deposit associated with the structure. The cultural deposit will be examined critically using a contextual approach. It will be shown that in this case such a contextual approach leads to conclusions vastly different from those which would be derived from a merely casual treatment of the data.

The Setting

Between 1986 and 1996, the Selz Foundation Yaxuna Project has undertaken an extensive program of mapping and excavation throughout the site of Yaxuna and in some of its satellites. Since the results of this research are not yet widely published, a background of the formal characteristics and history of the site is in order. Yaxuna is a rank 2 center located approximately 22 km south of Chichen Itza in the modern state of Yucatan, Mexico (Garza T. and Kurjack 1980). The site is dominated by four large acropolis groups, each containing monumental architecture in triadic arrangement. The monumental core of the site contains a number of other pyramidal structures, as well as numerous housemounds that typically housed non-vaulted architecture, the remains of which are low stone walls and foundation braces. South of the monumental core exists an area of dense residential occupation.

The chronology of Yaxuna has recently been worked out, predominantly on the basis of ceramic evidence (Suhler, Ardren, and Johnstone 1998). The site was established by the Middle Preclassic (Yaxuna Ia: 500–250 B.C.), as evidenced by ceramics recovered from construction fill throughout the site. By the Late Preclassic (Yaxuna Ib: 250 B.C.–A.D. 250), much of the monumental construction within the core of the site had been started. Large construction projects were undertaken during the Early Classic (Yaxuna II: A.D. 250–600), resulting in the pattern of four acropolis groups visible today. It is for this time that we see firm evidence of royal kingship in the form of a rich tomb, the ceramics from which indicate ties to the central Peten (Suhler, Ardren, and Johnstone 1998: 173). It is also for the Early Classic that we first see evidence of warfare and violent political takeover, a theme which was repeated throughout the history of Yaxuna. Associated with these episodes of warfare has been a repeated pattern of ritual termination of politically significant structures and monuments, as well as portable objects that presumably would have been imbued with power.

The following Late Classic period (Yaxuna III: A.D. 600–700/750) at

Yaxuna has been somewhat an enigma. Initial results from survey and excavation suggested that the Late Classic was a time of virtual abandonment at the site, when an impoverished community there did not control the necessary resources to build public structures (Freidel 1987, 1992). These initial findings have recently been challenged by members of the project based on further ceramic analysis (Suhler, Ardren, and Johnstone 1998: 176–177), specifically the isolation of Arena Red ceramics that are diagnostic of the Late Classic in the northern lowlands (Brainerd 1958; Robles C. 1990). As a result, we can now date to the Late Classic at least one new vaulted structure and certain modifications to some existing public structures. Additionally, Sacbe 1, which runs 100 km east to Coba, can now be dated to the Late Classic occupation of Yaxuna (Suhler, Ardren, and Johnstone 1998: 177).

On the basis of ceramic evidence from throughout the northern lowlands, a situation of hostility between two regional powers, Coba to the east and Chichen Itza to the west, has been hypothesized to have been in existence during the Terminal Classic (A.D. 750–1150) (Andrews and Robles C. 1985; Robles C. and Andrews 1986). Although Chichen Itza lies only 22 km away, Yaxuna did not participate in the Sotuta ceramic sphere characteristic of the former. Rather, Terminal Classic (Yaxuna IVa) ceramics at Yaxuna are part of the Cehpech ceramic sphere and hold similarities to ceramic inventories in Coba and Puuc sites to the west. The Terminal Classic period at Yaxuna saw major modifications to public architecture and the construction of two buildings that would be classified as Puuc palaces. Additionally at this time, a portion of the site center was fortified and the northern boundary between Yaxuna and Chichen Itza secured (Ambrosino, Ardren, and Manahan 2001; Ardren 1997).

Puuc Palaces at Yaxuna

Two Terminal Classic (Yaxuna IVa) palaces exist at Yaxuna. Both were constructed in the Classic Puuc architectural style (Figure 9.1). Yaxuna lies within the easternmost area known to contain Puuc-influenced architecture. Extensively studied by Pollock (1965, 1980), Classic Puuc architecture is characterized by a thin veneer of finely dressed stone blocks, commonly square in shape, over a concrete and rubble core or hearting. Rather than slab vaults, Classic Puuc buildings tend to have boot-shaped vault stones that are likewise finely dressed on the outside. A number of other stylistic attributes are common to Classic Puuc architecture, including decorated cornices, rounded doorway columns, half-columns or colonnettes repeated

FIGURE 9.1. Structure 6F-68 at Yaxuna, a small Classic Puuc palace.

in long rows, three-member moldings in which the middle member is often decorated, and stone mosaics on upper facades with lattice and stepped fret designs common (Coe 1987: 114–118; Pollock 1980; Velázquez M. et al. 1988: 46–47). Buildings that are given the term "Puuc palace" tend to be long, multiroom range structures that are constructed on low basal platforms. However, some examples combine this typical form with a temple pyramid form in various ways; for example, the Palace at Sayil in its final construction phase was a three-story structure essentially consisting of three separate range-style constructions, one on top of and recessed back from the other.

The larger of the two Puuc palaces at Yaxuna represents a two-story addition to the back of Structure 6E-5 on the East Acropolis. The other palace, Structure 6F-68, is a small range structure that was constructed as an addition to the south side of Structure 6F-4 on the North Acropolis (Figure 9.2). Both of these palaces, representing late additions to their respective acropolis groups, were oriented away from the central plazas of the acropoli. In fact, the two-storied palace did not rest on the raised acropolis surface but rather on the original ground surface to the north side of the acropolis. This palace faces Sacbe 1 at a point very close to its terminus. It is possible that the construction of this palace was intended to redirect the focus of the East Acropolis toward the *sacbe* as a political statement. However, it must be emphasized that only minor test pit operations have been performed on

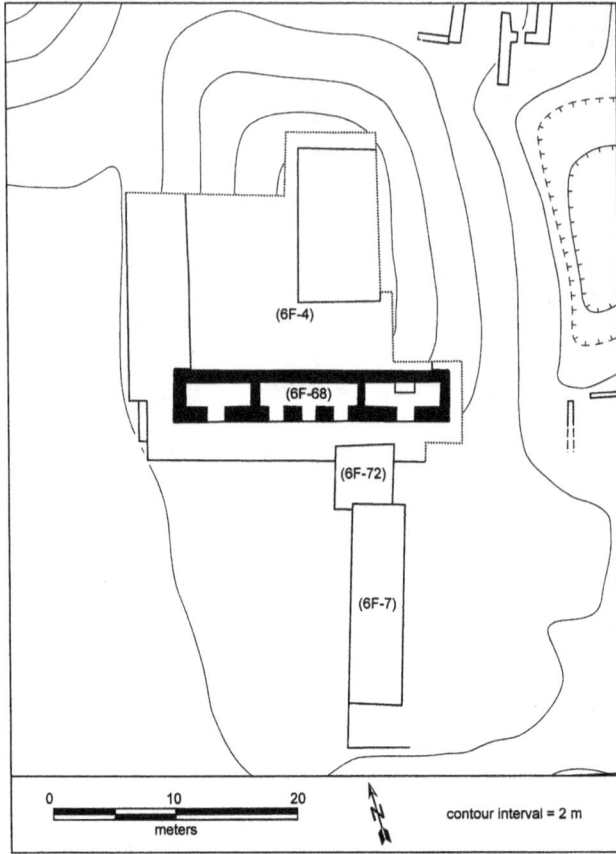

FIGURE 9.2. Plan of Structure 6F-68, including the long platform extending to the south.

the East Acropolis, thus limiting our understanding of the Terminal Classic occupation of the original structures there. It is interesting to note that a test pit placed at the summit of Structure 6E-2, the large central pyramid of the triadic group, produced no Cehpech ceramics but rather Postclassic (Yaxuna V) sherds directly underlain by Early Classic (Yaxuna IIa or possibly even Yaxuna Ib) ceramics (Freidel, Suhler, and Krochock 1990: 10). Unfortunately, such limited excavation merely indicates that Terminal Classic modifications were absent on the summit of this structure, and clearly further excavation is required before conclusions can be reached. The palace itself also did not receive any excavation; therefore, the only information we have concerning its plan and decoration is based on features visible on the surface. We also know that the palace currently exists in an extensive state of ruin, as none of its vaults are standing and much of its decorative veneer lies in a heap at the base of the structure.

The smaller Puuc palace, Structure 6F-68, has received extensive excavation and reconsolidation of its standing architecture between the 1992 and 1996 field seasons (Ambrosino et al. 1995, 1996; Ardren et al. 1994; Suhler and Freidel 1993). Like the other palace, Structure 6F-68 was appended to an existing pyramid in such a way that it reoriented the focus away from the central plaza of the North Acropolis (Figure 9.2). The original pyramid, Structure 6F-4, had a long gallery running along the western side, the original front of the building, which was partially collapsed while Structure 6F-68 was occupied. In fact, it is hypothesized that the west side of the building was deliberately demolished as a political statement by the individuals who undertook the construction of Structure 6F-68 (Ambrosino et al. 1996; Suhler 1996). The new focus was to the south, where a large corner of the acropolis plaza was raised approximately 1 m above the central plaza level.

Structure 6F-68 was built according to a popular Classic Puuc plan consisting of three rooms set in a line, all facing the same direction (Pollock 1980: 567). The building represents a small palace, measuring 26 m east-west by 5 m north-south. Stylistically, the exterior of Structure 6F-68 was constructed in the western Puuc tradition as defined by Pollock (1980: 586). Certain design features, particularly the basal molding, indicate that the building is rather unique when compared to the corpus of known Puuc-style civic/elite architecture. The basal molding is a three-member type, with the upper and middle members decorated (Figure 9.3). The upper member is a repeated scalloped or feathered design, while the middle member includes sets of three colonnettes interspersed with groups of veneer blocks carved with various images, including human forms in a number of postures and iconographic motifs. Additionally, the middle member of the basal molding includes banded colonnettes at regular intervals around the building. The only other Puuc building known to contain a basal molding elaborately carved with images is Structure 2C6 at Kabah (Pollock 1980). Although the basal molding of Structure 6F-68 at Yaxuna is unique in many respects, it is similar in layout to a few examples from the eastern Puuc region (Pollock 1980: 570–571) and the basement from the east wing of the Monjas at Chichen Itza (Bolles 1977). The upper facade of the building also included carvings of iconographic motifs and human likenesses; many of these were found in the collapsed rubble around the structure.

The iconography on Structure 6F-68 includes crossed geometric patterns, stepped fret designs, woven mat images, tasseled rosettes, sun-faced

FIGURE 9.3. Detail of Structure 6F-68 showing the decorated basal molding.

rosettes without tassels, and stylized faces. The cross and stepped fret patterns, although common in late Puuc architecture, are difficult to interpret. Many of the other designs seen on the building carry warfare symbolism. These include the tasseled rosettes that are very similar in design to battle standards portrayed at a number of lowland Maya sites; the sun-faced rosettes representing the heads of battle standards and possibly relating to the Sun-Jaguar, one of the supernatural beings that presided over war and sacrifice; and the stylized faces, one of which clearly represents a flayed sacrificial visage with its crescent moon–shaped eyes and skeletal jaw (Freidel, Schele, and Parker 1993: 293–336; Suhler and Freidel 1993: 87–89). A human figure, once decorating the upper facade and found in the rubble at the base of the building, probably represents a warrior, since he is depicted clutching a tasseled rosette to his chest as a shield. Similar circular, feathered shields are seen being used by warriors in battle in the murals of the Upper Temple of the Jaguar at Chichen Itza.

The woven mat, also present on Structure 6F-68, is a common symbol of rulership among the Maya. Archaeologists working at Copan have argued that a small building at that site decorated with mat imagery, Structure 10L-22A, functioned as a Popol Nah, literally "house of the mat" (Fash et al. 1992). According to sixteenth-century accounts, a Popol Nah was a Council House, a place where government officials and elders of the community would meet. In fact, the upper facade of this structure at Copan was decorated with human figures wearing large feathered headdresses, seated within niches atop place-name glyphs. They likely represent important nobles or council members from different areas throughout the Copan polity, each represented by an individual place-name (Fash et al. 1992). The basal molding on Structure 6F-68 at Yaxuna also contains images of seated lords with feathered headdresses. In this case, there are seated individuals portrayed in profile surrounding a fourth, centrally located individual carved in a frontal view. A diminutive individual who is dressed in a similar fashion accompanies this central lord. Similar assemblies of individuals are known to adorn buildings in the immediate region around Yaxuna, particularly at Chichen Itza and at X'telhu, a small satellite southwest of Yaxuna (M. Robertson 1986; Suhler and Freidel 1993: 89–90). Barbara Fash (cited in Freidel, Schele, and Parker 1993: 152, 437 as personal communication) has also suggested that the Popol Nah at Copan was associated with the teaching and performance of ritual dance, as a large dance platform stretches out in front of the building. A similar long, rectangular platform measuring approximately 5 m wide by at least 15 m long existed in front of Structure 6F-68 at Yaxuna (Figure 9.2).

Structure 6F-68 was found to be in an extensive state of ruin. The entire vault had collapsed except for a single line of semi-boot-shaped stones running along the rear of the building. Interestingly, a large proportion of the vault stones were encountered around the exterior of the structure, indicating that the southern half of the vault had likely fallen outward en masse with the front wall of the structure. None of the five lintels were in place, and only one stone large enough to be a lintel was encountered during excavation. Additionally, a number of elements from Structure 6F-68, including large veneer columns and stones from the unique upper member of the basal molding, were found scattered about the North Acropolis at great distances from the building. The columns, which originally decorated the lower facade of Structure 6F-68 as evidenced by in situ examples, each weigh over two hundred pounds and could only have arrived at their positions by human agents. A few columns consistent with those from Structure 6F-68 were also found within the ballcourt plaza to the southwest of the North Acropolis, yet it is possible that these were once part of an as yet unexcavated building. The nature of the collapse, along with evidence of percussion damage to the stones that remained intact, led us to conclude that human agents were involved in the destruction of the building.

Structure 6F-68 after its collapse directly overlay a dense deposit of artifactual material mostly comprised of ceramic sherds but also including lithics, groundstone implements, and faunal remains. At a glance, such materials might suggest midden accumulation in an area well lived in but infrequently, if ever, cleaned. But given their location along the entire front of the structure, including within doorways, this appears odd. Likewise, a consideration of these remains as the random effects of architectural collapse on post-abandonment floor assemblages without a closer examination of the remains would ignore potential information and possibly suggest misleading conclusions concerning the overall function of the building in question. If we are to arrive at meaningful conclusions concerning the possible functions of this Maya palace, we must first seek to understand the surrounding archaeological deposit.

Excavation of Structure 6F-68

The excavation of Structure 6F-68 at Yaxuna was initiated during the 1992 field season and continued through the 1996 field season. Excavation began in the interior of the eastern room, which was a clearly visible starting point due to surface indications of wall lines (Suhler and Freidel 1993: 78–91). During the initial clearing of a wide trench through the middle of this room, it was first noted that very little time had elapsed between the abandonment and the collapse of the building. Laying directly on the plaster floor of the eastern room were vault capstones. Excavation next proceeded through the doorway of this room to the exterior of the structure. This led to the discovery of the elaborate basal molding with its well-preserved iconographic motifs. Since a major goal of the Yaxuna project concerned research into Terminal Classic iconography, the next course of action decided upon was the exposure of the entire basal molding of Structure 6F-68. This was done within the time frame of the 1992 field season by the excavation of a narrow, 1.5 m wide trench in front of the edifice.

It was during the excavation of the narrow trench that Charles Suhler first noticed some unusual qualities of the archaeological deposit associated with Structure 6F-68. Banked against the base of the building, directly between the terrace floor and the stones of the collapsed upper facade, was a massive amount of cultural material composed primarily of large ceramic sherds. Also, within this deposit there appeared to be some unique concentrations. One of these was a concentration of very large reconstructible vessel fragments from liquid storage jars, encountered against the basal molding in front of the doorway to the eastern room. Also, the section of floor between the doorjambs was damaged; the smoothed plaster was absent and a large proximal fragment of a chalcedony stemmed point lay within the damaged floor. Overall, this deposit resembled a type of ritual deposits, referred to as termination deposits, first noticed and explicitly discussed at Cerros (Freidel 1986; Garber 1983, 1989).

Excavations continued during the following two field seasons and resulted in the total clearing of the eastern and central rooms; however, the most intriguing finds came from explorations outside of the structure. As clearing progressed along the plaza immediately west of Structure 6F-68 in an effort to define the basal platform on which it sat, we came across a thick deposit of pure white marl banked within a small corner. This marl deposit averaged about 20 cm thick and covered a small, benchlike protrusion. Incorporated into the marl was a dense concentration of ceramic sherds, including numerous examples that were quite large, representing significant sections of vessels. A similar situation was observed within the doorway to the western room, only here the white marl and sherd deposit measured over 50 cm in thickness. Upon excavation of the interior of the western room, it was apparent that the white marl existed only within the doorway. This suggests a special deposit, which we interpret as a part of the ritual termination of Structure 6F-68.

An extensive deposit of large ceramic sherds was also encountered in front of Structure 6F-68 resting on the building platform (Figure 9.4). A large horizontal exposure of this area was undertaken in two parts because of time constraints, the eastern half being excavated during the 1995 season and the western half following in 1996. Significant cultural debris was noted in front of the eastern room, but the area in front of the western room contained especially dense concentrations. The area fronting the central room, on the other hand, had relatively little cultural debris. Much of the deposit was found to rest directly on the hearting of the basal platform. The plaster that once covered the platform had been removed prior to the deposition of the dense sherd concentrations here. A sharp break in the plaster could be seen running along a rough line between 1.5 and 2 m away from the structure, indicating that it had been chopped out and removed rather than merely degraded along a portion of the platform.

The absence of plaster flooring that appeared to result from intentional cutting and removal was also noted within room interiors and on the platform extending from Structure 6F-68 to the south. These floor cuts tended to be circular or oval in shape, measuring roughly 1 m in diameter, or semicircular when oriented in a corner, and penetrated the plaster flooring. They typically resembled holes dug for dedication caches but lacked the smoothed plaster patch repairing them. Their placement was also similar in different rooms, as such features were encountered in the exact centers

FIGURE 9.4. Dense deposit of large ceramic sherds encountered in front of the western room of Structure 6F-68. (Photograph courtesy of Traci Arden)

of both the western and central rooms. Floor cuts in the central room and in the floor of the platform south of it contained ceramics that have been shown to be associated with the archaeological deposit atop the basal platform of Structure 6F-68.

The hole in the center of the western room was found to extend downward to a desecrated burial crypt (Figure 9.5). The crypt was lined with rough cobbles and covered with long, flat capstones. The hole was positioned over a gap in the capstones above the upper portion of the pelvis of the interred individual, who proved to be an adult female buried in an extended supine position. The lower torso of the skeleton was intact and fairly well preserved; however, only a portion of the upper torso was present. Two teeth were found scattered within this area, as well as a jumble of ribs and small bone fragments that mostly overlay the pelvis, which appeared to have been shifted slightly. Some of the ribs, some human teeth apparently from the buried individual, and smaller undifferentiated bone fragments were found within the soil matrix that filled the gap between the capstones and lay above the level of the burial. Furthermore, part of the matrix appeared very dark gray and was rich in charcoal, while a section bordering it was reddish brown and of a texture consistent with heat alteration. It appears that the cut into the floor within the western room was performed

FIGURE 9.5. Desecrated burial in the western room of Structure 6F-68; view after excavation.

as an act of desecration, with the burial entered and portions of the skeleton, including the skull, pulled out. A fire was then lit in the hole that remained.

Excavations in the vicinity of Structure 6F-68 revealed other evidence of localized fires throughout the area. A number of these were located in the interiors of the rooms, usually confined to the corners. Here both plaster floors and the walls above them appeared blackened. Two other areas of intense burning were located on the basal platform in front of the western and eastern rooms. On the western side, portions of the dry core fill representing the hearting of the basal platform were scorched on their upper surfaces, with the surrounding soil being very dark as well. Numerous burned sherds were located in this area. Within the northeast corner of the platform extending south from Structure 6F-68, four flat stones were arranged on end in a rectangular formation to house a fire. All four stones were firecracked into numerous pieces, and the soil within the rectangular box was blackened and contained a few burned sherds. Finally, immediately west of the marl deposit west of the building into the level of the central plaza, a large oval fire pit had been constructed. The matrix within this feature was very dark and rich in carbonized particles. Stones from the veneer of Structure 6F-68 were encountered within the pit, many of which bore evidence of fire damage including black stains and spalled surfaces.

A Contextual Approach to the Meaning of the Deposit

As stated above, the resemblance of the archaeological deposit associated with Structure 6F-68 to the previously recognized pattern of ritual termination was noted early in the excavation. A contextual analysis of the ceramics in the deposit has only strengthened our conviction that the structure was in fact ritually terminated and that the deposit represents the remains of this ritual activity.

First, as an aggregate, the ceramics in the Structure 6F-68 deposit were compared on the basis of sherd sizes against ceramics in other contexts at Yaxuna. Sherd sizes are thought to vary between termination and other types of refuse deposits, with the former type containing higher proportions of large sherds. The assumption is that refuse deposits such as swept zones tended to be trampled and extensively reworked after deposition. Also, a number of ethnoarchaeological studies in the Maya area have documented the retention of large ceramic sherds and vessel fragments for various purposes, which resulted in a tendency for middens to contain smaller, unusable sherds (Deal 1998; Hayden and Cannon 1983; Smyth 1989, 1991).

The samples that were compared with Structure 6F-68 came from deposits excavated in the site center where firm residential functions were suggested, and from a dense midden excavated north of the site center that was situated well away from its associated dwelling structures. Sherd size was measured by the areal size of individual specimens rather than by sherd weight, a more imprecise but common method. The method chosen is similar to techniques that are commonly used in the sorting of lithic debitage, in which items are sorted into discrete classes based on areal size. Also, only Terminal Classic slateware sherds were compared, to avoid problems inherent in differing ceramic composition, that is, different wares tending to break in different manners and thus into different sizes. When Structure 6F-68 deposits were compared to the residential deposits derived from the site center, a Chi-square test indicated that they behaved differently with regard to sherd size at a significance level of 0.022. The test was even more significant, with $p < 0.001$, when the midden from the north was included in the comparison. In both cases, the deposit associated with Structure 6F-68 contained significantly greater amounts of very large sherds. Thus, if the Structure 6F-68 deposit did represent a midden or residential trash, it was clearly different from other trash deposits encountered at Yaxuna.

If we accept that the deposits are not middens left by the final occupants of the building or area in general, what then could they represent? Two remaining possibilities are very different in their implications, yet both can be understood within the context of warfare and the rapid fortification of the North Acropolis, for which we have evidence (Ambrosino, Ardren, and Manahan 2001). The first possibility is that the deposits could represent the vessel and tool assemblages of the building that were abandoned in a quick evacuation of the site. This is exactly the situation that has been hypothesized at Aguateca from the recent work there (Inomata 1997). If that were the case here, it is clear that these deposits would directly reflect the function of this particular Maya palace. As appealing as this possibility is, it is complicated by a second one, namely, that the deposits represent the remains of the violent termination of Structure 6F-68 as a result of Terminal Classic warfare. Given this as the origin of the artifactual deposits, it follows that the materials need not reflect the actual functions of the building, except as a general statement of its perceived significance within the elite power structure at Yaxuna.

The decision between these two possibilities rests on the spatial distributions of vessels within the deposits that are particular to each scenario. In the quick abandonment scenario we might expect ceramic vessels, especially large jars, to have been left near their place of use or storage. Furthermore, entire vessels should be found broken within very localized areas, if in fact they were destroyed by the collapsing architectural material. On the other hand, previous investigations of termination have shown this to involve the scattering of purposefully smashed ceramic vessels and artifacts in addition to other activities, including the layering of white marl, the systematic defacement of architectural facades, and the burning of ritual fires on the structure being terminated (Freidel 1986; Freidel and Schele 1989; Garber 1983, 1989; R. Robertson 1983). Thus, the expected vessel distributions across space are very different under this scenario, with partial vessels predominating and complete vessels found scattered over wide expanses.

In order to discern how individual vessels were spatially distributed within the 6F-68 deposits, a program of ceramic refitting was undertaken. To make this task manageable, especially considering the recovered sherds totaled over twenty-five thousand, it was necessary to concentrate on rim sherds, except where very unique vessels could be identified. As a result of the refitting exercise, a total of 137 vessel fragments, deriving from over one hundred distinct vessels, were pieced together. The fragments ranged from practically complete vessels to a mere 2 refitted rim sherds. Very few of the vessels (less than 5 percent) could be considered complete, based on percentage of rim representation. Some of the complete vessels were found in localized areas, while fragments from others were found in widely scattered locations. The sherds of one of the complete vessels, a Xuku Incised grater bowl (Figure 9.6), were found on the basal platform in front of the western room, on the surface of Structure 6F-72 (a low platform in front of the central and east rooms of 6F-68), and within cuts into the floors of Structure 6F-72 and the central room of Structure 6F-68.

The incomplete vessels were likewise found in both localized and widely scattered contexts around Structure 6F-68. Eight different incomplete vessels were made up of refits deriving from both the doorway of the western room and the thick deposit west of Structure 6F-68. Within both of these areas, the sherds were encountered within white marl matrix. One area immediately outside of the doorway to the west room produced two different slateware bowls that had been neatly broken in half and set in place. A number of incomplete vessels were pieced together from sherds scattered over a roughly 10 × 3 m area on the basal platform in front of the western room.

Overall, the distribution of vessels around Structure 6F-68 appears consistent with the termination scenario. The ceramic assemblage is dominated by partial vessels, and although some complete vessels were encoun-

FIGURE 9.6. Reconstructed Xuku Incised grater bowl found scattered within the deposit associated with Structure 6F-68.

tered in localized areas, others were found widely scattered throughout the deposit. In the case of the Xuku Incised grater bowl noted above (Figure 9.6), large pieces of this vessel were found both inside and outside the structure, with some pieces coming from intentional cuts into floors that have been interpreted as distinct termination features. Thus, the assignment of residential functions to Structure 6F-68 on the basis of the various cookware and servingware sherds located in its immediate vicinity clearly would be a hasty one.

Discussion

In order to understand the functions of individual Maya palaces, both the formal attributes and the associated archaeological deposits must be considered. According to its formal attributes, the particular palace in question here, Structure 6F-68 at Yaxuna, had important political functions during the Terminal Classic period. The iconography on the building identifies the building as a Popol Nah or Council House. Moreover, warfare-related imagery is prominent on the building facade. The layout of the building, as well as its close association with a long platform probably used for dance performances, is nearly identical to that of a previously identified Popol Nah at Copan (Fash et al. 1992). As a Popol Nah, this example of a Puuc palace would have served as a meeting place for a council of elders and leaders of the Yaxuna polity to discuss political policy and, given the prominent warfare imagery, to plan warfare and defense strategies. Following the suggestion of Barbara Fash (cited in Freidel, Schele, and Parker 1993: 152, 437 as personal communication), Structure 6F-68 may have also been associated with the performance and teaching of ritual dance.

An initial look at the archaeological deposit associated with Structure 6F-68 revealed the presence of large quantities of domestic items, possibly suggesting a residential function for the structure. However, a closer examination of this deposit demonstrated that much of it resulted from the ritual termination of the building. Aspects of this termination—e.g., the near total destruction of the building, the wide scattering of facade elements, the evidence for extensive burning, and the desecration of the burial within the western room—indicate that this was a violent act performed with intentions of desecration. Given the fortification of the North Acropolis immediately prior to this, it appears that the termination of Structure 6F-68 was an outcome of the defeat of Yaxuna in warfare. Ceramic and other indicators within the termination deposit implicate forces from Chichen Itza as the perpetrators of this termination and the victors over Yaxuna at this time (Ambrosino, Ardren, and Stanton in press).

Since the domestic artifacts are the result of ritual termination, they cannot be assumed to have been associated with Structure 6F-68 prior to this event, and thus cannot be used to suggest a residential function for the building. Also, many of the ceramic vessels incorporated within the deposit are Sotuta varieties used at Chichen Itza but foreign to Yaxuna prior to this event. Essentially, these particular vessels were likely imposed on the structure post-abandonment rather than having been used at the structure by its occupants. Their forms say nothing directly about the function of the building, but their context does. Looking at the archaeological deposit associated with Structure 6F-68 contextually, the notion that the building served an important political function at the site is supported. The extensive termination deposit, the destruction of the building, and the elaborate desecration of the structure represent a massive undertaking and a decisive statement of victory. That this building received such attention in the defeat of Yaxuna suggests that it was considered to be essential to the power base of the polity.

A question that remains concerns the function of the other Puuc palace at Yaxuna. Although similar in general construction technique, this structure is formally very different from Structure 6F-68. There is some evidence, on the basis of surface remains, that this palace may have also been terminated as part of the same warfare event that saw the destruction

of Structure 6F-68 and much of the North Acropolis. However, this remains to be tested through excavation and a detailed analysis of its associated archaeological deposit. This is the crux of the matter, for it is
only through such an analysis that we can hope to understand how the
two buildings, both classified as Maya palaces, functioned within Terminal
Classic society at Yaxuna. Once this is done, we will be on firmer ground
for interpreting the dynamic past on the basis of the static remains of the
present.

ACKNOWLEDGMENTS

The excavations at Yaxuna discussed in this chapter were done under the direction
of David Freidel and were made possible through the generous support of the Selz
Foundation of New York. I must also thank multiple individuals who assisted in
the excavation of Structure 6F-68 and its surroundings including Traci Ardren, Dave
Johnstone, Kam Manahan, Jonathan Pagliaro, Justine Shaw, Travis Stanton, Charles
Suhler, Tania Wildman, and, of course, the men of Yaxuna.

REFERENCES

Ambrosino, James N., Traci Ardren, and Kam Manahan
2001 Fortificaciones defensivas en Yaxuná, Yucatán. In *Yucatán a través de los
      siglos*, edited by Ruth Gubler and Patricia Martel, 49–66. Mérida: Universidad
      Autónoma de Yucatán.
Ambrosino, James N., Traci Ardren, and Travis W. Stanton
in press The History of Warfare at Yaxuna. In *Warfare and Conflict in Ancient
      Mesoamerica*, edited by M. Kathryn Brown and Travis W. Stanton. Tuscaloosa:
      University of Alabama Press.
Ambrosino, James, David Freidel, David Johnstone, Justine Shaw, and Charles Suhler
1996 *The Selz Foundation Yaxuna Project: Final Report of the 1995 Field Season.*
      Dallas: Department of Anthropology, Southern Methodist University.
Ambrosino, James, David Freidel, David Johnstone, and Charles Suhler
1995 *The Selz Foundation Yaxuna Project: Final Report of the 1994 Field Season.*
      Dallas: Department of Anthropology, Southern Methodist University.
Andrews, Anthony P., and Fernando Robles Castellanos
1985 Chichen Itza and Coba: An Itza-Maya Standoff in Early Postclassic Yucatan.
      In *The Lowland Maya Postclassic*, edited by Arlen F. Chase and Prudence M.
      Rice, 62–72. Austin: University of Texas Press.
Ardren, Traci
1997 The Politics of Place: Architecture and Cultural Change at the Xkanha Group,
      Yaxuná, Yucatán, Mexico. Ph.D. dissertation, Department of Anthropology,
      Yale University.
Ardren, Traci, Sharon Bennett, David Freidel, David Johnstone, and Charles Suhler
1994 *The Selz Foundation Yaxuna Project: Final Report of the 1993 Field Season.*
      Dallas: Department of Anthropology, Southern Methodist University.
Bolles, John S.
1977 *Las Monjas: A Major Pre-Mexican Architectural Complex at Chichen Itza.*
      Norman: University of Oklahoma Press.

Brainerd, George W.
1958   *The Archaeological Ceramics of Yucatan.* University of California Anthropological Records, vol. 19. Berkeley: University of California Press.

Coe, Michael D.
1987   *The Maya.* 4th ed. London: Thames and Hudson.

Deal, Michael
1998   *Pottery Ethnoarchaeology in the Central Maya Highlands.* Salt Lake City: University of Utah Press.

Fash, Barbara, William Fash, Sheree Lane, Rudy Larios, Linda Schele, Jeffrey Stomper, and David Stuart
1992   Investigations of a Classic Maya Council House at Copán, Honduras. *Journal of Field Archaeology* 19: 419–442.

Freidel, David A.
1986   Introduction. In *Archaeology at Cerros, Belize, Central America*, vol. 1: *An Interim Report*, edited by Robin A. Robertson and David A. Freidel, xiii–xxiii. Dallas: Southern Methodist University Press.
1987   *Yaxuna Archaeological Survey: A Report of the 1986 Field Season.* Report submitted to the Committee for Research and Exploration, National Geographic Society, Washington, D.C.
1992   Children of the First Father's Skull: Terminal Classic Warfare in the Northern Maya Lowlands and the Transformation of Kingship and Elite Hierarchies. In *Mesoamerican Elites: An Archaeological Assessment*, edited by Diane Z. Chase and Arlen F. Chase, 99–117. Norman: University of Oklahoma Press.

Freidel, David A., and Linda Schele
1989   Dead Kings and Living Temples: Dedication and Termination Rituals among the Ancient Maya. In *Word and Image in Maya Culture: Explorations in Language, Writing, and Representation*, edited by William F. Hanks, and Don S. Rice, 233–243. Salt Lake City: University of Utah Press.

Freidel, David, Linda Schele, and Joy Parker
1993   *Maya Cosmos: Three Thousand Years on the Shaman's Path.* New York: William Morrow.

Freidel, David A., Charles Suhler, and Ruth Krochock
1990   *Yaxuna Archaeological Survey: A Report of the 1989 Field Season and Final Report on Phase One.* Dallas: Department of Anthropology, Southern Methodist University.

Garber, James F.
1983   Patterns of Jade Consumption and Disposal at Cerros, Northern Belize. *American Antiquity* 48 (4): 800–807.
1989   *Archaeology at Cerros, Belize, Central America.* Vol. 2: *The Artifacts.* Dallas: Southern Methodist University Press.

Garza T., Silvia, and Edward Kurjack
1980   *Atlas Arqueológico del Estado de Yucatán.* Mexico City: Centro Regional del Sureste, Instituto Nacional de Antropología e Historia.

Hayden, Brian, and Aubrey Cannon
1983   Where the Garbage Goes: Refuse Disposal in the Maya Highlands. *Journal of Anthropological Archaeology* 2: 117–163.

Inomata, Takeshi
1997   The Last Day of a Fortified Classic Maya Center: Archaeological Investigations at Aguateca, Guatemala. *Ancient Mesoamerica* 8 (2): 337–351.

Pollock, H. E. D.
1965   Architecture of the Maya Lowlands. In *Handbook of Middle American Indi-*

ans, vol. 2: *Archaeology of Southern Mesoamerica*, part 1, edited by Gordon R. Willey, pp. 378–440. Austin: University of Texas Press.

1980   *The Puuc: An Architectural Survey of the Hill Country of Yucatan and Northern Campeche, Mexico.* Memoirs of the Peabody Museum of Archaeology and Ethnology, vol. 19. Cambridge: Harvard University.

Robertson, Merle Greene

1986   Some Observations on the X'telhu Panels at Yaxcaba, Yucatan. In *Research and Reflections in Archaeology and History: Essays in Honor of Doris Stone*, edited by E. Wyllys Andrews V, 87–111. Middle American Research Institute Publication 57. New Orleans: Tulane University.

Robertson, Robin A.

1983   Functional Analysis and Social Process in Ceramics: The Pottery from Cerros, Belize. In *Civilization in the Ancient Americas: Essays in Honor of Gordon R. Willey*, edited by Richard M. Leventhal and Alan L. Kolata, 105–142. Albuquerque: University of New Mexico Press.

Robles Castellanos, José Fernando

1990   *La secuencia cerámica de la región de Cobá, Quintana Roo.* Mexico City: Instituto Nacional de Antropología e Historia.

Robles Castellanos, [José] Fernando, and Anthony P. Andrews

1986   A Review and Synthesis of Recent Postclassic Archaeology in Northern Yucatan. In *Late Lowland Maya Civilization: Classic to Postclassic*, edited by Jeremy A. Sabloff and E. Wyllys Andrews V, 53–98. Albuquerque: University of New Mexico Press.

Smyth, Michael P.

1989   Domestic Storage Behaviour in Mesoamerica: An Ethnoarchaeological Approach. In *Archaeological Theory and Method*, vol. 1, edited by Michael B. Schoffer, 89–138. Tucson: University of Arizona Press.

1991   *Modern Maya Storage Behavior: Ethnoarchaeological Case Examples from the Puuc Region of Yucatan.* University of Pittsburgh Memoirs in Latin American Archaeology 3. Pittsburgh, Pa.: Department of Anthropology, University of Pittsburgh.

Suhler, Charles K.

1996   Excavations at the North Acropolis, Yaxuná, Yucatán, Mexico. Ph.D. dissertation, Department of Anthropology, Southern Methodist University.

Suhler, Charles, Traci Ardren, and David Johnstone

1998   The Chronology of Yaxuna: Evidence from Excavation and Ceramics. *Ancient Mesoamerica* 9: 167–182.

Suhler, Charles, and David Freidel

1993   *The Selz Foundation Yaxuna Project: Final Report of the 1992 Field Season.* Dallas: Department of Anthropology, Southern Methodist University.

Velázquez Morlet, Adriana, Edmundo López de la Rosa, Ma. del Pilar Casado López, and Margarita Gaxiola

1988   *Zonas Arqueológicas: Yucatán.* Mexico City: Instituto Nacional de Antropología e Historia.

CHAPTER TEN

Palace and Society in the Northern Maya Lowlands

Edward B. Kurjack

The houses of the ancient Maya nobility were carefully made of durable masonry, so some of the structures still stand with their roofs intact. Nineteenth-century explorers referred to these buildings as palaces or castles if the buildings were situated on hilltops. Archaeological surveys encounter hundreds of elite dwellings in various states of collapse, as well as the less substantial remains of ordinary housing. This chapter compares the Maya palace with other kinds of domestic architecture and explores the social significance of their similarities and contrasts.

Problems of Definition and Interpretation

Palaces are best understood in the context of the entire range of domestic construction. Maya settlements contained three kinds of homes: a few big, expensive palaces where numerous relatives lived together in a communal architectural complex; many small, simple structures that could only shelter a few people; and a number of dwellings that are intermediate between the two extremes. Because palace masonry is highly visible and other kinds of houses are harder to find and study, it is difficult to confirm the expected ratio of a few palaces to a modest number of intermediate buildings to many common houses.

Comparison between palaces and other kinds of housing highlights features that distinguish elite dwellings from those of others. These variations reveal inherent architectural advantages that facilitated the distinct activities of their inhabitants and shed light on some of the ways behavior in the grand structures contrasted with the life of ordinary Maya. The differences indicate a way of life for palace dwellers conforming to a "great tradition," while the subcultures of commoners involved separate material, social, and ideological patterns.

Diversity of house form and cost is an unmistakable sign of social complexity and stratification. Northern Maya palaces are all-masonry structures that represent substantial labor investment. The builders had to quarry, select, and shape blocks of limestone. Lime was burned and marl (*sahscab*) dug up for mixing in mortar and plaster. Once walls were high enough, the distance between them was covered with a corbeled vault or some other variation of the Maya arch. Palaces required thick walls to support these heavy roofs. Floors of elite dwellings were paved and the walls covered with stucco. These features all added to both the durability, or permanence, and energy cost of the palace.

Northern Maya palaces are characteristically divided into a number of small chambers that consist of one or rarely two or more rooms. A few palaces have only one room, most have three to five rooms, but some key elite dwellings have one hundred rooms or more. Solid partitions between rooms and groups of rooms block communication; for this reason, the occupants had to exit the buildings in order to speak with people living in adjacent chambers. Landa (Tozzer 1941) called these rooms or groups of rooms "cells" (*celdas*), such as those of a monastery or prison. The cellular plan of a typical Maya palace suggests that the organizations once housed in the buildings were markedly divided into small subgroups consisting of related nuclear families which probably lived in the individual cells. Together the inhabitants of a palace formed a large, composite family.

High cost, durability, numerous small, cell-like rooms, and impressive overall size, then, are the traits that identify elite dwellings. Quality housing constituted wealth, and more people could potentially fit into a house with many rooms than into a small one. Judging from the extent and cost of these structures, palaces sheltered the wealthiest, most populous, and therefore most significant domestic organizations of northern Maya society. Military, economic, and political power derived from the number, concentration, coordination, and wealth of palace occupants.

Mayanists consider a variety of buildings palatial. While all agree that the many-chambered, multilevel structures at Sayil, Labna, and Santa Rosa Xtampak fit the definition, most scholars include many smaller vaulted buildings as well. Both H. E. D. Pollock (1980) and George Andrews (1995) believe that the majority of the buildings with masonry roofs that they examined were once residences, but they correctly maintain that these structures served other purposes as well. Andrews reserves the term "palace" for a structure with rows of rooms surrounding a solid core and refers to many of the architectural configurations others might consider palaces as "range" and "core/wing" buildings. Earlier, however, Pollock (1980: 565) did not define palaces beyond reporting that elite dwellings conforming to that general category were found "in great numbers and in a large range of sizes and designs." The present chapter uses the term "palace" in this sense. In addition to the great palaces at Sayil, Labna, and other sites, I include many small vaulted structures with one to five or more rooms in the palace category.

Andrews and Pollock both call attention to the frequency of the courtyard group, a complex of buildings surrounding a patio or open court. Although separate edifices, together they were comparable to a single communal residence. Following Pollock's lead, such a complex is herein regarded as the equivalent of a single palace. A group of buildings such as the Nunnery Quadrangle at Uxmal, therefore, is deemed a palace.

Some Mayanists, thinking that the term "palace" should be reserved for the dwellings of territorial rulers, might prefer to consider only the largest dwelling at a key site to be the palace. A perusal of site maps, however, shows there are several candidates for such designation at almost any large Maya settlement. Palaces of almost equivalent size may be clustered at the site center or situated some distance from each other. The size of Structure 1, the Palace at Labna, is not much greater than that of Structures 4-13, the Temple Group (Pollock 1980: 7-51). Xcanalcruz (Maler 1971) is another large palace situated only a short distance to the north. It is therefore difficult to identify the one building that was a regal residence. Careful measurement of the total floor space or a count of the number of rooms might show that a structure is indeed the largest at a given site, but other nearby architectural complexes are usually only slightly smaller and therefore compete with the grandeur of the biggest palace.

So where did the ruler actually live? Some large architectural complexes include a suite of rooms that, to judge by size and position, was the home of the "first family" of that palace. The bigger apartments, however, are seldom much more sumptuous than others in the same communal dwelling. Nor does the largest chamber in one palace greatly overshadow that of the other elite residential complexes at the site. Several groups of rooms in different palaces of an ancient community might be considered candidates for designation as the royal residence. This observation—together with the presence of multiple palaces at any site—is significant for any interpretation of Maya political structure.

Chronology also confuses the picture. Since vaulted architecture is a hallmark of the Classic stage in the Maya area, Preclassic elite families probably lived under thatched roofs. Most Early Period palaces are much smaller than their later Pure Florescent counterparts, and the largest residential structures at protohistoric Mayapan and Tulum are diminutive by comparison with many earlier palaces (E. W. Andrews IV 1965). While all-masonry roofs or vaults are a key characteristic of Classic palaces, most elite protohistoric dwellings had thatch or beam-and-mortar roofs. The largest, best-known palace-type buildings at Labna, Sayil, Kabah, Santa Rosa Xtampak, and Uxmal are apparently Late Classic phenomena.

The study of pre-Columbian palaces in northern Yucatan has a venerable history. Stephens, Charnay, Holmes, and Maler all made special reference to these elite Maya dwellings. More recently, Karl Ruppert (1952), H. E. D. Pollock (1980), Ignacio Marquina (1951), E. Wyllys Andrews IV (1965), E. W. Andrews V (E. W. Andrews IV and E. W. Andrews V 1980), George Andrews (1995), Paul Gendrop (1990), and Anthony Andrews (E. W. Andrews IV and A. P. Andrews 1975) have all produced authoritative surveys of pre-Columbian architecture in northern Yucatan.

Excavators find metates and domestic ceramic in and around palaces; therefore, most students agree that these structures served as homes for Maya notables (see Cottier 1982; Kurjack 1974; Folan, Kintz, and Fletcher 1983; Garduño 1979; Gallareta 1984; Benavides 1987; Manzanilla 1987). Despite a century and a half of exploration, however, crucial questions about palace functions remain unanswered. Although many investigators delight in discussing traces of religious and political activities, any review of the literature reveals the reluctance of the Mayanists to say much about domestic uses of palaces. In part, this may be due to the unequivocal views of J. Eric Thompson (1966: 57–58), who insisted that palace-type structures were too dark and damp to have been used as houses. Thompson's well-deserved stature in the field requires investigators to confirm or refute his outlook by reporting in detail the evidence for mundane activities they find in palaces.

Mexican anthropologists believe conserving the rapidly deteriorating monuments of the pre-Columbian past to be an all-pervasive moral imperative, and scholars from other countries have aided in that effort and worked diligently to catalog architectural details. This necessary focus on stabilizing buildings and recording their features has channeled effort away from interpretation. Conservation and recording activities tend to focus on standing edifices, but pottery and other artifacts that would help to identify the functions of these wide-open structures have been hopelessly scattered over the centuries.

Interpretation is hindered because most buildings at Maya sites have collapsed. The relatively few examples of standing architecture cannot be considered a representative sample of palatial construction. Moreover, the majority of the buildings that remain intact belong to the relatively late concrete-veneer or Pure Florescent style. Early Period "true masonry" structures from the previous phase are seldom encountered with masonry roofs in place.

Numerous palaces have been excavated, but the information made available from these investigations seldom enables consideration of palace functions. Evidence about the ways that palaces and their component rooms were used is derived from precise information about the distribution of sherds, metates, and other artifacts inside and around the structures. In order to be useful, excavations must encompass not only the buildings and masonry platforms on which the palaces were constructed, but the surrounding areas as well. Artifact concentrations are often encountered just outside the walls of palaces or adjacent to platform retaining walls. Published reports seldom focus on such details, so questions about where people cooked, bathed, and disposed of wastes have yet to be answered. Ongoing studies of palaces at Xkipché (Reindel 1997) and Labna (Gallareta et al. 1999) will be welcome additions to the Maya database—especially if they can shed light on such problems.

Cost-effectiveness of Maya Houses

Pre-Columbian murals and sculpture depict dwellings resembling the traditional cottages found in rural Yucatan today. These houses may have lacked the permanence and size of fine palace masonry, but they were inexpensive, efficient, and quickly constructed. Empty lots in villages that have been occupied for hundreds of years do not contain the kinds of surface traces that archaeologists record on site maps, so we can be certain that little remains of such ancient wattle-and-daub structures. Surveyors did, however, find clear evidence of the traditional Maya house both at Coba on the east side and Dzibilchaltun on the west side of the Yucatan peninsula.

Commoners built dwellings from primary resources that were readily available in the forest. This reliance on inexpensive, easily found, and quickly worked raw building materials partly determined the shape of common houses.

Most traditional one-room cottages in Yucatan today have an oval or apsidal plan. Instead of trying to bend branches to form sharp right angles, the Maya construct wattle walls and roof frameworks with rounded corners. Native carpenters bundle thin rods and bend them to the necessary shape to form the curved end purlins (see Wauchope 1938: 48). This technique, an efficient match of shape and material, produces added interior space at the ends of the house. The resulting dwellings, with their distinctive layout, can be rapidly constructed at minimum cost. This advantage facilitated migration for part of the population.

Those who must move often and abandon their homes are best served by low-cost housing. Lincoln (2000) and Repetto Tio's (1999) studies of seventeenth- and eighteenth-century church records from Yucatan show that while some families remained in the same town for generations, new settlers were constantly arriving from all directions. Evidently, each community had both a core population and a sizable transient group. The strength of a family's ties to a settlement was probably reflected by the energy cost of their dwelling, for even today the leading families in a Maya village indicate their status by constructing masonry homes. On the other hand, Farris (1984) underscores documents written by colonial officials complaining that the migrating Maya had so little that they could carry all of their possessions and quickly build new homes in the forest. People who move frequently, of course, have little time to improve their properties and acquire belongings. A subcultural contrast between shifting and permanent villagers probably predates the conquest and suggests a practical explanation for some of the differences between ancient Maya dwellings.

Few archaeologists have reported physical proof for the existence of thatched houses with apsidal plans. Wauchope once considered the absence of such buildings from the detailed map of protohistoric Mayapan to be conclusive. Until the research at Dzibilchaltun proved otherwise, he thought that the contemporary style of apsidal cottage was a late introduction to the northern lowlands (see Wauchope 1940: 236; Scholes and Roys 1948: 71–72). Some scholars, finding only rectangular rooms at their sites, still refuse to accept the importance of the round-ended shape as a Maya architectural form.

The few places where surveyors have encountered round-ended structures show that they had a wide distribution. Folan, Kintz, and Fletcher (1983), Garduño (1979), and Gallareta (1984) report numerous apsidal houses at Coba, while Benavides (1987) presents detailed plans and photographs of wall foundations for such buildings at the site.

Kurjack (1974; Garza and Kurjack 1980; see Ochoa 1995) describes evidence from Dzibilchaltun, where one of the well-preserved structures with rounded corners even had a Late Classic burial cyst symmetrically placed under the floor. The reason that so many ancient wall foundations for apsidal structures still exist at Dzibilchaltun is probably linked to the popularity of a special type of thatched cottage in the communities surrounding that site. Due to the quantity of loose rock scattered over the surface of the area, contemporary villagers often prefer this material to wattle-and-daub for the walls of their houses. Many traditional, round-ended dwellings there have stone walls erected without the use of mortar. Wauchope (1938: fig. 25) illustrates one of these buildings. Villagers everywhere build wooden or wattle-and-daub walls on low limestone foundations, but the basal courses of masonry for houses with stone walls usually consist of especially large, thick slabs set upright. Difficult to move without great effort, many such foundation blocks from similar ancient houses remain in place.

Although many wall foundations for apsidal structures are present at Dzibilchaltun, I assume that other round-ended structures for which no readily visible surface traces have been found also formed an important component of the settlement. Some of the platforms now devoid of any construction on their surfaces may have once supported such structures. Considerable blank areas on the published map of Dzibilchaltun would have allowed even at the center of the site for apsidal structures that subsequently disappeared without leaving surface traces. Excavations in some of these "empty" zones have already revealed considerable evidence of human occupation (Lizama 2000).

Pre-Columbian houses that combined some palace characteristics with simpler features reflect patterns intermediate between model elite and ideal commoner behavior. Elite dwellings were not all as large as the Sayil palace. While the biggest palaces contained a hundred or more chambers, most houses with masonry roofs had only a few rooms, and a few all-masonry dwellings had only one room. Multiroom structures with thatched roofs and plans similar to the layout of two- or three-room palaces constitute another well-known type of Maya domestic architecture. Moreover, single-room houses with walls of stone, wattle-and-daub, or other perishable material and thatched roofs also varied greatly in energy cost (see Kurjack 1974). Thus Maya society was more complex than a simple dichotomous elite-commoner system; nevertheless, the contrasts between the largest palaces and the simplest cottages indicate differences between two ideal sets of behavioral tendencies.

Functions of Palatial Architecture

Maya palaces were dwellings for nobility and royalty. The summary descriptions of the buildings included here serve to outline the characteristics of elite versus common housing and explore their functions. We can interpret the contrasts between the different kinds of residential architecture by studying the potential of features that make palaces different from ordinary houses. These features are high cost, durability or permanence, and large size.

The special characteristics of a palace are all closely related to the stratification system, for palaces were sumptuous by comparison with other dwellings. Wealth invested in architecture reflects the social position of its occupants, so in complex societies the elite demonstrate their superior standing by maintaining monumental homes. The riches of the elite, including natural resources in the vicinity of their houses and communities, had to be protected; therefore, whether or not the Maya conceptualized the palaces as military centers, these concentrations of manpower functioned as strongholds.

The permanence of the Maya palace derives from the higher quality of the materials used in its construction. Vaulted masonry used to build Classic Maya elite houses is much more substantial than wattle-and-daub walls and layered palm roofs. Storms that periodically cross the Yucatan peninsula damage thatch, but while palaces are not immune from the elements, some of these buildings have withstood tropical winds and rains for hundreds of years. Evidently palace dwellers and their elegant belongings had better protection from the elements than common houses could offer.

In addition to providing the material benefits that came from living in a durable shelter, the added effort and cost that went into palace construction was a deliberate attempt to gain social prestige and historical significance (see McAnany 1995). The grandeur of elite dwellings was used to justify both the political pretensions of occupants and territorial rights of a broader population.

Contemporary ethnic conflict involving destruction of monuments historically linked with opposing groups—their places of worship, schools, homes, and even their gravestones—reflects the symbolic meaning that humans give to monumental architecture. While ordinary houses can be taken and reused, castles, sacred buildings, and schools that legitimize the old order are often destroyed.

Similar attempts to rewrite history can be viewed at the central plaza of Dzibilchaltun. The breaking up of stelae and their reuse in the walls of new temples, the demolition and reorientation of buildings on the Great Plaza, and the sixteenth-century construction of a chapel there with material taken from earlier architecture are all examples of this kind of activity (E. W. Andrews IV and E. W. Andrews V 1980; Maldonado 1995).

Palace construction even influenced Maya domestic tranquility. As constant reminders of enduring elite power and the futility of resisting established rulers, the monumentality of palaces constituted a relatively inexpensive alternative to the use of force in the maintenance of social control. Similar relationships between architecture and political organization exist all over the world.

Historically, however, the splendor of the palace tends to impress external enemies in another way: opulence draws the attention of predatory neighbors. If monumental dwellings functioned to create stability within a community, these buildings also served as foci of competition and conflict between major settlements.

The durability of Maya masonry, however, added a further advantage: vaulted houses could be quickly and easily prepared for defense. Narrow doorways could be barricaded with minimal effort. Vaulted roofs cannot be set on fire, so without laboriously breaking through masonry walls or carrying out a frontal attack against easily defended positions, it would have been hard for enemies to harm those inside a palace. Mounting a decisive sudden raid would have been particularly difficult, for Maya towns had extensive, lightly settled peripheries, with prominent palaces situated near the centers surrounded by smaller buildings. This type of settlement layout protected the central palaces from surprise assaults. If more security was needed, the Maya would build fortifications around the central buildings (see Kurjack and E. W. Andrews V 1976; Webster 1980; Garza and Kurjack 1980). Thus some palaces functioned at least to some degree as forts and may be considered military architecture.

In those parts of the Yucatan peninsula with haystack-shaped hills, the Maya sometimes situated palaces at the tops of these formations. People living on the hilltops had to climb up and down steep slopes in order to carry out most activities. The potential for defense is the best explanation for such efforts; the ease with which the heights could be protected was the most likely reason behind the selection of these locations.

The difference between the potential of a large, many-chambered palace and that of a one-room cottage to shelter people is evident. Most of the cells or chambers of a palace are about equal in size to the single-room homes of contemporary villagers. Each palace cell contained sufficient room for a nuclear family, so until contrary evidence is found, I continue to believe that nuclear families inhabited most of the individual chambers of a Maya palace.

One advantage of the larger northern Maya palaces was its capacity to concentrate elite kinsmen in multifamily dwellings. The size of houses and house groupings at pre-Columbian sites indicates that people at all levels of society formed extended families (see Manzanilla 1987). The plan of some palaces, however, suggests that the elite often exaggerated this pattern by congregating their kin in large communal dwellings. Commoners may have lived and worked as extended families too, but the size of their domestic groups was smaller and the spatial arrangement of their dwellings was much less compact. It was therefore easier for elite groups with members already living together to organize for a joint project than it was for more widely scattered, loosely associated commoners to assemble for concerted action.

Ethnohistorical sources describe multiple family residences for the period prior to the conquest and ethnographers confirm the importance of extended families for contemporary Maya social organization. At any given moment, however, few multiple-family domestic groups can be found in rural Yucatan. While almost all dwellings in any village contain nuclear families, careful inquiry reveals that the eldest children of most couples are born in patrilocal extended-family settings. As this extended family grows to be too large, it breaks up. New houses are then constructed and younger couples move out. Therefore, despite the low frequency of extended families, this cultural pattern underlies both past and present social organization.

The choice of a one-room dwelling for a nuclear family or a structure that can expand to house a larger organization is at least partially determined by the original layout of the architecture. Robbins (1966) and Flannery (1972) describe the sociological significance of round versus quadrilateral ground plans. Adding three walls to existing structures efficiently enlarges buildings with four sides, but circular dwellings cannot be made bigger without complete reconstruction. Inhabitants of a community with round houses must erect an entirely new building when additional floor space is needed. While additions to quadrilateral plans result in larger buildings that are closely packed into dense settlements, the space between even those round buildings that are very close together inhibits the formation of compact architectural masses.

The two types of plans commonly used by the northern Maya for their houses—quadrilateral buildings for the elite and apsidal structures for the commoners—have these same advantages and constraints. When the farmer's family, housed in a cottage with thatched roof and apsidal plan, grows large enough to need additional space, another structure is put up. Rather than enlarge an existing apsidal house, rural Maya families construct a separate cottage. While palaces often form compact masses of architecture, the traditional Maya cottage is associated with settlements that are spread over a broad expanse of land.

Palaces sheltered large, well-organized domestic groups. The chambers of Maya palaces provided housing for many more individuals than did the typical houses of the common families. Living together in the same palace requires organization. Construction, maintenance, and operation of a multiple family dwelling, as well as the leadership needed to resolve the increased conflict related to life in close proximity, necessitated conformity to a powerful authority. The same coordination that was necessary for communal existence in a large building, together with the concentrated palatial manpower, allowed palace dwellers to dominate the more dispersed segments of the community.

The greater number of people living in a palace constituted a potential military force, for those elite homes with significant manpower could readily defend themselves or attack others. As houses for large groups that habitually acted in concert, the palaces could function as barracks containing teams of men available to do battle as organized units. The male residents of a palace constituted a standing force, around which those living in a dispersed mode could rally as auxiliary troops. Moreover, some palaces are situated in high, easily defended places while others are frequently associated with defensive features such as fortification walls. Over a century ago, Lewis Henry Morgan (1880), whose writings initiated academic study of Maya society, pointed out the likely link between communal life in Maya palaces and warfare (see Kurjack 1974: 20).

The concentrated population of a large palace had economic as well as military potential. Procurement of exotic materials for elite consumption is linked with military activity in many early civilizations. As leading organizations of Maya society, palaces had the manpower and organization to undertake long-distance trading expeditions.

Palace dwellers were also a source of mass labor for productive activities. Weaving was an important occupation in the Maya country, for richly dressed individuals frequently appear in sculpture and murals. Although contemporary use of cloth-making machinery cheapens the cost of cloth, we know that the preindustrial world placed high value on textiles. As the result of long and tedious work, pre-Columbian cloth was a light, easy to transport form of wealth. Certainly palaces in other early civilizations were production centers for textiles, and ethnohistorical accounts attest to the significance of Maya trade and tribute in this commodity.

Construction is another productive endeavor that is linked with military activity in many early civilizations. While it is doubtful that the Maya nobility mixed mortar or worked as hod carriers, the management personnel of large projects probably came from palace groups.

A key question for future palace research is to determine the degree to which the elite residences constituted such production centers. Certainly, the manpower inherent in the palace population should have facilitated economic specialization; however, relatively little obvious evidence for manufacturing has been found in excavated palaces in the northern Maya Lowlands.

Spacious storage facilities in and around the Maya palace complex supported domestic, economic, and military functions. The presence of underground cisterns for water storage was one of the first features to fascinate early explorers. These chultuns, usually associated with palace-type architecture, were excavated in order to secure the marl (*sahscab*) needed as building material and then adapted to trap and store the water required to mix mortar. Some palace areas or rooms contained many large, striated jars that were particularly well suited for water storage. The specific purpose of some special palace features has not yet been exactly determined; the unique vaulted and thickly plastered *"chultuns"* at Labna and Dzula are examples of such structures (see Zapata 1989).

The palace complex usually includes areas such as temples, special tombs for significant individuals, and large halls that were probably reserved for political and religious gatherings. Plazas and patios served as sites for mass meetings.

The number of entrances leading into a palace chamber is a clue to the degree of privacy associated with its use. Most vaulted rooms are about 5 m long and have a single door. Other chambers, however, have multiple doorways or a column at the front. While one doorway appears restrictive, two or more doors invite entrance by the ease of access they present. Thus vaulted chambers with many doors constituted semipublic space and those with single doors were more private areas. I suspect that rooms with several doorways or columns, lacking the intimacy of ordinary palace cells, functioned as Maya *megarons* similar to those of Bronze Age Greece. These halls were likely used to entertain visiting nobles and for other public activities.

A series of doorways begins to resemble a colonnade, particularly if the room they enter is longer than the typical palace cell. Structure 44 on the south side of the principal plaza at Dzibilchaltun is a great hall, the plan of which contrasts with the cellular layout of Maya domestic architecture (see Maldonado 1995). Multiple entryways are characteristic of the colonnaded halls at Chichen Itza and similar structures elsewhere. These buildings, the key to "Early Postclassic" organizational innovations at that site, probably functioned as men's houses or clubhouses for warriors. (Kowalski interprets Structure 44 as a Popol Nah or community administrative center for the Dzibilchaltun polity; see Chapter 8, this volume.)

Elite Interaction

Structured interaction between individuals results in group formation and maintenance. These kinds of contacts are strongly conditioned by the geographical distribution of a population, for prior to the invention of telephones and other communication devices, humans had to be close to each other in order to associate, talk, and work together. The distance between architectural complexes inhibits direct contacts with people housed elsewhere and thereby enhances interaction within the home. Therefore, residents of the same building work in concert more often than they deal with others. While social ties do not depend solely on the space between households, the potential for contacts within a neighborhood is greater than the chances for meeting people living farther away. People deal with their nearest neighbors more often than they do with others in their settlement, and inhabitants of the same settlement interact to a greater degree with each other than with outsiders from nearby towns or villages. The organization of a community depends on such interaction and is therefore closely linked to the settlement plan.

Any study of stratified societies suggests that inhabitants of the palaces dealt with each other in ways that were different from their transactions with commoners. Separate kinds of artifacts, housing, and kinship norms were key differences between the Maya "Great" and "Little" traditions. Elite and commoners lived close to each other and worked together, but not in the same manner or as intensely as the elite interacted among themselves.

The organization of the pre-Columbian community included a pattern of strong divisions within and between elite domestic groups. Palaces at a Maya archaeological site are not adjacent or concentrated in a single place; instead, these elite dwellings are deliberately separated from each other. The solid partitions between the chambers of a palace divide the inhabitants into small subgroups; and in the same manner, the distance between palaces enhances interaction with coresident neighbors and inhibits opportunities for dealing with elite individuals living farther away.

The distribution of vaulted palaces at archaeological sites is the basis for viewing the core of a Maya community as a cluster of elites mutually linked through social ties that were forged by generations of reciprocal acts. Since intermarriage between neighboring families is a typical form of interaction that is strongly influenced by the distance between people's homes, it would be difficult to imagine a stratified community in which the elite were not linked by ties of descent and marriage alliance. Palaces are seldom found in total isolation; always there are other elite dwellings nearby. The nucleus of the simplest form of Maya settlement had two major interacting palace populations, while larger, more complex communities contained additional palaces. Political authority and control derived from this alliance between palatial establishments.

This vision of Maya communities is inspired by the map of Labna, a site centered around two palace complexes of similar size that were connected by a short causeway (*sacbe*). The causeway constitutes a physical link between the two elite residences, demonstrating that a particularly close connection united the two extended domestic groups that once lived in the palaces. Construction of the causeway required the two groups to collaborate with each other, and the existence of this elevated walkway facilitated interaction between the inhabitants of the two buildings.

Smaller palaces and common houses surround the central buildings and causeway at Labna. The site is essentially a cluster of dwellings surrounding the causeway complex. Other major palaces are found a short distance from Labna; Maler (1971) considered Xcanalcruz, a major palace situated a little over a kilometer to the north, to be part of the Labna settlement. Recent excavations (Gallareta et al. 1999) show that the organization of the site may have been quite complex, but the outline presented here still pertains.

Various scholars have postulated that differences between palace establishments were the basis for symbiotic dependency between the elite groups of a community. At Labna the presence of a pyramidal structure and the portal arch in the "Temple Group" accentuate the contrasts in forms of the two palaces at either end of the central causeway. Perhaps one elite domestic group specialized in temporal affairs while the other focused on the spiritual. The existence of a strong relationship between people that once lived in the two sets of buildings, however, is undeniable. The effect of those ties was maintenance of their mutual position of dominance over the settlement.

Conclusion

Domestic organizations housed in palaces were the essential social groups of Maya society. The larger palaces of a community, with their populations involved in numerous activities, were early manifestations of urbanism, analogous to miniature cities. Palace dwellers conformed to rules governing their composition, activities, internal organization, and external relations. Together, these norms constituted a key institution. While the concept of palace establishments as economic, social, and political foci is beginning to become explicit in Mesoamerican studies, future research will reveal much of the substance of pre-Columbian Maya life by elucidating the combination of endeavors carried out in these elite dwellings.

REFERENCES

Andrews, E. Wyllys, IV
1965   Archaeology and Prehistory in the Northern Maya Lowlands: An Introduction. In *Handbook of Middle American Indians*, vol. 2, pp. 288–330. Austin: University of Texas Press.

Andrews, E. Wyllys, IV, and Anthony P. Andrews
1975   *A Preliminary Study of the Ruins of Xcaret, Quintana Roo, Mexico.* Middle American Research Institute Publication 40. New Orleans: Tulane University.

Andrews, E. Wyllys, IV, and E. Wyllys Andrews V
1980   *Excavations at Dzibilchaltun, Yucatan, Mexico.* Middle American Research Institute Publication 48. New Orleans: Tulane University.

Andrews, George
1995   *The Collected Works of George Andrews.* Vol. 1, *Architecture of the Puuc Region and the Northern Plains Areas.* Lancaster, Calif.: Labyrinthos.

Benavides, Antonio
1987   Arquitectura doméstica en Cobá. In *Cobá, Quintana Roo: Análisis de dos unidades habitacionales mayas del horizonte clásico*, edited by Linda Manzanilla, 25–67. Mexico City: Universidad Nacional Autónoma de México.

Cottier, John W.
1982   The Dzibilchaltun Survey: Consideration of the Test-Pitting Data. Ph.D. dissertation, University of Missouri, Columbia.

Farris, Nancy M.
1984   *Maya Society under Colonial Rule.* Princeton: Princeton University Press.

Flannery, Kent V.
1972   The Origins of the Village as a Settlement Type in Mesoamerica and the Near East: A Comparative Study. In *Man, Settlement and Urbanism*, edited by P. J. Ucko, R. Trigham, and G. W. Dimbleby, 23–53. London: Duckworth.

Folan, William J., Ellena R. Kintz, and Laraine A. Fletcher
1983   *Cobá: A Classic Maya Metropolis.* New York: Academic Press.

Gallareta, Tomás
1984   Cobá: Forma y función de una comunidad prehispánica. Tesis profesional (licentiate thesis), Universidad Autónoma de Yucatán.

Gallareta, Tomás, Lourdes Toscano Carlos Pérez, and Carlos Peraza
1999   Proyecto Labná, México. In *Land of the Turkey and the Deer*, edited by Ruth Gubler, 85–96. Lancaster, Calif.: Labyrinthos Press.

Garduño, Jaime
1979   Introducción al patrón de asentamiento del sitio de Cobá, Quintana Roo, México. Tesis profesional (licentiate thesis), Escuela Nacional de Antropología e Historia.

Garza T. de González, Silvia, and Edward B. Kurjack
1980   *Atlas arqueológico del estado de Yucatán.* Mexico City: Instituto Nacional de Antropología e Historia.

Gendrop, Paul
1990   *Arte prehispánico en Mesoamérica.* 5th ed. Mexico City: Editorial Trillas.
Kurjack, Edward B.
1974   *Prehistoric Lowland Maya Community and Social Organization: A Case Study at Dzibilchaltun, Yucatan, Mexico.* Middle American Research Institute Publication 38. New Orleans: Tulane University.
Kurjack, Edward B., and E. Wyllys Andrews V
1976   Early Boundary Maintenance in Northwest Yucatan, Mexico. *American Antiquity* 41: 318–325.
Lincoln, Elena K.
2000   Yucatec Maya Marriage and Political Alliances. Ph.D. dissertation, University of California, Los Angeles.
Lizama Aranda, Lilia
2000   Salvamento arqueológico en Dzibilchaltún, Yucatán, México. Tesis profesional (licentiate thesis), Universidad Autónoma de Yucatán.
McAnany, Patricia Ann
1995   *Living with the Ancestors: Kinship and Kingship in Ancient Maya Society.* Austin: University of Texas Press.
Maldonado Cárdenas, Rubén
1995   Proyecto Arqueológico Dzibilchaltún: La Estructura 44. *Revista de la Universidad Autónoma de Yucatán* 192: 67–75.
Maler, Teobert
1971   *Bauten der Maya.* Monumenta Americana IV. Berlin: Ibero-Amerikanisches Institut Preussischer Kulturbesitz.
Manzanilla, Linda
1987   Consideraciones finales. In *Cobá, Quintana Roo: Análisis de dos unidades habitacionales mayas del horizonte clásico,* edited by Linda Manzanilla, 261–286. Mexico City: Universidad Nacional Autónoma de México.
Marquina, Ignacio
1951   *Arquitectura prehispánica.* Mexico City: Instituto Nacional de Antropología e Historia.
Morgan, Lewis H.
1880   A Study of the Houses of the American Aborigines. *Archaeological Institute of North America, Annual Report of the Executive Committee* 1: 29–80.
Ochoa Rodríguez, Virginia
1995   Un contexto habitacional en Dzibilchaltún, Yucatán, México. Tesis profesional (licentiate thesis), Universidad Autónoma de Yucatán.
Pollock, H. E. D.
1980   *The Puuc: An Architectural Survey of the Hill Country of Yucatan and Northern Campeche, Mexico.* Memoirs of the Peabody Museum of Archaeology and Ethnology, vol. 19. Cambridge, Mass.: Harvard University.
Reindel, Marcus
1997   Eine Maya-Siedlung im nördlichen Yucatán, Mexiko. *KAVA Sonderdruck aus Beiträge zur Allgemeinen und Vergleichenden Archäologie,* vol. 17. Mainz am Rhein: Verlag Philipp Von Zabern.
Repetto Tio, Beatriz
1997   *Demografía histórica de la población maya-yucateca colonial; Maxcanú, Yucatán (1682–1756).* Tesis de maestría (master's thesis), Universidad Autónoma de Yucatán, Mérida.
Robbins, Michael C.
1966   House Types and Settlement Patterns: An Application of Ethnology to Archaeological Interpretation. *Minnesota Archaeologist* 27 (1): 3–30.

Ruppert, Karl
1952 *Chichén Itzá: Architectural Notes and Plans.* Carnegie Institution of Washington Publication 595. Washington, D.C.

Scholes, France V., and Ralph L. Roys
1948 *The Maya Chontal Indians of Acalan-Tixchel.* Washington, D.C.: Carnegie Institution of Washington.

Smith, A. Ledyard
1962 Residential and Associated Structures at Mayapan. In *Mayapan, Yucatan México,* by Harry E. D. Pollock, Ralph E. Roys, Tatiana Proskouriakoff, and A. Ledyard Smith, 165–319. Carnegie Institution of Washington Publication 619. Washington, D.C.

Thompson, J. Eric
1966 *The Rise and Fall of Maya Civilization.* 2d ed. Norman: University of Oklahoma Press.

Tozzer, Alfred M.
1941 *Landa's Relación de las cosas de Yucatán: A Translation.* Papers of the Peabody Museum of American Archaeology and Ethnology, vol. 18. Cambridge, Mass.: Harvard University.

Wauchope, Robert
1938 *Modern Maya Houses: A Study of Their Archaeological Significance.* Carnegie Institution of Washington Publication 502. Washington, D.C.
1940 Domestic Architecture of the Maya. In *The Maya and Their Neighbors,* edited by Clarence L. Hay, R. Linton, S. Lothrop, H. Shapiro, and G. C. Vaillant, 232–241. New York: Dover.

Webster, David
1980 Spatial Bounding and Settlement History at Three Walled Northern Maya Centers. *American Antiquity* 45: 834–844.

Zapata Peraza, Renée
1989 *Los Chultunes.* Serie Arqueología. Mexico City: Instituto Nacional de Antropología e Historia.

CHAPTER ELEVEN

The Tripartite Layout of Rooms in Maya Elite Residences

SYMBOLIC CENTERING, RITUAL MEDIATING, AND HISTORICAL GOVERNING

Jessica Joyce Christie

The purpose of this chapter is to analyze the pattern of a tripartite floor plan in Maya palaces and elite residences of the Late Classic and to show its symbolic significance. Based on comparisons with Classic Maya imagery and ethnohistoric sources, possible functions and uses of these rooms will be reconstructed, as well as the kinds of events that took place in them. This study does not focus on one specific palace-type structure but outlines a pattern observable throughout the Maya area.

In the last decades, epigraphic studies and iconographic analyses have demonstrated that many Maya images document historical events. Epigraphy entered this new direction in 1960 with Tatiana Proskouriakoff's discovery that certain dates on the Piedras Negras stelae record the births and the accessions of historical rulers (Proskouriakoff 1960). Archaeological excavations at numerous Maya sites have unearthed costume elements that match precisely the costumes worn by rulers on Classic Maya stelae, for example, jade earflares and necklaces of jade beads. Such correspondences justify the assumption that Maya imagery is one source of information in our efforts to reconstruct use and function of Classic Maya architecture. What we see on Maya stelae, lintels, and tablets physically took place in the temples and palaces.

To begin with, a brief overview of Maya cosmology as it relates to cosmic space is provided because the interpretation of architectural space will draw on this type of symbolism. Three specific case studies of palaces and elite residences with tripartite floor plans follow, and then an interpretation of this spatial layout will be offered.

Summary of Maya Cosmology

The Maya understood the world as a flat surface oriented to the four cardinal directions. There is some confusion in the literature as to exactly which form the earth assumed. If it was a square, the corners or the sides indicated the four directions. If it was conceived as round, the focal point was the center, from which four roads departed toward the four directions. Finally there are sources that describe the earth as a turtle or a fishlike caiman floating on the surface of water (Taube 1988: 153–174). In all three cases, the earth constitutes the second of three pan-Mesoamerican vertical divisions, with the watery underworld below and the upper world of the sky above. The sun rising in the east, climbing to the zenith at noon, setting in the west, and passing through the nadir at night, united the tripartite vertical and four-part horizontal divisions of the world into a holistic cosmogram.

Evidence that such a cosmological model existed and continues to exist abounds in Classic Maya iconography, site layout and orientation of buildings, and ethnohistoric sources, as well as in the more recent ethnographic literature (see, for example, Christie 1995; Freidel, Schele, and Parker 1993; Tozzer 1941; Taube 1988; Sosa 1986). Already in the Early Classic, in Tomb 12 at Río Azul, glyphs of the four cardinal points were painted on the four walls, each on the wall corresponding to its direction. The deceased was placed in the middle of the tomb, designating him as the center of the world. Most Classic Maya cities were laid out along north-south and east-west axes.

At Palenque, the Tablet of the Cross and the Tablet of the Foliated Cross, as well as the Sarcophagus lid, incorporate tree imagery. The central axis in all three compositions is formed by a tree that exhibits a skeletal mask in the root zone, symbolizing the underworld. The tree trunk displays branches terminating in snake heads and personified maize representative of the world of man, and a celestial bird perches on top. These trees function as channels of communication between the vertical cosmological levels through which K'inich Janaab' Pakal I enters the underworld and is eventually reborn (Sarcophagus lid).

In the *Books of Chilam Balam*, five great trees were set up in the four directions and in the center of the world. Further, Bishop Landa records that Maya villages in the Yucatan had four exits leading toward the four directions and that each direction was associated with a specific color and deity (Tozzer 1941: 135–140).

Even today, the highland Maya in Zinacantan, Chiapas, identify the four corners as well as the center of their world by specific hills and mountains. The solar path is conceived of as a celestial band that traverses the sky daily from east to west (see Vogt 1969, 1993).[1] Zinacantan's neighbors in Chamula personify the sun's path as Htotik (Sosa 1986: 189).

This tripartite arrangement of space and a form of centering, which attempt to materialize such cosmological concepts, are also present in the layout of Classic Maya palaces and elite residences.

The Tripartite Layout of Rooms in Maya Elite Residences

Central Acropolis at Tikal

In 1971, Peter Harrison presented a preliminary functional analysis of the Central Acropolis during the Late Classic period (Harrison 1971). He grouped the buildings according to room arrangement into four primary categories: tandem present/transverse present; tandem present/transverse not present; tandem not present/transverse present; tandem not present/ transverse not present (Harrison 1971: 94–107). Tandem rooms are rooms parallel to each other and extending along the longitudinal axis of the building. Transverse rooms are those at right angles to the longitudinal axis of the building. Harrison's functional analysis was based on architectural elements, as well as on ethnohistoric and ethnographic analogy. In his conclusions, he interpreted the structures of category 1 (tandem present/transverse present) as permanent residences (Harrison 1971: 298–300) (Figure 11.1). In most buildings of this category, the tandem and transverse rooms form a tripartite layout in which the tandem rooms are centralized and symmetrically flanked by transverse rooms.

Benches are an important architectural element and occur in buildings that have a category 1 room arrangement with greater frequency than in buildings of the other three categories. In particular, all of the tandem/ transverse structures have rooms containing benches with two sidescreens, which Harrison interprets as thrones. Ethnohistoric sources report that Maya lords of the sixteenth century had throne rooms in their houses in which they received visitors and held court (Harrison 1971: 257–259). Benches with sidescreens may thus provide evidence that elite Maya residences had multiple functions.

Buildings with tripartite floor plans also exist in the further outlying residential areas of Tikal. In the late 1950s and early 1960s, William Haviland excavated Groups 4F-1 and 4F-2, two distinct structural clusters occu-

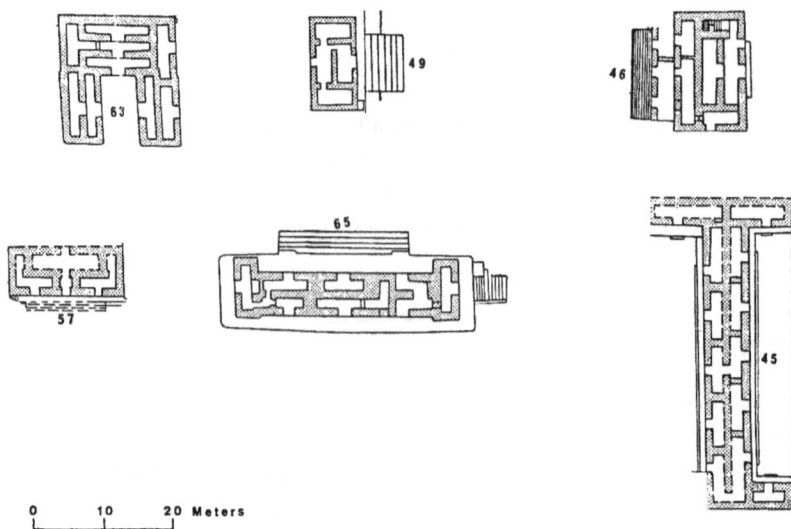

FIGURE 11.1. Central Acropolis at Tikal. Buildings of category 1 room arrangement: tandem present/transverse present. (Courtesy of P. D. Harrison)

pying an oval hillock near the Tikal Reservoir. Haviland and his team found that one building, 4E-31, dominated and was clearly set apart from all the other edifices. Structure 4E-31 is the westernmost building and faces east toward Groups 4F-1 and 4F-2. It has three doorways. The outer two provide access to two single rooms, 1 and 3, while the central doorway leads into the larger Room 2, which is divided into three spatial units by two partition walls extending approximately half of the width of the room. All three rooms had rectangular interior platforms covering the western half of the floor space.

Structure 4E-31 is the largest known in either Group 4F-1 or 4F-2 with regard to volume, substructural area, and height. It is unique for its plastered building walls, red-painted floors, and architectural features shared with temples on the North Acropolis, and it contained a dedicatory cache and initial burials (Haviland 1985: 179).

Haviland does not believe that Structure 4E-31 was "originally designed as a residence" and interprets it as "a place for people who lived in Gp.4F-1 and 2—heads of families, perhaps—to gather for special purposes" (Haviland 1985: 179). At the same time, he admits that architecturally the building was suitable for habitation and that there is material evidence for a late occupation, such as metates and burned spots found on the most recent floors (Haviland 1985: 179).

I think Haviland's data further confirm the pattern this chapter is outlining: Structure 4E-31 has a tripartite, centered floor plan, it has interior platforms which could have been used as benches, and its function was at least temporarily or partially residential. Based on my own observations among the Maya and on Landa's account (Tozzer 1941: 87 in Harrison 1971: 257–259), I believe that the Maya did not strictly separate residential from political or judicial functions. Houses could be lived in and serve as formal gathering places on special occasions. And I think this is exactly what Structure 4E-31 was.[2]

Takeshi Inomata and Daniela Triadan made very similar observations at Aguateca. For example, Structures M7-35, M8-4, M8-8, and M8-10 all had three main rooms. The center rooms had few associated artifacts that may have belonged to the household heads. These rooms were likely used for gatherings and receiving visitors. One of the side rooms in each structure housed a great quantity of objects, including large storage jars. These side rooms probably functioned as locations for storage and food preparation. The other side rooms contained only small numbers of artifacts and may have been places for living and sleeping (this volume). Such data indicate that formal and private uses commonly overlapped. The important point in the context of this discussion is that the central spaces appear to have had official and public functions and could be centered within an otherwise domestic context.

House of the Governor at Uxmal

The most thorough investigation of the House of the Governor was conducted by Jeff Kowalski (1987). Kowalski concluded that it was constructed around A.D. 900 to 915, shortly before the abandonment of Uxmal and other Puuc sites (Kowalski 1987: 51). Thus the House of the Governor may be seen as the culmination and final triumph of Puuc architecture.

Kowalski believes that the House of the Governor today still represents the original design and that it is the result of an uninterrupted and unified building project (Kowalski 1987: 114). The floor plan is based on two parallel vaulted galleries extending in an approximate north-south direction (Figure 11.2). A tripartite layout has been achieved by dividing the structure into three bodies separated by two great transverse vaults. The two small buildings flanking the central structure to the north and south each contain five chambers and, viewed together, they share a symmetrical room arrangement. The central structure consists of two central, parallel, and elongated rooms and eight side rooms of equal size. As a consequence, the complete design exhibits a double tripartite layout: the two flanking build-

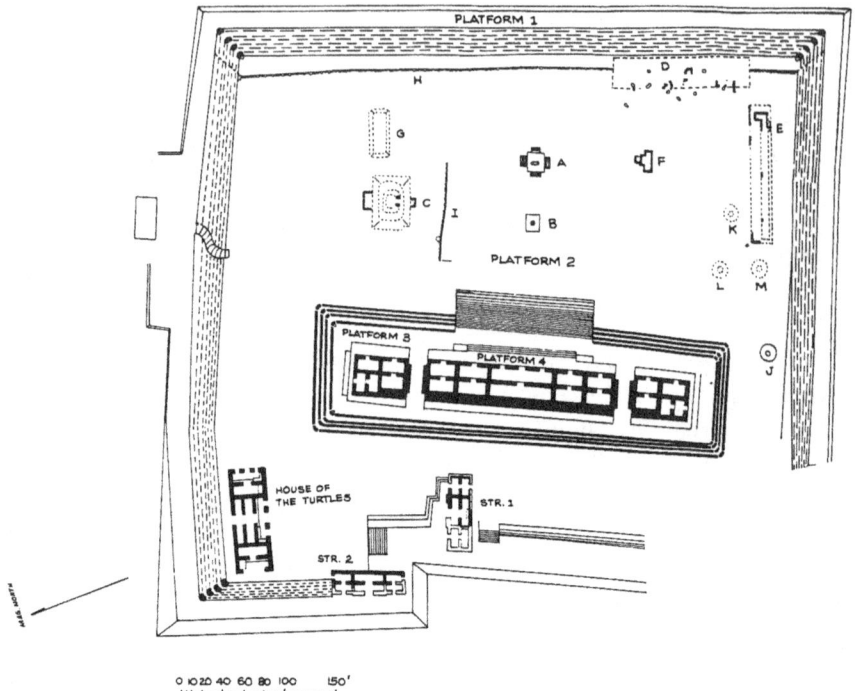

FIGURE 11.2. Plan of the House of the Governor at Uxmal. (Courtesy of Jeff Kowalski)

ings versus the central structure and within the central structure the two
middle rooms versus the four side rooms on both ends. Starting in the flanking buildings, the rooms gradually increase in size toward the center, so
that the symmetry appears consistent and unified throughout the plan.

The House of the Governor faces east, and it sits on a total of four platforms (Figure 11.2). Platforms 1 and 2 establish a large, almost square foundation for the House of the Governor and a number of smaller structures.
Platform 3 supports the House of the Governor only, and a monumental
central stairway leads up on the east side. Platform 4 further elevates the
three bodies of the building but not the spaces covered by the transverse
vaults. The arrangement of the House of the Governor and its neighboring
buildings is unusual because they do not line the sides of the first two platforms and do not form a courtyard. Instead, the House of the Governor is
centrally placed as the dominating focal point of the elevated space defined
by Platforms 1 and 2.

The tripartite layout is repeated and further emphasized by the figural sculpture. Above the doors of the entire east facade spreads a series of fully three-dimensional human figures sitting on thrones or cushions and wearing tall feather headdresses (Figure 11.3).

The largest human figure sculpture is placed above the central doorway of the middle section of the building. He is seated at the center of eight bars terminating in double serpent heads. Kowalski's thorough study of the iconography and inscriptions demonstrates that this figure must be Lord Chaak of Uxmal, who ruled at the time the House of the Governor was constructed. By him, the entire edifice was commissioned and to him it was dedicated (Kowalski 1987: 149–181; see also Kowalski, this volume, for an interpretation of its function).

Lord Chaak is flanked by two smaller figures sitting upon upturned serpent-head podia and wearing tall feather headdresses. Two human figures of medium size are placed between doors 4 and 5 and doors 9 and 10 of the central building. They are smaller than Lord Chaak but taller than the flanking figures. Like Lord Chaak, the medium-sized figures are flanked by smaller figures wearing feather headdresses and sitting upon the open jaws of serpents. A similar tripartite figure arrangement is repeated on the east facades of the South and North Wings.[3]

FIGURE 11.3. East facade of the House of the Governor at Uxmal. (Photograph by the author)

Thus the east facade of the House of the Governor displays five tripartite figure groups. While all individuals wear similar headdresses and sit on similar thrones and serpent podia, hierarchical scale is used to distinguish the personage in the middle from the flanking figures. Lord Chaak is further set apart by a different type of throne. These figures represent the ruler, Lord Chaak, and possibly Uxmal nobles performing public ceremonies or participating in political events.[4]

Historical ritual and political events took place below in the rooms and in front of the House of the Governor. During the ceremonies, the historical protagonists were likely positioned in architectural space in an order similar to that of the sculpted figures on the upper facade.

Of special interest with regard to ritual space is the bicephalic jaguar throne (Figure 11.3). It is composed of two crouching jaguars facing away from one another and joined at midsection.[5] The throne does not stand inside the middle chamber but outside on a small, radially symmetrical platform that is located directly in front and on the central axis of the House of the Governor (Figure 11.3). This alignment of the throne with the center doorway of the building suggests that the two are closely related and that they were planned as a unified complex.

On Stela 14 from Uxmal, Lord Chaak stands upon a bicephalic jaguar throne whose basic form resembles the one at the House of the Governor. Kowalski concludes that the jaguar throne on the stela was intended to depict the actual sculpture in front of the House of the Governor and that the bicephalic jaguar throne was used as a royal seat by Lord Chaak (1987: 180).

It may thus be argued that Lord Chaak occupied the jaguar throne outside the House of the Governor or perhaps appeared in the central doorway underneath his sculpted portrait during public ceremonies. The platform with the throne has four stairways radiating out from the center. This platform sits in the open space of Platform 2. The layout of architectural space suggests that officials could have surrounded the jaguar throne on four sides when Lord Chaak occupied it. When Lord Chaak stood in the central doorway of the House of the Governor, officials could have come out through the doors of the side chambers, all of which are oriented and open to the east, just like the central room. Participants would have observed the king either seated on the jaguar throne with his people grouped around him or highly elevated above the crowd. In this manner, the layout of architectural volumes and space mirrored the four-partite horizontal and the tripartite vertical orders of the cosmos. This carefully planned design always placed Lord Chaak in the center, symbolizing his control over the Maya world.

Las Sepulturas near Copan

A similar tripartite layout of architectural space has been observed in the elite residential compounds of Las Sepulturas. Las Sepulturas is located in the Copan Valley to the east of the main ceremonial center. As part of the second phase of the Proyecto Arqueológico Copán, from 1981 through 1984, directed by William T. Sanders, extensive, long-term excavations were carried out in the residential compounds of Las Sepulturas. The excavated structures were classified into three groups containing multiple patios: Group 9N-8 with Patios A through F and H; Group 9M-22 with Patios A and B; and Group 9M-24 with only one patio.

Two dissertations that attempt to analyze the uses of individual structures were submitted by Julia Ann Hendon (1987) and Melissa Diamanti (1991). Hendon isolates two types of special structures, one of which consists of residences that can be considered dominant structures because of certain qualities (see Hendon 1987: 535–545). Dominant structures possessing similar qualities have been observed at numerous Maya sites. Gair Tourtellot describes dominant structures in the following way:

> Most units have one larger, fancier, or formally distinct dwelling. At Seibal this dwelling was usually built as early as any other structure in the unit. Despite the greater bulk of its platform, it was usually built in a single effort. This dwelling is usually located on the north or west side of the patio, adjacent to the kitchen . . . shack if one is present. On an average, slightly more and finer artifacts are associated with it. At Tikal somewhat finer burials are also found in the more impressive platforms. . . . The most impressive dwellings in low-cost units may be smaller than the least impressive dwellings in higher-cost units (Tourtellot in Hendon 1987: 535).

Hendon proposes that the following Las Sepulturas buildings qualify as dominant structures: Gr 9N-8 A-82C, B-67, C-69, D-63, E-97, F-91; Gr 9M-22 A-194B, A-195B, B-189; Gr 9M-24 211 (Hendon 1987: 535–539). The majority of them are located on the north side of their patio, have associated middens and caches, and show evidence of plaster, paint, sculpture, and cordholders (Hendon 1987: 536). Eight of these ten dominant structures also have the tripartite room layout.

Structure 82-C is the central building on the south side of Patio A in Group 9N-8. Patio A is generally considered the highest-status compound because of its superior architectural construction, presence of sculpture, and large quantity of artifacts. Structure 82-C has a central room (Room 1)

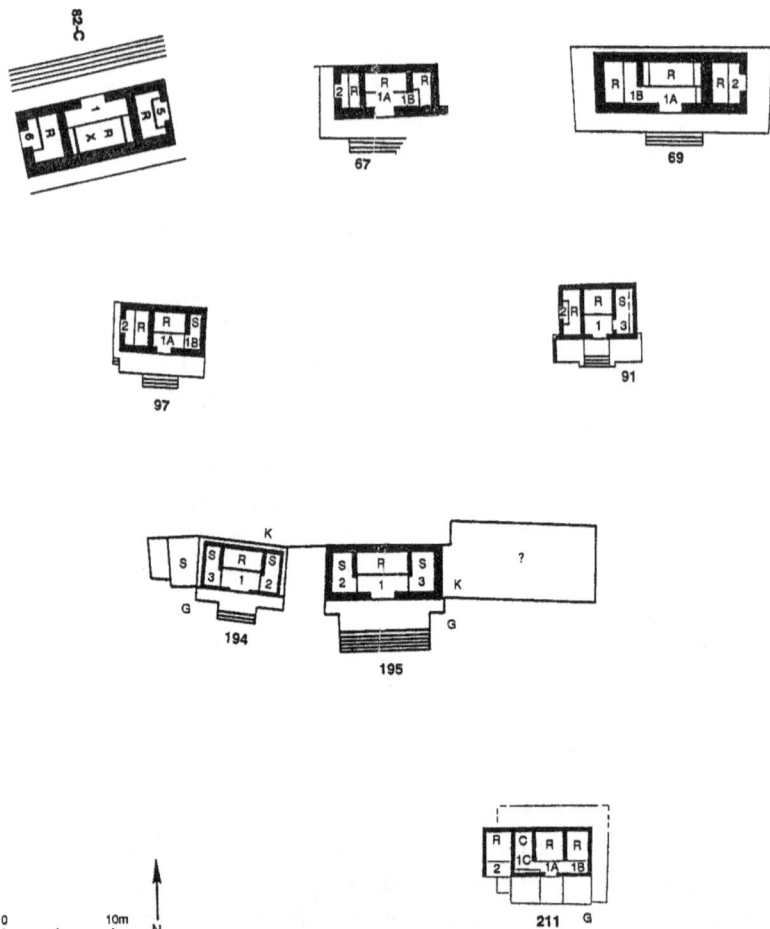

FIGURE 11.4. Las Sepulturas at Copan. Dominant Structures with tripartite room layout in Groups 9N-8, 9M-22, and 9M-24. (After plans from Melissa Diamanti)

and two side rooms (Rooms 5 and 6) (Figure 11.4). Room 1 faces toward the courtyard and contains a bench carved with figurative images and hieroglyphic text. Room 5 faces east and is almost filled by a U-shaped bench. Room 6 has an L-shaped bench and faces west.

The two-tiered facade of Structure 82-C displays three-dimensional figures of scribes (Figure 11.5). On the lower level, two half-figure stone busts of scribes holding pens and paint pots frame the central doorway. They emerge from open serpent jaws placed over the glyph *naah*. The *naah* glyphs and the pens and paint pots identify them as scribes.[6] In an earlier version of the building, a burial of a male individual was placed, accompanied by the statue of the patron god of scribes. Such evidence suggests that at least two generations of male members in the family living in Structure 82-C worked as royal scribes. Scribes were nobles in Maya society, and it is very appropriate that they resided in the highest-status patio.

Two members of the scribe family are individually identified on the hieroglyphic bench. This bench is supported by six legs adorned with figures. Four of the figures depict Pauahtuns,[7] while the two images in the middle are portraits of family members.

The glyphs of the inscriptions form the body of a celestial monster which stretches across the front of the bench. God N, the god of scribes, emerges from the front head of the monster. Grube and Schele reconstruct the initial date as 9.19.3.2.0 11 Ajaw 3 Yax (1987), which places the bench and the building within the reign of Yax Pasaj, the last of the powerful Classic kings of Copan. According to Schele's reading, on the above date Structure 82-C was dedicated by Mak Chaanal. His portrait is shown on the right inner leg. The text gives Mak Chaanal's father's name as Quetzal–God K, and his portrait is the left inner figure (Schele 1987). Mak Chaanal and Quetzal–God K were the scribes who worked for Yax Pasaj and likely the household heads of Patio A, who erected and embellished Structure 82-C.

FIGURE 11.5. Las Sepulturas at Copan. Group 9N-8, Patio A: Structure 82-C facade. (Photograph by the author)

Diamanti's functional analysis of Structure 82-C revealed that all three rooms were residential but that the central Room 1 with the hieroglyphic bench was also used for ritual and/or political purposes (Diamanti 1991: 239–245). Sanders as well argues that initially the central room functioned primarily for ceremonial and political gatherings of high-status individuals. The household head of Patio A, who was probably the head of the lineage occupying Group 9N-8, would have been seated on the hieroglyphic bench. The east room was likely his sleeping quarters, while the west room may have been the residence of his head wife or may have housed daughters of marriageable age. When the western corridor was created and the building to the west was added, following Sanders, the west room became the head's dormitory. Sanders thinks that one of the newly added rooms served as a private ancestral shrine where the lineage head made offerings to his ancestors (1989: 97).

Structure B-67 is located at the northeast corner of Patio B. It has a tripartite room arrangement and is accessed by a stairway that bends around the corner and also serves Structure 74-N. The central room of Structure 67 is larger than the two side rooms and has a rectangular bench and a central doorway facing toward the patio (Figure 11.4). The eastern side room opens into the central room and has an L-shaped bench. The two rooms are separated by only a short transverse bench wall. The western room is sealed off from the central room and faces west. More than half of its floor area is taken up by a rectangular bench.

Hendon notes that the architecture of Structure 67 is superior to that of its neighbors. Dressed tuff masonry was used and it had a vaulted roof as well as red-painted, stuccoed surfaces. The facade of Room 1 is decorated with a frieze composed of small rectangular tuff blocks set in the wall at an angle to create a woven, matlike pattern (Hendon 1987: 155).[8] Similar mats carved in mosaic stone decorate the upper surfaces of Structure 22A in the Main Group of Copan. This building has been identified as a Popol Nah or Council House and the mat designs refer to the mats upon which the councilors were seated.[9] Structure 67 was perhaps some type of lower-level Council House of the elite families who resided in Patio B and of the surrounding patios. Perhaps the lineage head of Group 9N-8 was centrally seated to make local political and judicial decisions.

It thus appears that the Maya replicated the political structure of the ceremonial center on a smaller scale in the residential units. It is important to note that not only the Council Houses but also some of the Early Classic royal palaces underneath the Acropolis (see Traxler, this volume), as well as the residence of Yax Pasaj (see E. W. Andrews V et al., this volume), exhibit similar centralized tripartite floor plans. Thus lineage heads conducted business in a less sumptuous but similar way to that in which royal business was conducted and enjoyed central authority on a local level.

At the same time, the rooms of Structure 67 were also used for living purposes. Diamanti's functional analysis makes it clear that the Maya did not set aside rooms for separate activities but that uses could overlap (Diamanti 1991: 234–306).

Structure C-69 fills the north side of Patio C. The building has a tripartite room layout and sits on its own platform, which is approached by three steps (Figure 11.4). The central Room 1 is larger than the two side rooms, it has a rectangular bench in front of the rear wall, and it opens toward the patio. The western side room is connected with the central room and contains a rectangular bench that covers the entire western wall. The eastern side room cannot be accessed from the central room. It has an eastern doorway, and a rectangular bench was placed in front of its west wall.

Originally, at least eight glyph blocks were set on either side of the entrance to Room 1. According to Fash et al., they give a date and the name of a protagonist who is not Mak Chaanal, the lineage head whose residence was Structure 82-C (Fash et al., in Hendon 1987: 170–171). In the interior of Room 1, the rear wall above the central bench was decorated with a frieze depicting a snake.

It is apparent that Structure 69 was the residence of a powerful local family. The head of Patio C may have conducted business from the central bench of Room 1 while his family pursued domestic activities in and around the building.[10] The presence of inscriptions on Structure 69 is evidence that the elite residents of Las Sepulturas were literate and that, like the Copan royalty, they used writing in order to legitimize their claims to power. I think Structure C-69 constitutes another piece of evidence for the complexity of the political power structure among the Maya: beside the royal family, there was a large elite class which used some of the same trappings as the king—e.g., writing, the tripartite room layout, possibly a Council House—to display their own local authority.

Structure E-97 occupies the north side of Patio E and has a tripartite room arrangement (Figure 11.4). The building sits on a tightly fitted platform that projects beyond only the southern and western facades. This platform is accessed by a central stairway on the south side that leads to Room 1. Room 1 is the middle room and has a rectangular bench. The eastern side room opens into Room 1, and the two are separated only by a short partition wall. The western side room has no access to Room 1. It faces west and contains a rectangular bench. In front of the west room, the platform leaves a narrow ledge to which two steps ascend.

Structure E-97 can be considered another local seat of power because of its tripartite floor plan and its superior architecture. It is the only building in Patio E that is vaulted and constructed of dressed tuff masonry. At the same time, it was used as a residence and as a storage place for food and ceramic vessels (Diamanti 1991: 271–272).

Patio F was only partially excavated, but it appears that Structure 91 was the dominant structure. Structure 91 is located on the north side of Patio F and has a tripartite room layout (Figure 11.4). It rests on its own platform, with a central stairway leading to Room 1. Room 1 is central, slightly larger than the two side rooms, and has a rectangular bench. The east side room opens into Room 1 and is furnished with a narrow ledge along its eastern wall. The west side room has a doorway in the western wall, which leads to Structure 90-N. Most of its floor area is taken up by a U-shaped bench. Structure 91 was the residence and place of business for the family head of Patio F.[11] Diamanti's analysis also shows that the eastern side room was used for storage of food and domestic items (Diamanti 1991: 277–278).

Pure symmetrical examples of the tripartite floor plan were found in Structures 194 and 195 of Patio A in Group 9M-22. Both buildings with their associated open platforms fill the north side of the patio. They have a large central Room 1, with a rectangular bench and two smaller side rooms that open into Room 1 (Figure 11.4). They rest on platforms that project beyond the south facades and are reached by means of central stairways.

Structure 194 is smaller, and attached to its west side is a platform of uneven shape. There are no traces of a superstructure. Structure 194 was decorated with sculpture made out of small tuff blocks forming a circular flat face (see Sheehy in Hendon 1987: 258–259).

Structure 195 is larger and has a higher substructure than Structure 194, and is connected with a large platform on its east side. This platform may originally have supported a cobble and *bajareque* (wattle-and-daub) superstructure (Hendon 1987: 260–261). The exterior of Structure 195 was decorated with figurative sculpture. A series of mosaic stone masks, representing jaguar faces with elaborate headdresses, and four carved and tenoned heads were attached to the outside walls of the superstructure. Two of the heads displaying a human and a jaguar were set into the front wall, a bat head in the east wall, and another human head in the west wall (Hendon 1987: 260).

The symmetrical tripartite room layout, the presence of sculpture, the red-painted floors, wall, and bench, and the superior architecture—Structures 194 and 195 were built of dressed tuff masonry and vaulted—indicate that both were high-status residences and important seats of power. In all likelihood, the lineage heads of Group 9M-22 were centrally seated on the bench in Room 1 and flanked by lower officials and family members when they made local political and judicial decisions and oversaw family rituals.

Very important is the fact that there were two dominant structures, which raises questions about the identity and relationship of the two leaders.[12] The family in Structure 195 was evidently more influential, and the repetitious and prominently exhibited jaguar faces may relate this family to a jaguar clan.

Another question is the function of the platforms associated with both buildings. Diamanti identifies them as storage and kitchen areas (1991: 283). It thus appears that the platforms as well as the structures formed the families' living quarters, and that business was conducted in Room 1 and the side rooms when the need arose.

A final point of interest is the spur of the main Sepulturas *sacbe* or roadway that reaches the patio between Structures 194 and 195 and is blocked off by a low wall. Hendon interprets the wall as a means of controlling movement from the *sacbe* into the patio (Hendon 1987: 255). The entrance of the *sacbe* between the two dominant structures and the attempt to control access establish further evidence of the power and authority the two families enjoyed.

Group 9M-24 has only one patio, which is surrounded by the residences of individuals of lower social status than those residing in Groups 9M-22 and 9N-8. There was no evidence of sculpture or paint on any one of the buildings. The dominant structure is Structure 211, located on the west side of the patio and facing south. It shares the tripartite floor plan, with a fourth room added to its west side (Figure 11.4). The central Room 1A is slightly larger than the side rooms and contains a rectangular bench. This bench continues into the eastern side room, and the two rooms are separated only by a transverse bench partition wall. The only furniture in the west side room is a small ledge built against the south wall west of the entrance. The fourth, add-on room on the west has a rectangular bench and faces south. It had no front wall.

The building was constructed of roughly shaped blocks of tuff and cobbles and had a perishable thatched roof. It rests on a low platform, while two elevated terraces or benches flank the entrance to Room 1A. A niche was built into the west retaining wall of the eastern terrace.

Diamanti's reconstruction of use patterns indicates that Rooms 1A, the east side room, and the westernmost room were fully residential, while craft production occurred in the west side room (Diamanti 1991: 293–294).

It thus appears that the pattern of a dominant structure with a tripartite floor plan can also be encountered in lower-class patios. Household and lineage heads may have tried to imitate the power structures of their lords with their own means and in their own environment.

This pattern could also be seen as one piece of evidence in support of the theory that the Classic Maya had a "segmentary state." David Webster and William Sanders believe that

> the mature Copan polity was characterized by a high degree of segmentation. By this we mean that, although the system was politically centralized around a group of preeminent titled elites (the royal lineage), kinship was still the dominant mechanism in overall social, political, and economic organization. . . . our argument is that there were multiple, effective political interest groups in the polity, which we conceive of as maximal lineages with their own internal ranking structures and, most importantly, their own corporate identity and resources. . . . In such a society the effective power of rulers is to a high degree circumscribed by the presence of lesser magnates with their own power bases. Leaders of such corporate groups . . . would be occupants of such impressive Type 3 or 4 groups as 9N-8, and their supporters/kin would consist not only of other occupants of the elite households, but of segments of the rural population as well. These second-level elites at Copan, at least some of whom seem to have enjoyed the possession of court titles and ranks, were stewards of large corporate, kin-based land holdings. (Webster 1992: 153–154)

Sanders adds that the resulting political situation was a highly volatile one and that the power of the Copan rulers depended on how long and how well they were capable of controlling such rival elites (1989: 102–104).

It has to be emphasized that there is by no means a consensus in the literature about the general applicability of the segmentary state model to Maya society. Diane and Arlen Chase, for example, argue that such a model "does *not* fit the Late Classic Maya of the Southern, and presumably Northern, lowlands" (1992: 308). I think the architectural pattern of the tripartite floor plan can be interpreted as one type of material evidence for a degree of segmentation in the political power structure of the ancient Maya.

William Fash has compared the social organization in the Copan Valley with that of the Chorti Maya documented by Charles Wisdom. Among the Chorti, a series of subcommunities occupies the area between towns. These subcommunities are called *sian otot* (many houses) and are made up of a number of fairly self-sufficient families. Marriage occurs generally between members of the same subcommunity. Applying this model to Las

Sepulturas, Fash interprets the largest patios, A and B, with the most elaborate buildings as the residences of the oldest segments of two families. The
smaller and irregular patios would have been inhabited by younger generations who, after marriage, established their own households scattered
throughout the subcommunity (2001: 156–158).

It will now be shown that tripartite compositions were popular in architecture as well as in other media of the visual arts throughout Maya
history.

A Short History of Tripartite Designs and Compositions in Maya Art

The pattern of a tripartite division in Maya architecture is widespread and
of great antiquity in the Maya area. Kowalski presents a historical summary of the three-part division in Maya buildings (Kowalski 1987: 120–125).
It thus seems sufficient to only point out some of the major examples.

Variants of the three-part plan can be traced back to the Preclassic
period. At Tikal, the substructures of the North Acropolis consisted of tripartite temple groups. Each temple was set on a pyramidal platform and
accessed by a central stairway. They were arranged so that a central temple
facing south was always flanked by two side temples facing east and west.
After a period of use, each temple group was filled in with rubble to form
a higher platform on which a new temple group was erected. Excavations
have exposed the substructures, so that today a series of three-part temple
groups are visible.

An Early Classic example has been documented at Uaxactun. The first
building phase of Structure A-V consisted of three vaulted temples facing
inward on a small elevated courtyard (see Kowalski 1987: 121).

Late Classic examples of the tripartite division abound. At Palenque,
the Group of the Cross is made up of three temple buildings placed on top
of pyramidal platforms of differing heights. On the rear wall, each temple
displays a large tablet carved with portraits of K'inich Kan B'alam II and
long hieroglyphic inscriptions. Analysis of the iconography and the texts
revealed that the three tablets refer to different stages of the accession ceremonies for K'inich Kan B'alam II.

In a recent paper, Claude Baudez interpreted each temple as "the locale
of a definite cosmic zone: Heaven, Underworld and Earth" (1993). He derived evidence for his interpretation from the iconography surrounding the
protagonist of the three tablets (K'inich Kan B'alam II). He concluded that
the three temples were the stations of a ritual perambulation performed

by the king during major political and religious celebrations (Baudez 1993). Andrews et al. (this volume) demonstrate that Structure 10L-32 in Yax Pasaj Chan Yoaat's palace compound had a similar tripartite room layout. Inomata and Triadan (this volume) record the same pattern of a centralized tripartite floor plan in Structure M8-10 at Aguateca.

Kowalski lists numerous examples in the Yucatan (1987: 122–125). At Xpuhil in the Río Bec area, Structure 1 consists of twelve interlocking chambers, above which rise three steep towers with ornamental stairs and mock temple buildings. The central tower is recessed, enhancing the tripartite division and creating the impression of three adjacent buildings rather than a unified facade. At Culucbalom, Structure 1 offers another solution to the three-part composition. Here the central building is located on a pyramidal platform, while the two wings sit on a lower level. The taller central building is further foregrounded by richer ornamentation, but the ensemble is unified by the three roof combs and shared upper profiling.

A very important aspect in a tripartite plan is the orientation and interconnectedness of the three units. Temple buildings generally have one doorway opening into one courtyard. The orientation of rooms in residential structures is much more complex. Many side rooms open into the same courtyard as the central room, particularly in royal residences with a tandem present/transverse present plan—for example, the House of the Governor—but others do not—for example, Structure 5D-65 in the Central Acropolis at Tikal. At Las Sepulturas, none of the side rooms face the patio as the central rooms do. Orientation of rooms certainly influenced the use of space, and I suspect that the side rooms at Las Sepulturas may not have shared the official and public function of the central rooms.

Access between rooms—specifically the interconnectedness between the central and side rooms—varies even more greatly, and I have not been able to discern any patterns. I think what this variety within the unity of the tripartite plan means is that what mattered was centrality and not precise geometric symmetry. And centrality was linked with political power. This desire for centering the built environment in space has been observed throughout Mesoamerica (Freidel, Schele, and Parker 1993: 123–172). Karl Taube has noted that the Maya often associated radial stairway pyramids with the concept of the three hearthstones that denote the mythological first central place (see below), through which the axis mundi passes to establish the vertical divisions of the cosmos. For example, when the Late Preclassic E-VII-Sub at Uaxactun was covered up, a lip-to-lip cache vessel was placed on the stucco floor near the top of the principal stairway. This cache vessel contained three simple stones. At Seibal, Structure A-3 is a

FIGURE 11.6. Palace at Palenque. Drawing of the figures on Palace Tablet. (Copyright Merle Greene Robertson, 1976)

radial stairway pyramid, and one stela fronts each stairway. A fifth monument, Stela 21, was placed in the very center of the structure on top. Again, a cache containing three jade boulders was found directly below this monument. At Tonina, Structure 5D-1 is a radial stairway building and a temple structure sits on top of the pyramidal platform. The Early Classic Stela 74 stood in the temple interior and portrays a ruler with three smoking hearthstones in his headdress (Taube 1998: 441–442).

The centering of significant personages is also an important theme in the iconography. A recently published Late Preclassic stela from Kaminaljuyu displays a protagonist centrally seated on a throne and flanked by two kneeling subordinate figures who may be captives. This composition was repeated twice and probably three times, but the lower right section is broken off (Kaplan 2000: 188–189).

At Palenque, sculptors repeatedly depicted the king and his parents in a tripartite arrangement. The Palace Tablet depicts the accession of K'inich K'an Joy Chitam II in A.D. 702 and records the events leading up to it.[13] K'inich K'an Joy Chitam II is shown seated in a central position, flanked by his parents. His father, K'inich Janaab' Pakal I, and his mother, Lady Tz'akb'u Ajaw, are handing him the regalia of the royal office. K'an Joy Chitam II is represented in a frontal view, while his parents are in profile. All three figures are seated cross-legged upon thrones from which zoomorphic heads project.

Robertson associates the three thrones and their supernatural heads with the Palenque Triad (Robertson 1985b: fig. 259).[14] Furthermore, the

image of the thrones closely resembles the throne stone glyph in the creation passages on Quirigua Stela C (for an illustration of the text with para-
phrase see Freidel, Schele, and Parker 1993, p. 67, fig. 2: 5). This text narrates
the creation of the world at the beginning of time. On 4 Ajaw 8 Kumk'u,
three stones were set: the first stone, a jaguar throne stone, was planted in
the sky; the second stone, a serpent throne stone, was planted on earth;
and the third stone was a waterlily throne stone. These events happened
when sky and earth were not yet separated. However, the stone plantings
mark the point in time when the sky was lifted up and the three vertical
orders of the cosmos were formed (Freidel, Schele, and Parker 1993, fig. 2:
5; Christie 1995: 85–104).

Schele and Barbara MacLeod have pointed out that the three thrones
on the Palace Tablet are variants of the first Three Stones of Creation
mentioned on Quirigua Stela C (personal communication 1992). They are
marked with the heads of a jaguar, fish, and serpent and thus correspond
to the three stones in the creation account, which are described as jaguar,
water, and serpent thrones (Taube 1998: 456). The thrones on the Palace
Tablet are replicated on a horizontal level and emphasize that the reign of
K'inich K'an Joy Chitam II marked the beginning of a new era. He is seated
centrally, occupying the middle level of the world of humanity. His close
interaction with his parents, who died before he acceded to the royal office,
demonstrates that he is mediating and is in close contact with the otherworlds above and below.

Conclusions

Architecture was designed in a similar fashion. Temple buildings were clustered in groups of three and rooms were laid out on a horizontal axis with a
foregrounded central space flanked by two smaller units. The Three Stones
of Creation and the resulting tripartite vertical order of the cosmos constitute one of the basic concepts through which the Maya tried to make sense
of the world in which they lived.

They re-created the tripartite vertical and the four-partite horizontal
divisions of the cosmos in multiple ways and built microcosms in their
daily lives.[15] The tripartite house plan was one such way of visualizing the
tripartite vertical order on a horizontal level. It was a way of centering in
which the king assumed a commanding position of authority when he was
seated in the central room, usually on a throne. Here he displayed his actual
and symbolic power to mediate in political as well as religious ritual. The
three-part room arrangement became an effective political tool with such

profound symbolic associations that it was copied on a more modest scale by lineage and household heads in outlying areas surrounding the ceremonial centers. It proclaimed the king or lineage head the pivot of the community or family and centered the daily life of the group around him. In this manner, the tripartite floor plan contributed to solidifying and sanctifying Maya social hierarchy.

The architectural space was sacred and used for ceremonies and official events, but it was also residential because the domestic, religious, and public lives of the Maya were integrated. Maya existence was not and is not divided into a public and a private life; both aspects coexist and overlap, and so do the uses of Maya houses. And this is why the tripartite order of the world is such a deep belief structure and is replicated in so many contexts in Maya life.

NOTES

1. For a more thorough discussion of Classical as well as contemporary Maya cosmology, see Freidel, Schele, and Parker 1993 and Christie 1995.

2. Building groups like Group 4F-1 and 2 raise important issues about social structure. The formal comparison between Structure 4E-31 and tandem present/ transverse present buildings in the Central Acropolis uncovered important similarities, such as the tripartite floor plan. Can we legitimately argue that formal and spatial similarities establish sufficient evidence for social similarity? Or, to put it in other words, did people with comparable social status reside in houses with similar material and spatial layouts? And if the answer is yes, what does this imply about Maya social organization in general? What were the political ties between the inhabitants of Groups 4F-1 and 4F-2 and the royal household at the Central Acropolis? Some of the authors in this volume address this issue further; see Guderjan, as well as Inomata and Triadan.

3. For a detailed description of the human figure sculpture on the House of the Governor illustrated by high-quality photographs, the reader should consult Kowalski 1987: 149–181.

4. Annabeth Headrick (1995) has offered an alternative interpretation of the secondary figures on the facade of the House of the Governor. She agrees that they represent individuals of high social status based on their overall naturalistic rendition and elite attributes, but she sees the open-mawed serpent heads as "vision serpents" and the seated figures as "the ruling lineage's ancestors." In this interpretation, the individuals would have been recalled in the ritual of the vision quest conducted by Lord Chaak. I think this explanation is quite possible, because the Maya frequently showed humans and supernaturals within the same composition.

5. Kowalski, this volume, presents a thorough iconographic analysis of the jaguar throne. See also Kowalski 1987: 229–236.

6. For a full discussion of the iconography of the facade, the reader should consult Schele and Miller 1986: 140–142.

7. There are commonly four Pauahtuns. These deities stand or sit at the four corners of the world and hold up the earth over the underworld and the sky over the

earth. Here they support the bench. Linda Schele presents a detailed analysis of the iconography and the text of the bench in Copan Note 24 (Schele 1987).

8. Hendon presents a detailed and thorough description of the architecture and the associated loci and artifacts; see Hendon 1987: 120–412.

9. This identification was first made by Barbara Fash et al. (1992). Since then, numerous other buildings at various sites have been interpreted as Popol Nahs (see Kowalski, this volume; Ambrosino, this volume). While some of these interpretations present convincing evidence, it is highly questionable that mat designs alone justify the conclusion that Structure B-67 actually functioned as a Popol Nah. I would like to emphasize that this identification is only offered as a possibility.

10. The Maya performed many domestic chores outside. Kitchen areas were often exterior open platforms. Interior spaces, including certain benches, may have been used mainly for sleeping.

11. Some of the artifacts found in Structure 91 also suggest that an elite family resided there: one flask and one perforated flat disk were recovered from above the floor of Room 1. The perforated disk was most likely a piece of personal adornment, perhaps an earflare or part of a necklace belonging to an official costume.

12. There is no evidence that the Maya ever had a social system based on moieties, as can be documented in many Native American and Andean cultures.

13. The Palace Tablet was originally located in the northern corridor of House A-D in the Palace. It was mounted on the center of the north-facing wall, oriented outward. A small throne was probably attached to the front of the tablet.

14. The Palenque Triad is three deities (GI, GII, GIII) with various connotations who figure prominently in Palenque iconography. The face of GI often displays the barbels of a fish. GII is identical with God K or K'awil. GIII is often represented with a looped band between the eyes and with jaguar ears.

15. For example, see Freidel, Schele, and Parker 1993; Christie 1995; Vogt 1969, 1993; Bunzel 1952.

REFERENCES

Baudez, C. F.
1993 Royal Journeys through the Universe: The Cross Group at Palenque. Paper presented at the 20th Mesa Redonda, Palenque, Mexico.
Bunzel, R.
1952 *Chichicastenango. A Guatemalan Village.* Seattle: University of Washington Press.
Chase, D. Z., and A. F. Chase (eds.)
1992 *Mesoamerican Elites: An Archaeological Assessment.* Norman: University of Oklahoma Press.
Christie, J. J.
1995 Maya Period Ending Ceremonies: Restarting Time and Rebuilding the Cosmos to Assure Survival of the Maya World. Ph.D. dissertation, Department of Latin American Studies, University of Texas at Austin.
Diamanti, M.
1991 *Domestic Organization at Copan: Reconstruction of Elite Maya Households through Ethnographic Models (Honduras).* Ph.D. dissertation, Pennsylvania State University. Ann Arbor: University Microfilms.
Fash, W. L.
2001 *Scribes, Warriors, and Kings.* London: Thames and Hudson.
Fash, B. W., W. L. Fash, S. Lane, R. Larios, L. Schele, J. Stomper, and D. Stuart
1992 Investigations of a Classic Maya Council House at Copan, Honduras. *Journal of Field Archaeology* 19 (4): 419–442.

Freidel, D., L. Schele, and J. Parker
1993   *Maya Cosmos.* New York: William Morrow.
Grube, N., and L. Schele
1987   *The Date on the Bench from Structure 9N-82, Sepulturas, Copan, Honduras.* Copan Note 23. Austin: Copan Mosaics Project, Instituto Hondureño de Antropología e Historia, and Art Department, University of Texas at Austin.
Harrison, P. D.
1971   *The Central Acropolis, Tikal, Guatemala: A Preliminary Study of the Functions of Its Structural Components during the Late Classic Period.* Ph.D. dissertation, University of Pennsylvania. Ann Arbor: University Microfilms.
1994   Spatial Geometry and Logic in the Ancient Maya Mind, Part 2: Architecture. In *Seventh Palenque Round Table, 1989,* edited by M. G. Robertson and V. M. Fields, 243–252. San Francisco: Pre-Columbian Art Research Institute.
Haviland, William A.
1985   *Excavations in Small Residential Groups of Tikal: Groups 4F-1 and 4F-2.* Tikal Report 19. Philadelphia: University of Pennsylvania Museum of Archaeology and Anthropology.
Headrick, Annabeth
1995   Las Monjas and the Tradition of Founder's Houses. Paper presented at the XIth Texas Symposium: The Maya Meetings at Texas, Austin, March 10, 1995.
Hendon, J. A.
1987   *The Uses of Maya Structures: A Study of Architecture and Artifact Distribution at Sepulturas, Copan, Honduras.* Ph.D. dissertation, Harvard University. Ann Arbor: University Microfilms.
Kaplan, J.
2000   Late Preclassic Kaminaljuyu. *Ancient Mesoamerica* 11 (2): 188–189.
Kowalski, J. K.
1987   *The House of the Governor: A Maya Palace at Uxmal, Yucatan, Mexico.* Norman: University of Oklahoma Press.
Proskouriakoff, Tatiana
1960   Historical Implications of a Pattern of Dates at Piedras Negras, Guatemala. *American Antiquity* 25 (4): 454–475.
Robertson, M. G.
1985a   *The Sculpture of Palenque,* vol. 2. Princeton: Princeton University Press.
1985b   *The Sculpture of Palenque,* vol. 3. Princeton: Princeton University Press.
Sanders, William T.
1989   Household Lineage and State at Eighth-Century Copan, Honduras. In *The House of the Bacabs,* edited by David Webster, 89–105. Washington, D.C.: Dumbarton Oaks Research Library and Collection.
Schele, L.
1987   *The Figures on the Legs of the Scribe's Bench.* Copan Note 24. Austin: Copan Mosaics Project, Instituto Hondureño de Antropología e Historia, and Art Department, University of Texas at Austin.
Schele, L., and D. Freidel
1990   *A Forest of Kings: The Untold Story of the Ancient Maya.* New York: William Morrow.
Schele, L., and M. Miller
1986   *The Blood of Kings.* Fort Worth: Kimbell Art Museum.
Sosa, John R.
1986   Maya Concepts of Astronomical Order. In *Symbol and Meaning Beyond the Closed Community: Essays in Mesoamerican Ideas,* edited by Gary H. Gossen, 185–196. Vol. 1. Studies on Culture and Society Series. Albany, N.Y.:

Institute for Mesoamerican Studies, University at Albany, State University of New York.

Taube, Karl

1988   *The Ancient Yucatec New Year Festival: The Liminal Period in Maya Ritual and Cosmology.* Ph.D. dissertation, Yale University. Ann Arbor: University Microfilms.

1998   The Jade Hearth: Centrality, Rulership, and the Classic Maya Temple. In *Functions and Meaning in Classic Maya Architecture,* edited by Stephen D. Houston, 427–478. Washington, D.C.: Dumbarton Oaks Research Library and Collection.

Tozzer, A.

1941   *Landa's Relación de las Cosas de Yucatán: A Translation.* Papers of the Peabody Museum of American Archaeology and Ethnology, vol. 18. Cambridge, Mass.: Harvard University.

Vogt, E. Z.

1969   *Zinacantan: A Maya Community in the Highlands of Chiapas.* Cambridge, Mass.: Belknap Press, Harvard University Press.

1993   *Tortillas for the Gods.* 2d ed. Norman: University of Oklahoma Press.

Webster, D.

1992   Maya Elites: The Perspective from Copan. In *Mesoamerican Elites: An Archaeological Assessment,* edited by D. Z. Chase and A. F. Chase, 135–156. Norman: University of Oklahoma Press.

CHAPTER TWELVE

Conclusions

Jessica Joyce Christie

Given the large amount of data about palaces and elite residences and the multidisciplinary approaches in this volume, the conclusions will attempt to isolate patterns and discuss points of agreement and disagreement among the authors. I do not think that it is possible to identify specific patterns that would apply to all Maya elite residential architecture. Nevertheless, the Maya shared strong enough cultural ties regarding their political and religious systems for their palaces and elite residences to exhibit certain similarities in form and function. At the same time, there was always flexibility and openness to local solutions and changes over time. With this in mind, my conclusions must be seen to some degree as generalizations.

This chapter is divided into four sections. Section one will address form. Repetitive formal and material elements, room layout, and spatial arrangement of royal and elite houses will be examined; and, based on shared aspects, four palace types will be introduced. Section two will look at location. The issue of residences in the core area versus the periphery of Maya cities will be evaluated, palace structures attached to temples will be addressed, and the symbolic context of sacred geography will be explored. Section three will discuss function. The extent to which the uses and functions of Maya elite residential architecture can be reconstructed at this time with reasonable certainty will be examined. There are structures that have been identified as the royal residences of specific historical rulers based on hieroglyphic inscriptions that are directly associated with them. Others are now understood as scribes' houses because in situ materials and iconography clearly refer to this profession. Furthermore, there is multiple evidence for a number of activities that took place in palace buildings besides the daily routine of sleeping and eating: rituals—most importantly, Period Ending ceremonies—and formal receptions and audiences. Section four will analyze the information palaces and elite residences provide about social structure. The fact that numerous elite residences can be found in every Maya city implies that an organized political and possibly religious hierarchy existed in Maya society. The number of elite residences may also provide insights into the hierarchy of different sites, while the general increase in elite residences in virtually every Maya city during the Late Classic reflects changes in the political organization from a system based on the sovereign to a governing body made up of members from multiple lineages. Section four cites numerous ongoing archaeological investigations, as well as recent studies in epigraphy (Schele, Grube, and Martin 1998), and leads to a holistic perspective of investigating Maya palaces.

Section One: Form

Looking at the formal and material elements of the royal and elite houses analyzed in this volume, one can conclude that the fundamental descriptions of Maya palaces by such early scholars as Tozzer, Spinden, and Smith are still valid. It is correct that most palace structures and elite residences sit on low platforms, contain large numbers of rooms and doorways, and are usually arranged around courts. These features define what I call palace-type I in the context of this volume. Palace-type I is by far the most common form of Maya palaces. In royal palaces, the buildings forming the courtyard are often two stories high and usually contain two rows of parallel longitudinal or tandem rooms and one or two transverse rooms at either end. They are furnished with benches, and their facades face the court and in some cases are decorated with sculpture.

Prominent examples abound; the Central Acropolis at Tikal is composed of palace-type I structures arranged around multiple courtyards (see Harrison, this volume; Liendo Stuardo, this volume; Christie, this volume). Some of the facades were adorned with extraordinary sculptural programs, some of which have not been professionally drawn and published and are therefore excluded from any functional analysis. Another just as well known example is the Palace at Palenque, which also consists of three clearly defined major and one minor courtyard, forming palace-type I complexes (see Liendo Stuardo, this volume). The sculpture, inscriptions, and wall paintings in the Palenque Palace have been thoroughly documented by Merle Greene Robertson (1985a, 1985b), whose painstaking work has provided invaluable insights into the events that took place in the Palace and the people who performed them. Thus we know that the throne under the Oval Palace Tablet in House E was the location where K'inich Janaab' Pakal I and probably some of his successors became king, and that the throne in House C facing the East Court and probably also the original throne under the Palace Tablet in House A-D were the focal points of important political receptions and audiences.

At Copan, Early and Late Classic palaces were organized around patios (see Traxler, this volume; Andrews, this volume). Some of the very early compounds, such as the residence of the lineage founder Yax K'uk' Mo', were constructed as closed patio groups with perimeter walls, while the later compounds are generally more open and irregular. The latter is true for Plazas A and B, which contain the house of the Late Classic king Yax Pasaj. Andrews also notes that nondomestic structures, such as temples and dance platforms, formed these plazas, together with the residences.

Palace-type I compounds reoccur in the further outlying residential areas. This can be shown particularly well at Las Sepulturas, which is an outlier of Copan located east of the ceremonial center. The excavated structures form multiple patios that are surrounded by mostly range-type houses resting on low platforms. It is important to note here that the quality of architecture greatly varies. There are buildings of dressed tuff masonry, roughly shaped tuff blocks, cobbles, and *bajareque*; most houses had thatched roofs, some had beam-and-mortar roofs, and a small number of structures were vaulted. Some had more interior furnishings than others, and a few displayed facades decorated with sculpture. It thus appears that the residents in some patios were wealthier and enjoyed a higher social status than the residents in others. In turn, the highest-status patios at Las Sepulturas are smaller and contain buildings with fewer rooms and less permanent construction materials than the royal compounds in the ceremonial center. It follows that palace-type I compounds constituted a very popular form of residential architecture that was commonly used by royal and elite families alike. Size as well as the quality of construction materials and decoration reflected the social and economic status of the particular residents and functioned as markers of social hierarchy (Hendon 1987; Diamanti 1991).

These findings tie in well with the site typology established for the Copan Valley by Richard Leventhal and Gordon Willey. They differentiate between type I, II, III, and IV sites, which are all patio groups. They differ, however, in the number of plazas, the number of surrounding mounds and structures, height, construction materials, roofing methods, and sculptural decoration. Type I defines the smallest and most perishable house compounds, while types III and IV are characterized as minor ceremonial centers and rank only one level below the Copan main center (Hendon 1987: 52–53).

Palace-type II buildings are large, multiroom structures that are self-contained and usually do not form part of a patio group. Type II palaces may be several stories tall and are often accessed by a central monumental stairway.

The best known example of a palace-type II is Structure 2B1, commonly referred to as "the Great Palace," at Sayil. This monumental palace contains ninety-four rooms, which are arranged in three stories and can be reached by two stairways on the north and south sides. It rests on a low platform, together with Structure 2B2, which stands detached from the palace. The south facade of the second story exhibits sculptural decoration of anthropomorphic masks and images of the Diving God flanked by serpents. Hieroglyphic inscriptions, however, are completely absent, so that the monumental building cannot be connected with any specific historical figure.

H. E. D. Pollock believes that the present form of Structure 2B1 does not represent one coherent architectural design but that the second and third stories were added on following the completion of the story below (Pollock 1980: 101).

In the context of site layout, Structure 2B1 forms the northern end of the north-south causeway, which terminates in smaller palace buildings in the south. It should also be noted that palace-type I compounds are abundant to the southwest and northeast of this causeway.

The site of Kabah contains possibly the largest number of palace-type II buildings. Following the plans, maps, and descriptions by Pollock, Structures 1A1, 1A2, 2A1, 2C2, 2C3, and 2C6 all fall into the category of palace-type II (see Liendo Stuardo, this volume). Pollock mentions the date A.D. 879 on a sculpted doorjamb in Structure 2C6 (Pollock 1980: 140). It appears that these building complexes grew in several phases, that rooms were added on over time, and that the visible remains represent their Terminal Classic and/or Early Postclassic appearance (Pollock 1980: 140–204). It should also be pointed out that palace-type I compounds do occur at Kabah, for example, Structures 1A3, 1A4, and 1A6.

An example of a palace-type II structure physically close to Kabah is the House of the Governor at Uxmal (see Kowalski, this volume; Liendo Stuardo, this volume; Christie, this volume). This building appears relatively small in size when compared to Structure 2B1 at Sayil; it consists of "only" twenty rooms and is one story tall. The House of the Governor does not form part of a courtyard but rests on four platforms which diminish in size as they go up and elevate it above the surrounding buildings. Platform 2 extends well beyond all sides of the House of the Governor and provides the space in front of the east facade where official activities were conducted. A low platform with radial stairs which supports a bicephalic jaguar throne was placed east of the building along its central axis. Interestingly, at Uxmal the royal throne stood outside in the open air, with the palace building as a stage set of royal power behind it, whereas thrones were placed inside centrally located chambers at most other sites, for example, Palenque.

As was noted for Sayil and Kabah, palace-type I groups were also constructed at Uxmal. The best-known example is the Nunnery Quadrangle, dated to A.D. 890 to 910, which implies that it was built at the same time as the House of the Governor (see Kowalski, this volume). Important questions that must be asked are whether the social status of the occupants of the two palace types differed and concern the purposes for which both palace types were used. Kowalski argues that the Governor's House "may have been a local version of a Popol Nah, where the ruler met in council with his subordinate lords to discuss affairs of state and plan community festivals" (see the discussion of Popol Nahs below) and that the courtyard of the Nunnery Quadrangle was a prestigious and public space where rituals reenacting creation myths and sanctifying and legitimizing rulership were conducted (Kowalski, this volume).

Another monumental example of a palace-type II building is the Caana at Caracol, which is now interpreted as a royal residential palace by Chase and Chase (1998, 2001). Chase and Chase's archaeological investigations showed that it contained minimally sixty-six contemporaneously used rooms in four palace units integrated with three temples. They counted between forty-five and forty-eight benches within rooms in palace structures. Twenty-four rooms are located in a single building placed halfway up the south facade of Caana. This palace exhibits a tandem plan, with two transverse rooms at the western and eastern ends.

Caana's summit plaza is delimited by a palace on its south side that contains at least fifteen rooms and nine benches, by three temples to the west, north, and east (Structures B18, B19, B20), and by entrances to two palace units set to either side of Structure B19. What is of particular interest at the summit of Caana is the close proximity of palaces and temples. The associated stucco sculpture and painted decoration, a Giant Ajaw altar, tombs, and in situ artifacts help in the reconstruction of the kinds of events that took place in this so highly physically elevated and thus symbolically charged location (see Chase and Chase 2001).

Palace-type III buildings are the gallery-patio compounds at Chichen-Itza (see Kowalski, this volume). These are open, colonnaded galleries surrounding an—often sunken—courtyard. A characteristic example is the

Mercado complex at Chichen Itza, which dates to the Early Postclassic. While the interior space is open and unpartitioned, the building can only be entered from the north side. A broad stairway leads to an elongated colonnaded vestibule, from which one doorway provides access to the galleries and patio. The galleries of the Mercado contain benches and daises, and some of the artifacts found in situ suggest domestic use. Arguments for public as well as residential functions of the Mercado compound have been made (see Kowalski, this volume). What is significant about palace-type III buildings is their open space and lack of privacy and their late appearance in Maya architecture.

Arthur Demarest, Kim Morgan, Claudia Wolley, and Héctor Escobedo have identified a "presentation palace" at Dos Pilas, which I will include in this discussion as palace-type IV (see Demarest et al., this volume). Presentation palaces are structures with thrones behind very open facades oriented toward public space. The particular building they identified, Structure N5-3, probably had wooden posts supporting a large canopy on the north side. The interior space therefore remained open on one side and directly faced the procession path, which connects the West Plaza Group with the eastern Duende complex (see Demarest et al., this volume). Presentation palaces thus clearly exemplify the public and official functions of Maya elite residential architecture. Juan Antonio Valdés has classified Structures 32 and 33 of Group B in Tamarindito, Structure M7-35 at Aguateca, and Structure 10L-18 at Copan as presentation palaces. These examples do not share the canopy roof and wooden posts of Structure N5-3, but have masonry facades with unusually wide door openings in front of a central throne. They were built specifically so that the main personage when seated on the throne appeared in plain view to all the participants in public ceremonies, and activities that took place inside and outside the palace were integrated (Valdés 2001: 150–153).

Space constitutes the complementary component of architecture that the material elements delineate. In fact, architectural theory has claimed that "the primary purpose of a building is the ordering of space, not the physical object itself. . . . Because the ordering of space influences modes of social interaction. . . ." (Ferguson 1996: 11; see also Hillier and Hanson 1984). This is exactly the aspect Rodrigo Liendo Stuardo's investigation of access explores. He uses two graphic methods to analyze access patterns in three Classic palaces in the lowlands and in four Early Postclassic residences in Yucatan. His results show that access was more simplified in the Early Postclassic buildings. He attributes this to the fact that his Yucatan examples from Sayil, Labna, and Kabah represent palace-type II structures (my terminology), while his lowland examples from Palenque, Tikal, and Uaxactun constitute palace-type I compounds (my terminology). He suggests that changes in access may be indicative of changes in the functions of Maya palaces. Liendo Stuardo proposes that the Classic palaces in the lowlands combined residential with political and ritual functions, while in the Postclassic these functions became disassociated and some political and ritual functions were transferred to elite residences.

The site of Xunantunich provides another excellent example of how important access was and how the Maya altered it over time. Xunantunich is laid out along a north-south axis. The northern endpoint is formed by a palace-type I compound surrounding Plaza A-III. This palace was most likely the residence of the ruling family at Xunantunich. The southern endpoint is marked by the Castillo. The Castillo is a tall temple building which is decorated with a stucco frieze in the upper areas of its pyramidal platform. The iconography of this frieze provides evidence that the Castillo functioned as an ancestor shrine for the ruling family.

Richard Leventhal and others' (1997) thorough archaeological work has demonstrated that access to the palace was increasingly and steadily restricted during the Late Classic. Initially a large and open public plaza existed between the palace-type I compound and the Castillo. Toward the end of the Late Classic, a temple building was set in the middle of this plaza and walls were erected that effectively separated and isolated the royal residence from public space. Access to the palace itself was limited at about the same time by the construction of additional platforms and buildings (Yaeger 1997). In this manner, domestic activities were neatly set apart from public gatherings and religious and ritual observances, which were restricted to the remaining section of the plaza in front of the Castillo. This reflects a profound change in the relationship between the ruling family and their subjects. One possible reason for such changes may be increased competition from rivaling elite families. In fact, Yaeger suggests that the palace-type I around Plaza A-III was largely abandoned by the middle to end of the Late Classic but that people continued to live at the site and perform rituals in the Terminal Classic (Yaeger 1997: 42).

Access analysis should be expanded to a broader discussion of the use of outdoor space. This very issue was addressed in a symposium entitled *Archaeological Ethnographies: Outdoors as Living Spaces*, organized by Nan Rothschild and Cynthia Robin at the sixty-fourth annual meeting of the Society for American Archaeology in 1999. Robin presented a comparison between a contemporary Yucatec village and a Late Classic site in Belize regarding the use of outdoor space. While direct cultural continuity cannot be demonstrated, Robin argued that many ancient Maya houses were probably surrounded by open workspaces and orchards and gardens, just like houses in the Yucatan are today (1999). Stacy Barber and Karen Holmberg identified *bodegas*, or workspaces and roofed storage areas, next to elite residences at the site of Ceren (1999).

I think archaeologists must pay more attention to the extramural spaces surrounding palaces and elite residences and include them in their functional analyses. This was done to some extent at Nakbe, where a retaining wall was found in association with one palace building. This wall had been erected solely to retain fertile imported soil. The soil was analyzed for plant remains by Steve Bozarth (Bozarth, personal communication 1998). His findings establish solid evidence that this palace at Nakbe had a garden. One would expect to encounter more gardens in other Maya cities. The presence of gardens is not surprising, considering that it has long been known and accepted that gardens were an integral element of Aztec as well as Inka palaces.

Section Two: Location

A second very important aspect in the discussion of Maya palaces is location and site layout. Where were the palaces located in the context of a Maya city? Is there any evidence about the relations between palaces and surrounding buildings? Such questions must be integral components of a holistic analysis of elite residential architecture, because their answers illuminate social behavior.

The chapters confirm the observation of early scholars that royal palaces are located centrally, in the core area, of Maya cities while elite residences are encountered further out, at the periphery. This pattern is so consistent that distance from the center can be used as an indicator of social status.[1] In multiple settlement surveys, the more remote house mounds have been from the center, the simpler their construction has turned out to be.

The widest-known examples are the royal palaces of K'inich Janaab' Pakal I at Palenque and of Chaak Tok Ich'aak I in the Central Acropolis at Tikal, the Early and Late Classic residences of K'inich Yax K'uk' Mo' and Yax Pasaj Chan Yoaat at Copan, and the large house of Lord Chaak at Uxmal, all of which were erected in the center of their city. Elite residences have been documented at all sites, and they are normally found outside the immediate core areas. Las Sepulturas presents a significant case. As noted above, Las Sepulturas is located a few miles east of the Copan ceremonial center. The residences follow the palace-type I layout. They differ widely in size, quality of materials, construction, and interior furnishings, which are considered indicators of social status (see above; Hendon 1987; Diamanti 1991). The most distinguished residence was Structure 82-C on the south side of Patio A in Group 9N-8. The facade on the lower level displays two half-figure busts of scribes holding pens and paint pots. The writing implements suggest that the male members of the family living in Structure 82-C probably worked as royal scribes. Two members of this scribe family are individually identified as Mak Chaanal and Quetzal–God K on the hieroglyphic bench set in the central room. The date in the same text places the bench, the house, and its scribal occupants within the reign of Yax Pasaj Chan Yoaat. It follows that Mak Chaanal and Quetzal–God K were scribes who worked under Yax Pasaj Chan Yoaat and perhaps enjoyed the privilege of residing in a high-status palace-type I compound close to the ceremonial center because they maintained a close relationship with the ruler (Grube and Schele 1987; Schele 1987).

Another pattern which the chapters in this volume clearly identify is the close proximity of palaces and temples. Many palace structures are not only located close by the main temples in core areas of Maya cities but are directly and physically attached to temple buildings. In palace-type I compounds, temples may occupy one or more sides of the courtyard. Caracol offers multiple examples: the summit plaza of Caana is delimited by a palace to its south; temples to the west (Structure B18), north (Structure B19), and east (Structure B20); and entrances to two palace units set on either side of Structure B19 (Chase and Chase, 1998, 2001). These buildings form a palace-type I group that includes three temples. The recovered stucco sculpture and texts, in situ artifacts, and tombs provide evidence that the summit plaza and its surrounding buildings constitute a carefully designed location where religious and political power was transferred and publicly displayed. In the B Plaza, Structures B4 and B6 were added to the sides of the Structure B5 temple. Both Structures B4 and B6 consist of two tandem rooms and a bench in the front room (Chase and Chase, 1998). The Barrio, a palace-type I compound, contains a temple on the north side and the Central Acropolis, which also forms its own palace-type I and includes temples and mortuary shrines on the north and east sides (Chase and Chase, 1998, 2001).

Similar relationships between palaces and temples have been documented at Dos Pilas. In the Murciélagos palace complex, Structure N5-7 was one of the earliest constructions. It is a tall funerary temple built in pure Tikal style. A royal throne room and presentation palace were discovered overlapping the bottom and the stairway of the N5-7 temple. Demarest and coauthors speculate that the purpose of this deliberate abutment of the throne room against the possible tomb of a Tikal ancestor was to publicly legitimize the descent of Dos Pilas Ruler 4 from Tikal (Demarest et al., this volume). A second example of a funerary temple with a throne room stood in the same courtyard. Structure N5-71 is another tall temple with a royal tomb but, unlike Structure N5-7, built in Petexbatun style. A throne room with an uncarved stone bench abutted this temple to the north. It thus appears that in the Dos Pilas examples the throne rooms attached to temples make a calculated political statement. Other sites should be examined for similar cases, especially Caracol.

The final point in the discussion of palace locations is the extent to which Maya palaces took advantage of sacred geography. In Maya cosmology, the earth constituted the middle plane between the underworld and the realm of the sky. Deities, ancestors, and supernaturals resided in both otherworlds. Natural openings in the earth, such as caves, springs, waterholes, and lakes, were understood as sacred portals through which the supernaturals in the underworld could be contacted. Elevations, such as trees and mountains, were seen as communication channels with the celestial level. Rich offerings were found at such natural portals to the otherworld—for example, in the famous cenote at Chichen Itza—and there is iconographic and epigraphic evidence that stelae symbolized trees and pyramidal temple platforms were conceived of as mountains (Freidel, Schele, and Parker 1993). Demarest et al. demonstrate that sacred geography also plays a role in the placement of elite architecture. The Murciélagos palace complex was erected atop a hill which contains a cave with a permanent spring. In particular, Structure N4-6, a funerary shrine on the east side of the northern residential courtyard, entombs a tunnel entrance that provides access to the subterranean cave system and its supernatural power. The location of the building on the east side and the general east-west orientation of the whole cave system further link it to the rising sun, so that communication channels were opened with the deities and ancestors inhabiting both otherworlds (Demarest et al., this volume).

Section Three: Function

This section will discuss the results of the functional analyses conducted by the authors. While many functions of Maya palaces and elite residences remain ambiguous and quite possibly always will be, an attempt will be made to pick out recurring use patterns for which at least two examples can be named and for which a general consensus exists among scholars.

The first function to be addressed is priestly residence. It was shown above that palaces and temples often stand in very close proximity. Temples form part of palace-type I compounds and palaces physically abut temple buildings. This pattern immediately suggests that palaces in direct association with temples may have been the residences of the priests in charge of the temples. Most scholars agree that priests enjoyed a high social status in Maya society. Consequently, we are justified in assuming that they would have lived in the core areas close to their sacred places of office. Chase and Chase's analysis of artifacts from Structures B4 and B6 at Caracol partially strengthens this interpretation. Both structures were added to the side of the Structure B5 temple (see above). Chase and Chase found "high status domestic trash," as well as an unusually high number of chert points that could be an indicator of some form of military function (Chase and Chase 2001).

On the other hand, Demarest and coauthors present a very strong case that Structures N5-3A and N5-3 at Dos Pilas, abutting the funerary temple N5-7, functioned as the royal throne room and presentation palace. The latter is a palace-type IV structure with an open facade and little privacy that contains a bench and faces the procession path running from the West Plaza Group to the east Duende complex. It becomes obvious that Structures N5-3A and N5-3 functioned primarily as a location for political display and official receptions and audiences rather than as a priestly residence (Demarest et al., this volume). This discussion makes it clear that both possibilities have to be checked whenever the function of a palace in close physical association with a temple is reconstructed.

A number of palaces have been identified as the royal residences of historical Maya kings. Thanks to the insights into Maya life offered by the enormous recent advances in epigraphy, such identifications are accepted by most researchers. The iconography and inscriptions link the Palace at Palenque closely with K'inich Janaab' Pakal I. We know that he sat on the throne below the Oval Tablet in House E when he acceded to the royal office in the year 615. At the same time, the whole Palace complex was not constructed solely during his reign. Merle Greene Robertson dates most of the Palace buildings from approximately 583, the accession of Lady Yohl Ik'nal to 783, the first k'atun anniversary of the rule of K'inich K'uk' B'alam II (Robertson 1985b: 94; Martin and Grube 2000: 72–74). These dates indicate that the Palace was also used by some of his predecessors and successors. But K'inich Janaab' Pakal I figures most prominently in the iconography and the texts.

At Tikal, the interpretation of Structure 5D-46 in the Central Acropolis as a family palace was confirmed by an inscription on a dedicatory vessel. According to Schele and Mathews' reading, the short text proclaims: "They say he ascended to his house, the Holy Place, the ninth successor lord of Ch'akte-Xoc, Six-Sky-Turtle Holy Building, True-Great-Jaguar-Claw, Mutul Lord" (1998: 78).

At Copan, the identification of the founder's group and residence of Yax K'uk' Mo' is based primarily on stratigraphy. It constitutes one of the earliest large-scale patio groups beneath the Acropolis (Traxler, this volume). Andrews identifies Yax Pasaj Chan Yoaat's house in Group 10L-2 with the help of inscribed monuments. Structures 10L-32 and 10L-30 are located next to each other in Plaza A and are associated with altars exhibiting texts in which Yax Pasaj Chan Yoaat is the protagonist. He is named the sixteenth and final ruler in the dynasty started by Yax K'uk' Mo' (see Andrews et al., this volume).

The association of the House of the Governor at Uxmal with Lord Chaak is again based on iconography and inscriptions, in particular Stela 14. The sculpted images on the east facade and the two-headed jaguar throne in front of the House of the Governor further strengthen this interpretation (see Kowalski, this volume).

In many cases, archaeology can provide dates which confirm the chronology of the texts. These are situations in which archaeology and epigraphy truly complement and reinforce each other, as, for example, in Structure 5D-46 at Tikal (see above). However, the connection of palaces with specific historical rulers still leaves open the question of how these buildings were used and what kinds of activities took place in the individual rooms. Where did the kings sleep and eat? Where did they hold formal audiences? And perhaps most importantly, did they live in these palaces permanently or did they maintain secondary houses? The extent to which it is possible to reconstruct what happened in Maya palaces and elite residences, using the present data, will now be addressed.

Most scholars agree that people ate in palaces, that they slept on some of the benches, and that palaces also provided space for rituals and political receptions. Evidence for the domestic activities comes from the numerous midden deposits that are found inside and in proximity of most palaces and elite residences. But it is difficult to conclude from the middens whether the occupation was continuous or interrupted, and it is impossible to tell if the same individuals spent their entire lives in one palace compound or whether the occupants changed. To shed light on this question, authors have resorted to the help of ethnography. Harrison lists a series of possible temporary residents, from people on religious retreats to artists and support staff (Harrison, this volume). Edward Kurjack refers to colonial documents, which reveal that Yucatec Maya communities had both a core population and a sizable number of transient members who moved and settled quickly wherever they could find economic opportunities (Kurjack, this volume). I think the possibility of temporary residency should receive more attention from archaeologists, even though it can hardly be documented archaeologically.

Finding an answer to the question of what kinds of rituals and ceremonies were performed in palaces is also difficult. Here again the main body of evidence is provided by carved monuments. As mentioned above, texts and iconography document that K'inich Janaab' Pakal I became king of Palenque on the throne below the Oval Tablet in House E of the Palenque Palace. House E was the historical place of accession of the Palenque kings and probably also a Council House (see below).

Other ceremonies which were performed in and around Maya palaces were Period Ending rites. Period Endings were of critical importance in the Maya worldview because they believed that the universe could come to an end on major year endings in their calendar and that only powerful rituals were capable of successfully bridging the transition from one period to the next. Such rituals attempted nothing less than to symbolically rebuild the cosmos by creating material manifestations of cosmological concepts (Christie 1995).

Two fascinating examples are recorded at Piedras Negras and at Caracol. Court 1 is a palace-type I compound located on the ascending hillside of the Acropolis at Piedras Negras. Structures J-2 and J-6 occupy the southeast and northwest sides of this court, with Structure J-6 higher up the hill because of the slope. Structure J-6 underwent four construction phases, and in the last phase a shallow niche was inserted into the center of the rear wall of Room 1, into which Throne 1 was set (Satterthwaite 1935: 36–43). Throne 1 is a beautifully carved monument depicting an underworld deity whose eyes are formed by two Piedras Negras lords—possibly the king's parents (Martin and Grube 2000: 152), as well as having a lengthy inscription. The terminal date of this inscription is the Period Ending 9.17.15.0.0., which places the throne within the early reign of Ruler 7 and which was most likely the occasion that motivated this last remodeling effort. It follows that the 9.17.15.0.0. Period Ending rites would have been held in a magnificent setting: Ruler 7 was centrally seated on Throne 1, overlooking Court 1 where his audience was gathered. His position marked the highest point of the central axis of Court 1. The placement of the palaces suggests that the hill of the Acropolis represented a sacred mountain and that the terraces on which Court 1 and the surrounding buildings were erected were its cosmological divisions.

At Caracol, Caana provided another spectacular setting for the 10.0.0.0.0. Bak'tun ending rites. Giant Ajaw Altar 16 exhibits a large 7 Ajaw glyph in the center. It was carved in the Early Classic to commemorate the K'atun ending 7 Ajaw 3 K'ank'in 9.7.0.0.0. and repositioned in the Caana summit plaza at the Bak'tun ending 7 Ajaw 18 Sip 10.0.0.0.0. Chase and Chase identified the pit in the stair balk of Structure B19-1st that had been dug for the placement of Altar 16 and associated offerings (see Christie 1995: 289–293). The iconography of the altar and its location evoked powerful cosmological concepts and the sacred geography of the natural environment; the towering Caana complex itself symbolized the Creation Mountain in the Popol Vuh where the first humans were fashioned from maize and life was renewed, and the quatrefoil shape on top of the altar marks an entrance point to the underworld into which the Ajaw glyph that personifies the outgoing Bak'tun descends and from which the new Bak'tun will rise. It is implied that the underworld is accessed inside the Caana mountain (for a more detailed discussion of the symbolism see Freidel, Schele, and Parker 1993: 138–139; Christie 1995: 265–298).

Furthermore, there is consensus that formal receptions and political audiences were held in Maya palaces and elite residences. Such receptions and audiences usually took place in rooms containing benches, particularly in rooms marking the center of a palace (see Christie, this volume). Multiple examples have been found on vases, as well as on carved monuments, that show a ruler seated on a bench or throne and interacting with his subjects, for example, Lintel 3 from Piedras Negras. Harrison addresses the images on vases that depict the reception of tribute, judiciary scenes, lessons, and the presentation of prisoners (see Harrison, this volume). All these are undoubtedly palace scenes. Archaeological investigations have brought to light material evidence of elite residences with centrally placed benches exhibiting figurative images and texts, which in all probability served as thrones in formal meetings. Beautiful examples are Throne 1 in Structure J-6 at Piedras Negras, the throne below the Oval Tablet in House E of the Palace at Palenque, and the well-known hieroglyphic bench in Structure 82-C at Las Sepulturas, Copan (see Christie, this volume). Claudia Wolley excavated Structure N5-3A, the throne room next to the funerary temple N5-7 at Dos Pilas. This throne also contains an inscription, but it was ritually destroyed and accompanied by offerings (see Demarest et al., this volume).

However, not all benches functioned as thrones and focal points of political gatherings. Some were possibly beds and others may have been used for multiple purposes, for example, as seats, altars, work benches, or for storage. In his dissertation, Harrison analyzed the benches in the Central Acropolis at Tikal and offered several interpretations (Harrison 1971). It follows that benches had multiple functions and the presence of a bench alone does not justify the interpretation of a room as throne room.

A special kind of palace primarily designed for meetings is the Popol Nah. Barbara Fash first identified Structure 22-A at Copan as a Popol Nah or Council House (Fash and Fash 1990). These were the places where the ruler met with local and regional lords to discuss the affairs of the city and state. Fash presents further evidence that sacred dances were initiated, performed, and taught at the Popol Nah (Freidel, Schele, and Parker 1993: 152–153, 437). The following elements may identify a palace structure as a Popol Nah. First, the architecture must provide for open meeting spaces; for example, a wide porch is located in front of Structure 22-A at Copan. Second, open platforms that could have been used for dance performances should be located close by. Popol Nahs also display sculpture, most importantly mat designs and portraits of the rulers and lords who converged there to hold council. At Copan, project epigraphers have interpreted the figures seated upon glyphs on the facade of Structure 22-A as lords from specific regions that are named by the glyphs which form their thrones (Freidel, Schele, and Parker 1993: 437).

Popol Nahs have now been identified at a number of sites. Kowalski interprets Structure 44 at Dzibilchaltun and the House of the Governor at Uxmal as Popol Nahs (Kowalski, this volume). The Council House at Yaxuna was probably Structure 6F-68. This building displays human images as well as mat symbols (Ambrosino, this volume). Schele and Mathews have argued that House E of the Palenque Palace and the North Building of the Nunnery Quadrangle at Uxmal constituted Nikte' il Nahs or flower houses because their facades exhibit flower iconography (Schele and Mathews 1998: 269). A Nikte' il Nah is a version of the Popol Nah and was used for the same activities: political meetings, planning of festivals, and dance performances. Another possible Popol Nah is the northwest palace unit next to Structure B19 on the summit plaza of Caana at Caracol. A huge stuccoed mat design covered the side of Structure B18 facing the interior plaza of this palace.[2]

Finally, we know of two buildings that were without question the residences of scribes. The first building to be identified as a scribe's house was Structure 82-C, located on the south side of Patio A in Group 9N-8 of Las Sepulturas, Copan. The two-tiered facade displays three-dimensional figures of scribes associated with *naah* glyphs. *Naah* is a Maya word for "house."[3] Structure 82-C also contains the hieroglyphic bench in its central room. The text dates the house to the reign of Yax Pasaj Chan Yoaat and names the scribes and lineage heads of Patio A, who most likely worked for Yax Pasaj (Grube and Schele 1987; Schele 1987). This line of thinking would suggest that scribes enjoyed a high social status in Maya society. This has indeed been confirmed by discoveries in epigraphy. Two titles for scribes are now known: *ah tz'ihb*, which means scribe and refers to the physical act of writing, and *ah ch'ul hun*, which also means scribe but in the sense of "keeper of the holy books" and "literati" of society (Harrison, this volume). Both scribal titles are connected with the royal court and reinforce the great prestige and high social standing of scribes.

The second scribal residence is Structure M8-10 at Aguateca. The Aguateca Archaeological Project found numerous implements for scribal activities, such as shell ink pots and mortars and pestles for pigment preparation, associated with this building. Archaeologists further discovered high-status ornaments, for example, carved shells and jade beads, as well as domestic objects, including storage and serving vessels and manos and metates (Inomata and Triadan, this volume). Based on the artifactual analysis, Inomata and Triadan conclude that Structure M8-10 was the house of a scribe. The luxury ornaments also confirm the high position of this scribe in the Aguateca hierarchy.

Section Four: What Can Palaces and Elite Residences Tell Us about Social Structure?

I think this is the aspect in which the contributions to Maya palace research have been and will continue to be most significant. Maya social structure is without question a very complex issue and has to be approached from an interdisciplinary perspective. Here archaeology, anthropology, ethnography, epigraphy, and art history truly link hands to shine light on how Maya society was organized and how individuals and cities interacted with each other. Some of the interdisciplinary approaches which are utilized in the chapters will be discussed below.

First and most importantly, we know that Maya political power had multiple levels and that there was a hierarchy of political offices.[4] I do not believe that Maya cities had palaces comparable to the Versailles of

Louis XIV, which functioned as the exclusive royal residence and seat of government. However, Harrison presents exactly such a comparison and does see important similarities (Harrison, this volume). Archaeological investigations at all the sites mentioned in the chapters have shown that royal palaces were located in the core areas and that elite residences of considerable high status existed in the near vicinity. These findings suggest that Maya city government was formed by the king and a number of high officials.[5] Inomata and Triadan (this volume), following Chase and Chase (1992: 3), further caution that not all elites may have left material evidence of their existence. Some individuals with social prestige may have lived in simple houses and will never be able to be identified by means of archaeological methods. This could imply that the actual number of elites and their political power was greater than the number derived from recorded elite residences.

Such interpretations are confirmed by epigraphy and iconography. At this time, three titles are known that were used for different positions in the social hierarchy. The *kalomte* held the highest political leadership office. Epigraphic studies have shown that no *kalomte* was ever possessed or governed by another person. Second in the hierarchy was the *ajaw*, which is the most common term for a city leader. It is, however, a term that can be possessed in written texts, meaning that the *ajaw* could be subordinated to another individual in a higher position, which would have been a *kalomte*. The third term in the hierarchical order is the *sajal*. Most *sajals* recorded in the texts were possessed by someone with more power. The term may be translated as an "underlord," usually subservient to an *ajaw* (Harrison, this volume). It follows that the *kalomte* most likely resided in the palace in the core area, such as the Palenque Palace, the Central Acropolis at Tikal, or the Sayil Palace, and that the *ajaw* and *sajals* lived in the elite residences located further away from the center. The distance between the houses and the ceremonial center probably diminished as the rank of the occupants increased.

Additional proof of a stratified social hierarchy comes from the images painted on vases. There are numerous palace scenes in which a ruler is shown seated centrally on a throne, surrounded by nobles and officials of descending rank (Kerr 1989–1997).

Second, Maya palace research may provide information about the hierarchy of sites and their relationships. Simply speaking, a Maya city with a great number of palaces and elite residences may have been more powerful and exerted influence over another city with a very small number of elite residences. In Hillier and Hanson's terminology, the rulers and elites at different cities formed a noncorrespondence sociospatial system (1984: 256–261). In such a system, there is a split between spatial groups and transpatial groups who are the rulers and elites at different cities and who must operate across space to relate individuals in different spatial groups, in this case the cities, to each other and promote interaction between them. To what degree did Maya upper classes form a noncorrespondence system?[6] I think investigations of residences may help to illuminate answers to this question.

In this research direction, archaeology and epigraphy again complement each other. At the 1998 "Maya Hieroglyphic Forum at Texas," Linda Schele, Nikolai Grube, and Simon Martin presented new models of hierarchical relations between Classic Maya polities. They looked not only at emblem glyphs, as previous scholars had done, but also at a number of verbs and clauses that indicate supervision and subordination (Schele, Grube, and Martin 1998). Recent settlement surveys in Belize have documented new sites of various sizes and probably importance. In response, speakers at the symposium "The Social Implications of Ancient Maya Rural Complexity," organized by Gyles Iannone and Samuel Connell for the 1998 meetings of the Society for American Archaeology, added "middle level" as a site category for minor centers to the two preexisting categories, urban and rural settlements. It would be a meaningful project to investigate the extent to which archaeological and epigraphic evidence match—provided, of course, that middle-level sites were mentioned in the hieroglyphic record. Such an approach was followed at the 2002 "Maya Hieroglyphic Forum at Texas," during which Simon Martin, Marc Zender, and Nikolai Grube investigated the relationships between Palenque and its neighboring sites of varying hierarchical levels (Martin, Zender, and Grube 2002).

Finally and most importantly, Maya palace research has shown that the number of elite residences changed over time. The chapters report an increase in elite residences in the Late Classic at Tikal, Caracol, and Blue Creek (see Harrison, this volume; Chase and Chase 1998, 2001; Guderjan, Lichtenstein, and Hanratty, this volume). In general, these findings might signal a decentralization of power throughout much of the Maya area in the Late Classic (Guderjan, Lichtenstein, and Hanratty, this volume). In some cases, changes in elite residences may provide deeper insights into the power struggles within one specific Maya city, for example, Blue Creek (Guderjan, Lichtenstein, and Hanratty, this volume). But I think the greatest promise of Maya palace research lies in its potential to help illuminate not only local but also regional political organization.

NOTES

1. On the other hand, high-status residences have been encountered in close proximity of royal palaces. Harrison points to the West Plaza, the G and F Groups, the so-called Bat Palace, and the South Acropolis at Tikal (Harrison, this volume). At Caracol, it is not entirely clear where the ruling family lived, but Chase and Chase (1998) identified a number of elite residential compounds within the core area.

2. It must be clearly stated, however, that mat designs alone do not constitute sufficient evidence for the interpretation of a building as a Popol Nah. The northwest palace unit on top of Caana and Structure B-67 at Las Sepulturas (see Christie, this volume) both remain weak candidates unless additional lines of evidence can be brought forward.

3. For a full discussion of the iconography of the facade of Structure 82-C, the reader should consult Schele and Miller 1986: 140–142.

4. The nature of Maya courts is examined carefully in *Royal Courts of the Ancient Maya* (Inomata and Houston 2001).

5. Harrison (this volume) interprets elite residences located close to the Great Plaza of Tikal as possible secondary settings to which the Royal Court could move when necessary. I think it is more likely that these were the houses of political and religious officials who enjoyed considerable power and influence in the city government. A general increase in the elite class in the Late Classic has been well documented in the literature (Chase and Chase 1992; Guderjan Lichtenstein, and Hanratty, this volume).

6. Looking at Maya society from the perspective of a noncorrespondence system would be an innovative approach because it would focus on the relations between individuals of the same or similar social status but at differing locations. Traditionally, researchers have examined the relations between social groups at only one site at a time. The former methodology can be described as horizontal, while the latter is vertical.

REFERENCES

Ashmore, W.
1981   Some Issues of Method and Theory in Lowland Maya Settlement Archaeology. In *Lowland Maya Settlement Archaeology*, edited by W. Ashmore, 37–69. Albuquerque: University of New Mexico Press.
Barber, S., and K. Holmberg
1999   Ceren and the Great Outdoors. Paper presented at the sixty-fourth annual meeting of the Society for American Archaeology, Chicago.
Chase, D. Z., and A. F. Chase
1998   A Consideration of Classic Maya "Palaces" at Caracol, Belize. Paper presented at the sixty-third annual meeting of the Society for American Archaeology, Seattle.
2001   The Royal Court of Caracol, Belize: Its Palaces and People. In *Royal Courts of the Ancient Maya*, vol. 2, edited by T. Inomata and S. Houston, 102–137. Boulder: Westview Press.
Chase, D. Z., and A. F. Chase (eds.)
1992   *Mesoamerican Elites: An Archaeological Assessment.* Norman: University of Oklahoma Press.
Christie, J. J.
1995   Maya Period Ending Ceremonies: Restarting Time and Rebuilding the Cos-

mos to Assure Survival of the Maya World. Ph.D. dissertation, Department of Latin American Studies, University of Texas at Austin.

Coe, W. R., and W. A. Haviland
1982 *Introduction to the Archaeology of Tikal, Guatemala.* Tikal Report 12, University Museum Monograph 46. Philadelphia: University of Pennsylvania.

Diamanti, M.
1991 *Domestic Organization at Copan: Reconstruction of Elite Maya Households through Ethnographic Models (Honduras).* Ph.D. dissertation, Pennsylvania State University. Ann Arbor: University Microfilms.

Fash, W. L., and B. Fash
1990 Scribes, Warriors, and Kings. *Archaeology* 43: 26–35.

Ferguson, T. J.
1996 *Historic Zuni Architecture and Society.* Tucson: University of Arizona Press.

Freidel, D., L. Schele, and J. Parker
1993 *Maya Cosmos.* New York: William Morrow.

Grube, N., and L. Schele
1987 *The Date on the Bench from Structure 9N-82, Sepulturas, Copan, Honduras.* Copan Note 23. Austin: Copan Mosaics Project, Instituto Hondureño de Antropología e Historia, and Art Department, University of Texas at Austin.

Harrison, P.
1971 The Central Acropolis, Tikal, Guatemala: A Preliminary Study of the Functions of Its Structural Components during the Late Classic Period. Ph.D. dissertation, University of Pennsylvania.

Hendon, J. A.
1987 The Uses of Maya Structures: A Study of Architecture and Artifact Distribution at Sepulturas, Copan, Honduras. Ph.D. dissertation, Department of Anthropology, Harvard University.

Hillier, B., and J. Hanson
1984 *The Social Logic of Space.* Cambridge: Cambridge University Press.

Inomata, T., and S. Houston (eds.)
2001 *Royal Courts of the Ancient Maya.* 2 vols. Boulder: Westview Press.

Kent, S. (ed.)
1990 *Domestic Architecture and the Use of Space.* Cambridge: Cambridge University Press.

Kerr, J., with M. D. Coe et al.
1989–1997 *The Maya Vase Book.* 5 vols. New York: Kerr Associates.

Leventhal, R., et al.
1997 *Xunantunich Archaeological Project: The Final Field Season.* University of California at Los Angeles.

Martin, S., M. Zender, and N. Grube
2002 *Palenque and Its Neighbors: Notebook for the XXVIth Maya Hieroglyphic Forum at Texas.* Austin: University of Texas.

Martin, Simon, and Nikolai Grube
2000 *Chronicle of the Maya Kings and Queens.* London: Thames and Hudson.

Ortiz, A.
1969 *The Tewa World: Space, Time, Being, and Becoming in a Pueblo Society.* Chicago: University of Chicago Press.

Pollock, H. E. D.
1980 *The Puuc.* Memoirs of the Peabody Museum of Archaeology and Ethnology, vol. 19. Harvard University, Cambridge, Mass.

Proskouriakoff, T.
1960 Historical Implications of a Pattern of Dates at Piedras Negras, Guatemala. *American Antiquity* 25: 454–475.

Robertson, M. G.
1985a *The Sculpture of Palenque*, vol. 2. Princeton: Princeton University Press.
1985b *The Sculpture of Palenque*, vol. 3. Princeton: Princeton University Press.

Robin, Cynthia
1999 Changing Living Spaces: Outdoor Domestic Space Use in Modern and Ancient "Maya" Communities. Paper presented at the sixty-fourth annual meeting of the Society for American Archaeology, Chicago.

Satterthwaite, L.
1935 *Palace Structures J-2 and J-6*. Piedras Negras Preliminary Papers 3. Philadelphia: University Museum, University of Pennsylvania.

Schele, L.
1976–1997 *Notebooks for the Maya Hieroglyphic Workshops*. Austin: University of Texas.

Schele, L.
1987 *The Figures on the Legs of the Scribe's Bench*. Copan Note 24. Austin: Copan Mosaics Project, Instituto Hondureño de Antropología e Historia, and Art Department, University of Texas at Austin.

Schele, L., and D. Freidel
1990 *A Forest of Kings*. New York: William Morrow.

Schele, L., N. Grube, and S. Martin
1998 *Notebook for the XXIInd Maya Hieroglyphic Forum at Texas*. Austin: University of Texas.

Schele, L., and P. Mathews
1998 *The Code of Kings*. New York: Scribner.

Schele, L., and M. Miller
1986 *The Blood of Kings*. Fort Worth: Kimbell Art Museum.

Smith, A. Ledyard
1950 *Uaxactun, Guatemala, Excavations of 1931–1937*. Carnegie Institution of Washington Publication 588. Washington, D.C.
1962 Residential and Associated Structures at Mayapan. In *Mayapan, Yucatan, Mexico*, edited by Harry E. D. Pollock, Ralph E. Roys, Tatiana Proskouriakoff, and A. Ledyard Smith, 165–319. Carnegie Institution of Washington Publication 619. Washington, D.C.

Spinden, H. J.
1913 *A Study of Maya Art, Its Subject Matter and Historical Development*. Memoirs of the Peabody Museum of American Archaeology and Ethnology, vol. 6. Harvard University, Cambridge, Mass.

Stephens, J. L.
[1841] 1988 *Incidents of Travel in Central America, Chiapas and Yucatan*. London: Century.

Thompson, J. E. S.
1959 *The Rise and Fall of Maya Civilization*. Norman: University of Oklahoma Press.
1963 *Maya Archaeologist*. Norman: University of Oklahoma Press.

Tozzer, A. M.
1911 *A Preliminary Study of the Prehistoric Ruins of Tikal, Guatemala*. Memoirs of the Peabody Museum of American Archaeology and Ethnology, vol. 5, no. 2. Cambridge, Mass.: Harvard University.

Valdés, Juan A.
2001   Palaces and Thrones Tied to the Destiny of the Royal Courts in the Maya
       Lowlands. In *Royal Courts of the Ancient Maya*, edited by Takeshi Inomata
       and Stephen D. Houston, 138–164. Boulder: Westview Press.
Wauchope, R.
1938   *Modern Maya Houses: A Study of Their Archaeological Significance.* Carne-
       gie Institution of Washington Publication 502. Washington, D.C.
Yaeger, J.
1997   The 1997 Excavations of Plaza A-III and Miscellaneous Excavation and Ar-
       chitectural Clearing in Group A. In *Xunantunich Archaeological Project: The
       Final Field Season*, 24–55. University of California at Los Angeles.

Index

www.ingramcontent.com/pod-product-compliance
Lightning Source LLC
Chambersburg PA
CBHW020334270326
41926CB00007B/176